Wedding Planning

FOR

DUMMIES®

A Wiley Brand

by Dominique Douglas, Bernadette Chapman, Marcy Blum and Laura Fisher Kaiser

Wedding Planning For Dummies®

Published by: **John Wiley & Sons, Ltd.,** The Atrium, Southern Gate, Chichester, www.wiley.com

This edition first published 2014

© 2014 John Wiley & Sons, Ltd, Chichester, West Sussex.

Registered office

John Wiley & Sons Ltd, The Atrium, Southern Gate, Chichester, West Sussex, PO19 8SQ, United Kingdom

For details of our global editorial offices, for customer services and for information about how to apply for permission to reuse the copyright material in this book please see our website at www.wiley.com.

For general information on our other products and services, please contact our Customer Care Department within the U.S. at 877-762-2974, outside the U.S. at (001) 317-572-3993, or fax 317-572-4002. For technical support, please visit www.wiley.com/techsupport.

A catalogue record for this book is available from the British Library.

ISBN 978-1-118-69951-5 (paperback); ISBN 978-1-118-69948-5 (ebk);
ISBN 978-1-118-69949-2 (ebk)

Printed in Great Britain by TJ International, Padstow, Cornwall

10 9 8 7 6 5 4 3 2 1

Contents at a Glance

Table of Contents

Introduction

● ●

A wedding, whether it's a quiet civil ceremony or a pull-out-all-the-stops extravaganza, requires equal parts creativity, planning, diplomacy and nerve. We admit that the whole ordeal can seem overwhelming at times. After all, getting married is a profound rite of passage. But we're here to tell you: *please don't panic.* You're in good hands (as long as you have this book in *your* hands)!

The mission of *Wedding Planning For Dummies* is to demystify and simplify myriad details that go into the Big Day, inspire you with wonderfully innovative ideas to personalise your wedding celebration, instil confidence in you to pull off a memorable ceremony and reception (no matter what your budget or wedding style) *and* hopefully enable you to have some fun while doing it.

About This Book

Wedding Planning For Dummies isn't just for brides. Because a wedding (not to mention a marriage) is a joint venture, we recommend that the bride and groom participate equally in its creation. If you've done zero planning, we'll get you up and running. No matter what stage you're at, however, we won't make you go back and start over because you've done something wrong. Generally speaking, no single right way exists. Whatever makes you and your intended happy is the right way for you.

Packed with wit and wedding knowhow, *Wedding Planning For Dummies, UK Edition,* helps you figure out your own wedding style and guides you through each stage of the planning process. What size wedding is right for you and your budget? Where's the best place to have the ceremony and reception? How can you make sure everybody will show up at the church on time? How can you save money without looking cheap? Whatever the wedding-related issue, the answer is here in this easy-to-use reference.

We've organised this book to make planning your wedding as stress free and logical as possible. Each chapter is divided into sections, and each section contains useful information, such as:

- How to set a budget and stick to it
- Tips for evaluating prospective venues for the ceremony and reception, whether for a local or destination wedding

  ✔ Thoughtful ways to make guests feel welcome

  ✔ Ideas for creating memorable menus, music playlists and party favours

  ✔ How to keep your wedding day running smoothly by creating a
    no-surprises schedule

Although some wedding guides love to dictate timelines for when to do
what, we find that contrived deadlines produce more anxiety than efficiency.
A wedding can be two years or two months in the making. Rather than lay out
a strict protocol or chronology, we've organised this book according to what
makes sense for real brides and grooms, for many of whom the demands of
work or family leave little time for wedding planning. We say: let *your* priorities determine the timing for everything from setting the date to jetting off on
honeymoon.

The great thing about this book is that you decide where to start and what
to read. It's a reference you can jump into and out of at will. Just head to the
table of contents or index to find the information you want.

Foolish Assumptions

Every book is written with a particular reader in mind, and this one is
no different. As we wrote *Wedding Planning For Dummies* we made a few
assumptions about you:

  ✔ You're a newly engaged couple and you've just begun really thinking
    about the kind of ceremony and reception you want to have.

  ✔ You haven't had much experience with planning weddings or even large
    parties, and yet you know you don't want a wedding-by-numbers.

  ✔ You want basic information – tips from the pros – but you don't want to
    be bombarded with minutiae.

  ✔ No matter what size your budget, you're starting to feel panicky, wonder-
    ing just how much the wedding of your dreams is going to cost and how
    you're going to afford it.

We can't tell you what kind of wedding to have – that decision is completely
up to you. But we can tell you how to make the most of your resources and
budget. We realise that you want to know not only the traditional ways of
celebrating your big day, but also, in some cases, innovative ways to tweak
the official rites and rituals. We can help you figure all that out. And, dare we
say, make the process *fun*.

Icons Used in This Book

Icons are the nifty little pictures in the margin of this book. They each grab your attention for a different reason:

Contrary to what some sexist ninnies think, the bride *and* groom should be responsible for pulling the wedding together. Of course, a natural delineation of duties may occur, but some decisions require input from both parties. When you see these entwined wedding rings, it signals a matter where you should consult each other.

Yes, we realise that your Aunt Betty graduated with honours from the TJTWID (That's Just The Way It's Done) Etiquette Academy, but we're here to tell you that times have changed, and so have certain iron-clad rules of decorum. When you see this icon, expect either an alternative way for handling a sticky wedding situation or simply a heads-up on making everyone feel comfortable.

Although we don't advocate being a slave to calendars and endless to-do lists, every now and then a timely reminder is in order. When you see this symbol, adjust your personal wedding timetable accordingly.

No matter the budget, anyone planning a wedding wants to get the most bang for their buck. This symbol means we're about to impart vital information regarding a practical money matter. Although many times we tell you how to save money, we just as often explain why pinching pennies in a particular area may not be wise. We also use this icon to flag information that may save you precious time, and simply help you out in the planning.

Weddings, like life, can be unpredictable, but certain mistakes, pitfalls and tacky traps are easily avoided. Defuse these little bombs before they explode.

Beyond the Book

As you work your happy way through planning your wedding, you can augment what you read here by checking out some of the access-anywhere extra information that we've hosted online. You can find the book's e-cheat sheet at www.dummies.com/cheatsheet/weddingplanninguk, and by going to www.dummies.com/extras/weddingplanninguk you can access four bonus articles and an extra Part of Tens chapter.

Where to Go from Here

You may find that you need to fast-forward to the reception chapters because the space you want gets booked a year in advance. No problem. This isn't a Stephen King novel – you can jump around all you want without missing any major plot twists. Check out the table of contents to find a topic that suits your fancy.

If you're just getting started, you may as well turn to Part I. Chapter 1 starts you off easily. Before you know it, you'll be planning like a pro.

Part I

Getting Started with Wedding Planning

getting started

with

wedding planning

web extras

For Dummies can help get you started with lots of subjects. Visit www.dummies.com to learn more and do more with *For Dummies*.

In this part...

✔ Get straight down to business – work out what is important to you and what kind of wedding you want.

✔ Stay on track from the start by working out what you can afford to spend, devising a budget – and sticking to it.

✔ Remember that your wedding day isn't just about photographs and partying and understand the legalities involved in tying the knot with your loved one.

Chapter 1

First Things First

So here you are, engaged! Congratulations. Finding your perfect partner and the person you want to spend the rest of your life with is such an amazing thing. Organising your wedding is often the first major event you experience together and it should set you off, hand in hand, on your wonderful journey.

Whether you're planning a large wedding or an intimate event, you need to take certain steps to ensure that your dream wedding turns into reality. In this chapter, we set out the first steps you need to take to get it all started.

The 'Ise' Have It

In spite of what you've heard, the time between your engagement and your marriage needn't go down in the history of your relationship as the Dark Ages. What follows is a series of 'exercISEs' to kick off your wedding planning and set you on the right track to pulling off the wedding of your dreams. As you familiarISE, fantasISE, prioritISE and so on, the goal is to figure out what's important to both of you and to achieve your vision with as little acrimony and heartburn as possible. Okay – we admit this ISE thing is cheesy, but it really works.

Familiarise: Spreading the news

Some etiquette books still advise that a man ask a woman's parents for her hand. However, some brides may be offended by the connotation of ownership. Nonetheless, after someone has proposed, we recommend that you demonstrate respect and courtesy by telling your parents first. This isn't the time, however, to ask them to foot the bill. Give them oxygen. Let them bask in the glow a bit. (If there's no glow in sight, proceed directly to Chapter 22 and start planning your honeymoon – it may be time to elope.)

This is a natural time for the first communiqué between the bride's and groom's parents if they don't already know each other. We recommend you rely on your own sense of whose parents should initiate contact. If it's a toss-up, you can fall back on tradition and suggest that the groom's parents call the bride's.

If either of you has children, tell the kids before you tell other people (or other people tell them). Life isn't like *The Brady Bunch*; the merging of families can be highly charged, even if everyone seems to get along famously.

We realise that you're overjoyed with your decision to marry, but don't let your enthusiasm lead you to draft 82 people for your wedding party as you spread the news among your friends and relatives. If you've known since you were two years old who your best man or maid of honour is going to be then by all means that person should be among the first few people to know. Otherwise, hold off broadcasting even tentative plans until you know how many of your 2,000 closest friends you can actually invite.

Fantasise: Envisioning your dream wedding

All too often, people begin planning their wedding by setting a strict budget and then trying to shoehorn in all the things they think they *should* have in their wedding. This process not only doesn't work, but it can also leave you feeling like you can't afford to have your dream wedding in any way, shape or form. We suggest that you work backwards. Before you rein in your dreams, imagine that no budgetary or logistical constraints exist. Start thinking about all the elements that would go into your fantasy wedding. Be as specific as you can, using all your senses. Are there aspects you've dreamed of since you were a child? How big is the wedding? Where are you? What time of day is it? What colour are the bridesmaids' dresses? What does the band sound like? Who's there? What does the venue smell like? What are you eating? What are you drinking?

Guest-imating your costs

You can never make a preliminary guest list *(in writing)* too early. Thinking about whom to invite and who will actually show up has a tremendous impact on the way your wedding planning evolves. The number in your head may not correspond to the reality, and seeing the names on paper helps check your natural tendency to invite casual acquaintances. While certain costs such as venue hire, ceremony costs, music and the wedding dress are usually fixed, items such as centrepieces, food and beverages change in proportion to the number of guests attending. The difference between 100 and 125 guests may mean three more tables and everything that entails at the reception. Only you can decide whether those people make the day more special or simply blow your budget. In simple terms, remember that every guest adds to the cost.

Including everyone who *really* matters while not inviting everyone either of you or your parents have ever met is a precarious juggling act. Before you ask your prospective in-laws to submit a list of names and/or an estimate of the number of people they'd like to see there, give them some parameters upfront so no confusion occurs later. After you've agreed on a tentative number of guests, you can go out looking for venues with a much more realistic idea of what will accommodate your group as well as your budget.

Remember that the mysterious folk who calculate wedding statistics say that you can expect 10 to 20 per cent of those invited not to attend. That's the national average, but it could be irrelevant to your situation, so don't bank on this when planning the size of your venue or determining your budget's bottom line. You may be the lucky ones blessed with 100 per cent attendance.

Write down these thoughts on a piece of paper and exchange them with your spouse-to-be. Collect images that express the style for your dream wedding and then compare; do you see any similarities between your perfect weddings? You may feel more comfortable brainstorming out loud together, but the point is that you should both be honest and open-minded. Take each other's fantasies seriously. Refrain from making dismissive snorting sounds. This type of open exchange is neither a mind game nor an exercise in futility, but rather a very helpful step in discovering what both of you really want.

Prioritise: Deciding what's really important

Now, take all your fantasy elements and put them in some order of importance. Are towering bouquets of white lilies more important than drinking vintage Champagne? Are you flexible on the time of year? The time of day? Must you have a couture dress, or are you willing to go with something less lavish and instead spend more money on an eight-piece band? Does the venue have to be a dream castle or would the local hotel serve the same purpose?

Compare your priority list with your intended's. Maybe you both agree that having a sit-down dinner isn't so important. Perhaps you've always pictured a rustic country wedding in a barn but your better half thinks only a country manor house will impress everyone. What compromises are you both willing to make? (This is good practice for the rest of your lives.)

Visualise: Making a reality checklist

The next step is to take these priorities and paint the picture of where you're going to spend your money. Start by estimating the cost of each of the most important elements. These estimates provide you with a rough budget, a way to set some parameters; you'll flesh it out later. (See Chapter 2 for more information on setting a budget.)

Remember that none of this budgeting is set in stone, so you can afford to be flexible. Assuming you can't afford the world's most exotic flowers or vintage champagne, assess which parts of your prioritised fantasy line-up may really work. Although you both may have in mind a caviar-and-blini bar, you may also see a band that sets you on fire. Because having both will blow your whole budget, one has to go. To facilitate that decision, think back to what sticks in your memory about great weddings you've been to. Was it the food? The setting? The music?

Weddings aren't planned in a vacuum. Nor do they end when the cake is cut. You'll encounter both familial and interpersonal ramifications that last far longer than this one day. A good idea, therefore, is to find out at the very beginning what the highly charged issues are – and when in doubt, compromise. Doing so makes for a happier day and a happier future family life.

Dealing with kiddie complications

One of the wonderful things about weddings is that they can bring many generations together under one roof. On the other hand, you may not be delighted to have screaming infants punctuating your vows, or paying for even the most adorable Shirley Temple clone to take up a seat at your reception.

Whether to invite children to your wedding is one of the more emotional issues you may face during your premarital meanderings. As you may have noticed, people can get positively fierce when it comes to their little darlings. So what are your choices, and after you make your decisions, how do you impart them most graciously?

Don't count on guests being versed in the nuances of invitation addressing. (In other words, they probably won't realise that their children aren't invited if their names aren't on the envelope.) After you've made your decision,

be gracious but firm when people call and ask whether the exclusion was an oversight. The easiest way to start an all-out family war is to cave in and make an exception for some children but not others. Specifying an age cut-off is difficult. If you have young ladies and gentlemen involved in your ceremony as junior ushers and bridesmaids, they'll undoubtedly be crushed if they aren't invited to the reception. What's more, depending on your families, you may be pressured to invite other relatives of the same age if you're including these kids. And for an evening reception, trying to have any children whisked away at their witching hour without having to bid farewell to their parents is next to impossible. One solution may be to arrange a quiet area adjacent to your reception where this age group can be deposited to nap – under the supervision of a wedding nanny – until their parents are ready to leave.

Organise: Breaking down the details without breaking down

If the word *organise* strikes fear into your very core then you really need to read this. And even if you're uber-organised, you may benefit from reading the following tips on getting organised and setting a budget.

Approach your wedding as any other big project in your life: divide it into manageable pieces. Group several little steps into segments and plot them along a timeline or calendar, setting deadlines that fit in with everything else going on in your life:

- ✔ **Jot down tasks and deadlines on your calendar.** Use a pencil or an electronic calendar in case things change. They will change. Count on it.

- ✔ **Organise your time to make things easy on yourself.** If you're starting university, changing jobs or moving, this probably isn't the time to plan a complex wedding with a cast of thousands. Although weddings are happy occasions, they are, nonetheless, stressful. Ask yourselves, 'How much are we willing to give up?'

✔ **Create a planning folder.** An expanding file with several sections or clear plastic sheet protectors (the kind that fit into a ring binder) are handy for keeping track of all the ephemera that multiplies as you plan your big day: contracts, menus, wine labels, brochures, guest lists, fabric swatches, stationery samples, photos, plane tickets, receipts, magazine articles and so on. When the wedding's over, a lot of this stuff makes great scrapbook fodder.

✔ **Use technology to ease the planning.** Most households have a smartphone or tablet, making wedding planning a far more portable task. You can download various apps that allow you to enter wedding tasks, with an action date, and set reminders. Create an account at `Pinterest.com` and collect images that you can then show suppliers, like the cake designer and florist, to express your wedding vision. And use the note function to record thoughts and light-bulb moments as they happen.

✔ **Start keeping track of your guests as early as possible.** Use a computerised spreadsheet. Each entry contains data on everyone to whom you send an invitation – the correct spelling, address, RSVP, gift, spouse or significant other, and who invited them. Such a compilation proves invaluable when planning your seating chart (see Chapter 5).

Just as you collect ideas and pictures of things you want for your wedding, it's equally important to note things you *don't* want. That way you have a better chance of remembering, for example, to tell the caterer that Aunt Myrtle is fatally allergic to nuts or to tell the band that under no circumstances are they to play 'Agadoo'.

Synchronise: Dispelling the timetable myth

With the exception of invitations, which can take up to four months to print and mail, you can accomplish almost every aspect of a wedding in less than two months. Not that we suggest waiting until the last minute, but you don't have to be a slave to someone else's timetable. Okay, now here's the big shocker: *Wedding Planning For Dummies* doesn't have the ubiquitous wedding timeline that tells you, for example, 'Two days before: Polish your left toenail.' We believe this set-in-stone manifesto strikes terror into the hearts of even the most courageous couple. In devising your customised timetable, allow your priorities, budget, personal schedules and reality constraints to come into play.

Having everyone's contacts at a glance

As you plan your wedding, you'll make a lot of phone calls and send a lot of emails, so pull together everyone's contact information in one place. As you assemble your nuptial team, keep an up-to-date contact sheet of all the key players. Include their phone numbers – home, office and mobile – as well as postal, email and website addresses. For suppliers, include the company name and contact person. At some point during your planning, the following players – listed here alphabetically – may be on your speed-dial:

- Attendants' attire (company or store)
- Best man
- Bride
- Bridesmaids
- Bride's parents
- Cake maker
- Calligrapher
- Caterer or banquet manager
- Ceremony musicians
- Ceremony contact
- Decorations and party favour company
- Dress designer
- Drinks company
- Florist
- Groom
- Groom's parents
- Hair stylist
- Hire company
- Jeweller
- Lighting designer
- Maid of honour
- Makeup artist
- Mobile toilet company
- Photographer
- Reception musicians
- Reception wedding co-ordinator
- Registrar or priest
- Stationer
- Suit-hire shop
- Tailor
- Transportation company
- Travel agent
- Videographer
- Wedding planner

First things first

We do advise that you attend to certain details sooner rather than later. In fact, even before you've finalised the date of your wedding, you should get moving on aspects that are hard to find, in great demand or simply take a long time to accomplish. Generally speaking, these include:

- **Band:** Like popular venues, good bands (and DJs) require that you book them several months in advance. (See Chapter 20 for info on finding musicians.)

✔ **Photographer:** If photos are incredibly important to you, sourcing a photographer as soon as you have your venue and date organised is a good idea. Great photographers can get booked 12 or more months in advance.

✔ **Invitations:** Traditionally, you mail invitations six to eight weeks before the wedding, but most couples post them much earlier, especially if the wedding is in the summer holidays. A way to get around posting the wedding invitation earlier is to post a save-the-date card a year in advance, meaning key friends and family pencil in your wedding date. (See Chapter 8 on invitations and other stationery needs.)

✔ **Location:** You're not the only two people getting married in the foreseeable future, so if you want to get married in high season at a popular venue, you may have to book up to a year in advance. (See Chapter 4 on choosing a space and Chapter 17 on working with a caterer.)

✔ **Wedding dress:** The source of much pre-wedding anxiety, the hunt for the perfect wedding dress is unpredictable. Even if you score the first time you go shopping, you need to allow time for the dress to be altered. Then you have to get the veil, shoes, bra . . . see Chapter 11 for the gory details.

Picking the date

When it comes to picking the date, keep in mind the following:

✔ **Don't get in knots trying to please everyone.** Maybe your maid of honour goes on a spa retreat at the same time every year. Or your future mother-in-law already has tickets for a three-month Caribbean cruise next summer. People may put in requests, but you can't please everyone. In the end, you must decide what's best for you and the majority of your guests. When you've set the date, stick to it. Your guests will have to deal with it. And most of them will deal with it very well.

✔ **Work around availability.** Perhaps you want a specific photographer or venue, so you set the date with availability in mind.

✔ **Consider carefully before piggybacking.** Having a wedding coincide with another major holiday is often tempting. (See the nearby sidebar 'Dates to bear in mind'.) This can work if your family usually gets together anyway at this time, or if people coming from out of town need a few extra days' cushion and the holiday provides some extra time off work. But holiday weddings can be costly (think how much you'd charge to work on a holiday; the service staff feels the same way). And sometimes people resent having their precious holiday time eaten up with a social obligation. If they must sacrifice, however, they may expect the gracious host to make sure there's plenty to keep them entertained.

Dates to bear in mind

Some holidays or three-day weekends seem like a perfect opportunity to have a wedding. Other times can be off limits depending on your religion or nationality. Although you can marry in a church over Easter and Christmas, your local vicar/priest may decline due to how busy he is at this time. Still other dates may be anniversaries of painful events such as a death in the family. In any case, here are some days to take into consideration when choosing a date.

New Year's Day
St. Patrick's Day
Palm Sunday
Passover
Good Friday
Easter Monday
Mother's Day
Father's Day
Bank holidays

Christmas Eve and Day
Boxing Day

✔ **Don't let sentimentalism become an issue.** Some couples are sentimental about dates – they want to get married on New Year's Eve to symbolise their new start together, or on one of their birthdays, or on the anniversary of their first kiss. Although this may seem sweet, watch out – your special spot on the calendar may fall on another holiday, an inconvenient day of the week or at the *peak* (read 'more costly') time of year. January, February and March are typically slow months in most parts of the UK. The most popular time to get married is May to October, and December.

Think about marrying mid-week and off season for the best deals.

Deputise: Choosing your team

We presume you've purchased this book because you have some vested interest in producing your own wedding. However, like it or not, in our society money means power. Consequently, if your parents or in-laws are paying for a portion of the wedding, they do get a vote. This situation may prove to be one of the trickiest you face, requiring utmost diplomacy. Other people often have specific fantasies regarding *your* wedding that may be diametrically opposite yours.

Measure the importance of financial contributions against your resolve for certain aspects of your wedding. This ratio is something only you can determine. If you're accepting a great proportion of money from others, be prepared to take a great proportion of their advice. Decide which is more important to you: more financial help or total control.

Should people become overbearing, try to turn the situation around. Listen to every word of their input, thank them with all the grace and charm for which you're undoubtedly known, and then quietly make decisions with your fiancé(e) and announce them sweetly but firmly.

Before meddlers become too meddlesome, put them to work on a simple project, such as researching places for out-of-towners to stay or making biscuits for the favours. We strongly advocate the gentle exploitation of family and friends, but keep in mind that involving someone in your wedding means inviting them. Ask favours only from close friends, or from people who have nothing to lose or gain from helping you. The best way to solicit help is to ask for recommendations from family or friends who've been through this. That way they feel they've done something to help you and are absolved from the responsibility of interfering further.

Think over all offers of help before accepting them. Just because your best friend says she can do calligraphy doesn't mean she's very good at it. Delegate sensibly. The idea is to save you time, not make more work, cost more money or cause hurt feelings.

Working with a Wedding Planner

Professional wedding planners used to be considered an extravagance for the rich and famous only. In the past decade, however, more couples have begun to rely on their expertise.

You may want to consider hiring a planner if:

- You can't spare at least 12 hours per week doing the job yourself – and twice that much time as the wedding date draws near.
- You want to invite more than 80 guests.
- You're holding your wedding in a home, garden, barn, museum or other location that isn't a full-service venue.
- You're getting married in a far-off location.

When looking at weddings you like the look of in magazines or on blogs, check the credit list to see whether a wedding planner was involved. Try the UK Alliance of Wedding Planners (www.ukawp.com) to find a local planner; all members are insured and vetted. Ask key suppliers whether they've worked with a wedding planner they can recommend.

Be careful of wedding businesses that list wedding planning as a service, examples being florists, caterers, mobile bar companies and even stationers. You want to work with someone whose sole job is wedding planning so you can be sure of their dedication to you and your wedding. You want your planner to have a passion for wedding planning, not to have it as an aside to their current passion.

Another point to remember when hiring a planner is to check whether they take commission. Some planners charge a fee but also receive a commission from suppliers and venues every time one of their clients book them. You need to ask yourself whether you're comfortable with this. Ask yourself whether you feel you can trust that they are recommending the best suppliers for you, or simply those that pay commission to wedding planners.

Understanding different wedding-planning services

The best time to hire a wedding planner is at the beginning of the process. Some planners, however, can be brought in at any point to handle just a few aspects or serve as the project manager of events on the actual wedding day.

Most often, planners charge in three ways: a flat fee, hourly or a percentage. Expect to pay between 10 and 15 per cent of your total wedding budget for a planner to organise the entire wedding. Check the planner's website for a price guideline.

You have two options for wedding planning, the full monty and some tailored help:

- **Full planning:** Following an initial consultation, your planner works with you to plan your wedding. They produce a timeline or schedule and an outline budget to which you both work. They manage all the elements of your wedding, involving you as much as you choose. Duties include finding your venue, short-listing suppliers to meet your brief and designing the overall look and feel of the day. Your planner has regular meetings with you, is available for ideas and advice, and attends your wedding day, managing all suppliers.
- **Partial planning:** This ranges in scope as follows:
  - **On-the-day management:** You may choose to arrange everything yourself but decide you'd like a professional to manage your day. Your planner works to your schedule to co-ordinate suppliers and oversee the day.

- **Final few weeks:** If you prefer to do your own planning but would like support for the last few weeks and on the day, many planners offer this service. Following an initial consultation, your planner visits your venue, communicates with and co-ordinates all the suppliers you've arranged, tweaks your schedule to ensure it flows well and manages the big day.

- **Venue search:** Many planners offer a service whereby you provide a brief of the venue you're seeking, stating county, venue type, licensing needs, minimum numbers and other requirements, and they produce a shortlist of venues that meet these criteria. Prices vary depending on whether or not you require the planner to visit the venues or simply undertake desk research on your behalf.

- **Supplier search:** You may be planning your wedding yourself but find yourself struggling to find the perfect DJ or florist. Your planner takes a brief from you and comes up with a shortlist to your specifications.

- **Consultancy:** Couples who perhaps can't afford the full services of a planner or who want to plan the wedding themselves can buy bundles of hours from a planner and use the planner as a consultant. In essence, the planner will guide you with what tasks you need to be completed and in which order. They may give you supplier or venue recommendation, but you make the appointments and negotiate before booking. The planner just helps keep you on track.

- **Design/styling:** Couples nowadays feel the pressure to create very stylish and unique weddings. Those who are unable or unwilling to spend the necessary hours researching and implementing the design can hire a planner to create the design for them. Normally, this means the planner creates a mood board to show the design and colours. A *mood board* can either be an electronic collage of images or a physical board showing the colours and theme of the wedding through a mix of photos gathered from the Internet or magazines. After the design is agreed the planner recommends suitable supplies and providers that match the design; for example, cakes, stationery, lighting and linen.

Interviewing prospective planners

Before you talk to a planner, do a little homework. When you pick up the phone, be prepared to tell the planner when you expect your wedding to take place, where you want it to be (or at least some possibilities), how many guests you plan to invite and what your estimated budget is. Schedule an appointment to meet in person. Questions to ask:

- How long have you been in business and how many weddings have you organised?
- Where did you study?
- Do you belong to any professional organisations?
- What services are included in your contract?
- Are you comfortable working within my budget?
- Will you be able to work with suppliers I choose?
- Are you insured?
- How do you charge – hourly, flat fee or a percentage of my total budget? And do you also take commission from suppliers?

You and your intended are in this together, so both of you should meet with prospective planners. Even if your ideas haven't totally jelled, just describing them to a planner is a useful exercise. Also bring magazine clippings featuring fashion or decor elements that appeal to you. That way, the planner can get an idea of your taste and style.

Remember, you're looking for someone who has taste, style and creativity, and is organised, detail-oriented and objective (a plus in charged situations). You want someone who's utterly dependable and who has a terrific sense of humour so you can laugh through the stressful times. Your wedding planner should be someone you actually *want* to spend time with.

As in any great relationship, the bond you form with your wedding planner should be based on trust, honesty and mutual respect. With that kind of foundation, you can create a day that you and your guests will remember fondly.

Chapter 2

Avoiding Those Wedding-Bill Blues

In This Chapter

▶ Creating a budget spreadsheet
▶ Sticking to your budget
▶ Negotiating contracts
▶ Scouting deals online

*B*ooks and magazines that depict excruciatingly perfect weddings create a sense of false expectation. Couples may feel entitled to their own fairy-tale wedding or pressured to throw the ultimate fête. Then, as estimates from suppliers start rolling in, they snap back to reality (or plunge into despair). Just figuring out how to afford this single event becomes all-consuming and, for many couples, strains their relationship.

In this chapter, we help you get a grip on the big financial picture by explaining how to set a budget and stick to it, negotiate contracts and avoid costly surprises. We also highlight a few of our favourite cost-cutting tips, many more of which you'll find throughout the book.

As you look for ways to stretch your wedding budget, remember that you have smart ways to cut costs, and not so smart ways. You don't necessarily want to go with the supplier who quotes the lowest, and nor do you want to assume that the priciest supplier will provide the best goods or services. Always get references, ask lots of questions, get everything in writing and weigh your options carefully. If a deal seems too good to be true, it probably is. Sometimes penny wise really is pound foolish.

Love is a Money-Spender Thing

First, the bad news: we can't give you a cut-and-dried formula that tells you how much to spend on your wedding. Who's to say what percentage of your budget needs to go to food, wine or your dress? That's a matter of your personal taste, finances and circumstances.

Now, the good news: you *can* have an awesome wedding without breaking the bank. All it takes is the right attitude, savvy shopping, creative planning and diligent budgeting.

The most important idea to remember about your wedding day is that you're getting married to the person you love. Whether your budget is £3,000 or £300,000, the party's success ultimately depends on the way you conduct yourselves, the love and respect you show for each other, and the way you express your happiness. This isn't about putting on a show. It's about forging a new life as a married couple and commemorating that. The hospitality you provide should reflect your values.

In fact, we can't stress enough what a wedding should *not* be: a cause of grief and anxiety. Perhaps in the back of your mind you're worried that guests will dissect every aspect of the reception, playing that tacky guessing game, 'How Much do You Think This Cost?' Stop. Such thoughts can drive you crazy and make you skew your budget based on someone else's priorities. Besides, if you have friends who really think such things, why are you inviting them to your wedding?

Whatever you do, don't go into debt to get married. Yes, this is an important day, but it's not worth struggling to pay it off for years to come. Have the wedding you can afford and make it the best it can be. Remember, the vows say 'for richer or poorer', not 'to our credit card limit'.

Knowing What You Can Afford

Before you even think about booking a venue or supplier, you need to know what you can afford. Sit down with your fiancé(e) and family to work out a realistic budget for the wedding. Consider where the money's going to come from:

- ✔ **Who'll contribute financially?** Just the bride and groom, or will family members pay for part of the wedding?

- ✔ **Who'll offer services/goods for free?** Will some family members provide a service or skill as their wedding gift to you?

- ✔ **What savings do you have?** Do you have money set aside for the wedding? If not, work out your expenditure versus your income and determine a realistic amount to save each month, and then multiply this figure by the length of time you plan for your engagement. So, if you're planning to marry in 18 months' time and you can afford to save £100 per month, you can save an additional £1,800 for the wedding pot.

Previous generations managed big weddings on small budgets by relying on the generosity of family and friends. So why not ask around. Consider whether you know someone who can contribute a service or item to your wedding. Perhaps you know someone who is a genius in the kitchen and who can make your cake? Maybe you have a friend who owns a nice car that you'd be able to use or your local taxi company has some *executive cars* – smarter, valeted cars used for local businesses. These are cheaper than a wedding car, but if you add some wedding ribbon they're perfectly suitable. Perhaps you have a relative with green fingers who can plant pots of beautiful flowers for table centres?

Be realistic with how far your budget can spread. If you want to invite 200 guests but your budget is £10,000, you have to compromise. Plenty of ways in which you can do this are out there. Instead of a formal sit down meal, for example, perhaps you can settle for an evening reception instead? If you need to cut costs, decide on your priorities by working out what is really important to you. Those are the areas where you should be spending your money.

Start Spreadsheeting the News

For tracking your wedding expenses and sticking to the bottom line, nothing beats a simple computerised spreadsheet. To the uninitiated, spreadsheets may look intimidating, but they're really a breeze to use. They'll also become your new best friend while planning the wedding. And after you figure out how they work, you have an easy way to see at a glance what this wedding is costing.

As shown in Figure 2-1, start at the bottom line by putting in the amount for your total budget. Based on that figure, fill in guesstimates for various items. As you research suppliers and quotes, make adjustments in the Estimated Cost column. You may have wildly overestimated the cost of wedding invitations or been dreaming when you thought silk flowers where cheaper than real ones. Typically, you may find suppliers' estimates much higher than your guesses. Don't panic. This spreadsheet is simply to help you get some perspective. Seeing the numbers laid out helps you deal with denial – that is, thinking that somehow all the numbers will magically work themselves out.

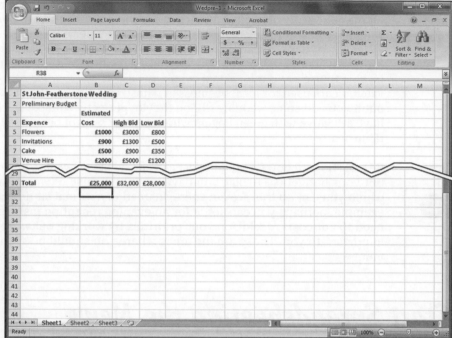

Figure 2-1:
Set up a
spreadsheet
to help you
compare
quotes.

Alternatively, instead of the Estimated Cost column, you can include a Percentages column where you allocate a percentage of your budget to various items. Here is an example breakdown:

- **Ceremony (including fees, bell ringers, choir, organist):** 3 per cent
- **Cake:** 2 per cent
- **Entertainment (including music):** 7 per cent
- **Florist:** 5 per cent
- **Film/video:** 5 per cent
- **Hair and make-up:** 1 per cent
- **Photographer:** 5 per cent
- **Reception (including venue, food, styling and drinks):** 45 per cent
- **Stationery:** 3 per cent
- **Transportation:** 2 per cent
- **Wedding dress/suits:** 8 per cent
- **Wedding planner:** 14 per cent

These percentages are just guidelines. Nothing is set in stone, so if you want to blow your budget on a great band, that's fine – just remember to reduce your spending elsewhere!

The percentage method can also be a good guide on knowing what you can't afford, for example if your budget is £10,000, allocating 5 per cent for photography allows you £500 for a photographer. If this was too much, you'd need to make a decision whether to forego something else in the budget so that you can afford the photographer. Remember that in some instances you may not be paying for a particular category – perhaps your future mother-in-law is making the cake or no transport is needed, for example. If so, great – just redistribute that percentage elsewhere within your budget.

After you've chosen your suppliers, set up another spreadsheet to help you keep track of money coming in and going out. The spreadsheet in Figure 2-2 shows you how to record expenditures, deposits paid and outstanding balances. Comparing estimates against actual amounts is helpful because invariably if you overspend in one area, you underspend in another. Creating a column that shows when payments are due is a good idea as well. You can get as elaborate as you want, adding columns to track additional payments, record contact information or make notes to yourself. The spreadsheet can also get quite long as you add line items. (See the 'And another thing . . . ' sidebar in this chapter for a list of possible expenditures you may want to include on your spreadsheet.)

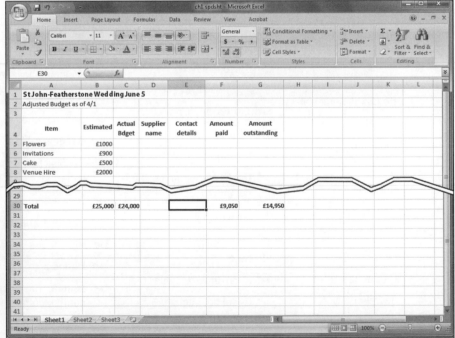

Figure 2-2: Create a more detailed spreadsheet to keep track of money coming in and going out.

And another thing . . .

Although we can't give you standard formulas to make budgeting a whizz (because, frankly, they don't exist), we do provide here a definitive list of the items you may need to include in your budget. If your goal is to avoid unpleasant surprises later, read on:

Ceremony

- Aisle runner
- Bell ringers' fee
- Church fee
- Registrar fee
- Organist fee

Clothing

- Alterations
- Bride's outfit

    Dress

    Gloves

    Hair

    Headpiece and veil

    Jewellery

    Make-up

    Nails

    Shoes

    Underwear

- Bridesmaid(s') outfit(s)

    Dress

    Hair accessories

    Jewellery

    Make-up

    Shoes

- Flower girl(s') outfit(s)

    Dress

    Hair accessories

    Jewellery

    Shoes

- Groom's outfit

    Cufflinks

    Shoes

    Suit

    Shirt

    Tie/cravat

    Waistcoat

- Page boy(s)/ushers

    Shoes

    Suit

    Waistcoat

    Tie/cravat

Drinks reception

- Canapés
- Corkage
- Drinks (recommend three per guest)
- Garden games
- Waiting staff

Flowers

- Altar/registrar table
- Bridal bouquet

- Bridesmaid(s') bouquet(s)
- Buttonholes
- Corsages
- Ceremony entrance (arch/urns/trees)
- Confetti (fresh or freeze-dried)
- Flower girl posy/basket
- Miscellaneous flowers (additional urns/occasional tables/cake posy)
- Pew ends
- Table centres

Gifts

- Attendants
- Bride and groom (to each other)
- Parents
- Party favours
- Welcome baskets

Hire companies

- Banquet chairs
- Banquet tables
- Candles (candelabras/lanterns)
- Dance floor
- Garden furniture
- High chairs
- Linens
- Lounge furniture (sofas/pouffes/coffee tables)

✔ Marquee

    Air-conditioning/heat

    Catering annexe

    Floor

    Electricity generator

    Lighting

    Windows

✔ Mobile bar

✔ Table settings (crockery/cutlery/glassware)

Music

✔ Band(s)

✔ Ceremony musicians, choir, singers

✔ DJ

✔ Drinks reception

✔ PA system for speeches

✔ Piano rental

Other events

✔ Next-day brunch

✔ Rehearsal dinner

Photography

✔ Albums

✔ Assistant(s)

✔ CD or memory stick of high-resolution images

✔ Copyright

✔ Engagement portrait

✔ Photographer's attendance fee (possibly including):

    Reprints/enlargements

    Videography

Rings

✔ Engagement

✔ Wedding

Stationery

✔ Calligraphy

✔ Escort cards

✔ Guest book

✔ Thank-you cards

✔ Invitations

    Information sheets

    Map and direction cards

✔ Menus

✔ Order of services

✔ Place cards/tags

✔ Postage

✔ Reply cards

✔ Save-the-date cards

✔ Signage

✔ Table names/numbers

✔ Table plan

Transportation and accommodation

✔ Bride and groom

✔ Guests

✔ Parents

✔ Wedding party

Venue hire

✔ Ceremony fee

✔ Drinks reception room

✔ Evening party room

✔ Wedding breakfast room

Wedding breakfast

✔ Cake – including stand and knife

✔ Drink

    Table water

    Table wine (½ bottle per person)

    Sparkling wine/Champagne for the speeches

✔ Food

    Adult meal

    Child meal

    Waiting staff

    Additional meals (Band/non-catering staff)

✔ Photographer

✔ Videographer

✔ Wedding Planner

Wedding planner

✔ Additional staff

✔ Expenses

✔ Planning fee

Some venues may charge an additional service charge on top of the catering bill. Before signing any contract make sure you are happy with this clause.

Include a column in your budget for a 10 per cent contingency on all expenses and for the bottom line. Unless you're a psychic, you're bound to underestimate some costs and overestimate others. This 10 per cent represents the highest amount you're willing to spend if need be. Just knowing that you're prepared with this contingency can save you from having a premature budgetary meltdown. Also, include Value Added Tax (VAT) in all your budgeting, where appropriate. Many suppliers give quotes that just say 'plus VAT'. Take a moment to calculate the amount and add it to your costs.

Whether you use a spreadsheet or some other system for keeping track of expenses, the key to watching your bottom line is to make sure you record every single deposit you put on a credit card and every transfer you authorise. Slacking off in this department is a good way to overspend.

Controlling Costs

Because weddings tend to cost more than may seem reasonable or possible, bear in mind these ways to make the most of what you have to spend:

- ✔ **Know your limits.** If you're paying for the entire wedding or a large portion of it, schedule a session with a wedding planner (who can tell you what things cost).

- ✔ **Open a wedding account.** The simplest way to manage your wedding budget is to open a dedicated wedding account so you know exactly how much money goes in and how much comes out.

- ✔ **Get donations upfront.** If someone else is contributing to your wedding, try to get the money in a lump sum.

- ✔ **Earn credit card points.** When it comes to paying for big-ticket items such as the dress or the venue hire, charge them to a credit card that gives you something in return (like frequent-flier miles). Do, of course, remember to pay the balance before that interest starts accumulating!

- ✔ **Elope.** Just kidding.

- ✔ **Be punctual.** Stay organised and stick to your wedding-day schedule so you can avoid overtime charges. (See Chapter 14.)

- ✔ **Read the fine print.** Examine contracts and costs carefully and ask questions. Is VAT included?

- ✔ **Negotiate.** Asking suppliers for reasonable discounts is perfectly acceptable if you have a good reason for them to reduce the costs, such as holding your wedding on an unpopular day or arranging a last-minute wedding.

✔ **Shop in the sales.** This seems obvious, but you may not realise how many wedding-related items you needn't pay retail prices for. Be on the lookout for sample sales for dresses (see Chapter 11), wine sales at supermarkets/wine merchants, department store sales for attendants' gifts, shoe sales – you get the picture.

✔ **Cut the head count.** Invite fewer people. Put simply, every guest costs you!

✔ **Keep checking the bottom line.** Being diligent is the best way to avoid magical thinking. If you've exceeded your budget in one category, look for another area where you can make up the difference. Remember – something's got to give!

✔ **Call in favours.** Weddings normally bring out the best in friends and family, so why not ask them to actively help you with the wedding? Perhaps someone has a hidden talent, like cake-making or hair-styling, or does someone have a luxury car you can use as the wedding transportation?

Comprehending Contracts

Just assuming that a booking is confirmed can be a costly mistake; always making sure that you have a signed contract filed away neatly in your wedding folder is a good practice to get into.

In this section, we give you some guidelines on what should be included within contracts and we draw up a list of items to check off when reading the small print. And make sure you do read that small print, as invariably there is a hidden clause somewhere which may just affect your wedding.

Making written contracts with suppliers

For every supplier you hire for your wedding, you should have a *written* contract that specifies the deposit paid and the amount due. If you're dealing with professionals (which we hope you are), the contract should contain a list detailing the specific services agreed upon. If you're dealing with a friend or relative, have at the very least a letter of agreement spelling out the service(s) to be provided. Make no exceptions. Verbal agreements are legally binding, but they're subject to amnesia and harder to prove in court. At any rate, the point is certainly not to prepare for possible lawsuits, but rather to make your wedding day as flawless as possible.

Contracts should be as specific as possible. Instead of 'rose bouquets', say 'three hand-tied bouquets of yellow and orange roses, finished with lace ribbon; one hand-tied bridal bouquet of pink, yellow and ivory roses, hand-tied with ivory satin ribbon'.

Most businesses have their own formal contracts, but if a supplier fails to produce one, you may want to take it upon yourself to draft a letter or contract detailing the goods or services you ordered, the pertinent details of your wedding and the amount you expect to pay. Ask the supplier to sign a copy; if the supplier refuses, find a new one. You don't want to do business with people who aren't willing to take responsibility for their work.

Before signing a contract, read it carefully and don't be shy about writing in additions or changes. However, ask suppliers how they want you to write them in. The supplier and you must both initial all changes before signing. Never sign a partially or entirely blank contract. A supplier may try to hurry things along by saying the details can be filled in later. Don't assume the supplier has criminal motives – the supplier may in fact just be trying to speed things up. But you're nonetheless better off waiting or finding a different supplier.

If you and a supplier discuss changes by telephone or email, you need to follow up with an actual letter reiterating the changes. Keep a copy for your files. (Also keep hard copies of email correspondence.) In fact, keep *all* receipts and copies of contracts in your wedding file. You'll need to refer to them several times before and after the wedding.

Depending on the type of supplier, your contract should include:

- ✔ Business name, address and phone number
- ✔ Contact person
- ✔ The person responsible for your event
- ✔ A complete description of the product or service
- ✔ The quantity you're ordering
- ✔ The number of people to be served
- ✔ Date and time service or product is to be available
- ✔ Date and time service is to end
- ✔ Exact prices for product
- ✔ Where and at what time product is to be delivered or set up
- ✔ Fees for delivery and set-up

- ✔ When overtime begins and the fee per hour or half-hour
- ✔ Policies regarding returns, postponement or cancellation
- ✔ Price escalation policies and when quoted rates expire
- ✔ Payment installments
- ✔ Acceptable payment methods (cheque, cash, credit card or bank transfer)
- ✔ Business representative's signature and date
- ✔ Your signature and date

Forking out a little at a time

Giving a deposit is actually in your interest: it tells suppliers that you're serious and further commits them to your event. If you can negotiate for deposits to be refundable, more power to you. However, most suppliers insist that they be non-refundable as a way to protect themselves from fraud.

No doubt you've come across contracts with suppliers before, maybe when you've bought a brand-new kitchen or conservatory, and you probably didn't have to pay in full until all goods or services were delivered to your satisfaction. But the event world runs a little differently. Many suppliers insist on full payment before the day of your wedding and specify so contractually.

Remember, after you pay a deposit and sign a contract, you're legally bound to pay in full.

As you make deposits, update your wedding budget. If you pay with a cheque, note on the memo line exactly what the deposit is for. For example, '50 per cent of wedding cake'. Paying deposits with credit cards is also a good idea because if the supplier fails to deliver, goes out of business before your wedding date or commits some error – and you can convince the credit card company of that – the charges may be reversed. Buyers' remorse doesn't qualify for a reversal of charges.

If you cancel or postpone your wedding, don't expect a full refund of your various deposits. Some businesses charge 50 per cent of their estimated fee regardless of the reason you cancel. They may have turned away other business on your wedding date; your deposit compensates them for this loss. Some suppliers return deposits if you cancel because of a death in the family or if they're able to rebook the date and recoup the revenue. If you don't cancel but merely postpone, you may face a price increase.

Covering your bash

If you're the sort who always sees the glass not only half-empty but also cracked in six places, you may consider taking out a wedding insurance policy. These policies generally cover postponement, photographs, dress/attire, gifts, additional expenses, personal liability and medical payments. Just imagine, for example, the horror of discovering your venue has burnt down a few months before the wedding. A good insurance policy would not only cover your costs but also cover you for legal obligations with suppliers you've hired. Of course, this is a worst-case scenario and we would hope another local venue would come to the rescue, but being safe is always better than being sorry.

Is the one-time premium worth it? Like all insurance, it may seem like money down the drain until something goes horribly wrong. But read the fine print. A policy may cover postponement or cancellation only in cases when non-refundable expenses are incurred due to circumstances beyond your control. These circumstances may include sickness or bodily injury to the bride or groom or anyone *essential* (whatever that means) to the wedding party, damage or inaccessibility to the premises where the wedding or reception is to be held, loss or damage to the wedding dress or other wedding attire, or job loss. Not surprisingly, insurance doesn't cover change of heart.

Bargain-Hunting Online

Thanks to the Internet, you can plan almost your entire wedding without getting up from your desk – from taking virtual tours of venues to ordering invitations to buying wedding outfits.

The first stop on any Internet shopping expedition should be your favourite search engine such as `Google.com` or `Yahoo.com`. Depending on what you're in the market for, first try a search for exactly what you seek (for example, 'vintage headpiece'). If that doesn't produce enough results, expand with general terms (such as 'bridal headpieces').

Most search engines are sophisticated enough that you can enter a string of words with no quotation marks or connecting words. However, quotation marks can help narrow the search faster: typing in wedding dress can bring up thousands of entries on anything having to do with Christmas or angels, but 'wedding dress' with quotation marks would give you more precise hits.

In many cases, shopping on the web saves you money, but not always. To get your money's worth as you scour the Net, remember to:

- **Bare your gifts.** When shopping for attendants' gifts, be aware that you pay extra for gift-wrapping online orders. But some stores, such as Tiffany and Fortnum and Mason, send their goodies in boxes that are so pretty they make wrapping paper superfluous.

- **Pit prices against each other.** Consumer sites compile databases of products sold at online stores and sort them according to price. In some cases, these sites also provide product reviews and customer-service scores, and even tally the cost of shipping for you.

- **eBay it.** With millions of items for sale in hundreds of categories – including one for 'Wedding Supplies' – you can find almost any accessory for your wedding on eBay (www.ebay.co.uk). Type in 'wedding' or 'bridal' on the site's search engine and you'll discover rings, dresses, veils, shoes, tiaras, jewellery, invitations, favours, flowers, candles and just about anything else you can think of – often at far below retail prices. To get the best deals, read all the instructions and policies on the site and have a good idea of retail prices.

Chapter 3

Making It Legal

In This Chapter

▶ Knowing the law and how it applies to your wedding

▶ Pondering prenups

▶ Changing your name

▶ Calling off a wedding

*W*eddings aren't all fluff and festivities. All that is window dressing for an extremely serious rite of passage. You still have to make it legal. Besides getting a licence, you need to figure out whether to change your name and, depending on your circumstances, whether a prenuptial agreement is a good idea. In this chapter, we walk you through these tasks, and take a look at what you need to do if the wedding plans grind to a halt.

When you start organising your ceremony be sure to check with the relevant registrar or minister regarding any law changes that may have occurred since the publication of this book.

Registering Your Wedding: Understanding UK Law

First things first: a *marriage licence* (*marriage schedule* in Scotland and Northern Ireland) is the piece of paper that authorises you to get married, and a *marriage certificate* is the document that proves you're married. For the easily confused, be aware that you may see a 'marriage licence' referred to in some places as a 'certificate for marriage', which isn't the same thing as a 'marriage certificate'! Similarly, depending on which county you're in, you may come across the place you go to give notice for your marriage being referred to as a 'registry', 'register' or 'registrar' office.

When you've got your head around the lingo, you need to move on to the rules.

Playing by the rules

The following rules apply for weddings that take place in the UK:

- ✔ The couple should be over 16 years of age to be legally married. Parental consent is necessary if under 18 in England, Wales and Northern Ireland, but is not necessary in Scotland.

- ✔ Couples should be free to marry, which means not closely related or already married to another person.

- ✔ There should be two witnesses to the ceremony. They should be mature enough to understand the legalities of the marriage in order to sign as a witness.

The sections that follow outline the legalities for different kinds of ceremonies.

When you get your marriage certificate, order an extra copy or two because you must submit an original copy – not a photocopy – when applying for a new national insurance card and driving licence. That way, if you mail your marriage certificate, you don't have to worry about your only bona fide copy returning to you in several pieces or stained with coffee rings or forever disappearing into the bureaucratic black hole.

Civil ceremonies

The civil ceremony is the most popular type in the UK, accounting for 70 per cent of all marriages. The ceremony is equally open for heterosexual and homosexual marriages (same-sex couples follow the same legal rules as different-sex couples).

To have a civil ceremony you must marry in a licensed venue or register office. The venue must be open to the public and the doors must be unlocked. The venue must be a 'permanent structure', so a pavilion can be licensed but not a marquee. A boat would only be acceptable if it was permanently moored. Contact your local authority for a list of licensed venues in your chosen areas.

You can book civil ceremonies only exactly 12 months in advance (minimum 15 days); very rarely will a registrar provisionally hold a date. This can be difficult when you want to book a venue two years in advance to get a popular date.

You must have lived in the district you're giving notice in for at least seven days (a hotel can count if based abroad). If your venue isn't in your district you still need to register in your district first, and then you can contact the register office where your venue is located to book the registrar for your wedding.

Some venues appear to offer an outside ceremony. For example, you may find a venue with a licensed room whose doorway leads into a garden or gazebo. It may be possible for guests to sit outside in the garden while the couple marries inside the structure, whether that's under an archway, doorway or gazebo.

After you've chosen the venue for your ceremony, you need to call your local register office to make an appointment to go and give notice. Both bride and groom must go in person to the register office in the district(s) that you each live in. The registrar asks a few personal questions about each partner and then enters the details into the marriage notice book. You need to provide these documents to give notice:

- ✔ Birth certificates.

- ✔ Change of name deed, if applicable.

- ✔ Decree absolute, if one or both are divorced.

- ✔ Marriage certificate and death certificate, if one or both are widowed.

- ✔ Passports (couples who don't have a British passport need to check their eligibility to marry in the UK with their consulate; European passports are generally fine provided they meet the residency requirements, but Americans and other nationalities need to check their visa status and individual status).

- ✔ Proof of current addresses.

Papers are posted within the register office for public view. Anyone who wants to oppose the marriage has 15 days to do so. Assuming no one does object, you can collect the marriage license after 15 days if you're marrying in another district; otherwise you can leave the license with the registrar, who'll take it to the ceremony. If marrying in another district, you need to forward the licence on to that district.

The marriage licence is only valid for 12 months and for that particular ceremony venue. If you want to marry after 12 months or you change your mind about the venue, you have to go through the whole procedure again.

Faith weddings

A religious wedding can take place at a church, chapel or other registered religious building (and religious blessings can take place in a religious building after a civil ceremony in a register office). Even if you've decided on a religious ceremony, however, you may still need to 'register' your marriage at your register office (see the preceding section).

You don't usually need to give notice with the register office if you're getting married in an Anglican or Church of England church; the officials who perform these marriages will both give notice *and* register your marriage. For some religions, however, you need to give notice with the register office at least 16 days before the ceremony, and although the ministers and priests of other religions can be authorised to register marriages, some may not be authorised to do so. Check with your officiant whether or not they will give notice and register your marriage; if not, the responsibility is yours. If the official performing the actual ceremony is not authorised, either a registrar must attend the religious ceremony or you need to have separate religious and civil ceremonies.

Here we take a look at the various rules for the main faith weddings that take place in the UK. (For further information on other religious ceremonies head across to Chapter 15.)

Anglican and Church of England weddings

Weddings must take place in a recognised religious building between the hours of 8 a.m. and 6 p.m.. The doors need to be unlocked throughout the ceremony. The ceremony can take place on any day of the week provided the vicar, reverend or minister agrees. They normally don't like Sundays for weddings, however!

Officially, you can confirm wedding dates only 12 months in advance, although this depends on the flexibility of the vicar.

When you have your meeting with the vicar you need to take:

- ✔ Baptism certificates
- ✔ Birth certificates/passports
- ✔ Decree absolutes/death certificates for divorced/widowed people
- ✔ Written consent from guardians if under 18

The vicar reads out the *banns* on three consecutive Sundays before the wedding within three months of the ceremony date; these declare the couple's intention to marry and give any regular worshippers an opportunity to object. If the couple live in a different parish to which they are marrying then the banns need to be read there as well. Be careful to check parish boundaries because they don't follow modern-day geographical/postcode boundaries. The church where the wedding takes place should be able to advise.

In some cases it may be necessary to marry by common license or special license (if the couple aren't resident in the parish). Please review the Church of England website for full details (www.yourchurchwedding.org).

At the ceremony, the vicar issues and signs the marriage certificate.

Catholic weddings

Couples marrying in a Catholic church must give notice as if they're having a civil wedding (see the earlier 'Civil ceremonies' section) with the Catholic church listed as the venue of marriage. In some situations a civil registrar needs to attend the Catholic church, not to conduct the ceremony but to be there to arrange the signing of the register/paperwork. Sometimes an appointed person at the church is allowed; it varies greatly but we recommend checking early because civil registrars get notoriously booked up in some areas.

The same often applies to Greek and Russian weddings.

Jewish weddings

Although Jewish weddings often take place in synagogues, they aren't subject to the same licensing restrictions as civil weddings, which must be performed under a permanent structure, so they can be held anywhere. You see lots of weddings taking place at private venues, particularly in gardens under the *chuppah*, or canopy, which symbolises the home that the couple will share.

Couples being married by a rabbi give notice at their local register office as if they are having a civil ceremony (see the earlier section) and pass those notices on to the rabbi. In some situations a civil registrar needs to attend the ceremony to sign the paperwork, but in most cases the rabbi brings an appointed person to sign the certificate or officiate at the ceremony.

Live abroad but marrying in the UK?

If one of you lives abroad but you're planning on marrying in the UK, you may be able to give notice of your intention to marry in the country where you reside, if that country has signed up to the British Subjects Facilities Act. Visit www.gov.uk/marriages-civil-partnerships for up-to-date information.

Drawing Up a Prenup

Prenuptial agreements don't have a long history in the UK but are gaining popularity. They may sound daunting, but these agreements offer couples-to-be a legally binding way of safeguarding their own property in the event that the marriage fails somewhere down the line.

Contrary to popular belief, prenuptial (or 'prenup') agreements aren't enforceable in England and Wales. However, a recent case in the Supreme Court has made it much more likely that the divorce court will hold a couple to the terms of the agreement. For a prenup to stand up in the courts of England and Wales it is advisable that both parties have:

- ✔ Entered into the agreement of their own free will, without duress or undue pressure.

- ✔ Understood the implications of the agreement, because the court will look at the intentions the couple had when they signed the agreement.

A court will also consider whether holding the parties to the agreement is fair and look at whether the parties obtained independent legal advice, the level of financial disclosure in the agreement and how long before the wedding the agreement was written.

Think about getting a prenup in these circumstances:

- ✔ If one of you has property that you would want to keep if the marriage were to end – for example, if it brings you a considerable income or if the property is home to a family business.

- ✔ If one or both of you want to retain as much property as possible for children or grandchildren from prior marriages. A prenup can assist in ensuring that the bulk of a spouse's property passes to the children or grandchildren rather than to the current spouse.

Some couples find that going through the prenup exercise helps them come to terms with each other's needs and values before certain issues become irresolvable problems later on in the relationship. Sometimes, many of the issues that get hashed out in prenup preparation become simple private pledges rather than part of a potentially legally binding document. That said, arranging a prenup or negotiating its terms can lead to psychological repercussions. Before you broach the subject of a prenup with your partner, ask yourself whether such an agreement is worth the effect it may have on your relationship. Even if both of you agree to enter into an agreement, be aware that prenups can be stressful to negotiate, especially in the run-up to the wedding.

If you do decide to negotiate a premarital agreement, both you and your partner should obtain legal advice so that you're aware of the proper procedures to follow – and you each need a different lawyer. Instruct your lawyer to write the agreement in plain English, not legalese, and aim to negotiate the specifics and sign the agreement as early as possible in the wedding-planning process. Getting a head start makes sense because an agreement signed under duress may not hold up in court and because you really don't want financial negotiations to be on your mind as the banns are read or, even worse, as you walk down the aisle. Be flexible and certain that every negotiation reflects your love for each other.

Playing the Name Game

Deciding what to call yourselves after your marriage isn't the simple wife-changes-her-name-to her-husband's scenario it once was. Although many newspapers still feel compelled to note when the bride is keeping her name, upon marriage, a woman's *surname* (her family or last name) doesn't automatically change to her husband's, nor is she legally *required* to change it. A woman must choose to change it and then take certain measures to make the change official (that is, legal). Note that if you're one of the 36 per cent of women who opts to retain your maiden name, you're still entitled to a portion of your husband's pension, income or other rights associated with the marriage contract.

Deciding whether to change your name

These days, a variety of options are both possible and socially acceptable:

- The bride takes the groom's name.
- The bride keeps her birth name.
- The bride keeps her birth name for professional circumstances, but takes her husband's name in all other cases.
- The bride and groom use both their last names, with or without a hyphen.
- The bride uses both her birth and married surnames, with or without a hyphen.
- The groom drops his name and takes the bride's.
- The bride and groom meld their names into a new one altogether.
- The bride and groom pick out an entirely new name.

For a woman, adopting her husband's name can have some drawbacks. If a man has been previously married or comes to the marriage laden with some unfortunate financial or legal baggage, a new bride can find herself being harassed by credit-collection agencies as a result of mismerged data – that is, when an ex-spouse's financial information winds up in a new spouse's credit report. If your hubby-to-be owes back-taxes, has tax liens on his property, has been the victim of identity theft or has some other complicated financial history, you may want to hold off changing your name until those issues are resolved so you can protect your own assets.

Another issue to consider is whether your career will suffer by changing your name. People are marrying later in life (the average UK woman marries at age 25 to 29 today, up from 20 years old in the 1980s) and many women find that they've established themselves enough that changing their name would confuse colleagues. This is particularly true in industries where referrals and networking are integral to the job. On the other hand, announcing your new name can be a wonderful opportunity to touch base with clients and colleagues.

If you decide not to change your name, you may find that older relatives (mothers, grandmothers, aunts and so on) don't understand this decision and they may insist on calling you by your husband's surname. Don't get stressed over it; we advise to go with the flow.

Updating your records

You should decide by the time of your wedding what names you'll use legally, professionally and socially. If you change one or both of your names, start using them as soon as you're married and then be sure to change your name on all your identification, accounts and important documents. And if marrying also means moving house, be sure to change your address on all records too.

Follow these steps:

1. **Notify HM Revenue & Customs.**

   Getting any other institution to acknowledge your new identity is hard until Big Brother does. HMRC automatically updates your benefit- and tax-related matters, such as child benefit, national insurance and your pay-as-you-earn or self-assessment (but you need to take charge of notifying the student loan company).

2. **Change your passport and driving licence.**

   You can apply for a new passport in your new name up to three months before the ceremony, during which time your old passport is cancelled. The new passport is postdated so you can't use it before the ceremony. You can download a passport form via www.gov.uk/changing-passport-information/marriage-and-civil-partnership.

   You must book your honeymoon flights in the name you plan to use on your passport: the name on the passport must be the same as on the tickets. Check that your postdated passport in your new name is acceptable by the country you're visiting for any necessary visa.

   To change your driving licence, go to www.dvla-driving-licence.co.uk and download an application form.

3. **Update all other records.**

   Here are a few things you need to change:

   - Bank accounts (order a new cheque book too)
   - Business cards
   - Credit cards
   - Electoral roll
   - Email address (home and professional)
   - Frequent flyer programmes
   - Insurance policies (change your beneficiaries as well)
   - Retirement accounts (again, change your beneficiaries)
   - Stationery
   - Work records (tell the finance department and your manager)

Many companies allow you to update your information by phone or email. However, others, such as banks and credit card companies, require a written request and, in some cases, a copy of your marriage certificate. Be sure to sign each letter and, if circumstances require it, have your spouse sign as well.

Take a copy of your marriage certificate with you when you travel or have to sign anything official, such as the papers when you're closing a home sale. After you have new forms of ID, you can leave the certificate at home.

Unplanning a Wedding

If you're in the throes of planning your wedding and you need to cancel or postpone it, we realise that what you're going through is traumatic. Whatever the culprit, you're faced with an awful task, made all the more unpleasant by unnecessary financial losses in addition to the psychological stress.

For details on the social aspects, such as alerting guests that the wedding is off, see Chapter 8. To figure out what to do with gifts you've already received, see Chapter 9. Continue on, dear reader, for tips on dealing with contracts and money matters, and deciding what to do with the engagement ring.

Settling up

Depending on how far along you are in your planning, you must call your venue, caterer and other suppliers, and attempt to get all or some of your deposits back. If you've managed to specify a refundable deposit clause in your contract, that'll make things easier and less of a financial hardship. If a supplier refuses to refund any money you're due, you can dispute the charge on your credit card statement (if you read Chapter 2 and paid by credit card, that is) or take it up with a third-party mediator such as the Citizens' Advice Bureau. In general, suppliers assess the cause of the cancellation, the possibilities of their rebooking the date and the amount of time they've already invested in your wedding to calculate a possible refund.

The potential pitfalls involved in unplanning a wedding is another excellent reason to take out wedding insurance (which we discuss in Chapter 2). Do remember to check that your policy covers you for postponement and cancellation.

Even if your attendants were going to pay for their own dresses or other attire, you now need to reimburse them for the money they've spent or the deposits they may have lost. If they ask you to pay them back for the shower they threw in your honour, you're not obligated to do so. But do return their gifts to them (or, if used, an identical gift) with a note of 'Thanks, but . . .' as we describe in Chapter 9.

If you need to iron out some financial details of your split with your ex (such as reception payments spent), retaining legal counsel is probably a good idea so that you keep discussions businesslike.

Deciding who keeps the ring

Whether she's the jilter or the jiltee, every bride wants to know: 'Do I have to give the ring back?' The answer is usually yes, although many legal cases have grappled with this question and reached different conclusions. The main point of contention is whether an engagement ring is just a gift or contains an implied condition of marriage. And though some judges think the ring should go back to the purchaser, regardless of who broke up with whom, others think that if the man (the 'donor' in legal parlance) broke off the engagement, he can't recover the ring.

We happen to feel that, no matter whom or what is to blame, the ring should go back to the person who gave it.

Part II
Preparing for Your Big Day

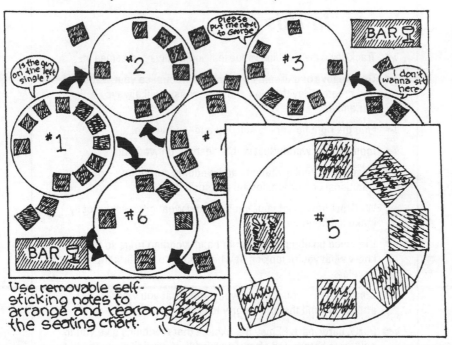

For a free bonus article about what part your usher can play in making a success of your wedding day, head online and take a look at www.dummies.com/extras/weddingplanninguk.

In this part...

- Track down the wedding venue that you've always dreamed of.

- Get creative and dream up ways to personalise your wedding and create a day that you and your guests will always remember.

- Find the right flowers to suit you and your venue.

- Indulge your wanderlust with a destination wedding.

- Design beautiful invitations and wedding stationery – whether traditional or modern, formal or informal.

- Work out how to let your guests know what gifts would really make a difference to you.

- Get clued up about engagement and wedding rings so that you know what you're looking at when you take that first trip to the jewelers.

- Consider what you want to wear, and what you want your attendants and the bridal party to wear.

- Party, party, party! Enjoy the excuse that weddings give you to celebrate before and after your wedding, as well as on the big day itself.

Chapter 4

Finding the Perfect Venue

. . . .

In This Chapter

▶ Finding the right place

▶ Considering how you use the space

▶ Visiting venues

▶ Holding a reception in a marquee

. . . .

*W*hether you choose a religious ceremony followed by a reception in a marquee or a civil ceremony and reception at the same venue, finding a tie-the-knot spot is one of the first tasks to cross off your list. Sought-after venues are often booked up a year in advance, and, in popular areas, hotels and B&Bs fill up quickly as peak season approaches. And, of course, until you know where you're getting married, moving on to other decisions, such as ordering invitations and finalising the menu, is impossible. So read on to get the lowdown on location, location, location for your wedding reception or all-in-one venue (for the lowdown on locations for the ceremony, head to Chapter 15).

Which venue you choose has a huge impact on all other factors of the wedding, so spend time getting this decision correct.

Looking for Love in All the Right Places

You may already know where you want to hold your wedding reception. Perhaps you have romantic visions of a castle or a rustic country barn. Regardless, you've many factors to consider when choosing a venue.

Deciding on location

Start with the big picture. Will the wedding take place where you currently live or near to your family? Think about whether you want a city location or would prefer to be in the countryside.

If guests are travelling long distances then good access is important, along with parking.

Considering popular choices

The UK offers an array of beautiful venues. Here are our top options:

- **Historical castle:** Some brides dream of a fairy-tale wedding, so where better to hold it than in a castle? This truly is a wedding fit for a princess. Check capacity levels and whether you can dine inside or whether you must hire a marquee.

- **Chic hotel:** Perhaps you like the fast-paced city life? If so a chic hotel may be the venue for you. Catering is in-house but you have the bonus of guests being able to party and sleep at the same venue.

- **Country barn:** Whether you want a truly rustic barn or a modern renovated version, you've plenty of choice. Most allow you the opportunity to bring in your own caterers and booze, which can help bring the wedding budget down.

- **Country manor house:** If you've always wanted to be a lord and lady at your country estate for the weekend, a manor house may be the choice for you. Steeped in history with many original features, a country manor house offers you a taste of exclusive luxury for 24 hours. Catering is normally in-house. And many have venue wedding co-ordinators to assist you with making key decisions.

- **Private marquee:** If you or your family have a beautiful large garden, you can plan a reception at home. Your ceremony legally has to take place elsewhere, but you can hold the rest of the proceedings inside the marquee (see 'Planning a Marquee Reception', later in this chapter).

Venues that are open to the public may not allow access until late afternoon, so bear this in mind in terms of the wedding schedule and supplier logistics when shortlisting venues.

Following your nose

Your own attitude plays a key role in your search for an original, magical place to get married.

✔ **Be gutsy:** Get personal suggestions from people whom you consider arbiters of taste and style, including bridal magazine editors.

✔ **Be curious:** Perhaps you or someone you know attended a wedding that was stunning, but for some reason – cost, location, size – the venue isn't quite right for you.

Find out what other spots the couple passed up. Their reject list may contain your dream site.

✔ **Be creative:** Enquire about unconventional spaces to hire, such as private homes, museums, galleries, boats and private gardens. Owners who've never thought of renting out their property may consider it for a wedding.

Choosing between 'on-premise' and 'off-premise'

Find out whether a prospective reception venue has in-house caterers or whether you need to hire your own. In general, *in-house* means a venue that provides the food and drink, whereas *venue-only* means just the venue itself is included within the hire fee, meaning that you'd need to hire your own caterers and possibly a mobile bar company.

Some venues have lists of caterers that they either allow or recommend. Whether you've fallen in love with a particular venue-only space or have designs on a brilliant caterer, be certain they can work together. If you feel the food is equally or more important than the space, start by finding a caterer, who in turn may lead you to the space. (See Chapter 17 for tips on finding a great caterer.)

Doing your homework

Before you set out on a wild goose chase, spend some time amassing as much material on various locations as possible. You can find information about wedding sites in a variety of places, including

✔ **Bridal magazines:** Buy a load of bridal magazines one month and browse the real weddings as well as the advertisements. Also check out bridal magazines like *Wedding Venues & Services,* which has a large directory on venues, broken down by county.

✔ **Caterers:** Because venue-only locations are their stock in trade, caterers are tuned in to what's available. To find a unique space, interview caterers for suggestions or review their websites for venue links and mentions on their social media regarding venues they've recently worked at.

✔ **Historical organisations:** If you're set on using a historical venue then visit the websites of the National Trust (www.nationaltrust.org.uk) and English Heritage (www.english-heritage.org.uk) to see which of their venues host weddings. Likewise, if you wanted to hold your reception in a museum, check the website of the museums you're interested in for information on their wedding hire.

✔ **Internet:** If you've determined what type of venue you want, use the Internet to search for suitable venues in your chosen area. For example, search 'wedding barn in Essex'.

✔ **Personal recommendation:** Never underestimate the strength of recommendations from family and friends. Ask them about weddings they've been to recently and details of any venues that especially wowed them.

✔ **Venue directories:** A few specialist web directories have venue listings on them. Try www.wedding-venues.co.uk, www.squaremeal.co.uk and www.landedhouses.co.uk.

✔ **Wedding fairs:** Some venues exhibit at the larger wedding fairs, but also some venues host the smaller fairs, which gives you the perfect chance to visit the venue and meet local suppliers.

✔ **Wedding planners:** Wedding planners have an abundance of venues they can recommend to you. In some cases these venues may be little-known gems you wouldn't find otherwise. The planner will ask you various questions to determine the type of venue you require and then prepare a list of recommended venues for you to consider. In some cases these venues give a discount to clients of wedding planners.

✔ **Your local authority:** Especially useful as a first stop for planning an out-of-town wedding. Contact your local authority and ask them to send a list of approved and licensed wedding venues in the area. Some have fabulous websites and brochures they can send you.

Vetting the venues

For ease you may decide to email the venue in the first instance to check availability. After confirmation that the venue is indeed available, we recommend calling for further information. The phone interview lets you preview the service you may receive. Do they return calls promptly? Do they seem flexible, or do they have a more 'take it or leave it' attitude? Do you get a sense the venue staff would be happy (not desperate, just pleased) to host your wedding? Are they too busy to talk to you? Condescending? Rude? Evasive?

During the initial phone call:

✔ Get the name and title of the person on the other end of the phone.

✔ Ask what room(s) are available for your wedding date and time.

✔ Ask for food and beverage price estimates. (For a breakdown of what those estimates may be, see Chapters 17 and 18.)

✔ Ask whether you'll have exclusive use of the venue, or whether other events or guests will be at the venue.

A good venue encourages you to visit for a personal show round. Refer to the later section 'Taking a Space Walk'.

Determining Whether You Need More Than One Space

If you're not going to be married in a church or other religious building, you need a place to have a ceremony, a drinks reception, the wedding breakfast and an evening reception (if you have one). Your first choice should be a site that can handle all four in separate spaces.

The turning of the room

Finding versatile, multi-roomed spaces isn't easy. Consequently, you may need to *turn a room*. This term refers to resetting a room for another function. A space that must double for wedding breakfast and evening reception requires that chairs be moved and tables positioned while guests are in the room. If the ceremony and wedding breakfast are in the same room, guests are ushered to a separate area while staff turn the ceremony room.

Elaborate decor may involve extra labour costs or may be impossible to pull off in the time between the ceremony and reception. Your decor concept should not dictate the length of the drinks reception. By the time they're seated, some guests may be too sloshed to notice or care whether they have a rose tree or a redwood towering above them.

Ceremony here, reception there

Even if getting married in a church isn't a priority, you may opt to have the ceremony and reception at different locations to avoid any room-turn awkwardness. Doing so, however, may incur additional expense, such as fees for the ceremony site, dual sets of flowers and other decor for both sites, and transportation for your guests.

What's more, the timing between the two sites must work. When drawing up your schedule, don't forget to factor in the time it takes for guests to get in their cars, plus the actual journey time to the reception venue. For a sample wedding-day schedule, see Chapter 14.

Taking a Space Walk

After you've done your preliminary nosing around, investigate spaces in person with your fiancé(e) or a close friend whose opinion you trust. Don't take your parents or future in-laws on this qualifying round. You want to have intelligent, researched responses to the possible downsides before they spot them and panic.

When you go to see a venue, take copious notes. Ask for brochures and photos of other events that have taken place there. If none are available, snap a few photos – because by the time you've seen the 12th place, you won't remember one manor house from another. But ask permission before taking photos because some places consider their layout and decor proprietary information.

Remember, you're still in the preliminary stages. Go with your gut reaction. Hiring a venue is a bit like finding your dream home: in short, you know it when you see it. Some venues look perfect on paper, but when you're walking round the venue your heart doesn't stutter. Don't settle for 'it's okay'. This isn't the time to start thinking about how you can transform a space you basically don't like. If the place depresses you or offends any one of your five senses, move on.

Asking the right questions

As you scout various options, you need to ask different questions, depending on whether the space is in-house catering or venue-only (see the earlier section on deciding between the two) and whether you intend to use the site for both the ceremony and reception or just the reception.

For starters, ask specifically what parts of the space are available. You may envision the venue's exquisite rose garden as the perfect backdrop for photos, only to find out, the day before, that it's off-limits.

Also, if another event will be taking place at the same time, ask the manager how staff keep guests from running into each other. A 'bridal crossing' experience can put a real dampener on your day.

The list of questions in Figure 4-1 helps you zero in on the specifics.

Venue Checklist

Date and times
- ❏ Does the venue book other weddings or events on the same day? (How does the venue ensure the two separate events don't clash?)
- ❏ How far in advance can the venue confirm a booking?
- ❏ From what time do suppliers have access to set up?
- ❏ When does everything have to be collected; is it that evening or the following day(s)?

Capacity, logistics and floor-plan dimensions
- ❏ What rooms are included within the hire fee?
- ❏ How many guests can the venue seat (with dancing) for a formal sit-down meal? Ask to see floor-plans, diagrams and photos including pictures of previous events.
- ❏ What do they consider the optimum number of guests for the space?
- ❏ How does the space work? (Think about the flow of a wedding. Where do guests enter, how are they directed to the ceremony, drinks reception, wedding breakfast and evening reception?)
- ❏ Is sufficient parking available?
- ❏ Is the disabled access sufficient for guests with mobility issues?
- ❏ Is there a cloakroom?
- ❏ Which area is used for the drinks reception?
- ❏ If a room is used twice (for the ceremony and wedding breakfast, for example) how long does it take to turn it around?
- ❏ Where can the bride get dressed? The groom?
- ❏ Any restrictions on where the photographer can go on the day? What spaces work well in bad weather?
- ❏ What is the rain plan if part of the day will take place outside?

Possible restrictions
- ❏ Does the venue have a sound meter in place? If so, what decibel is it set to? (It's important you relay this information to any band/DJ you hire for the evening.)
- ❏ Does the venue insist on minimum numbers for the day and/or evening? In some cases if you have less than the minimum numbers, you have to pay the surplus in catering costs.
- ❏ Are there restrictions on which suppliers you can use? Some venues may have set caterers you must use, or only one company may be allowed for firework displays at the venue.
- ❏ Is dancing allowed? This may sound crazy, but some historical venues insist the evening celebration take place in an adjacent marquee. This is to protect their floor against high heels.
- ❏ What time does the party need to finish? Do they offer the opportunity to pay for an extension?
- ❏ Does the venue offer exclusivity? If so, do they make an additional charge to guarantee this?

Fees
- ❏ What is the venue hire fee? Is this for the whole space or is there an additional charge per room used?
- ❏ How many hours do you have the venue for?
- ❏ Does the venue have special offers for mid-week or low-season dates?
- ❏ Are all staff included within the fee?
- ❏ When are the deposit and further payments due?
- ❏ What is the cancellation policy?
- ❏ Can you reserve the date without paying a deposit in order to check availability with the registrar (if you're having a civil ceremony)? How long will they hold the venue for?

Lighting
- ❏ What lighting is in the venue? How does the lighting look best? Are any of the lights dimmable?
- ❏ Are candles allowed? Does the venue supply them?

Staff
- ❏ Will the person showing you around the space be working with you throughout the entire process? If not, who's your contact and will she be there on the day as well?

Figure 4-1:
Asking the right questions helps determine whether a site is viable for a ceremony, reception or both.

Many places refuse to hold tastings of their menus for shoppers, and we do empathise. Producing a meal for two (or four) is both costly and labour intensive, especially for off-site caterers. We feel, however, that after you've booked the facility or caterer, you're entitled to a tasting, and you should negotiate this upfront before signing the contract. If the food isn't up to par, you're entitled to repeat tastings until it is (but definitely take this as a warning sign).

As you question a prospective caterer or banquet manager, get a clear idea of the rules regarding bar service, because that affects overall cost and logistics. (For a complete rundown of your bar needs, see Chapter 18.)

In order to compare the total *real* costs for your food and beverage service at a venue-only site with those at an in-house site, you must get estimates from outside caterers for the venue-only site. Comparing sites based on rental fees alone doesn't give you enough financial information to make a decision. For this reason, we include the questions to ask in preliminary interviews with caterers in Chapter 17.

Planning a Marquee Reception

Many couples have always dreamed of a beautiful marquee reception, especially for summer weddings. A marquee can create a quintessentially English feel to the reception.

One of the main reasons you may decide to have a marquee is to ensure that you have complete control of your reception. In essence, a marquee gives you a blank canvas to work from. However, marquee events require a lot of organisation and come with logistical challenges along the way, so make sure you are very organised and think seriously about hiring someone to assist with the planning.

Locating a marquee site

A variety of places can be great locations for a marquee reception. Most people who opt for a marquee reception do so because they or their parents have a garden that they're desperate to use. However, if your wish is to have a marquee reception, but you don't personally have the space for one, do not fear. Here are some alternatives to consider:

✔ **Farmers' fields:** Some farmers hire out their paddocks. Ask around if anyone knows of a local field for hire. If you go for this route, you may need to hire security to supervise any hired stock held in the marquee.

✓ **Private manor houses:** Hiring the grounds of a local privately owned manor house is sometimes a possibility. You may not be allowed to use the actual house; instead, the hire fee will cover the use of their land to erect a marquee and their gardens for the drinks reception. Try finding one at www.wedding-venues.co.uk or www.landedhouses.co.uk.

✓ **Village halls:** It may be that your village hall is set in a picturesque field but you need a tad more space than the hall offers. Extending the space by having a marquee could be the perfect option. You'd need to check the council will allow this and, like the paddock site, ensure you have security on hand.

✓ **Wedding venues:** Some wedding venues have a *pavilion* (a permanent marquee) for weddings or a seasonal marquee (erected between May and September). So if you want a marquee wedding but with the reassurance of a venue team overseeing the event, this may be the option for you. Remember, though, that you won't have the flexibility or total control that you get from having a marquee in, say, your garden.

Speak with your local marquee companies for recommendations on local sites that you can hire for erecting a marquee.

Choosing your marquee

Marquees generally come in one of the designs shown in Figure 4-2, and the style you choose depends on the number of guests, where you want to place the dance floor and food stations, and the venue setting. The basic styles are as follows:

✓ **Dome:** A modern structure made from a lightweight aluminium frame and cotton canvas cover. Can be erected anywhere; no guy ropes or poles.

✓ **Frame:** Supported by an aluminium frame with no poles or ropes. Ideal if you can't use poles and guy ropes on the site, such as on tennis courts or concrete courtyards. Also called a *clear-span frame marquee*.

✓ **Giant tipi:** A beautiful alternative to an ivory marquee with Nordic wood poles and light tan-coloured canvases. With the sides down it looks like a traditional tipi and with the sides raised it resembles a witch's hat.

✓ **Geo marquee:** Similar to the dome, it's a stunning modern structure. Made from a timber frame and covered with natural canvas. Anchored to the ground using steel pins.

✓ **Stretch tent:** Relatively new to the UK, it offers amazing flexibility and can be pitched to work around buildings or trees, down slopes and stairs – literally 'stretched' to fit any location. Made from an ultra-strong white canvas, stretch tents give a modern feel to marquee events.

✓ **Traditional pole:** Perfect for a romantic reception, the marquee is supported by central poles, guy ropes and steel pins. You have to erect this marquee on grass surfaces and hammer stakes into the ground.

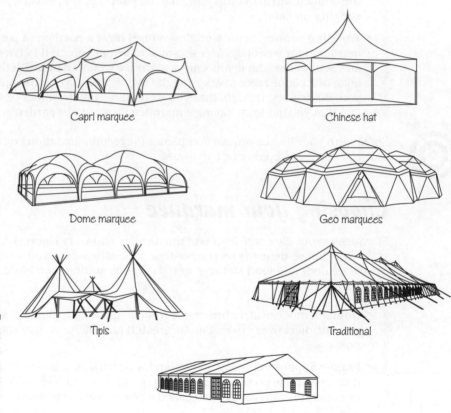

Capri marquee

Chinese hat

Dome marquee

Geo marquees

Tipis

Traditional

Figure 4-2:
Marquees
come in
various
shapes and
sizes.

Frame marquee

Covering all the bases

After you've decided to have a marquee wedding, you need to consider several issues:

- ✓ **A British summer:** You need to think through possible weather problems and work out contingencies for them in advance. For example, if the field allocated for parking floods then where can guests park? Is there a neighbour with a large courtyard or a local village hall? Or, if budget allows, consider hiring an industrial gridlock system for the field. Ask the marquee company to create walkways to and from the marquee to key areas like the toilets and the car park. And if you know you have a lot of smokers then you may want to have a gazebo on standby to position just outside the marquee entrance. We're big believers in being prepared for any eventuality!

- ✓ **Annexes:** In addition to the main marquee, you may need an annexe for the caterer and a separate lighted annexe for the mobile toilets (if weather is predicted to be wet).

- ✓ **Careful preparation:** Think about hiring a wedding planner to help with the logistics of organising a marquee reception. If this isn't possible, gather a team together who can help you decorate the marquee the day before the wedding. You need to get tables and chairs in position and possibly dress them (if your caterers don't undertake this task). But don't put any stationery, like table names or place cards, out until the morning of the wedding, otherwise the dampness in the air makes the card curl.

- ✓ **Comfort zone:** Even if it's a balmy summer, the temperature does still drop in the evening. Therefore consider hiring a heater; many also double up as air-conditioning units.

- ✓ **Decor dilemmas:** Consider how you'll light and decorate the marquee. Even if you plan something simple, you're looking at a great white expanse punctuated by glaring industrial tent poles. Disguising all this can be heart-stoppingly expensive. (See Chapter 5 for tent-decorating ideas.)

- ✓ **Deliveries/collections:** Schedule every delivery and/or collection. For example, the marquee company may want to take down the marquee on the Sunday, but most hire collections won't until the Monday. Send your schedule to the marquee company so they know what's being delivered/collected on what day. If you have a wedding planner, she can be on hand to supervise all deliveries and collections; if not, nominate some-one who can do this on your behalf.

✔ **The flushing bride:** In the category of 'Little facts you never dreamed you'd need to know but aren't you glad we're printing them here', the toilet situation requires utmost attention. Bathrooms shouldn't be an afterthought; adequate and 'commodious' toilet facilities are a crucial aspect of hospitality. When hiring mobile toilets check how many guests the unit is suitable for. Always go for the large unit where at all possible. You don't want a long queue of guests waiting to use the facilities or, heaven forbid, a unit running out of fresh water so that it doesn't flush any more.

Most mobile toilets are quite luxurious now, with male and female toilets within the same trailer (but separate compartments). The male toilet also has both a toilet cubicle as well as a few urinals. The units come with workable sinks, soap, hand cream and a facility for drying hands. Ask what power source they need and check the unit is delivered fully functional, so you don't need to fill it up with water on site.

✔ **Power reassurance:** Not hiring a generator to save a few pounds is tempting, but we strongly recommend you reconsider. Imagine the marquee going into darkness because of a power cut, or losing power in the middle of the band's set. Make sure you hire a quiet generator and position this somewhere out of sight and as far away from guests as possible. Check that it has a distribution board (this divides the electrical power to lighting, band supply, caterers and so on) and leads come with the generator.

Collect information from suppliers on what power they need and forward the information to the marquee company, or electrician if you have one. They will ensure power extensions are positioned in all key areas.

✔ **Proper placement:** Make sure you find an appropriate spot to put the marquee. Ask at least two companies to conduct a site visit. During this meeting the marquee companies will measure the site and discuss any logistical problems they can see. Think about dining, dancing, bar area and catering annexe. The companies will check access is suitable for transport vehicles and the toilet trailer. After the site visit they should send you a computerised drawing of the proposed layout.

✔ **Smart budgeting:** Even when the marquee quotation arrives, remember that you may need additional funds in other areas. Examples are lighting, bar unit, furniture, mobile toilets, generator, stage/dance floor, PA system, walkways and security (if the marquee is accessible by the general public overnight).

✔ **Walk steady:** Even if your budget is tight, erecting a marquee without flooring is risky. Floors can be prohibitively expensive because of the labour involved in laying them, but here's the conundrum: not having a floor leaves you vulnerable to potential fiascoes – off-balance tables and chairs, an uneven dance floor and, most ruinous, water seepage.

A downpour on your wedding day isn't the only weather report you have to worry about. If it has rained recently, water seeps up from the ground. Add a hundred pairs of high heels poking divots in the lawn and so much for the verdant expanse that made you decide your home was the perfect spot for the most important day of your life. (Anyone for a little white-water rafting?)

Anticipating special needs

If you have guests who are elderly, disabled or ill, make them as comfortable as possible. That means providing transportation and making sure the ceremony and reception – including mobile toilets – are wheelchair accessible when necessary. Because people who can't see or move well can often get left out of the fun, be especially gracious by seating them in places of honour, devoting quality time to them and appointing someone to keep on top of special hospitality needs.

Chapter 5

Setting the Scene

. . . .

. . . .

So, you've booked your venue, you're getting ready to send out your invitations, you've begun to hire your photographer, videographer, florist and perhaps even a wedding planner – and now what? Well, now it's time to make *your* wedding. Adding personal touches that set the scene for your wedding, and are unique to you and your groom, is what will make your wedding memorable for you and your guests.

Relax. This is going to be fun. Yes, the world of venue design and lighting comes with a lot of abbreviations, buzz words and jargon, and you may want to do a bit of research on some of the terminology, but ultimately, as long as you can explain what you want to the experts, you should be able to achieve the 'look' you want. And the way you decorate your venue doesn't have to cost a fortune, either. Being a little creative with printed materials, table settings and favours should cost you no more, but it can add a touch of sparkle to the whole day.

First step: do your homework. Amass ideas and tips, learn the venue's ground rules for decorating (see Chapter 4 for other pointers in evaluating a venue) and refine your own personal vision. At that point, you should be in good shape to meet with your florist, venue manager, lighting company and your wedding designer, or begin constructing your wedding fantasy yourself.

Knowing What to Contemplate Before You Decorate

No doubt with every passing day the wedding you've designed in your heads has morphed many times over. Be forewarned: you haven't seen anything yet. As your reconnaissance gathering goes into full throttle, make sure that you:

- ✔ **Get a floor plan** (as in Figure 5-1) of your reception space that shows, based on your estimated number of guests, the location of the tables, dance floor, bars, buffet stations, stationary pillars, furniture, kitchen and architectural features that may affect the set-up of your reception dinner and the party afterwards.

- ✔ **Try out different florists** every time you have an occasion to send flowers. Pay a call on the shop or design studio in person or, even better, order flowers for yourself. If you can, after you've selected your florist, ask them to do a flower 'rehearsal' so you can see one centrepiece and your bouquet, to ensure you're on the same page. Flick to Chapter 6 for details on flowers.

- ✔ **Create a mood board** by collecting swatches, clippings, sketches and anything else that helps you describe what you have in mind. Going through local bridal magazines is just the beginning. Peruse bridal magazines from other countries, interior design and food magazines, art books and classic movies. You may be inspired by something as minute as the way a curtain hangs or the way a vase is set on a table. If a window display at your favourite boutique catches your eye, find out whether the stylist is available to do weddings.

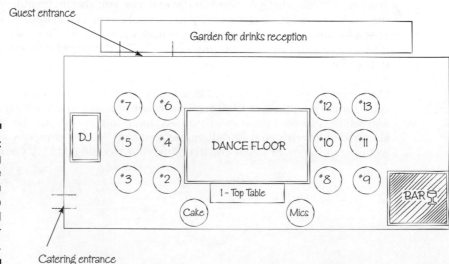

Figure 5-1:
Drawing up a simple floor plan helps you to visualise and design your reception.

✔ **Keep a 'Not at *My* Wedding' list** or 'anti-mood board' that may include odoriferous flowers such as Rubrim lilies, narcissus (daffodils) and daisies, or any arrangement styles that you find tacky or just *not* your style.

✔ **Solicit the input of the banquet/venue manager or the caterer,** but differentiate between that person's opinion and fact. They may know what has worked in the past in that space – and may be right most of the time – but you should feel free to make suggestions and ask questions.

 A common pitfall of wedding planning is a lack of communication about your wedding decor with the powers-that-be at your reception venue. Before things get too far along, meet with the banquet/venue manager and go over the ground rules. Among the details you want to get straight:

✔ What are the decor specifications? For example, is the ceiling so low that high centrepieces don't work?

✔ Do you like the chairs or do they need to be covered? (Hire chair covers if your venue's chairs are of the grubby, conference-shaped variety, or perhaps hire chairs – see the later 'Chairs' section for more details.)

✔ How much time does the venue allot for set-up and breakdown?

✔ Does the venue have another event either immediately before or after yours?

✔ What can be affixed to what? Some places have strict rules about stringing garlands, hanging things on walls, using nails and the like.

✔ What, if any, are the restrictions regarding prop hire, candles, additional lighting or fabric draping?

✔ Does the venue manager have a list of recommended and/or dictated suppliers who can work there, such as florists and lighting companies?

✔ Where do the bars, dance floor and DJ usually go?

✔ Where is the best spot for the top table, and where does the manager recommend the other tables go?

✔ Can you remove or cover decor elements that you find objectionable, such as pieces of furniture, lighting fixtures and pictures on the walls?

✔ Do the fountains and fireplaces work? Can the venue make them work in time?

✔ When will the venue make renovations (painting, cleaning and so on) promised in the contract?

✔ Are any new renovations or decor changes in the works before your wedding?

✔ Are any public or shared spaces off-limits for decorating?

✔ Will the room be *turned* (meaning, changed over) between the ceremony and reception? How long does that take? (See Chapter 4 for room-turning concerns.)

✔ Does the venue have air-conditioning and heating, and is it sufficient?

Choosing a Wedding Designer

For the purposes of this book, we use the term *designer* to refer to any person involved with the decor. You see, once upon a time, only florists were involved. They supplied flowers for parties and weddings, and you may have called them to send a dozen red roses to your sweetheart for Valentine's Day. Now we have floral designers, party designers, event planners, event producers, space stylists and even lifestyle consultants. You can't tell from the title alone whether a person designs the entire decor (including flowers, linens, lighting and props), designs solely flowers or even knows a poppy from a Popsicle.

If you've hired a wedding planner (see Chapter 1) then you probably don't need to hire a wedding designer too, because most professional wedding planners assist you in the design of your wedding. However, if you haven't hired a wedding planner then a wedding designer may be a useful supplier to have on board. (Be aware, though – a wedding designer is *not* a wedding planner and don't think of them as a replacement for a wedding planner. Wedding designers don't get involved in the overall project management of your wedding; they are only involved in the design of your reception venue.)

The first meeting with a designer you're considering can take place either at your reception venue or at the designer's shop or workspace. Set the parameters and be upfront about your budget; no reason to waste your time and theirs by offering them a price way below their usual rate or having them suggest outrageous concepts you could never afford. Ask to see photos of possible room treatments. After you choose a designer, take a walk through the venue *together* as early in your planning as possible, even if she's familiar with your space.

After you've hired your designer or company, and have agreed on budget and design details, you should be able to see a sample centrepiece a few weeks before your wedding. If possible, have the designer create a sample table replete with linens, place settings, candles and table numbers so you have a clear idea of the total effect. Be flexible: when it comes to flowers, what you see isn't always what you get. When possible, get a photo of the centrepiece. Your contract most likely stipulates that because of unforeseen events, such as frost, seasonal changes and shipping problems, certain substitutions can be made. Find out what those may be.

To prevent any misunderstanding, here are some other specifics to include in your agreement:

✔ Does the designer charge set-up and breakdown fees?

✔ How early will they need to start setting up and how long will it take to break down? (This factor is important for avoiding overtime fees on your venue.)

✔ Can the designer arrange to deliver leftover flowers to your home? For what fee?

✔ At the end of the event, what materials, such as tablecloths, vases, napkins and table numbers, do you own and what does the designer own?

✔ Can guests leave with the centerpieces intact, or do the flowers need to be wrapped or put in other containers?

What's in a Room?

Consider every aspect of your space that could use some decoration. The following overview provides ideas and solutions for design dilemmas, whether your wedding is in a hotel, a banquet hall or on a country estate.

First impressions

Think about the following that guests first notice upon arrival.

The driveway

Even before you hit the entrance, you can convey a celebratory air without spending a great deal of money. Create a glowing path of footlights by using *luminarias* (votive candles in paper bags). Either colour or plain-brown paper bags will do. Large silver lanterns or hurricane glass lanterns also look very welcoming. Make sure you have a few inches of sand in the bottom of all these to stabilise the candles.

Tiki torches, often found at gardening shops, are dramatic as well as inexpensive. When filled with citronella, these have the added bonus of repelling things that go buzz in the night.

For daytime weddings, use potted plants, staked balloons or nicely done billboard-type signs along the drive to guide the way.

The entrance

As guests enter, give them something to remember:

- An arched trellis adorned with flowers.

- A pair of large fibreglass urns faux finished to look like jade, pink marble or granite and stuffed with flowering branches.

- A welcome sign done as a whimsical garden plaque, a sports-type pennant or an illuminated medieval-looking scroll lettered in gold – especially in lieu of the generic black event board with white plastic letters that many hotels and conference facilities use.

- Waiters bearing trays of drinks just inside the door for an immediate display of hospitality.

The gift and guest book table

Guests bring presents to weddings less and less nowadays, so you may not need to have a fancy table waiting to be piled with packages. (We cover different traditions for displaying gifts in Chapter 9.) However, we would always suggest that you have some sort of gift table in the room for those who have decided to bring their gift to the reception. This table can also double up as your guest book table, if you're having one.

In many cases, guests bring cards, with or without a cheque or money inside, and you may want to have a nice 'post box' available so they can 'post' their cards to you. These post boxes are available to hire (type 'post box hire' for weddings into your Internet browser), or you may want to simply place a cardboard post box on the gift table, and they can add a touch of fun to your decor. Ensure you assign your wedding planner or a friend to be in charge of taking these boxes back to your hotel room or home before you leave the reception, so they're safely waiting for you.

Wait until you get home to open the packages and envelopes – doing so at the reception isn't appropriate.

And what about a guest book table? Although passing the guest book around during the evening is a good idea, we always think it's worth having a designated 'home' for it, too. The gift table is a good place, so that when people get a little worse for wear later in the evening, they can put the guest book back where it belongs so that it doesn't get lost somewhere.

For a guest book, buy a hardback album with blank pages (a photo album may work) that matches the style of your wedding. A truly meaningful guest book is more than a list of signatures. Besides, you presumably already have your guests' names and addresses from your invitation list, so you don't need them to sign in as if at a hotel.

Up, down and all around: Ceilings, floors and walls

Look at the big picture. What parts of the space are crying out for help and need to be disguised? What has potential and should be accentuated? Can you live with the bare acoustic ceiling tiles, or should you divert precious centrepiece funds to camouflage them? Does the space contain a singularly exquisite architectural feature – a cathedral ceiling, a sweeping banister, a fountain? You can create an entirely different environment by draping the walls, ceiling and every possible feature, but if your space requires such a total transformation, why did you book it in the first place?

When it comes to decorating, choose your battles. Neutral walls and even patterned wallpaper may disappear depending on the time of day. If the walls are decorated in a flamboyant way, go with it rather than trying to do a complete overhaul. Similarly, the flaming-orange carpet may be distracting during a day wedding, but inconsequential at night when the tables are set up and the lights are low. If you have a budget that allows for more than tabletop decor, such strategies as draping ceilings or walls and hanging floral chandeliers from the ceiling transform a space completely.

Fabric, table linens and other decorating materials must adhere to fire-safety regulations. Heath and safety officers have been known to spring surprise inspections at even the most glamorous locations and insist that everything be removed. Speaking of fire safety, by law you can't cover lighted exit signs and sprinklers.

Trees or huge plants such as ficus, palm or philodendron cover a multitude of sins for comparatively little money because you can hire them from nurseries. Some nurseries hire out large, hearty, flowering plants also.

Lighting

People often don't realise just how important lighting is for the look and mood of an event. A few shades can make the difference between intimate and institutional. You don't want lights dimmed to such a romantic level that waiters have to set off flares. Nor do you want the room so brilliant that sequin dresses spontaneously combust. However, a pin spot can make even a modest centrepiece pop, and something as simple as dimming the chandeliers for the first dance can conjure an aura of mystery and suspense.

Visit the space at the time of day your wedding will be. Even for afternoon events, where supplemental lighting is often a waste of money, you need to take into consideration the level of light. Ask your designer to detail the most appropriate light settings for your reception and mark them for the banquet manager. Some other questions to ask:

- Is the light so bright that blinds need to be closed?

- Do the windows have blinds?

- Should you change the time of your wedding because the light looks best at a certain time of day?

- If you're having your ceremony at the site, in which direction does the sun set and can you plan your ceremony around that?

- Do the lights have dimmers? What are the requirements or restrictions for a lighting designer?

Hiring a professional lighting company may seem extravagant – and it is – but creative lighting can transform a room in ways you never dreamt possible. Properly up-lit, an urn filled with branches not only appears larger but also throws dramatic silhouettes on the wall, turning a single arrangement into a forest. Think about restaurants and homes where you feel extremely comfortable. Chances are, the lighting there is very pleasing to both your eye and your psyche.

Some floral designers offer lighting services; others subcontract with companies that supply the equipment. If you're hiring a DJ for later in the evening, the chances are that they will bring lights for the disco. Don't be afraid to ask them if they can help create the right atmosphere for the dinner as well. Either way, here are some terms you may hear bandied about:

- **Ambient or diffused light:** The main light in the room, coming from either natural or artificial sources. This light should soften and flatter; use accent lighting to make specific areas or architectural features stand out.

- **Fairy or twinkle lights:** Strings of tiny lights like Christmas lights. Used behind opaque fabrics, on banisters or in trees, they add a magical touch. An inexpensive lighting trick is to drop strings of these like vines from the ceiling or against columns.

- **Gobos:** Custom-made or hired stencils that go over lights to project patterns such as stars, moons, snowflakes, monograms or musical notes on to walls, dance floors or draped fabric.

- **Pin spots:** Narrow beams that target centrepieces, the cake or anything demanding special attention. Hung from the ceiling or directed from light poles, they're frequently used in pairs to give cross-directional light. The darker the room, the more dramatic pin spots look.

- ✔ **Up-lights and down-lights:** Also known as 'light-cans', which are usually painted to match the space. Used to project beams of light upward from the base of an urn or tree or down onto a mantel or altar. A recent trend is to put battery-operated up-lights under Perspex tables to create a surreal glow.

- ✔ **Washes:** Colours (usually pastels) projected over large spaces such as bars or dance floors that bathe the area in a particular light.

- ✔ **Intelli-beams:** Also known as 'intelligent lighting', lighting engineers program these computerised systems to generate complex patterns and a multitude of colours.

To de-emphasise unattractive areas without spending a penny, simply remove some of the fluorescent tubes in the bathrooms or unscrew light-bulbs in wall sconces. If you need *some* light, replace the bulbs with pink or frosted bulbs.

Props

By *props* we don't mean big theatrical pieces. You may incorporate unique items that you own, such as ceramic pitchers, silver bowls, candelabras and vases, into your decor scheme. Antique stores often rent out items that aren't precious, and prop shops exist where you can find all sorts of goodies. Caterers and hotel banquet departments often own props that they wouldn't have thought to use for a wedding but that you may be interested in, such as huge fans, paper lanterns or even backdrops.

The drinks reception area

A secret to a lively party is keeping guests constantly amused and entertained with small surprises. To do this, try not to be too predictable with any of the facets of your reception, including the decor. If the dining room is romantic and classical, there's no reason that the drinks reception area can't be glitzy or very modern. Don't mimic a dining room with large centrepieces and tables – you want guests up and mingling, not planted like carrots.

Here are some other traffic-flow considerations:

- ✔ Place bars and food stations around the room, not all together.
- ✔ Bars should be visible to guests, but not near the entrance, which can cause bottlenecks.
- ✔ Don't set bars near the dance floor or music.
- ✔ In a tight space, don't use one-sided head tables; they take up too much room.

Seat and you shall find

Even for a buffet meal, unless you're lucky enough to have an entire guest list composed of a jolly group of people who all know and love each other, you want to have a table plan and perhaps seating cards. Otherwise, one table inevitably has 30 chairs crammed around it while your two oldest school chums eat in a corner by themselves.

You have many options for your table plan, whether printed or handwritten. Try to fit the table plan in with your theme, perhaps in the same style as your invitations – using the same colours and ribbon. And why not be creative with your table names (see the 'What's in a name' sidebar later on in the chapter)?

Tackle the seating chart first and then once you've placed everyone on their tables you can print a table plan; you can print this on A1- or A2-sized card at a local print shop. As shown in the illustration, to compose a seating chart, take a large piece of cardboard and sketch in the floor plan with numbered tables. Take a pad of self-adhesive notes and write the names of guests who've confirmed their attendance. Place the names around the tables, trying to fill one table at a time while taking into account whom guests may know at their table and at tables closest to them. Your parents probably want to sit near your table and their friends near them. Conversely, you don't want to antagonise your feuding aunts by seating them next to each other.

By about a week before your wedding, the seating chart should be firm, then and only then make an official print of your table plan. A charming option for a smallish wedding is a calligraphed seating list framed and propped on an easel.

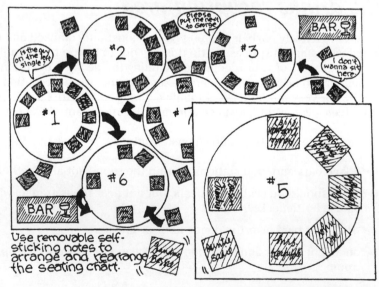

Think about tables. Bar-height pedestal (*poseur*) tables should be small, tall and large enough for no more than four people to stand around. Provide seating for about a third of the guests – but not more than a third – during the drinks reception. Having seats for, say, 75 per cent of the guests isn't gracious; it's silly and makes people think you forgot to hire chairs for the other 25 per cent.

A trestle table can serve as a bar, or the space may have rolling bars. In either case, avoid bottlenecks at the entrance by making sure the bar – and waiters passing drinks – are far enough inside so guests can grab a drink and keep on moving. Bar linens should be either skirted or boxed so the table legs don't show; choose the colour of the linens to work with your scheme. (For a full discussion of bars, see Chapter 18.)

For a truly dramatic effect, make a bar out of ice. An ice sculptor carves the entire bar out of ice and then lights it dramatically with coloured lights. Other popular but less-extravagant options include large ice sculptures that sit atop the bar and also serve as chillers for flavoured vodkas. However, make sure that the ice sculpture (or floral arrangement or candle arrangement) isn't overwhelming. The bar, after all, is a high-traffic spot and workspace.

Dining area arrangement

Even if you've had to shoehorn in more than an ideal number of tables, leave adequate room both near the entrance and between tables so guests can make their way gracefully without snagging tablecloths in their wake. Upon entering, guests should feel they're in a completely different atmosphere than the one they just left.

If you're having a buffet you need to place these tables where guests can line up and easily reach them without standing on someone's chair. Because the key decorative element of buffets is the food itself, they're best discussed within the context of planning the menu (see Chapter 17).

Position your ushers, or one or two waiters, as traffic police near the entrance of the dining room, with a floor plan that indicates table numbers and locations. Otherwise, Aunt Mary may still be looking for her table when dessert is being served.

The following sections consider each area of the space in turn.

Dining tables

One way of making a large room filled with guests look less institutional and more elegant is to vary the sizes and shapes of the tables. A successful floor plan can include squares, rounds and/or rectangles. The most efficient way of making sure you're devising a plan that works is to use a CAD (computer aided design) program, which many hotels and marquee companies have. But you can also simply measure the space and map out the floor plan on graph paper.

We're often asked 'What size of table do I need to seat ten guests?', and so on. If you're using round tables, the following guide may help you to understand how many people you can seat comfortably around your table:

Table	Seats	Maximum number of people
4 feet (approximately 1.2 metres)	6	8
5 feet (approximately 1.5 metres)	8	10
5 feet 6 inches (approximately 1.7 metres)	10	11
6 feet (approximately 1.8 metres)	11	12

Having the same number of guests at every table is virtually impossible. Still, you want to keep the number of people at each table and the table sizes in close range. You may have eight tables of ten and two tables of eight, for example, but not two tables of four, two tables of seven, three tables of ten and so on. This is a party, not a nightclub; people at smaller tables feel like the odd folks out. When you have your final guest count, ask the banquet manager or whomever is laying out the seating whether you should plan for fewer tables because space is tight or more tables because you have room to spare. If you do use different sized tables, inform the tablecloth and centrepiece suppliers as soon as possible so everything is in proportion.

Top table

Wherever the bride and groom sit is called the *top table* and is classed as *table number 1*. The most important aspect in planning the top table is where you put it, because everyone wants a view of the bride and groom. Two things affect the size of your top table: the size of your space and who you want to sit with you. For the latter, you can do one of two things:

✔ Seat both sets of parents, the officiant (if invited), grandparents and/or extremely close relatives such as aunts and uncles with you. Then you can sprinkle the wedding party and their significant others around the room, making them mini-emissaries for you.

✔ Give parents their own tables with friends and seat the wedding party and their significant others at your table.

In the UK, the bride and groom traditionally sit in the middle of the top table flanked by the bride's parents, then the groom's parents and finally by the best man and chief bridesmaid. This is one area, however, in which we feel you don't need to stick with tradition; choose a layout that suits you and your families. After all, it's your wedding!

Don't assume you're a seating psychic. If your parents are divorced or you have some other family drama that may erupt, ask before you blithely place people where you please. Even if you play the peacemaker at family events, remember that this isn't the normal family dinner. Your attention will be elsewhere during the reception. Are you brave enough to leave contentious relatives to their own devices?

Until recently, seating the entire wedding party on one side of a long table so they faced the room was standard operating procedure. But many couples now find the long top table either unattractive, silly or impossible to plan seating for, so they're opting to use a round table. If as a matter of diplomacy or personal taste you use a rectangular top table, you can make it a focal point, swagging the tablecloths, planting floral gardens down the length of the table or situating the table under an airy arbour or gazebo-type structure.

Some couples, perhaps out of the sheer frustration of determining who should sit at the top table, have a table for just the two of them, called a *sweetheart table*. Although it's not our favourite solution, it's likely to be a moot point where you sit because you'll both be working the room for most of the meal.

Cake table

Place this table prominently in the main dining area and decorate accordingly. (See Chapter 19 for a complete cake table report.) If possible, and if the cake is beautiful, spotlight it.

Dance floor

A built-in dance floor makes life easy, but if you need to hire one, interlocking 3-x-4-foot (approximately 0.9-metre to 1.2-metre) parquet squares are superior to the flimsy rolled-up variety. Dance floors, just like everything, come in many forms and can be relatively cost effective or expensive. If the dancing is really important to you, and you want to create a nightclub feel, try a white or black LED dance floor.

Staging

If you're having trouble fitting a large band directly on your dance floor, you simply don't want to give up precious dance floor space or you just want drama, you can hire platforms to be used as a bandstand or stage. Even though these risers generally run only 8 inches (or 20 centimetres) high, your designer should cover the gap between floor and platform with stapled material. Specify who's erecting the stage – the venue, the hire company or your designer – and make sure to get the size specifications from the band.

You can't do much about camouflaging speakers because they need to be placed between the musicians and the audience. Mixing boards are big and ugly no matter what, so place them as discreetly as possible on a table with a boxed cloth that matches the dining tables.

Lighted music stands are often emblazoned with the band's name. If having this free billboard for the band doesn't jibe with your decor, specify that you'd prefer the band use generic music stands or none at all. For more band information, see Chapter 20.

Chairs

Hotels and restaurants often spend a great deal of money on their chairs, which are designed to work with the room's decor as well as to seat the optimum number of people around each table. If you need to hire chairs, in most parts of the UK wooden and plastic folding chairs are available in various colours. A more elegant option is Chiavari (faux bamboo) chairs, which are smaller – though less comfortable – than most chairs and can seat more people at a table. Although Chiavaris cost more to hire, you may actually break even because you need fewer tables, tablecloths and centrepieces.

An expensive but very elegant option is the Chandelle chair. Chandelle chairs have round backs and usually come in white or cream. If the look of your wedding is really important to you and budget is not an issue, we think these are lovely.

If your venue's chairs are particularly hideous, you may want to hire chair-back covers, full slipcovers and/or simple sashes. Materials range from polyester-cotton blends in various colours to space-age-looking Spandex. A ribbon of tulle covered with a floral garland on the backs of the bride's and groom's chairs adds romance. For a funky chic look, swathe chairs with a few yards of transparent fabric (such as crystal organza or tulle) and tie it into a gigantic bow in the back.

Tabletops

A centrepiece alone does not a table make. The flavour and spirit of an event are conveyed through many details, which, repeated seat after seat, table after table, form a delectable impression as guests enter. After guests are seated, they have time to note and appreciate each and every nuance, from the colour of the napkins to the placement of the wine glasses. Consequently, the hours you invest planning these elements are well spent.

Before the guests file into the main dining room, have the head waiter or your wedding planner do a table-by-table inspection to make sure that the correct number of chairs and place settings have been set at each table, the tables are where you want them, every place is set correctly, the glasses have no spots, the candles are lit and the chairs are straight – in short, that every decorative detail has been taken care of.

The following sections give you a tour of all the elements to consider for your tabletops.

Tablecloths

Anything you can dream up for your wedding is available for hire – for a price, of course – and tablecloths are no different. The typical white restaurant tablecloth, darned and dingy, is best used as an undercloth. You can make just about any tablecloth look more festive, however, with a little creativity and sewing ability. Although sprucing up every table may be impractical it can look lovely for the cake table or top table.

Napkins

A subtle part of the decor, napkins can go on the service plate or directly on the tablecloth, but they don't work well fanned out in glasses when a low centrepiece is on the table.

TIP

If you're hiring napkins, hire plenty of extra for waiters' service and to replace dropped or soiled ones. For cocktail napkins, order at least three per guest.

Tie your napkins with a ribbon in your colour scheme, or use jewel-encrusted napkin rings. Perhaps add a long-stemmed rose or a sprig of lavender.

Tying napkins with wire-edged ribbon or raffia in your colour scheme is a lovely finisher and less expensive if you (and your helpers) do the tying. That means picking up the napkins a few days before your wedding if possible. For a couple of how-tos in creative napkin-folding, see Figures 5-2 and 5-3.

The Candle

Figure 5-2: This fold is handy for tucking in items – place cards, bread sticks or single flower stems.

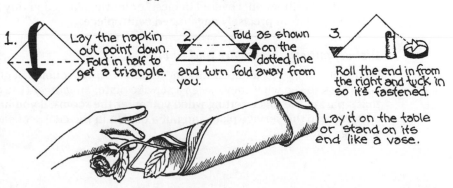

1. Lay the napkin out point down. Fold in half to get a triangle.

2. Fold as shown on the dotted line and turn fold away from you.

3. Roll the end in from the right and tuck in so it's fastened.

Lay it on the table or stand on its end like a vase.

The Single Fan

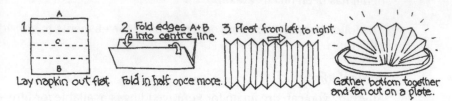

Figure 5-3:
This fan fold is one of the easiest to master.

1. Lay napkin out flat.

2. Fold edges A+B into centre line. Fold in half once more.

3. Pleat from left to right.

Gather bottom together and fan out on a plate.

TIP

When it comes to cocktail napkins, starched linen is elegant and formal but not inexpensive to hire. A standard monogram on paper napkins is fine, but creating your own logo by hand or computer and having it printed on paper cocktail napkins and hand towels may be more in keeping with the style of your reception.

Candles

Candles have long held a mystical appeal and, perhaps as an outgrowth of New Age trends, have become, if you'll pardon the pun, hot, hot, hot. Where once you may have seen two elegant tapers guarding each centrepiece at a reception, you now find a virtual conflagration composed of hundreds of candles in all shapes and sizes. Ask your venue whether it allows real candles because some venues only allow faux candles for health and safety reasons.

WARNING!

Tall tapers can turn into wax-spitting demons in rooms with cross-directional air currents. Even dripless candles can be hazardous. If you're at all unsure, ask the venue manager what he's seen work the best in the space. Also work out a contingency plan for when the candles burn down: either have staff replace the candles or adjust the lighting accordingly. And *never* use scented candles around food.

The glass holders for votive candles provide a base for decorating. They're frequently gold or silver leafed, covered with galax or lemon leaves, and tied with raffia, beribboned, covered in mesh or fabric, planted in tiny terra-cotta pots or hung from precisely engineered centrepieces.

Dishes, cutlery, stemware and so on

Frequently, in hotels and restaurants you don't have a choice of china and silver. Ask to see what they use as a service plate, or *charger* (the empty plate that's part of the place setting when you enter the room). If you hate the pattern, skip the service plate and put a napkin in the centre of each place setting instead.

For china, silver and glassware hiring, which you need at some sites, choices abound. At the inexpensive end of the spectrum are heavy, white china, flimsy silverware and chunky glassware. Attractive options do exist at various price points, and if you and your caterer can agree that one plate can be used for two courses (in other words, washed in between), hiring attractive china may be affordable. Just make sure that every element works with the overall table design. As you can see in Figure 5-4, outfitting a place setting for a five-course meal means a lot of hire charges.

Table accoutrements can be practical as well as enchanting:

- Individual salt and pepper shakers or cellars for each person
- Butter placed on lemon leaves
- Tiny silver tongs for sugar cubes
- Coloured stem or coloured glasses – sometimes just the water glass in a different colour can bring alive a table setting
- Metallic or faux jewel napkin rings, perhaps with a long-stemmed rose or a sprig of lavender
- Knife, spoon or chopstick rests

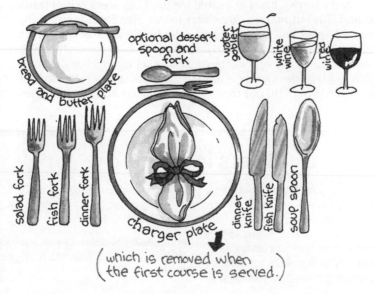

A Place Setting with the Works!

optional dessert spoon and fork

water goblet

white wine

red wine

bread and butter plate

salad fork

fish fork

dinner fork

charger plate

dinner knife

fish knife

soup spoon

(which is removed when the first course is served.)

Figure 5-4: Make sure that each place setting includes the specific plates, glasses and utensils needed for your meal.

If you're serving meat, be sure to order sharp knives. Regular hired knives usually aren't serrated, forcing guests to engage in Eating Olympics.

Table numbers

Make table numbers easy to read, but refrain from making them big enough for billboards. And put some thought into creative ways to avoid using generic table-number supports. These ways may include:

- ✔ Giant wooden numbers spray-painted in gold, silver or bronze
- ✔ Rococo frames displaying table numbers
- ✔ Leaves painted with numbers, affixed to a long tube and planted in the centrepieces
- ✔ Numbers on table tents that match place cards
- ✔ Different flowers or props on each table, with guests assigned to table names – 'Gardenia' or 'Tango' – rather than by number

Waiting staff should remove table numbers at the beginning of the meal – the table is probably too crowded as it is, and after guests are seated, numbers are unnecessary.

Place cards and seating cards

In times past, *seating cards* – which let guests know on which table they are to be seated – were a must at seated meals. They went out of fashion during the '60s and '70s but made a comeback in the '80s. Seating cards do not replace your table plan, but they can prevent a bottle-neck at the entrance of your wedding dinner as everyone tries to find their name on the table plan. If you have seating cards, you will need a table set up at your drinks reception on which to place the cards (in alphabetical order) and then an usher or wedding planner to hand out the seating cards to each guest as they arrive.

What's in a name?

Some couples want to push the boat out a little farther than Table 1, Table 2, and so on. This is where you can get really creative and, hopefully, bring a smile to the faces of your guests as they decipher the theme. Here are some other ideas – some work brilliantly with themes you already have, and others look great with props or photos:

- ✔ Your favourite shops, films, poets, authors, TV shows, artists/bands, songs, ice-cream flavours, wines, whiskies or gemstones.

- ✔ Places where you've lived, where you're going on your honeymoon or have been on holiday together.

- ✔ Meaningful dates to you both – your first kiss, your first date, the first time you said 'I love you'.

Place cards, on the other hand, tell guests where at the table they are seated, and are usually folded cards (folded tent-style) centred at 12 o'clock above each plate, or flat cards set on top of each napkin. Alternatively, for a more elegant feel, you can use placed holders such as silver balls or cubes, tree stands, heart-shaped stands or cute little miniature chairs. You can also use your favours instead of place cards (see 'Doing Your Guests a Favour'), personalising them with guests' names. Tie a name tag to them or print the name on a label.

Increasingly – and sensibly – names on place cards have become less formal, using first names and even nicknames so that members of the table know how to best address each other. Remember to write names on both sides of the folded cards so that guests across the table from one another can also read them.

Assigning tables is difficult enough and, admittedly, assigning seats is an even bigger pain. But guests really appreciate your having thought about whom they may have to talk to for several courses.

Menu cards

Pretty menu cards don't have to be expensive. You can design them yourself on your computer and have them either printed at a printing company or photocopied on card stock by a professional copy shop. Many stationery shops carry artistically bordered cards specially made for laser printers.

If you're having your wedding at a restaurant or hotel that laser prints its daily menu, the venue may be happy to do yours in the same fashion. Although you may have one menu per person, two or four per table is sufficient. If you've opted for a buffet with different food stations (see Chapter 17), menu cards are a real advantage. Otherwise, after the party you'll hear, 'I didn't know there was lobster somewhere!'

TIP

Designing a menu card

A handsomely printed or calligraphed menu card makes a nice memento. Here are some tips for making yours special:

✔ Put your names or monogram, the wedding date and the site at the top of the menu.

✔ List the wines to be served to the left of each dish – but only if they're interesting enough (not necessarily expensive) to mention.

✔ Use colourful and descriptive adjectives.

✔ Use the menu cards as place cards, writing each guest's name at the top.

Bathrooms

Women, in particular, get a kick out of bathroom baskets filled with goodies. We suggest throwing in everything from hairspray to breath mints to emergency pairs of tights in various sizes. In off-premise spaces, the bathrooms can be dreary at best, so bring in your own hand towels, scented candles, soaps and even toilet paper to replace the particularly torturous variety found in institutional toilets.

Transitional spaces

You don't have to bedeck vestibules, foyers and spaces between the drinks reception room and dining rooms in flowers and finery, but they should at least look like they're a part of the same event. Even if you've already blown your budget on more pressing design details, try to save a few pounds to place some votive candles around on ledges and tables, or to cover spare tables and chairs with tulle, the all-purpose wedding material. You can cover potted plants in plastic garden containers with tulle or other fabrics and group them together to soften otherwise neglected spaces.

Making the Most of a Marquee

We've seen the sad results of people who erected grand marquee tents but ran out of money to decorate them. Although their fantasy may have been to dine in a palace that had somehow magically dropped into their backyard, the reality ran more towards dining inside a great white laundry bag. If the tent itself puts such a gaping hole in your budget that you can't afford to hang a piece of greenery, you really should reconsider your choice of venue.

Some crucial aspects of marquee decorating include:

- **Banners:** Wide bands of fabric that cover part of the ceiling and are less expensive than a full tent lining, but serve the same purpose in drawing the eye away from the ceiling.

- **Fabric linings:** Most marquee companies rent out pleated fabric linings that cover the ceiling and/or the walls. Linings are rather pricey.

- **Flooring:** If you opt for the floor (and we recommend that you do), we suggest having carpet to muffle sound. A less-costly floor covering is black or green AstroTurf. (See Chapter 4 regarding floor issues.)

- **Interior lighting:** If your wedding is in the evening, the marquee requires lighting. Options include chandeliers, *starlighting* (pea lights), track systems, inexpensive globes, carriage lights (which look like old-fashioned gas lamps) and oversized Chinese lanterns.

✔ **Landscape lighting:** Used to emphasise natural features such as ponds or trees, as well as to guide guests to necessities such as bathrooms and driveways. Solar lights can work well and do not require an electricity supply.

✔ **Poles:** Depending on the pitch of the marquee, for a large tent poles can be up to 42 feet tall. When planning marquee seating, take into account how poles affect sight lines. Poles are metal and ugly and you need to cover them somehow. Besides painting them, you may wind them in floral garlands or ruche and tie fabric around them. For a touch of organic whimsy, cover the poles in cheap fabric and glue leaves in over-lapping rows pointing upward to completely camouflage the metal. For a country theme, corn husks work well.

✔ **Windows:** Marquee sides are clear plastic, opaque plastic or cloth, depending on the season, and often stencilled with windowpanes, arches and shutters.

Make sure all marquees, equipment and decor comply with local health and safety guidelines. The marquee company is responsible for getting the proper permits.

A nice touch for personalising marquee weddings taking place in a field: have some wellington boots available just in case it all becomes a bit too muddy for those stilettos!

Doing Your Guests a Favour

Although sending guests off from your reception with a small gift is very gracious, finding the right item, neither too cheap nor too grand, can be dif-ficult. With wedding memorabilia, the line between cute and kitsch can be mighty thin. If you either can't or don't decide to spend the money to give your guests something they may actually save until they get to their car, you should forego giving anything at all – it's not necessary. With a little creativ-ity, however, you can probably find or make the perfect party favour. Our suggestions:

✔ Traditional candied almonds, symbolising the bitter and the sweet of marriage, but packaged creatively to evoke your own wedding style (for example, small tins with calligraphed labels that double as place cards).

✔ If your wedding has a floral theme such as daisies or roses, a full-sized plant in a terracotta pot with a note on care and treatment.

✔ Herb plants such as basil or sage in a terracotta pot, with a printed card of your favourite recipe.

- Whole miniature wedding cakes, large enough to be a dessert portion, packaged in white glossy boxes and tied with chiffon ribbons.

- Small boxes made of sugar filled with tiny chocolates and packaged in decorative boxes.

- A tin of assorted homemade cookies in the shapes of tiered wedding cakes, bells and rings.

- Macaroons placed in a gorgeous trinket box.

- Homemade preserves or chutneys in jam jars with handwritten labels, or a custom tin of blended tea.

- For a summer wedding, little bags of fresh fruit.

- Your favourite tipple in a lovely mini-bottle – think whisky, limoncello, tequila and so on.

- Bottles of wine or vodka or beer with a custom label (these should be full-sized bottles; what can a couple do with a half bottle – rinse their mouths?).

- A book of love poems or quotes with a leather bookmark or a metal page-keeper that's embossed with your wedding date.

- A pair of hand-painted Champagne flutes.

- Small topiary trees in faux-antique pots.

- Your own blend of perfume that you've made especially for your wedding – a decadent but lovely touch. Try www.illuminumfragrance.com.

- A custom-burned CD of your wedding music.

- A handwritten note to each guest thanking them for coming to your wedding, placed in an organza bag to match your colour scheme with a few special chocolates (you can also place these in each bedroom if you're having a destination wedding – see Chapter 7).

Certain party favours must come in pairs. Giving guests (whether couples or single) a lone Champagne glass or bottle of beer is beyond useless – it's too sad to contemplate.

If favours aren't part of your tabletop decor, the best way to distribute them to guests is as they leave the reception. Put the favours in small bags with pretty tissue paper, and have an usher or your wedding planner hand one to each guest. Putting the bags on guests' chairs is rarely convenient; the bags end up on the floor, getting trampled every time someone gets up from the table.

For a wedding that ends in the wee hours of the morning, send your guests off with a special favour – a goody bag containing some ready-to-eat breakfast fare. Bagels and cream cheese, a mini-loaf of sourdough bread and a wedge of good cheese, or tiny croissants, breakfast pastries and a small pot of jam, along with some lovely chocolates, are sure to be appreciated.

Treating kids

Wedding dinners can last quite some time – delightful for the adults, somewhat boring for the kids. A little preparation goes a long way in ensuring happy, occupied children for at least the duration of dinner, and happy, relaxed adults all around. Instead of favours, why not place a few fun toys and activities in a brightly coloured bag and put them where the children will be sitting?

You may even hire a children's entertainer – she'll whisk the kids off to another room where they play games, read stories and have their dinner served to them. Giving parents just a few precious hours off to enjoy your wedding will win you many brownie points! For more on hiring entertainers, see Chapter 20.

Chapter 6

Flower Power

• •

• •

Flowers are, with rare exception, the dominant decorative element for a wedding. Even the horticulturally illiterate appreciate the symbolism and elegance that flowers impart. And although 'that which we call a rose by any other name would smell as sweet', a loosely tied bouquet of long stems creates a strikingly different mood than a composite of petals painstakingly wired to resemble one enormous blossom.

You want to find a florist who can handle all your floral needs, including ceremony, reception and personal arrangements. In this chapter, we help you find the perfect florist, decide exactly what you want and then infuse your special day with memorable, beautiful, scent-sational flowers.

Getting a Feel for What You Want

Before you start interviewing florists, you need to get an idea of the kinds of flowers you like. Here are four mediums for gathering flower inspiration:

> ✔ **Google:** Go to www.google.co.uk, type in 'flowers', 'bridal bouquet', 'reception flowers' or something similar, and then click on the Images tab. Hey presto: you have hundreds of pictures to scroll through. Click on an image you like and either print it out or send the URL to your florist.

✔ **Magazines:** Pop to the shop and buy every wedding magazine on the shelf, take them home and start browsing! Magazine articles and photos can be inspiring and offer new, exciting ideas – even other, non-wedding types of magazine such as fashion or interior home publications. If a picture within these magazines helps to define the style of wedding you want or your personality, keep them handy to show your florist.

✔ **Mood boards:** You may want to collate images that convey your wedding ideas into a mood board. Used by interior designers and professional wedding planners, *mood boards* help you to see how your different ideas can work together. They are a great way of testing the water with colour combinations, fabrics and concepts. As well as images, you can include the invitations you've chosen, ribbon to depict the colour of your bridesmaids' outfits and a picture of the venue you've chosen. Pin all these elements on to an A3 board and from there you simply remove any images that you fall out of love with and replace them with newer ideas that you love.

✔ **Pinterest:** Visit www.pinterest.com and type 'flowers' or 'bridal bouquets' into the search facility. Not only do you then see images, but you can collect them by pinning them on to your own virtual pinboard. Likewise, if you see a bouquet you like on a blog or website, you can use the Pinterest 'pin' button on your browser to pin the image on to your wedding board. Then you can show your board to any suppliers you've involved with your wedding design.

✔ **Wedding blogs:** So many wedding blogs are out there, it can be difficult to find a really helpful one. Start by typing 'wedding blogs' into your search engine, and view blogs from the US, Australia, South Africa and the UK for a variety of real weddings. Most blogs convey a particular style – some describe edgy weddings, some vintage, some whimsical and others contemporary. You can pin the flowers you like on to your Pinterest board.

Create a file of photographs you like. The images may depict floral bouquets and displays, or simply convey the feeling you want for your wedding. If a wedding stylist is credited in a photo you like, jot down the name; your florist may know the stylist's work and draw inspiration from it. Focus on the broad concept first, and then find the flowers that go with the image you want.

An oft-heard bridal refrain is, 'Can't we just use some heavenly wildflowers that we pick ourselves?' Sure you can – if you want to spend your wedding in a police cell. Under the Wildlife and Countryside Act 1981, which covers Britain, uprooting any wild plant without permission from the landowner or occupier is illegal. You're better off growing some wildflowers yourself or asking your florist to source them for you.

Every colour has a meaning

Ever wondered what different colours mean in relation to a wedding? Here's a quick list for you:

✔ **Green** reflects the natural elements around you and celebrates the fact that you're healthy. Green evokes a refreshing, calming feeling, as if you're at one with nature.

✔ **Orange** reflects the lust to be had in the marriage. It shouts out that you're fun and bold and that you're not afraid to show it on your wedding day.

✔ **Pink** represents youthful happiness, when pale, and the stronger pinks represent a vibrancy to life. Pale pink is soft and delicate and can represent your girly side. A stronger pink says that you want to be seen and heard, and goes with the slightly glitzier side of your personality.

✔ **Purple** represents royalty and, of course, you are royalty for the day! Purple is a serious colour that demands to be heard and seen. Using purple flowers in any arrangement creates a bold and striking reaction.

✔ **Red** represents the blood tie of the two families coming together. In essence, red is the colour of love and passion.

✔ **Yellow** is bright and optimistic, a cheerful colour that brings smiles to people's faces.

✔ **White** reflects the purity and innocence of your impending marriage. You can't help but look at white flowers and feel a calmness surround you.

Finding a Fab Florist

When choosing the right florist for your wedding, get recommendations for florists from friends, editors of local bridal magazines, wedding blogs, your chosen venue and other wedding suppliers. View the florist's website and any social media sites they're active on. Look at their floral style – does it fit with your vision for the wedding?

Call your shortlisted florists and arrange with each a meeting to discuss your wedding in detail, pass on your ideas, listen to the florist's suggestions and lay down the framework from which the florist can provide a quotation for the anticipated work.

At the interview, the florist should be able to back up any design concepts with photographs of weddings, individual bouquets and events for which they have supplied flowers and/or decor. Here are some questions to consider (of course, florists can be male or female, but we go with the masculine here for simplicity's sake):

✔ Has he worked at your venue before? If not, will he make a site visit before writing a proposal?

✔ What props, tablecloths, floral containers and other extras does the florist own? What would need to be hired and by whom?

✔ Do you like the environment of the florist's space or shop?

✔ Are his concepts original? How does he respond to your ideas? If you've brought clippings or mood boards, is he interested in them?

✔ How does he handle substituting flowers if the ones you've decided on become unavailable due to unexpected circumstances?

✔ Will he make a sample centrepiece or table set-up for you?

✔ What are the set-up and breakdown fees?

✔ From what time does he need access at the venue and can the venue accommodate this?

✔ When does he anticipate collecting his hired items like vases? Is this time acceptable to the venue?

✔ How soon can you expect a proposal?

✔ What are his payment terms?

✔ Does he think the budget you're estimating is realistic? If not, how much does he think your ceremony and reception flowers will really cost?

✔ Can he come up with alternative flower designs and decor concepts that fit with the overall wedding design and are within the budget? Perhaps he could use cheaper flowers to bring the cost down?

As you chat, carefully note the florist's answers. If you're on completely different wavelengths, move on to the next prospect – no point wasting each other's time.

Decorating the Ceremony Site

Whether your nuptial site is an old church with Roman arches, a historical manor house, a rustic barn or a register office itself, you'll want to add some floral decor for the occasion of your marriage. That may mean letting a grand site speak for itself with little or no embellishment, enhancing the most eloquent aspects of the space through equally elegant arrangements or undertaking a major overhaul to turn a secular site into one you deem appropriate for your vows.

Visit your ceremony site with your florist (or wedding planner) and think about the chronology of your ceremony in relation to what needs decorating. What do guests see as they arrive? What's the view from where they sit? Where are the musicians positioned? Where does the bridal party enter?

Where does everyone exit? By understanding how the space works, you can target areas where arrangements will add a great deal and those spots where they'd be wasted.

Sometimes an easy mistake to make can be to come up with a design without considering how it will work in the venue. For example, using a single orchid stem displayed in cylinder vases in a Tudor banqueting hall with high ceilings will look out of place; the singular stem will become invisible. So, working with and not against the venue decor is important, and doing so should also help your budget considerably. For example, say your colour scheme is pink and gold, but the banqueting chairs are green; you either need to hire in replacement chairs or cover them at an additional cost, or you can tweak your design to incorporate the green, which makes the chairs part of your design.

Remember, if you have an outdoor ceremony, it should be about the outdoors. Work with nature, not against it. Double check that the ceremony area has been well looked after, surplus dead leaves or flowers have been removed and pathways cleared, for example. If the flowers aren't in full glorious bloom, supplement them with homemade pots of flowers. You could even ask your florist to line the aisle with little pots of herbs or perhaps other commonly seen garden flowers like bulbs or daisies. (Using lots of tropical flowers may seem out of place in an English garden.) And don't forget to have a contingency plan for the UK weather. For example, if the ceremony site is very open and prone to strong wind, choose floral decorations that won't be blown away. Also ensure you discuss how to use the flowers if the ceremony ends up being indoors – birch trees lining an aisle outside look great, but won't work if the ceremony moves indoors due to weather.

Some people recommend using the registrar's table or altar flowers twice by whisking them from the ceremony to the reception. Separate venues, however, can make this practice unwieldy. Compare the cost of additional flowers with the moving expense and hassle. If the savings are truly significant, determine with your florist where to place these pieces so that their reappearance is least obvious.

If you're marrying in a religious building, typically someone on staff is responsible for specifying and enforcing the rules as to how you may or may not decorate, what time you can begin decorating and when all your decor has to be removed. Churches can be particularly strict about decor, so heed their rules carefully. For example, churches sometimes have set floral containers and/or candelabras for the altar and aisles. And before you lug your altarpieces to your reception, check the rules. Some churches insist that the flowers are a donation to be left behind for the congregation to enjoy. If you really want to use your church displays back at your reception site you could ask the florist to make a donation floral piece for the church instead.

If your church has booked another ceremony either before or after yours, consider splitting the cost of decorating with the other wedding party. Ask your vicar to put you in touch with the other couple.

Think about the following areas of the venue you want to decorate:

- ✔ **Altar flowers:** Usually, an altar is flanked by tall arrangements. Delicate blossoms disappear at a distance, so choose arrangements composed of large flower heads. You can use greenery and filler flowers in these pieces advantageously because the arrangements can be quite airy. Because churches tend to be dimly lit, light or vibrant hues work well, but keep the flowers in one palette. The flowers should enhance the couple and surroundings, not call attention to themselves.

- ✔ **Entrance:** Think about flagging the entrance. For a church you may create a floral arch, and at a wedding venue you may choose topiary trees to make a walkway to the door.

- ✔ **Font:** In churches, the baptismal font may seem the perfect piece of architecture for the wedding touch, but check first to make sure you can decorate it. If you can, filling the font with multicoloured rose petals or garlanding around the base adds a charming note to the surroundings. Garlands or small pots set on windowsills complete the vision.

- ✔ **Pew ends:** Decorative elements as simple as ribbons tied into beautiful bows or as lavish as elaborate rose topiaries may go on the ends of rows along the aisle – typically alternate rows – and be free-standing or attached to benches/chairs with floral holders.

- ✔ **Registrar's table:** Depending on space available, for a civil ceremony you may not be able to display large pedestals like in a church, so think about decorating the registrar's table. Some brides simply place their bouquet on the table for a cost-effective solution. Whatever you decide, remember to keep any display low enough so the registrar can actually see you.

Keep the size of the space in mind when choosing these arrangements. It doesn't make sense to overpower an exquisite country church that has a diminutive altar with flowers appropriate for St Paul's Cathedral. A church ambiance should remain intact after your design wizards alight.

Creating chuppahs

Although religious law requires Jewish weddings to take place under a *chuppah*, it cites no specifics regarding size or decoration. Generally, a *chuppah* is a canopy open on four sides and constructed just for the wedding. Some chuppahs are designed to be free-standing, and others are carried and held up by four people whom the couple wishes to honour.

Chuppahs can be beautifully simple and easy to make, covered with a fabric that's meaningful to the couple, such as a *tallit,* or prayer shawl, given to the groom by the bride and her family, or a material richly embroidered with symbols of married life or other personal notes.

More elaborate chuppahs are also often used in interfaith ceremonies that take place in manor houses or hotels. It's not unusual for the chuppah to appear to float above the congregation amid billows of organza, ivy and flowers suspended by invisible wires.

Choosing Personal Blooms

The term *personal flowers* refers not only to the bride's bouquet and groom's buttonhole, but also to all the flowers worn or carried by attendants, family members or others you want to honour. Men often have preferences, some quite specific, for the buttonhole they wear on their wedding day. And for brides, the flowers they carry as they walk towards married life are the ultimate – and very visible – accompaniment to their wedding dress.

Specify exactly where and when you want the florist to deliver your personal flowers and that you want them all labelled to avoid even the slightest chance that an usher may try to pin a mother-of-the-bride corsage to his lapel.

Bride and attendants

At the beginning of the 20th century, brides and bridesmaids carried such elaborate bouquets that the women practically needed a wheelbarrow to transport them down the aisle. Bouquets can be striking but they should never be distracting: you want all eyes on the carrier, not on her bouquet. As an accessory, the bouquet should complement the dress as well as the size and shape of the wearer. Bridesmaids' bouquets need not be dwarf versions of the bride's, but can be mini works of art in themselves.

Antique lace, organza, wired ribbon or fabric from the hem of the bride's skirt wrapped around the stems finish a bouquet beautifully, although not inexpensively.

You want to hold your bouquet by placing your elbows at your hipbones and grasping the stems or handle with both hands in front of your belly button. You should be able to do this while linking your arm with one person, unless you choose an overarm or presentation bouquet, which you must cradle in both arms. Figure 6-1 illustrates some of the following examples of bouquet types:

- **Shower:** Classic, elaborate shape with ivy and long-stemmed flowers that are wired or pulled out to droop gracefully in a teardrop shape.
- **Composite:** A flower constructed of hundreds of real petals wired together to look like one enormous flower.
- **Crescent:** Composed of one full flower and a flowering stem, often orchids, wired together to form a slender handle that you can hold in one hand. Designed as either a *full crescent,* a half-circle with a central flower and blossoms emanating from two sides, or as a *semi crescent,* which has only one trailing stem.
- **Hand-tied:** Round bouquets composed of flowers, greenery and, occasionally, sprigs of herbs.
- **Posies:** Smaller versions of hand-tied bouquets. Ribbons, feathers and brooches are sometimes integrated into them.
- **Presentation:** The overarm bouquet – long-stemmed flowers cradled in your arms.
- **Tossing:** A bouquet used for tossing so you can save the actual wedding bouquet for posterity. No need to duplicate the original.

Flowers, however dazzling and pure, can cause you grief if they aren't prepared with meticulous care. Before handing them to attendants, ask someone to check them to make sure they're dry and that any stamens that may stain dresses have been removed.

Instead of a bouquet, consider using fewer flowers in these innovative ways:

- A single long-stemmed flower, such as a calla lily, rose or Casablanca lily
- Flower buds worn in the hair
- A hat adorned with fresh flowers
- A comb, hair clip or headband covered in lace, ribbon and flowers

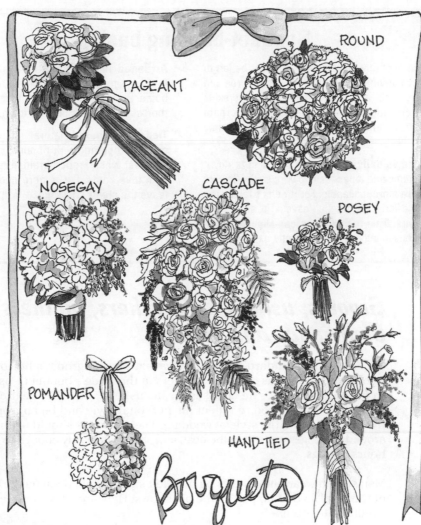

Figure 6-1:
A bouquet's shape and style are as important as the kind of flowers it contains.

Mothers, stepmothers, fathers' girlfriends and others

Many women think of corsages as being old fashioned, not to mention the pinholes that corsages make in their expensive outfits. Alternatives exist, including wrist corsages, flowers pinned to a handbag or floral heads combined with a jewelled bracelet. Many florists now offer magnets to hold corsages in place on a dress. Ask your florist for this option if a pinned-on corsage is a must-have.

Bouquet-building basics

A bunch of flowers can almost never be left to its own devices. Creating floral sculptures and even simple arrangements requires the skills of a few magicians. Here's how florists create various arrangements and why the prices may vary wildly:

✓ **Individually wired:** The florist cuts down stems and tapes them to wire so the flowers are more malleable. For greens such as ivy, the florist first stitches leaves with a fine silver wire. This technique is complicated, time-consuming and, consequently, expensive.

✓ **Arranged in holders:** The florist places floral foam soaked in water in a bouquet holder – a plastic cone with a handle, and then sticks flowers into the foam.

✓ **Tied in bunches:** A natural bunch of flowers tied together with ribbons, which are prettiest when French braided or finished with love knots. For a more natural look, leave the stems showing.

Grooms, ushers, stepfathers, mothers' boyfriends and others

No longer the standard-issue white carnation, the groom's buttonhole is normally the same as one of the flowers in the bride's bouquet – as if plucked from there. The ones he chooses for his ushers and other gentlemen he wants to honour need to reflect his personal style and be appropriate for their outfits – and the style of wedding. These flowers should neither brown around the edges nor wilt in the heat, and should be hardy enough to withstand hours of hugs.

Men should wear buttonholes on their left side and pin them on the underside of the lapel so that no part of the pin shows. Here are a few replacements for traditional buttonholes:

✓ English roses in vibrant colours set with a sprig of rosemary

✓ Hypericum berries backed with Galax leaves

✓ Lavender and sweet peas

✓ Orchids

✓ Peonies or hydrangeas

✓ Standing Amaranthus

✓ Twigs and foliage

    ✔ Variegated ivy, fern and mini pine cones

    ✔ White snowberries

Think about wrapping the stems in a fabric to match the wedding design. Or for rustic weddings, use twine.

Order extra buttonholes. They're relatively inexpensive and one or two may not survive ham-fisted attempts at pinning or may get crushed by well-wishers. Besides, it's good to have extras for any forgotten menfolk.

Little touches for little people

When dealing with flower children (or any children, for that matter), keep accessories in proportion to the child's size. You don't want your flower girl to look like an ungainly flowering plant moving down the aisle. Some simple floral alternatives to the traditional flower basket include:

    ✔ **Alice Band:** Selection of flowers worn on a headband.

    ✔ **Circlet:** A ribbon or twig band accented with blossoms and worn on girls' heads.

    ✔ **Garland:** Round garland of a selection of flowers to match the bride's bouquet; can be formal, like roses, or bohemian with daisies.

    ✔ **Hoop:** Made of vine strung with flowers and carried like a tambourine.

    ✔ **Pomander:** A polystyrene ball covered in lace and tulle and trimmed with floral heads; it hangs on the wrist (refer to Figure 6-1).

    ✔ **Slide and comb:** One of two flowers combined with a slide or comb; perfect for vintage weddings.

Fresh petals can be slippery. If you want to follow children strewing petals from baskets, show them how to sprinkle them, alternating sides of the path rather than straight down the danger zone. Don't forget to check whether your venue allows you to scatter petals.

The ring bearer's main accessory is the ring pillow, which may be sewn of luxurious fabrics such as satin, silk, velvet or organza. These pillows are sometimes embroidered or trimmed with silk, natural flowers or ornate tassels, and the rings are tied on with attached ribbons. As special as the pillow is, though, the ring bearer may be more interested in wearing a buttonhole identical to that of the ushers so that he feels as grown up as them, so make sure you include the ring bearer in your flower order.

We suggest that the ring pillow never have the real rings on it. To protect the child's ego, attach fake rings and have the best man make a display of untying them. The real rings are, of course, safe with the best man and maid of honour.

Decking Out Receptions

As the most important aspect of your reception's design, flowers are likely to eat up the bulk of your decor budget. (For a larger discussion on decorating your reception space, see Chapter 5.) Flowers themselves are generally expensive; in addition, someone has to select, prepare, transport and arrange these precious blooms – and that can add up to significant money. If you want them to last through your reception with heads up and colour intact, you can't just plop flowers in a vase. They must be conditioned – stems denuded of thorns, anthers, stigmas and extra leaves (which may decay in water, producing a foul odour), ends snipped or crushed, and stems wired. If you desire a certain look, such as fully opened roses, these must be blown open just enough but not one iota too much. Even the seemingly homespun wild-flowers-in-a-jug look isn't as simple as it appears. Studied casualness takes *work*.

Making floral arrangements measure up

Many hosts are obsessed with centrepieces being no higher than eye level when you're sitting at the table. Although this design raises arguments between designer and client, keep in mind that people tend to converse with those seated next to, rather than across from, them. People like to be able to at least nod at the smiling faces across the way, but in our opinion, as long as centrepieces are airy, you don't have to worry about partially obscuring the cross-table view. You just don't want a mini conifer hedge bisecting the table. Various table sizes and shapes are now used in tandem at the same reception, so designers must make different sizes and shapes of their floral pieces as well.

If you're fixated on giving guests a clear view across the table, use the elbow test. Rest your elbow on the table and raise your forearm perpendicular to the table, fingers extended. Centrepieces on the table should end below your fingertips (about 35 centimetres), and elevated centrepieces, where the flowers are above eye level, should start above your fingertips.

TIP

For the most part, use filler flowers and greenery sparingly. Ideally, greenery consists of leaves removed from the flowers themselves and used only to balance an arrangement or hide the mechanics – floral foam, chicken-wire cages, tape, wire and wired tubes – built in to add height and breadth. In any centrepiece, no matter how elaborate or simple, these materials should never show.

Centrepieces for wedding receptions no longer look as if they've come off a floral assembly line (see Figure 6-2). Designers create rooms as a whole, using a variety of colours, flowers and approaches for each table. Some tables may have low arrangements and other tables may feature an elevated centrepiece.

Figure 6-2: Gone are the days when centrepieces came in one-style-fits-all.

FLORAL CENTREPIECES

WARNING!

If someone in the immediate family suffers from hay fever, think about testing your preferred flowers in their home to check they don't affect them. Flowers that may affect those with hay fever include freesias, lilies, hyacinths and narcissi.

Styling your centrepieces

You have various styles and configurations of centrepieces to choose from:

- **Candle holder:** Hurricane vases are especially popular in winter. A glass vase and church candle with a ring of flowers surrounding it looks beautifully romantic.

- **Candelabra:** A tall candelabra that has four to six arms holding tall, tapered candles. Flowers start at eye level, stemming from an elevated bowl in the centre of the candelabra.

- **Collection of containers:** You could have delicate crystal posy vases lining a long top table, or Victorian teacups and jugs in the centre of a round table. Collections usually contain delicate blooms like Lisianthus, sweet peas and freesias.

- **Continental style:** An arrangement composed of flowers whose stems have been cut almost down to the head and arranged in low, mounded patterns. Well suited for side tables as well as centrepieces.

- **Country garden:** An abundance of flowers and foliage, such as roses and ivy tendrils, that look as if a small garden is growing in the middle of the table. The greens either completely obscure the container (which is therefore nothing fancy) or allow at most a peek of the container, such as a pretty basket or vintage jug.

- **Fish bowl or globe:** Round glass bowls stuffed with mounded flowers, such as roses or just a few calla lilies for a fairly low centrepiece.

- **Long and low:** Traditionally, this style is for the long top table. It's still popular, but lots of brides are choosing to have a long line of mini vases instead.

- **Organic:** Arrangements that have not only flowers but also colourful fruits and vegetables, using whatever's in season. Often displayed in tall clear vases.

- **Topiaries:** Either natural ivy grown around a metal frame and trimmed to resemble something as simple as spheres or as complex as cupids, or topiary trees made of Styrofoam balls covered with moss and finished with flower heads, fruits, ribbons and so on.

Flanking the band or bordering the dance floor with floral pieces is generally a waste of money, because you usually have to remove these when the music starts.

Don't forget to ask your florist if they have additional items – such as lanterns, shepherd crooks, candelabras, votive candles and vintage crockery – that you can hire. You may want to keep the number of suppliers you use to a minimum, and getting both flowers and design props from the same supplier is an excellent way to do this. If your florist doesn't have the items you require, local hire companies exist that may be able to help. Many have competitive rates compared with national suppliers, so do an Internet search to find out what's near you or ask your wedding planner to investigate on your behalf.

Additional floral displays

If budget allows, here are a few other areas in which you can have flowers:

- ✔ Backs of the top table chairs (pew-end arrangements are perfect for this)
- ✔ Beams in a barn
- ✔ Courtyard or occasional tables
- ✔ Doorways
- ✔ Fireplace in a manor house
- ✔ Top table
- ✔ Walkways – for example, hanging from shepherds' crooks

At some point, your florist (or wedding planner) should communicate with your cake maker. If your cake is to have sugar or icing flowers, you may want it to co-ordinate with the centrepieces or the bridal bouquet. If the cake is to have fresh flowers, the florist needs to know the colours and shape of the cake so he can provide them.

Making Your Own Arrangements

One of the biggest costs in the flower universe is labour. If you have the time and the inclination (or a group of loving aunts dying for a wedding assignment), you may go into do-it-yourself mode. Or, to cut your floral expenditure, you can ask your florist to come up with some simpler ideas that require less labour and/or fewer stems.

Bear in mind the time involved in any DIY arrangements, and the cost. The price of flowers has soared over the years, so make sure you price up your ideas properly, comparing DIY to hiring a professional florist.

The following strategies will help you create an eye-catching look with fewer flowers:

- Use elements other than flowers to create centrepieces: glass bowls of green apples with ivy, tiered plates laden with varieties of grapes, miniature pumpkins and acorns, or highly stylized, minimalist arrangements. The look of the room comprises all the tables as a whole, so alternating tables that have ornate arrangements with those that have smaller ones won't diminish the beauty of your reception.

- Float apples, limes or lemons in glass cylinders and finish the arrangement with cut flowers.

- Place candelabras on their own with just a few votive candle holders at the base and a single stem for colour.

- Use the available tablecloths for the underlay or bottom cloth and top them with a long coloured table runner of a contrasting colour. A family member proficient on a sewing machine could make the runner.

- Instead of mixed cut flowers, use potted plants or herbs that green-fingered friends can grow easily.

- Decorate the cake table with petals or gems in lieu of flowers.

- To accent an escort card table, use small pots of herbs, flowering plants or a bed of petals rather than an oversized floral piece.

- Tie napkins with ribbons, lace remnants or raffia and tuck in a sprig of ivy, rosemary or an inexpensive flower. Creating more visual interest around the entire table makes an imposing centrepiece less necessary.

 Instead of flowers, put scented candles with a few sprigs of ivy or rosemary in the toilets.

Keeping the Bloom On

If you choose not to toss your real bridal bouquet, you may want to preserve it, which you can do in one of several ways:

- **Air-dry:** Hang the bouquet (and the buttonhole, if you choose) upside down in a dark, ventilated space, separating the flowers by type for best results.

- **Freeze-dry:** Professionally done, this keeps the colours more vibrant than air-drying does. You can then display the flowers in a glass dome or shadow box.

- **Preserving with desiccants:** Simple but time-consuming, this arts-and-crafts project requires you to bury the bouquet in silica gel, available at hobby shops.

- **Potpourri:** Dry the flowers, and then remove the petals and mix them with fragrant oils, herbs and spices. Put in an airtight jar and shake once a day for six weeks.

In a spirit of generosity, many couples consider donating their leftover flowers to a local hospital. It's a nice thought, but, frankly, most hospitals don't want them. If, however, you want to do something truly charitable, make arrangements with a nursing home *before* your wedding as to when and where to drop off small, tidy bouquets after your reception. Negotiate the price for this delivery with your florist. Another possibility, if the timing is feasible, is to ask your florist to provide floral paper or ribbon, and then your wedding planner or any other assistant on the day can create amateurish bouquets from the centrepieces and other arrangements at the end of reception for your guests to take home.

Chapter 7

Planning a Destination Wedding

∙ ∙

In This Chapter

▶ Working out the cost

▶ Vetting venues

▶ Jumping through legal hoops

▶ Managing the organisation from afar

▶ Taking care of guests

▶ Celebrating back home after the wedding

∙ ∙

A *destination wedding* is one whose location requires some travelling on the part of you and the majority of your guests in order to spend a few memorable days with the group. Typically, these events take place over a long weekend and entail a special level of research, logistics and hospitality. But having your wedding in an exotic location or somewhere that's especially meaningful for you makes it all the more distinctive. In spite of the complicated logistics, destination weddings provide ample opportunity for originality, freedom and intimacy.

This chapter gives you the lowdown on destination weddings, to help you determine whether this is the type of wedding for you, and if so, how you go about arranging it.

Understanding Why Couples Pick a Destination Wedding, and Counting the Cost

People choose destination weddings for a range of reasons:

✔ To bring together friends and family that are separated by great distances.

✔ To provide neutral territory if concerns exist about family feuds or power issues.

✔ To have an exotic backdrop to the nuptials.

✔ To keep the event intimate and limit the guest list.

✔ To save money.

The final point is a big one – many people think that destination weddings are cheaper than marrying at home, and often that's true because:

✔ Destination weddings usually attract fewer guests.

✔ You can often get more value in an all-inclusive resort than in a major city.

✔ You can rely on a location's natural beauty instead of dressing it up to look like somewhere else. It makes no sense to try to turn a beach setting into a chandeliered hotel lobby, or an Italian villa into a cosmopolitan venue.

✔ You may have fee leverage with some suppliers if you're getting married in a wonderful, exotic location. For example, finding a first-rate photographer in an out-of-the-way spot is often impossible, but you may be able to barter a UK photographer's services in exchange for a few free days at the location plus airfare.

But all rules have exceptions, and the costs can mount up, especially if you have to 'import' what you need. Make sure you keep in mind these costs for a destination wedding:

✔ Any additional socialising you're hosting for guests

✔ Ceremony fee

✔ Flights and accommodation (but if you honeymoon in the setting that's a cost you were going to pay out for anyway, right?)

✔ Key suppliers like photographer, cake, flowers and music (but they tend to be a fraction of the cost back home because you won't have the photographer for long, you won't need many flowers and the cake is small)

✔ Spa treatments, hair and make-up

✔ Transfer fees for guests

✔ Visas, inoculations, an affidavit signed by a solicitor stating that no legal objection exists against your marriage, and renewal of passport

✔ Wedding meal and drinks

✔ Welcome packs for guests

Investigate when the off-peak times are at your chosen destination and check the weather is okay for then. Also ask your travel agent for discounts on group bookings.

The top 15 destinations for overseas weddings

Research shows that the countries in this list are the top destinations to which couples often head for their overseas weddings.

- America (especially Florida, Las Vegas and New York)
- Australia
- Austria
- Bermuda
- Canada
- The Caribbean (especially St Lucia, Jamaica, the Bahamas, Antigua and Grenada)
- Cyprus
- France
- Greece
- Iceland
- Italy
- Seychelles
- South Africa
- Spain
- Thailand

Finding a Faraway Venue

The destination you choose for your wedding could be one with which you're intimately familiar, such as a location where you've holidayed or perhaps a relative's villa, or it may be an entirely new, different and fascinating location. Which country you choose generally determines the type of wedding you can have when you get there. For example, in Australia, South Africa, Canada and the US you can hold your ceremony pretty much anywhere (a mountain setting or perhaps the Grand Canyon, anyone?), but in other countries the venue has to be licensed, just as in the UK. For this reason, having someone who can guide you on any licensing restrictions is essential. Whether this person is your destination wedding planner, the venue co-ordinator or the travel agent, having someone with knowledge of the area is a must. The other factors to consider when choosing your destination are distance and cost, and whether you plan to invite friends and family to the wedding. Locations in Europe, for example, are cheaper and quicker to fly to than say America or Australia.

You can source your ideal faraway destination venue in a number of different ways. To begin with, think about whether you want your wedding to take place at a private location, exclusively for you, or in a hotel, a wedding venue or out in the open. Just like in the UK, some of the best deals can be found when booking everything in-house at a place where guests can eat, celebrate and stay. If you opt for a hotel, ask the hotel wedding co-ordinator how many weddings typically take place there every day or week; you may be surprised at the 'conveyor belt' process of some resorts.

Many tour operators have specialised wedding departments that can assist you with the paperwork and recommend suppliers to hire, and many offer wedding packages that can be very good value, including flights, accommodation, registrar, photographer, cake, bouquets and a meal. Some offer a concierge service for an additional fee, and in many cases the actual wedding planning may be handed over to the venue co-ordinator who you meet upon arrival at the resort. Tour operators who have great resources for marrying abroad include First Choice (www.firstchoice.co.uk), Sandals (www.sandals.com), Kuoni (www.kuoni.co.uk), Thomson (www.thomson.co.uk) and Virgin Holidays (www.virginholidays.co.uk). You can also try specialist companies like Perfect Weddings Abroad (www.perfectweddingsabroad.co.uk) or Luxury Wedding and Honeymoon Hotels (www.luxuryweddingandhoneymoonhotels.com).

If you want to marry at a wedding venue or out in the open try contacting the local tourist board for a list of venues you can try.

Alternatively, you can hire a wedding planner in the UK who specialises in weddings for your chosen destination to organise everything for you. You may also choose to hire a wedding planner in the country where you're having your wedding – the US has a very well-established wedding-planning community, and wedding planning is a growing profession in many European countries, particularly in Italy and France. Some couples decide on two wedding planners – one in the UK and one in their destination. This may sound extravagant, but actually it can save you a lot of money in the long run and the two wedding planners can split the one fee as each does about half the work.

Honeymoon-weddings

You may choose a *honeymoon-wedding*: getting married with just each other (and two witnesses) in the same locale as your honeymoon. Some resorts (Walt Disney World and Sandals) specialise in intimate honeymoon-weddings, which are smaller and less complicated than full-blown destination weddings. These add-on weddings are inexpensive – even free in some cases. Ask the wedding department at your destination to send you a full description on how they do these ceremonies and mini-receptions. If details are important to you, take a trip to the destination to meet with the person who'll be overseeing your wedding. If you want something different than the resort ordinarily provides (and are willing to pay for special plans), notify your destination far in advance – in writing – and ask them to send back a letter of agreement.

Arrive a few days early to arrange things the way you want them. An on-site wedding co-ordinator should be able to assist you in whipping your wedding into shape.

Honeymoon-weddings can be the simplest to carry off – especially if the emphasis is on the honeymoon and you don't invite any guests. In such cases, the resort provides all the accoutrements, including the witnesses. You may send out announcements, or even have a celebratory bash when you return. These post-wedding parties tend to be less expensive and less stressful than the typical wedding ceremony followed by a same-day reception.

Destination Location Checklist

❏ What are the legal and religious requirements for getting married there?

❏ What are the residency requirements?

❏ How difficult is it for your guests to get to? Is a change of planes necessary?

❏ Is travel and accommodation affordable for guests?

❏ Are blood tests or immunisations required for marriage licences?

❏ Will guests require vaccinations?

❏ What are the necessary documents to get married In this destinatlon?

❏ Must proof of divorce or proof of being a widow(er) be certified?

❏ Do documents need to be translated into the native language? Are the original documents necessary?

❏ Do these documents need to be sent In advance?

❏ How long do you have to wait after your arrival to obtain a marriage liccnce?

❏ After getting the licence, how long is the waiting period?

❏ Are witnesses necessary? Must they be citizens of that country?

❏ Are civil ceremonies allowed? Which religious ceremonies are permitted?

❏ What is the name of a reputable wedding coordinator and/or a travel agent specialising in destination weddings who can help with bookings for your guests and with hiring suppliers?

❏ Can you make at least one site-inspection trip?

❏ Would you like to spend your honeymoon there?

❏ What's the weather like in the season you're planning to get married?

❏ How long before your wedding is It suggested you arrive?

Figure 7-1: Rescarch the perfect destination for your wedding.

Figure 7-1 offers a destination location checklist to help you consider all the factors you need to bear in mind to decide on a destination venue that works for you and your guests. The number of guests you invite (and you may per-haps ask only close friends and relatives) and the portion of their tab you pick up depends on what you decide is reasonable to spend when choosing a destination.

Understanding the Legalities of Marrying Abroad

The legal requirements necessary to make a wedding legitimate vary from country to country, so make sure you do your homework, otherwise you could find out you were never actually married legally (like Mick Jagger and Jerry

Hall whose Bali wedding was annulled). You want to make sure your wedding is legally recognised in the country you're marrying in *and* the country where you live.

In most cases, if you're marrying at a resort, the in-house wedding co-ordinator assists you with the legalities as part of the package, but it's up to you to provide the necessary paperwork on time so that the co-ordinator can take care of the red tape and ensure you're legally married.

Contact the UK-based embassy of the country you want to marry in, just to clarify what documentation you need for a wedding in that country. The embassy can give you the most up-to-date information regarding the legal requirements. And follow instructions to the letter: you don't want the wedding cancelled just because you didn't bring one requested document.

In most countries each party needs to produce the following documentation three months in advance as well as on the wedding day itself:

- ✔ An affidavit signed by a solicitor stating that no legal objection exists against your marriage
- ✔ Valid ten-year passport
- ✔ Full birth certificate
- ✔ If you're adopted, your adoption certificate
- ✔ If you're widowed, the death certificate of your former spouse and previous marriage certificate
- ✔ If you're divorced, your decree absolute

You may be asked by your venue or travel agent to prove that you're allowed to marry. In most cases, you can obtain a Certificate of No Impediment (CNI) for this purpose from your local register office. Check whether you need a CNI with the authorities in the country where you're getting married. A Nulla Osta is the Italian version of the Certificate of No Impediment. You can find further information at www.gov.uk/government/publications/certificate-of-no-impediment-and-nulla-ostas. Check with your destination contact whether the CNI as issued by your register office is acceptable, or whether it needs to be exchanged for a locally accepted version in the local language. (These can be issued by the local British Consulate or Embassy.)

Also look into residency requirements. Table 7-1 provides a guide, but do check with the relevant embassy before making any plans.

Should you want to marry in Bali you must declare a religion. Atheism is not recognised. The regular stated residency is ten days, but tourists can waive this by completing a guest registration form.

Table 7-1	Minimum Residency Requirements Pre-Ceremony
Residency Period	*Countries*
None (although in many instances you must meet the registrar a few days before)	Australia, Austria, Antigua, Bermuda, Barbados, Croatia, Gibraltar, Italy, Malta, New Zealand, Portugal, South Africa, Spain, St Lucia, Thailand, Turkey, US (do check because some states like New York require only 24 hours)
Between one and seven days	Anguilla, Bahamas, British Virgin Islands, Cook Islands, Greece, Cyprus, Dominican Republic, Grenada, Jamaica, Mauritius, Mexico, Seychelles, Sri Lanka
10 days	Bali
40 continuous days (or gain special permission from the local church)	France

If you're finding the residency issue daunting, consider marrying legally in the UK with just witnesses and then having a blessing/humanist ceremony at your chosen destination.

Organising from a Distance

Planning your dream destination wedding can be stressful, so give yourself enough time to do it well. Giving yourself plenty of time to organise your wedding also means that you don't get restricted by the availability of popular venues. When you have a confirmed booking at your venue, send out save-the-date cards to the people you want to invite so that you then give them time to save up and book time off work.

Don't feel that you have to go through the process of organising your destination wedding alone; you do have options:

✔ Hire a **wedding planner** in the location you're marrying. This is especially helpful if you're not using a fully serviced venue or you do not speak the language of the country you're visiting. The planner can recommend the best places to stay and vetted suppliers to use. They'll also be there on the day, setting up and generally running the celebrations for you. In addition, a local planner knows the location's customs and etiquette and can save you from blunders – like wanting the ceremony at siesta time, or hurrying along a laidback Caribbean supplier.

✔ Book a wedding through a **travel agent.** Although the service won't be as condensed as an independent wedding planner, the agent can advise on some suppiers to use and assist with accommodation and shuttles.

✔ Use a **wedding venue** that offers you a package so you don't have to plan much at all.

Things to think about when speaking with local suppliers, hotels and wedding planners:

✔ What's the time difference? What times are best to contact people?

✔ Can they conduct any meetings via Skype? Doing so enables you to build up a rapport in advance of the wedding and show swatches, invites and so on to them.

✔ Do you need an interpreter?

✔ Do they all have legally binding contracts you can sign, and more importantly are they in English?

Think about the climate, too, when organising your dress. Remember you expand in the heat, so don't have a corset too tight or you'll never sit down on your wedding day.

Don't forget to tell your bank or credit card company that you're heading abroad for a while. If you don't inform them before you go away, they may freeze your card when they see a number of unusual payments showing against the card, thinking they are being made fraudulently.

Going local for your flowers – or going expensive

If you really want white English roses for your bouquet then expect to pay far more if your wedding is in the Caribbean, because the flowers will be imported. We had a client who was married in Jamaica and created an English country garden feel to her wedding dinner. To keep costs from going through the roof, we transported almost all the decorations in our luggage – from the candles, ribbons and freeze-dried roses to cake decorations and confetti rose petals.

Wherever possible we recommend that you choose local flowers for your wedding, especially if you're keeping an eye on costs. You selected this destination for a reason, so embrace the culture, traditions and local flowers.

Don't forget to pack . . .

Remembering *everything* you need to pack for a destination wedding can be a daunting task. Not only do you need to pack the things you'll need for your honeymoon, you also need to remember the items required for the actual ceremony. Chapter 22 offers up a list of things to pack for your honeymoon. Here is a list of items to pack for the ceremony:

✔ **Wedding dress:** Arrange with the airline to take your dress on board the plane and ask if they can hang it up for you. Depending on who you fly with, the stewardesses will normally try to be accommodating. And ensure your dress is in a garment bag and not squashed into a holdall.

✔ **Wedding shoes:** Don't forget to wear them in prior to the wedding, and take appropriate shoes for your location – if you're getting married on a beach, could you walk in high heels?

✔ **Veil/tiara:** Also remember any other hair accessories you may need, including hair grips.

✔ **Wedding jewellery:** Take jewellery on the plane with you, within your hand luggage.

✔ **The rings and ring cushion if applicable.**

✔ **Wedding underwear:** Don't forget your stockings or garter belt.

✔ **Stationery:** Pack any stationery you've ordered for the ceremony or the celebrations afterwards, such as your order of service, place cards and table names.

✔ **Important paperwork:** Take copies of all your correspondence with your venue co-ordinator, travel agent and wedding planner confirming key decisions.

✔ **Your iPod loaded with your wedding music:** Even if you've booked live musicians, taking a playlist as a backup is a smart move.

✔ **The groom's outfit:** Don't forget the shoes, shirt, tie and cufflinks, if the outfit includes them.

✔ **Make-up:** Don't forget your make-up if you're doing this yourself.

Also put together a small emergency kit:

✔ **First aid:** Take bite-relief cream, allergy tablets, insect repellent, headache tablets, indigestion tablets and plasters.

✔ **Beauty items:** Pack body tape for cleavage, baby wipes (which are good for anything and everything!), deodorant, hair clips, brush, hairspray, make-up, nail file and clear nail varnish, perfume, sanitary products, sun cream (if you are heading to a hot destination), tissues, toothbrush and toothpaste.

✔ **Miscellaneous bits and bobs:** Remember your clothes brush, earring backs, a mini sewing kit, mints, flat shoes for dancing, travel shoe polish, and – top tip – a piece of white chalk to cover any smudges on your dress.

Checking Out a Typical Timeline

To give you an idea of how the festivities may unfold, here's a sample day-by-day breakdown of events for a four-day, Thursday-Sunday wedding weekend at a private villa:

- ✔ **Thursday evening:** Bride, groom, parents and perhaps siblings have dinner. May be anything from a casual at-villa dinner to elegant dining in a restaurant; gives the families a chance to spend some private, calm-before-the-storm time together. Other early arrivals are on their own, but try to have their welcome packages in their rooms when they arrive (see 'Ensuring winning welcomes', later in this chapter).

- ✔ **Friday:** The majority of guests start arriving and checking in. Although picking them up at the airport isn't necessary, make sure they know the easiest and least expensive ways to get to the villa or hotel where they're staying.

- ✔ **Friday, late afternoon:** Rehearsal takes place for those in the wedding party as well as people who are otherwise involved in the ceremony (readers, singers and so on). Usually (but not always), you rehearse where the ceremony will actually take place.

  Although you may be tempted to skip a formal rehearsal and just do a run-through on the day of your wedding, we strongly advise against that – the run-through will either be nerve-wracking or won't take place at all.

- ✔ **Friday evening:** After the rehearsal, the wedding party goes to a rehearsal dinner. Who else gets invited to this pre-nuptial event is a source of great debate in bridal circles. We believe that if you're asking people to travel to attend your wedding, you should entertain them in some way. Do provide transportation to and from the event.

  The rehearsal dinner (or luncheon) works well with a casual feel. A barbecue is ideal because guests can eat and mingle far more easily than at a formal dinner.

- ✔ **Saturday:** Wedding day! Schedule some group activities during the day – a football game, visit to a spa, for example – but make sure they're optional; some of your guests may want to sleep in.

- ✔ **Saturday afternoon:** If getting to and from the ceremony and reception sites from where guests are staying is tricky, provide transportation if possible. If your wedding doesn't go on until the wee hours, possibly offer a late-night bar or coffee-and-dessert option after the reception at the hotel where the guests are staying for those who want to party on.

- ✔ **Sunday:** Brunch, usually hosted by a relative or friend. Keep it very casual, more of a drop-in affair than a seated lunch. Although you're not obligated to attend the brunch (people understand if you've already left for your honeymoon), if you're still around, stop in and say your goodbyes.

Thinking About Your Guests

If you've chosen to marry abroad you need to think about looking after your guests as they may have gone to a lot of expense and effort to witness your marriage. The beauty of a destination wedding is that it is normally more intimate than a wedding at home, which means that you can really look after them and make them feel special.

In this section, we talk about ways to keep your guests informed of key information about the wedding schedule and how to produce little welcome packs.

Putting together the guest list

Choosing whom to invite is tricky regardless of whether you're marrying in the UK or abroad. Do you still want a lavish wedding with lots of family and friends, or is an intimate occasion more your style? Generally speaking, unless budget is no issue for you or guests, larger weddings are better suited for Mediterranean locations because travel costs are more reasonable for guests. If, however, you plan to invite just immediate family, you can look further afield.

Do the inviting and initial planning as early as possible so guests can book flights and accommodation and book time off work. We recommend you give your guests at least a year's notice if at all possible.

Telling guests what they need to know

In order for your guests to plan accordingly, give them a detailed idea of what to expect, including background on the destination and the wedding's itinerary. Even if you're so ahead of the game that you included this info with the save-the-date, you may decide to post it on a personal wedding web page for the less-organised half of the population.

A pre-wedding info package may include any or all of the following vital data:

- ✔ Reservations phone number for hotel(s), web addresses, general price variables and how your group is listed ('The Rawly-Pawly Wedding', for example).
- ✔ The name of a contact person at the hotel if applicable.

✔ Travel agent information or recommendations on booking air travel.

✔ Information on transportation to and from the venue.

✔ Travel requirements such as vaccinations, passports and visas.

✔ An overview of the destination, including a map.

✔ Typical weather for that time of year.

✔ A rundown of the festivities, a preliminary schedule of events, general dress codes and suggestions of what to bring, such as golf clubs or tennis racquets.

✔ Child-care information.

✔ Phone numbers and the contact details for services that guests need to book in advance, such as spa treatments, scuba diving or skiing lessons.

✔ A questionnaire that asks whether they're interested in spa services or sports such as sailing, tennis or diving. Although this may seem a bit much, at small resorts these services book up fast. Based on this questionnaire, you can give the management a heads-up so they're not caught short-staffed.

You could also include a festive touch such as a sun hat with your *combination monogram* (a logo or graphic that combines your initials or names) and wedding date on it (it's considered bad taste to use your married monogram before you're actually married) and instructions to wear upon arrival (very cool for group shots).

Generally speaking, guests pay for their own travel and accommodation, and you're responsible for the events that take place over the weekend.

Figure 7-2 shows a sample wedding preview letter that tells guests everything they need to know.

Molly and Joe are getting married!!!

By now you've heard the fantastic news that we are getting married on 6th April, 2006, in Jamaica. We are tickled pink that you are planning to join us for our wedding and a weekend of festivities to celebrate.

Why Jamaica?

There were many trips to Jamaica as single souls, where we both fell head over heels in love with this magical island, never knowing that each other existed. And then — one trip together that cemented our relationship and sealed our futures together. It seemed like the only place for us to commit to each other surrounded by our dear friends and family.

Air reservations

Due to the popularity of trips to the islands at this time, we urge you to call early to make your airline reservations. We have contracted with "Krebbs Travel" travel agents, at 09876 543210 or www.krebbstravel836.co.uk, for a discounted rate for our guests on both British Airways and Air Jamaica. If you wish to ask specific questions, please contact Celeste at extension 23 and tell her you are with the Fox-Hall wedding.

Accommodations

We have blocked rooms at a discounted rate at the Island Heaven resort and spa. The rates vary from rooms in the Lodge (£) and the Poolside Cottages (££) to the Fantasy Suites (££££). The rest of your stay is included in your room rate, or as our guests.

Please be certain to say you are a member of the Fox-Hall wedding party when booking. The rooms are reserved for us until 15th February, after which they will be released. Please call early so as not to be disappointed (and disappoint us, of course).

Transportation

A shuttle bus from Island Heaven will meet every flight upon which our guests arrive. There will be representatives from the resort directly outside the customs signage. If you prefer to rent a car (which we don't recommend as driving is on the "other side" of the road, and the roads aren't exactly state of the art), there is a rental agency at the airport, and our travel agent will reserve one for you in advance. Just ask her when you make your other reservations.

Figure 7-2:
Give your
guests the
pertinent
information.

Activities

There will be a beach barbecue on Friday evening, the main event on Saturday at 5 p.m., followed by dinner and dancing under the stars and a farewell brunch on Sunday atl 10 a.m. (for those of you who can tear yourselves away from paradise). We will be going into honeymoon seclusion after that, so be sure to get your fill of us beforehand as we will be definitely incommunicado!
Golfing. tennis. scuba. snorkeling. coladas, daiquiris. rum punch, naps, sun, naps. sun . ... If you wish to book any spa services, such as a massage or hair styling, it is best to book these early as well. Call the spa directly at 00 800 234 5678.

Weather

The average temperature is a perfect 29 degrees – balmy, not humid. A light sweater or jacket may be necessary at night. The rest of the time, wear plenty of sun block and something to keep it in place.

Dress

With the exception of our wedding ceremony and the celebration that follows on Saturday – which is island-dress-up (you interpret) – all other activities are strictly casual. Penalties for overdressing will be administered.

Babysilling

We are aware that many of you may be bringing your kids and making this a funily holiday. They are welcome to all events – WITH THE EXCEPTION of the ceremony and the party following. We have contracled with a bonded child care service that was recommended by our wedding consultant. They can be reached at We Be Kid-Care, 09876098765.

Questions

If there is anything we haven't covered here please call or e-mail either of us:

Molly: 01632 960998 or Mfox@baddabing.com
Joe: 01632 960997 or Jhall @baddabing.com

Watch for more mailings and information as April approaches. (You know we can't help ourselves!)

We are really looking forward to seeing you in Jamaica, mon.

Love,
Molly and Joe

Figure 7-2:
(continued).

Negotiate a group rate based on the maximum number of guest rooms you feel comfortable guaranteeing. These contracts can be complicated and often require you to furnish a credit card to hold the rooms until your guests furnish theirs. *Note:* Be certain you understand what you're financially responsible for if guests don't take the rooms you block booked. Negotiate other variables at the same time, such as a hospitality suite, farewell brunch and delivery fees for welcome baskets.

Don't be afraid to ask the resort for a room upgrade for yourself, perhaps to a suite, if you book a certain number of rooms for your guests.

Ensuring winning welcomes

A great way to show appreciation for those who've decided they can't miss your wedding, even if it's on the other side of the equator, is a welcome package that says, 'We're glad you're here.' One of the loveliest expressions of thanks is a little something in guests' rooms upon their arrival. The gift can be anything from a luxury hamper to a backpack. The contents don't need to be elaborate or expensive; just try to make them as thoughtful as you can. A creative welcome package may include the following:

- ✔ **Welcome note:** A brief but heartfelt message that welcomes and thanks guests for making the journey, provides a day-by-day synopsis of the weekend, reminds them exactly when and where the wedding and reception will take place, and gives directions to the hospitality suite, if you're having one.

- ✔ **Customised map:** Show the area and pinpoint your personal favourite places. In a city, you may add art galleries, flea markets, shops and restaurants. At a resort, you may highlight snorkelling spots or the best bar. Also include directions and transportation details.

- ✔ **Snack and beverage:** Local taste treats are best. For example, in New York City, you could include Zabar's bagel chips and New York State apple cider. In the Caribbean, you may offer the brand of rum the island is noted for (Cockspur in Barbados, for example) and tropical fruits. In Italy, pop in a regional red wine and a bag of biscotti.

- ✔ **Souvenir or two:** Something inexpensive, kitschy and fun – postcards, key chains or magnets.

- ✔ **Background material:** Brochures or other printed information on the destination, salient or fun facts ('Did you know the Ferris wheel was invented in Pittsburgh, USA?') or a good travel guidebook. Also include phone numbers of doctors, babysitters and other local troubleshooters.

✔ **Wedding-party particulars:** A separate insert just for bridesmaids, ushers and other wedding-party members that details where and when the rehearsal is and any other events that pertain to them. (See Chapter 14 for info on the wedding-day schedule.)

✔ **Goodies for kids:** A children's welcome gift (which should be different – and a lot less expensive – than the adults'). Depending on the age, sweets, a colouring book and crayons, a notebook or a scrapbook for them to fill with details of the trip will delight them and convey that you're especially glad they came.

Partying When You Get Home

If you decide to have a smaller destination wedding, you may throw a more lavish post-wedding party back in the UK. A party that occurs after you've returned from your honeymoon can be a great way to celebrate with *all* your family and friends. And for the bride, it's another chance to glam up and wear your dress.

Here are some ideas for the after-party:

✔ Theme the party to match your destination wedding. For example, if you were married in the Caribbean, you could serve local cuisine like jerk chicken, have tropical flowers and maybe welcome guests with traditional music in the background before your live music commences.

✔ Have a professional photographer take pictures of you and key family or friends, especially those who couldn't make the destination wedding.

✔ Set up a digital photo booth and give each guest props reflective of the country in which you were married.

✔ Set up a digital slideshow of your wedding photos or play your video; this helps guests feel more included in the wedding.

✔ Leave a copy of your wedding album on a table and frame your favourite wedding and honeymoon snaps.

✔ Incorporate traditions like cake cutting, informal speeches and the first dance.

Chapter 8

By Invitation Only

. . . .

. . . .

The invitation is meant to convey the necessary facts about your upcoming ceremony and the celebration following. If things were as simple as who, what, when and where, we could do away with this chapter and you could save a bundle by relaying the salient information via telephone calls, email or paper aeroplanes.

As you're well aware, that isn't the case. The wedding invitation – from its wording, design, form and addressing, to its printing style and ink colour – is the subject of etiquette controversies; long, long chapters in wedding books; and dictatorial outlines. Some people believe that to flout the rules these sources imply is to risk massive embarrassment, if not complete social disgrace. However, weddings have become a little more relaxed in recent years and it may be that you want to be a bit more modern in your style.

Whether you want to be traditional or modern, we believe you should be familiar with what the social wags consider proper before you get creative. Therefore, in this chapter we first cover all the rules for writing traditional, formal invitations. Then we move on to tips and ideas for giving your invitations a personal twist. No matter what kind of stationery you choose, it's helpful to know about card stock, print fonts and other technical details, so we provide a primer on that too, and we get to grips with the envelopes, addressing and posting.

How much effort you put into your wedding stationery is really up to you (and your budget). But there's something to be said for the idea you can tell the quality of an event by the quality of the invitation. So we suggest that you really take time to design your invitations and select the best option for your budget.

Preliminary Planning

Play it safe. Order your invitations at least three to four months – and send them no later than six to eight weeks – before the wedding. Send invitations to guests coming from abroad ten weeks in advance. If you plan on getting married over a bank holiday weekend, send out invitations to everybody eight to ten weeks ahead of time, unless you've already sent a save-the-date card.

In figuring the number of invitations you need, a classic mistake is to think that if you're inviting 200 people, you need 200 invitations. Guess again. Look at your list. Chances are that a good number of those people are couples, which means you need send only one invitation, not two. However, you do want to order 15 to 25 per cent extra; re-ordering afterwards is more expensive.

A way of theming your wedding is to select a motif, colour or typeface that appears on all your wedding-related stationery – from save-the-date cards to thank-you notes – as well as on such incidentals as cocktail napkins, menus and seating cards. A consistent colour palette gives your event cohesiveness and conveys the amount of thought that went into your wedding.

Ordering your entire stationery wardrobe, from invitations to thank-you notes, at the same time may save you money and it also helps ensure consistency in colour, paper weight and art. But this requires an enormous amount of fore-thought, particularly if you want to have a monogram or other emblem designed for use throughout. Unless you are the most organised person and never change your mind about anything, we don't suggest you order everything in one go – sometimes themes develop organically and you may not reach a final decision on your menu design, for example, until closer to your wedding.

If you're not up to placing your stationery order too far in advance, you may send an email or a save-the-date card with the basics of when and where you're planning to marry like this:

> *Sophie and Henry are getting married!*
> *11 August 2014*
> *Mayfair, London*
> *Please save the date.*
> *Invitation and details to follow.*

If you don't like the idea of sending save-the-date cards, you can find lots of clever alternatives, from refrigerator magnets (found on many wedding web-sites) to wall calendars with the day and month of your wedding circled.

Guest who?

Before you can figure out how many invitations to order, you need to get a grip on your guest list. The complete guest list can represent the merger of a minimum of four lists – the bride's, the groom's and that of both sets of parents. The recipe for the final number should comprise one part realism (budget and logistics), and two parts graciousness and hospitality. Consider this a casting call for all the supporting players in not only your two individual lives, but also in the lives of your two families together. Being stubborn now about someone who's important to your future mother-in-law may strain relations for eternity.

Be as tolerant as possible of your parents' requests. Nostalgia is a major draw for weddings, and later you may be very touched that

your parents' oldest friends and long-lost relatives care enough to reconnect as you realise that they in fact do make your circle complete.

If you're looking for where to draw the line, remember that weddings aren't an opportunity to pay back social obligations or recoup your investment on wedding gifts to others in the past. And never make the mistake of sending invitations to people you really don't want to come on the assumption they won't. They're often the very first souls to accept.

Some people may never speak to you again if they're not invited. If you can live with that, leave them off the list. Otherwise, add them and don't look back.

For a wedding held in a tourist area during peak season, when accommodation is at a premium, a longer letter or information sheet may be in order, detailing travel and accommodation options (see the later section 'Extra, extra'). Chapter 7 gives details on guest information for destination weddings.

Formalities First

In this section, we take you through the traditional rules for communicating with guests, from the invitation to the announcement. (We also include some information on cancellation and postponement notices, just in case.)

Creating formal invites

What constitutes a traditional, *formal* wedding invitation? It's written in the third person, engraved on folded paper or heavy card stock in black ink and posted inside two envelopes. The inner envelope has no glue. The invitations are usually ecru, although some couples prefer the look of pure white. For invitations engraved on card stock, the edge may be bevelled with gold or silver.

Read on for pointers on what to write, and how.

Getting the wording just right

The rules of composition for formal invitations are quite specific:

- ✔ **Abbreviate and punctuate (almost) nothing.** That means you spell out words like Doctor, Street, Road, Apartment and county names.

- ✔ **You may omit the county if the city is well known,** such as London or Manchester.

- ✔ Use *the honour of your presence* **for ceremonies in a house of worship.**

- ✔ Use *the pleasure of your company* **for ceremonies in secular locations,** such as a hotel, club or some other non-religious venue, or solely for the reception.

- ✔ **Write out the numerals for long numbers in street addresses,** unless the numbers are particularly unwieldy.

- ✔ **Write out times including the word** *o'clock.* For example, *two o'clock.*

- ✔ **Use 'half after' or 'half past' in lieu of '-thirty' for half hours.** For example, *half after five o'clock* or *half past five o'clock*, not *five-thirty o'clock.*

- ✔ **Write out years.** Whichever way you want to write this is fine: *two thousand and fourteen* or *twenty hundred and fourteen*. In the tradition of needless nuptial debates, whether to capitalise the year ranks as a biggy. We like the look of capitalising it, but whatever you choose is correct.

- ✔ **Always put the bride's name before the groom's.**

- ✔ **Note that while you use** *Mr* **with the groom's name, the bride's name doesn't take** *Miss* **or** *Ms.* In the case where the groom's parents are hosting the wedding, the rule is reversed.

- ✔ **Use professional or military titles for the groom and father-of-the-bride.** You don't have to use professional titles for brides or mothers, but use them if both mother and daughter are issuing the invitations.

Who's hosting the wedding?

The crux of traditional formal invitations lies in meticulous placement of names to convey who's related to whom as well as who's hosting the wedding.

If the **bride's parents** are hosting the wedding:

Mr and Mrs Charles Smith-Jones
request the honour of your presence
at the marriage of their daughter
Sophie Anne
to
Mr Henry James Featherstone
Saturday, the eleventh of August
Two thousand and fourteen
at half past four o'clock
Saint Mary's Church
Mayfair, London
and afterwards at the reception
The Wedding Society
Forty-two Pall Mall

RSVP

If the wedding is **not in a church,** you can word it this way:

Mr and Mrs Charles Smith-Jones
request the pleasure of your company
at the marriage of their daughter
Sophie Anne
to
Mr Henry James Featherstone
Saturday, the eleventh of August
Two thousand and fourteen
at half past four o'clock
The Wedding Society
Forty-two Pall Mall

RSVP

The **most formal** invitations contain the name of the recipient written by hand:

Mr and Mrs Charles Smith-Jones
request the honour of
Mr and Mrs John Clarke's
Presence
at the marriage of their daughter . . .

If the **bride's mother is a widow or divorced** and goes by her ex-husband's surname:

Mrs Catherine Smith-Jones
requests the honour of your presence
at the marriage of her daughter . . .

If the **bride's mother is divorced,** she may combine her maiden name and married surname:

Mrs Franklin Smith-Jones
requests the honour of your presence
at the marriage of her daughter . . .

Although etiquette experts have always maintained that no such person as *Mrs Annabelle Smith-Jones* (in other words, Mrs with a woman's birth name) can exist, because more women are combining their first name with Mrs, the rules seem to have relaxed of late. It's your call.

If the **bride's father is a widower or divorced** and he's hosting the wedding:

Mr Charles Smith-Jones
requests the honour of your presence
at the marriage of his daughter . . .

If the **bride's mother is remarried** and she and her new husband are hosting the wedding:

Mr and Mrs Malcolm Bridges
request the honour of your presence
at the marriage of her daughter
Sophie Anne Smith-Jones . . .

Note: You can use the words *Mrs Bridges' daughter* for *her daughter*.

If the **bride's widowed father is remarried** and he and his wife are hosting:

Mr and Mrs Charles Smith-Jones
request the honour of your presence
at the marriage of his daughter . . .

Note: You can substitute the words *Mr Smith-Jones's daughter* for *his daughter*.

If the **bride's father is deceased** and her stepmother is hosting the wedding:

> *Mrs Charles Smith-Jones*
> *requests the honour of your presence*
> *at the marriage of her stepdaughter*
> *Sophie Anne Smith-Jones . . .*

If the **bride's parents are divorced, both are remarried** and all are sponsoring the wedding:

> *Mr and Mrs Malcolm Bridges and*
> *Mr and Mrs Charles Smith-Jones*
> *request the honour of your presence*
> *at the marriage of*
> *Mrs Bridges' and Mr Smith-Jones's daughter*
> *Sophie Anne Smith-Jones*
> *to . . .*

The names of the bride's mother and her new husband go first. If you think your guests can assume whose daughter she is, you may omit the line before the bride's name (*Mrs Bridges' and Mr Smith-Jones's daughter*, in this case.)

If the **bride's parents are divorced** and her mother goes by her ex-husband's name:

> *Mrs Charles Smith-Jones*
> *and*
> *Mr Charles Smith-Jones*
> *request the honour of your presence*
> *at the marriage of their daughter*
> *Sophie Anne Smith-Jones . . .*

Listing the parents on separate lines, as shown, indicates that they're divorced or separated.

If the **groom's parents** are giving the wedding:

> *Mr and Mrs George Featherstone*
> *request the honour of your presence*
> *at the marriage of*
> *Miss Sophie Anne Smith-Jones*
> *to their son*
> *Henry James . . .*

Note: In the preceding case, use *Miss* for the bride and omit *Mr* for the groom.

If the **groom's father is deceased** and the groom's mother is hosting the wedding:

> *Mrs George Featherstone*
> *requests the honour of your presence*
> *at the marriage of*
> *Miss Sophie Anne Smith-Jones*
> *to*
> *Henry James . . .*

If you're **hosting your own** wedding:

> *The honour of your presence*
> *is requested at the marriage of*
> *Miss Sophie Anne Smith-Jones*
> *to*
> *Mr Henry James Featherstone . . .*

or

> *Miss Sophie Anne Smith-Jones*
> *and*
> *Mr Henry James Featherstone*
> *request the honour of your presence*
> *at their marriage . . .*

If the ceremony is **very small**, you can invite people either by phone or include a ceremony card with the reception invitation for the few invited to both:

> *The honour of your presence*
> *is requested at the marriage of*
> *Miss Sophie Anne Smith-Jones*
> *to*
> *Mr Henry James Featherstone*
> *Saturday, the eleventh of August*
> *Two thousand and fourteen*
> *at half after four o'clock*
> *Saint Mary's Church*
> *Mayfair, London*

You don't need to put *RSVP* on invitations that are for ceremonies only. Most likely, the place of worship will accommodate all guests.

If the recipient is **invited only to the reception:**

Mr and Mrs Charles Smith-Jones
request the pleasure of your company
at the wedding reception of their daughter . . .

This type of invitation is useful for belated receptions held, for example, after the bride and groom have returned from their honeymoon or if the ceremony was held in another town (see Chapter 7 for information on faraway weddings). This invitation also works for extremely small ceremonies consisting of just family or just you and witnesses. Bear in mind, however, that anyone you care enough to invite to the reception would probably love to see you walk down the aisle. Think twice before depriving them of this pleasure.

If the **reception and ceremony are in different locations**, or you can't fit all the information on the invitation, you may have a separate reception card:

Reception immediately following the ceremony
The Wedding Society
Forty-two Pall Mall
London

RSVP

If the reception isn't immediately following the ceremony, add a line indicating the time it will begin.

You ask for a reply by printing one of five things under the text or in the bottom-left corner: *Kindly respond*, *The favour of a reply is requested*, *RSVP*, *Rsvp* or *r.s.v.p.* The abbreviation RSVP is short for *Répondez, s'il vous plaît*, which is French for 'respond (if you please)'. Include the address where the response is to be sent because the return address on the envelope is often blind embossed, which is hard to read, and recipients often discard the envelope. Alternatively, include a reply card in the envelope.

In countries where **double invitations** are customary, two complete sets of text are printed side by side with the bride's on the left and the groom's on the right. This solution is perfect for invitations printed in two languages. A similar concept known as the *French-fold invitation* – folded in half twice, once horizontally and then vertically – is also back in vogue and useful for weddings hosted by both the bride's and groom's parents. The bride's information appears on the left, the groom's on the right, and the where and when is centered beneath:

Mr and Mrs Jaime Puente
request the honour of your presence
at the marriage of their daughter
Juanita
to
Mr Antonio Jicama

Mr Antonio Jicama
Mr and Mrs Geraldo Jicama
request the honour of your presence
at the marriage of their son
Antonio
to
Miss Juanita Puente

*Saturday, the fourteenth of November
at two o'clock in the afternoon
Our Lady of Angels Church
Manchester*

Sending announcements

You can send an announcement to anyone you didn't invite to the wedding but want to inform of your nuptials. In response, you should expect nothing more than a note of congratulations. Address and stamp announcements before the wedding so that they're ready for a friend to post the day after the wedding.

Wedding announcements can be from the bride's parents or both sets of parents:

*Mr and Mrs Charles Smith-Jones
and
Mr and Mrs George Featherstone
have the pleasure of announcing
the marriage of
their children
Sophie Anne Smith-Jones
and
Henry James Featherstone . . .*

The happy couple may announce their marriage themselves:

*Sophie Anne Smith-Jones
and
Henry James Featherstone
have the pleasure of announcing
their marriage . . .*

Extra, extra

As a minimum, we recommend including an information sheet with your invitation. Use a matching paper, but not necessarily the same card stock you have for your invitation, and by all means print it yourself if easier. You may include:

- **An introduction** from both of you, telling everyone how much you hope they can join you on your big day.

- **Accommodation details** for hotels in the area. Let people know if you've arranged special rates somewhere, and whom they should contact.

- **Contact details** for any queries or concerns. The named contact could be the bride's mother, maid of honour or your wedding planner.

- **Special dietary requirements** are something that more and more people have, and you need to let your caterers know if your guests have any such requirements (particularly if you're having a seated dinner rather than a buffet). Ask your guests to let you know any special requirements they may have by adding a line on your RSVP cards.

- **Maps** showing the location of the church and/or your reception venue. Also include info about any special transport arrangements, such as a coach departing from the church to your reception or taxis at the end of the evening.

- **Policy on children attending the wedding** (we discuss whether or not to invite children in Chapter 1). On your sheet, you may write something like: *Children at the wedding: In order to invite all our friends and family we are not able to accommodate children who are not named on the invitations. We hope that you understand and are still able to share in our big day.*

- **Wedding gift information,** if you've decided to send this (see Chapter 9).

If you get really stationery happy, you may end up with more enclosures than the *Readers' Digest*. Use them only if they serve your purposes, not because you think the bulkier the invitation, the more important it appears. Here are a couple of others you may add in:

- **Pew cards:** Small cards that say *Pew Number___* to tell close friends and family in which pew they're to sit. Cards may say, *Within the ribbon,* meaning that several pews (designated by a ribbon along the aisle) are reserved for special guests but no specific pew is assigned. You may include pew cards with invitations or send them later after receiving replies. In the latter case, cards must be sent in an envelope.

- **At-home cards:** Traditionally used to tell guests of the couple's new address after they move in together following the wedding. Because many couples today live together before marriage, these cards have a new purpose: to tell people how the bride and groom want to be known after the wedding.

When things don't go as planned

If the wedding is cancelled after invitations are posted, you (or your maid of honour, close friends or relatives) must call each guest personally if time doesn't permit you to send written word. If you do send a formal announcement, you're under no obligation to explain your decision.

A cancellation announcement may read:

> Mr and Mrs Charles Smith-Jones
> announce that the marriage of
> their daughter
> Sophie Anne
> to
> Mr Henry James Featherstone
> will not take place

If a wedding is postponed due to death or other unforeseen circumstances after the invitations have been posted, you may call with the information or print a formal announcement of the change:

> Mr and Mrs Charles Smith-Jones
> regret that
> owing to a death in the family
> the marriage of their daughter
> Sophie Anne
> to
> Mr Henry James Featherstone
> has been postponed
> to Saturday, the twenty-seventh of September

If the invitations have been printed but not posted, you may enclose a card (rush printed), saying:

> Kindly note that
> the date of the wedding has been changed
> to
> Saturday, the twenty-seventh of September

How Else Can We Put This?

You may feel that the style for your invitation lies somewhere between the (dare we say) anachronistic style of the ages and the wit and wisdom of a *Monty Python* sketch. You're up for something more creative, more ambitious, more modern – more *you*. In that case, you may adapt traditional wordings to your own means. Feel free to break the rules as long as you don't leave your guests scratching their heads or guffawing.

For starters, consider these alternatives to the tried-and-true wedding-invitation formulas:

- ✔ **Lose the formality.** Consider not using *honour of your presence* or *pleasure of your company* at all. (See examples later in this section.)

- ✔ **Use the first person** (*We cordially invite* . . .) as opposed to the third person (*Mr and Mrs Charles Smith-Jones request the pleasure* . . .) and close with your names at the bottom of the invite, similar to a signature.

- ✔ **Use *Ms* instead of *Miss*.** Or omit social titles altogether.

- ✔ **Skip *Mr and Mrs*.** Use the first names of both parents and step-parents instead.

- ✔ **Use professional titles for brides and their mothers, just as you would for the men.** The fact that they're doctors, dentists or judges isn't a national secret.

- ✔ **Include a stamped, addressed envelope with an RSVP card.** In addition, put *Kindly respond* in the lower left corner of the invitation.

- ✔ **Put *Respond by [date]* on RSVP cards.** If you're planning on issuing more invitations depending on the number of regrets you receive, have some response cards printed without a date. Remember, however, that yesses generally come in early, while nos delay their responses as long as possible.

Invitation turn-offs

The brief nature of invitations is intended to prevent you from oversharing. Some things to avoid in your creative frenzy include:

- ✔ Cloying poetry and trite, drippy sentiments

- ✔ Bad art

- ✔ Tiny, messy things such as confetti, glitter and adorable metallic musical notes that spill forth as you remove the invitation from the envelope and surface in carpets, chair cushions, underwear drawers and even more exotic places for years to come despite the use of industrial-strength cleaning contraptions

- ✔ Telling guests where you're registered for gifts and what particularly you're hoping to receive (see Chapter 9 on registry etiquette)

- ✔ Noting that children aren't welcome (however, you may want to handle this in the information sheet – see the earlier 'Extra, extra' sidebar)

- ✔ So many names as hosts that guests know without a doubt who's on the committee that's paying for the wedding

Striking a less-formal tone

As long as you're loosening up a bit, feel free to use more-informal wording. Here are some variations, starting with if **your parents are hosting**:

> *Mr and Mrs Charles Smith-Jones*
> *invite you to join us at the marriage of*
> *our daughter . . .*

or

> *Charles and Catherine Smith-Jones*
> *would be delighted to have you*
> *join them*
> *as their daughter*
> *Sophie Anne*
> *and*
> *Henry James*
> *pledge their love to each other . . .*

If you **host your own wedding**, the invitation may read

> *Sophie Anne Smith-Jones*
> *and*
> *Henry James Featherstone*
> *would be delighted*
> *to have you share*
> *in the joy of their marriage*
> *Sunday, 12th August*
> *at 1:30 p.m.*
> *St Mary's Church*
> *Mayfair, London*
> *and afterwards at the reception*
> *The Wedding Society, Pall Mall*

Another variation:

> *Sophie Anne Smith-Jones*
> *and*
> *Henry James Featherstone*
> *invite you to celebrate with them*
> *at their wedding . . .*

When the **ceremony and reception take place in the same venue**, you may think that mentioning both events is unnecessary. After all, you assume, guests know you wouldn't drag them all this way without feeding them. But you know what happens when you assume, don't you? To be absolutely certain that guests won't be making a fast break for the nearest restaurant after the ceremony, try:

Sophie Anne Smith-Jones
and
Henry James Featherstone
invite you to witness our vows
and join us afterwards for dining and dancing
under the stars
Saturday, the eleventh of August
Six o'clock in the evening
The Wedding Society, Pall Mall

If **the couple and both sets of parents host** the wedding:

Sophie Anne Smith-Jones
and
Henry James Featherstone
together with their parents
Mr and Mrs Charles Smith-Jones and
Mr and Mrs George Featherstone . . .

Many couples of all religions are adopting the Jewish custom of listing both sets of parents on the invitation, not necessarily because the groom's parents are helping foot the bill but simply out of respect:

Mr and Mrs Charles Smith-Jones
request the honour of your presence
at the marriage of their daughter
Sophie Anne
to
Mr Henry James
son of Mr and Mrs George Featherstone . . .

If, out of respect, you want to **include the name of a deceased parent**, make sure that it doesn't read like a dead person is hosting the wedding.

Mrs Charles Smith-Jones
requests the honour of your presence
at the marriage of
Sophie Anne
daughter of Mrs Smith-Jones
and the late Mr Charles Smith-Jones
to
Mr Henry James Featherstone . . .

RSVP remedies

Even if you don't have other events to worry about, a fill-in-the-blanks reply card is the most expedient method for the wedding itself:

Name (s) . . . .
. . . .
I/We will be delighted to attend the wedding
I/We will not be able to attend the wedding
I/We have the following special dietary requirement:
. . . .

Response cards never ask the number of guests coming. Guests should assume that only the people listed on the envelope are invited. They then write in only the names of the invitees who can make it.

A compromise between the traditional lack of a reply card and a fill-in-the-blank reply card is a card that says, simply, *Kindly respond by [the date]* or *The favour of a reply is requested*. Guests then write a gracious note in the blank space. If the thought of leaving your friends and relatives to figure things out scares you, consider adding *for [your wedding date]* at the bottom.

The date on the response card should be three to four weeks before your wedding, depending on how early you post your invitations. If you're really pressed for time and your wedding is informal, consider asking guests to RSVP by phone or email rather than by post.

Dress codes: Now wear this

One of the most difficult decisions for many couples is whether to dictate guests' attire. An engraved invitation or one for a wedding after 6 p.m. doesn't automatically direct people to dress in black tie. If it's important to you to see every male guest in a tuxedo and all the women in their fanciest dresses, print *Black tie* on the invitation. If you're determined that the aesthetics of your wedding will be marred if the guests are underdressed, you may consider these rarely used but *very* specific directions: *Black tie, Evening gowns, Very formal* or *Very black tie*. The rather trendy *Black tie optional* seems to encourage guests *not* to wear black tie, and *Black tie invited* is even more confusing.

Other dress codes you may specify include *Dress for an evening in the country* (hopefully, a hint for women to leave their spike heels at home), *Garden party attire, Festive dress* or *Creative tie*. Try to avoid *Smart/casual* – most people don't really know what this means and you could have everything from evening gowns to jeans at your wedding.

The non-printed invitation

If you're having an extremely small wedding, you may invite guests via a handwritten note:

Dear Emily,
Henry and I are getting married on Saturday, 11th August. We would be delighted
to have you join us for the ceremony at 3 p.m. on the town green in Henry's home-
town, Banbury, Oxfordshire, and afterwards for tea at the home of his aunt, Hazel
Twig, 42 East Bean Street.

Affectionately,

Sophie

Sorting Invitations for Other Events

Rehearsal dinners, which are usually hosted by the groom's parents, are all the rage in the US, and they're becoming more popular in the UK. If the rehearsal dinner is small, you may simply let invitees know when and where by word of mouth. These invitations may have a touch of fun depending on the sort of dinner you're organising (Chapter 13 looks in detail at organised rehearsal dinners) or you may rely on a classic format:

George and Diana Featherstone
invite you to a rehearsal dinner
in honour of
Sophie and Henry
Friday, 10th August
7 p.m.
Wick's Steak Palace
121 Smith Street
London, SW1

RSVP
020 7946 0000 (Diana Featherstone)

For a different twist, use the words 'prenuptial dinner' instead of 'rehearsal dinner'.

Often the bride's parents, grandparents or close friends host a brunch the morning after the wedding, particularly if several of the guests are from out of town (see Chapter 13 for details on other kinds of parties). If the same guests are invited to the rehearsal (or another pre-wedding event), wedding and brunch, for efficiency and economy you may combine the before-and-after events in one invitation and enclose them with the wedding invitation:

Please join us for a
prenuptial cruise and jam session
Friday, 10th August
The Thames Queen
boarding at 6:30 p.m.
setting sail at 7 p.m. sharp
Waterloo Pier
Bring instruments
– Sophie and Henry

~

Betty Smith
invites you to join her for a
post-wedding brunch
Sunday, 12th August
at her home
45 Pansy Way
Banbury, Oxfordshire

To make life easier, you may use one RSVP card for several events. Guests send the card back – in a stamped, pre-addressed envelope – to the person who has the most time to keep running tabs on the various head counts.

Please respond by 11th July
Name (s) _____ _____ will attend the wedding
Name (s) _____ will attend the cruise
Name (s) _____ will attend the brunch

Typefaces and Other Technicalities

To help you design the invitation you have in mind and ensure that your order gets placed correctly, it helps to understand a few points about the stationery trade. So in this section we start with a primer on paper and printing. Then we move on to considering fonts, colours, envelopes and proofreading the text.

Printing methods

The way your invitation is printed conveys as much about your wedding style as the words themselves. You may choose between several printing methods to suit your invitation, including:

- **Blind embossing:** Letters are etched into metal plates, which are pressed against paper without ink so that you just see the imprint, no colour. Usually used for monograms, borders and return addresses.

- **Calligraphy:** Handwritten with special pens and inks, usually for addressing. Can be done in a print style to match the invitation or use a calligraphed original to make a plate for an engraved invitation or as the prototype for an offset invitation.

- **Computerised calligraphy:** Done by a special machine with mechanised pen and laser printer. Meant to look hand-calligraphed; some fonts are more successful than others. Used for both invitations and addressing.

- **Engraved:** Letters are etched into a metal plate, which is then rolled with ink and wiped off. Ink remains in each etched letter. The paper is pressed on to the plate, leaving a raised image and a 'bruise' on the reverse side. Engraving in black ink is considered the appropriate mode for formal invitations. You may need to include a sheet of tissue paper over the type when posting to prevent it from smudging.

- **Letterpress:** Created on an old-fashioned, movable type machine. Raised type is inked and stamped on to the paper. Very popular for the hand-made effect it gives to invitations. Borders and other letterpress designs are quite beautiful. Unlike other processes, letterpress works well on handmade paper.

- **Lithography, offset or flat printed:** Produces a crisp, flat image. An inked impression is made on a rubber-blanketed cylinder and then transferred to paper.

- **Thermography:** A popular, less expensive alternative meant to mimic engraving. Heat-sensitive powder is sprinkled on to ink, which is heat-treated to form letters that are raised but not indented. Can be shiny.

Paper

Paper and card are measured in *gsm* (grams per square metre), which is the measurement of paper quality. The higher the gsm, the heavier and better quality the paper. The most desirable paper is acid-free, 100 per cent cotton rag, as opposed to paper that contains a high percentage of wood pulp.

Most invitations come in one of two standard sizes: A5 or A6. An invitation may be a single, heavy card or a single-folded sheet with printing on the outside or a double-folded sheet with the printing on the inside. In either case, the words can run horizontally or vertically. If you depart from these standard sizes, you may have to buy handmade envelopes, which can be pricey.

If you opt for a non-traditional style, you can use special papers for creative effect. *Vellum* is a strong, translucent paper resembling parchment and is used either as an overlay or as the actual invitation. Gilt-edged vellum, which is rimmed in gold ink, is expensive yet beautiful. Sold by the sheet, special handmade papers may have nubby textures and be embedded with leaves, dried wildflowers or metallic threads. Often impossible to print on, they make beautiful backgrounds for mounting invitations printed on plain card stock. If these options prove too expensive, consider using them for a smaller event such as the rehearsal dinner or brunch.

Fonts

Although some printing companies invent their own names for specific type styles, or *fonts*, they're all variations of the same styles. You may choose from several printing styles ranging from what's usually called Antique Roman, a fairly staid but respectable-looking block print, to Copper Plate, a swirly script. Many typefaces come in shaded versions that add a three-dimensional look to the font. Discuss the merits of various *point* (letter) sizes with your printer. Using a specific font on all your wedding stationery is one way of creating a unified look.

As shown in Figure 8-1, professional calligraphy is a really nice touch (although it isn't cheap). If you use a calligrapher to address your envelopes, you must provide an accurate, alphabetised guest list. If you don't know all the post codes, don't expect the calligrapher to. Look up post codes at `www.royalmail.com/postcode-finder`.

Figure 8-1:
The beauty
of various
calligraphy
styles, or
hands,
lies in the
quirks and
flourishes of
each letter.

Mr and Mrs Alexander H. London
Mr and Mrs Tyler E.R. American
Mr and Mrs Albert F. G. Daley
Mr and Mrs Kenneth Saint James
Mr and Mrs Raymond A. Shaw
Mr and Mrs Jackson S. Italic
Mr and Mrs Charles F. G. White
Mr and Mrs Franklin B. Langley
Mr and Mrs Sean Antique Roman
Mr and Mrs Randolph K. Tucker
MR AND MRS ROMAN B. CAPITAL
MR AND MRS SLANTED V. TALESWORTH
Mr and Mrs Samuel F. O. Bartholomew
Mr and Mrs Benedict S. Canyon
Mr and Mrs Parker Terrace Hamilton

Calligraphy courtesy of Glorie Austern

Some calligraphers are conscientious enough to catch mistakes and correct them free of charge. Mistakes that are your fault, however, will cost you in both labour fees and extra envelopes.

Ink colour

Aside from the traditional dark black, many colours are available, from deep grey to violet. If you want the type on your invitations to be the same shade of cornflower blue as your beloved's eyes, you can find a matching PMS (Pantone Match System) colour at your printer.

Envelopes

If you use double envelopes and you choose to spiff up your invitation with a lining, the lining goes in the inside envelope but not the outer. Linings can be anything from black satin moire to tie-dyed papers.

Tradition has dictated that the return addresses on outer envelopes are blind embossed at most, but you won't win any friends at the post office this way. Calligraph or print the return address – with no name for a private home, no apartment number for an apartment house – on the back flap. Traditionally, the address should be that of the wedding host(s), so even if the bride's parents are hosting the wedding in name only, the reply cards go to them. If you're keeping track of regrets and acceptances, the parents then pass on that information, or merely drop off the weekly returns in a pillowcase for you to tabulate. You may also want to have your wedding planner deal with all this for you, if you have one.

If you have oversized invitations, you may post them in oversized boxes (similar to a scarf box) with the invitation wrapped in tissue. Many companies sell transparent mailing tubes perfect for scroll-like invitations.

Besides taking into account special postal costs (not just for weight but for non-standard sizes as well), consider where the invitations are being posted. Your exquisite packaging may get karate-chopped and crumpled as the postie crams it into a tiny letterbox.

When recipients open the envelope, they should be able to read the invitation without turning it around. Traditionally, you insert the materials as follows:

- Folded invitations go in the envelope fold first.
- Enclosures go either on top of the invitation or in the fold. (The response card doesn't go behind the invitation, because some guests may not see it.)
- Reception response cards go under the envelope flap, not inside the response envelope.

Proof it all night

After ordering invitations from your printers, you receive a proof of the text. Read this proof over very carefully; any mistakes you overlook aren't considered the printer's fault. Then have someone else – preferably someone who knows nothing about your wedding and thus doesn't have the same blind spots you do – proofread everything. Obvious typos are often the easiest to miss.

With some engraved invitations, the proof is made from the actual printing die, on which all the text appears backward and requires a mirror to decipher. After the invitations are printed, if you can get the die from the printer, you may want to turn it into a small tray or have it mounted, a custom popular in Victorian times.

Creating Your Own Invitations

Many couples choose to design their own invitations or hire a graphic artist to assist them in creating something one-of-a-kind. But if you're *really* ambitious, creative and eager to save money, try *literally* making your own invitations. For something really homemade and whimsical, invent your own style.

With the software packages available today, you can produce an invitation that's nearly professional quality. However, unless you invest in your own printing press, you can't approximate an engraved product or even a thermographed one. But if you seek a casual style then the do-it-yourself route works fine.

Printing your own wedding invitations doesn't always save you money. Although you're eliminating the middleman – the printer – you may still have to buy the paper and the software – and don't forget the ink. And you should also take into account your own time, experience and anxiety level. How many sheets of gilt-edged vellum will you mess up before you master the process?

One way to go is to have the invitation card printed professionally and then assemble your own multifaceted creation. Many Internet companies offer such services and supplies.

With a little online searching, you can find all sorts of companies selling interesting papers for laser-printing your own invitations, place cards, orders of service and so on. And these days, crafts and stationery shops stock an impressive array of do-it-yourself supplies and embellishments. Among the items you may need are:

✔ **Deckle ruler:** A special tool with a wavy, sharp edge. You lay it on the paper and tear-cut along the sharp edge to create the hand-torn effect.

✔ **Embossing stamp:** Emboss a simple image or monogram on your card stock or envelope.

✔ **Glue sticks or a glue gun:** For mounting papers and attaching doodahs.

✔ **Hole punch:** For threading ribbons.

✔ **Ribbon:** A simple bow or wisp of organza is perhaps the least expensive way to transform a plain card into an elegant invite. Buy several rolls – you can extend the theme by using it to tie napkins, accessorise place cards and tie bows on favours.

✔ **Sealing wax:** Create an embossed seal on the outer envelope by using a decorative press and wax in a colour that matches your overall theme. True sealing wax doesn't fare well in the post, so use one of the many faux versions out there (you can find them advertised as such). They seal like wax but don't crack when put through a stamping machine.

✔ **Special papers:** Combine different textures – vellum, crepe, handmade flower paper and so on – to mat your invitation for a sophisticated layered look.

✔ **Trinkets:** A small brass charm glued on to the invitation is another quick way to add interest.

Addressing Traditions

If you're quite relaxed about your invitations, you may want to skip this section, in which we give you the lowdown on all the traditions for envelope addressing. But if formality matters to you, read on.

As with other aspects of traditional formal invitations, inner and outer envelopes subscribe to precise rules of decorum. For starters, you address envelopes by hand or have them calligraphed; you never use laser printers or labels. The following rules also apply.

Outer envelopes

Here are some guidelines for the envelope that contains the invite and any inserts:

✔ **Use formal names.** If you use middle names, you must use them in full. Middle initials won't suffice; if you don't know the middle name, skip it.

✔ **Spell out all words, such as Apartment, Avenue, Street and county names.** Abbreviate only Mr, Mrs, Ms, Jr, Messrs and Esq. Write out professional titles, including Doctor.

- You may address envelopes to married couples in the most common way – *Mr and Mrs Travis Twig*. However, etiquette authority Debrett's recommends that you address the invitation to both but the envelope to just the woman – Mr and Mrs Travis Twig (invitation), Mrs Travis Twig (envelope).

- Address envelopes to unmarried couples as *Mr Huck Porter and Ms Wanda Guernsey* with the names on separate lines.

- Send separate invitations to children over 13. (*Note:* Some experts say children over 18; use your discretion.)

- You may send joint invitations to siblings of the same sex younger than 13. Address them as *The Misses Twig* or *The Messrs Twig*. If you're sending to both boys and girls, write the names on the same envelope like this:

> *The Messrs Twig*
> *The Misses Twig*

- You may write *Miss Daisy Twig* or *The Misses Twig* under *Mr and Mrs John Twig*, but *The Messrs Twig* receive a separate invitation.

- Because adults should receive their own invitation no matter what, only use the phrase *and Family* when everyone under the same roof is invited. Such open-ended generalisations can, however, get you in trouble; some people have very large families, and you may not want to meet all of them on your wedding day.

Inner envelopes

If you're using double envelopes, address your inner envelope as follows:

- Address married couples as *Mr and Mrs Twig* with neither the first names nor address.

- Use only first names for children: *Pearl, Pablo and Gus*.

- Put a young daughter's name below her parents' if the outer envelope is addressed to both the parents and her: *Miss Felicity Twig*.

- You may address intimate relatives as, say, *Aunt Hazel and Uncle Woody* or *Grandfather*.

- If you ask a friend to bring a guest, write *and Guest* on the inner, but not the outer, envelope. Better yet, find out the guest's name.

In a perfect world, all your guests would realise that only those people whose names appear on the inner envelopes are actually invited. That's not always the case, however. This is especially true when it comes to children, and you may need to employ some proactive diplomacy where precious darlings are involved. You can include some information on your information sheet (see the earlier sidebar 'Extra, extra'). For more information on negotiating this sticky wicket, see Chapter 1.

Fit to be titled

As if you don't have enough rules to remember in writing a simple address, professional titles can put you out of your tree. Traditionally, the rule has been very simple: no matter what, you never list women with professional titles or, if they're married, their own first names. That's simple enough, yes, but these days, ignoring a woman's professional and personal identity strikes many people (including us) as sexist, to say the least. The fact that many women are keeping their names after marriage complicates matters even more.

We believe that you should use professional titles for either everyone or no one. If you're stumped about how to list the names, go with this simple rule: alphabetical order unless superseded by title. For example:

Doctor Jane Silk and Mr Ty Bickle

In the preceding example, although *Bickle* would normally go before *Silk*, because Jane Silk has a title – doctor – she goes first.

However, if the partners have different names and each has a title, list them alphabetically by last name:

Judge Felix Bipp and Doctor June Pickle

If the couple has the same last name, put the titled person first:

Doctor Whit Fink and Ms Camela Fink
Doctor Mathilda Burr and Mr Rip Burr

Unless you hobnob in royal or diplomatic circles or work as an executive assistant to some corporate titan or socialite, you probably don't have to worry very often about addressing personages with fancy royal, professional, political or religious titles. But now that you're getting married, here's your chance.

If you want to use titles, we suggest you visit the Debrett's website (www.debretts.com/forms-of-address.aspx), which gives you the correct forms of address for every title possible.

It's a Postage Thing

Don't forget to send invitations to your officiant and parents. You'd be amazed at how often these very important people get overlooked. Also send an invitation to yourselves before the others go out so that you can see how long it takes to arrive and in what condition.

In calculating the cost of your invitations, be sure to include postage. When you have a sample, including response card, information sheet, maps and all other inserts, take it to the post office to have it weighed (twice). If you're using special handmade papers or envelopes, bring several; some may weigh more than others, and you don't want any invitations to wind up back in your letterbox marked with the heart-stopping words 'insufficient postage' or, even worse, for one of your guests to be asked to pay for the under-postage! Be prepared to put up to three stamps on each envelope. Don't pinch pennies here: go for all matching stamps, which look more finished even if you have to pay a few more pence to mail the invitation.

When you're at the post office, enquire about commemorative stamps. You can sometimes find designs that tie in with your theme or colour scheme (preferably in the self-adhesive style). The post office can help you find out-of-the-ordinary stamps, too. You may even choose to make personalised stamps; visit `www.royalmail.com/personal/stamps-and-collecting/ smilers` for information on what can be done and the prices.

Putting stamps on the response envelopes encourages your guests to post them in. However, stamping reply envelopes for guests abroad is useless – they must use their own postage.

One for the record

The simplest way to preserve your invitation is to mount and frame it, or include it in your photo album. If you have a lot of time on your hands, you may decoupage it on a plate, serving tray or hope chest in which you keep other wedding mementos. Or save time by sending it to a company that backs invitations with velvet and mounts them in shadow boxes.

Chapter 9

Toasters Are Banned!: Putting Together Your Gift List

. . . .

In This Chapter

▶ Setting up a high-tech registry

▶ Requesting non-traditional gifts

▶ Sending out the thank-yous

▶ Dealing with unwanted presents

. . . .

Christofle claims to have invented the *bridal registry* (a service provided by retail stores or websites where you list the gifts you would prefer your guests to select for you) in 1856. The French silver manufacturer apparently figured out that wedding guests appreciate some guidance on what to get the happy couple – or else it grew tired of couples exchanging their umpteenth set of sterling-silver toast tongs.

Many shops recognise that wedding registries aren't only an entree to the profitable bridal market, but also a way of winning couples' shopping loyalty for life. Consequently, retailers have gone to great lengths to make the process painless, from dedicating a team of consultants who steer you through the aisles to equipping you with bar-code scanners to zap on to your list any item that your heart desires.

All this consumerist sophistication, and all the glee that comes with choosing gifts, however, doesn't mitigate all the emotional trauma of the process. Suddenly, you're shopping for *our* stuff, attempting to meld your personal tastes – and that can be very unnerving. If you doubt this, just go to the homewares floor of any department store on a Saturday afternoon and watch while one couple after another morphs from browsing Jekylls into snarling Hydes as they decide which china pattern to live with *for the rest of their lives*.

In spite of this dilemma, registering remains a brilliant concept – your defense against a deluge of this year's hot gift item as well as grotesqueries from well-intentioned but hopelessly taste-challenged gift-givers – and a growing trend that has become more and more acceptable. It can make the whole process of gift giving so much easier for you and your guests. For some couples, however, the idea of registering for gifts makes them feel uncomfortable – if it's not for you, then don't do it. So, in this chapter, we examine the many different ways in which you can inform your guests about your wishes.

Retail Details

To give yourself enough time to choose your items carefully, begin planning your registry soon after you're engaged. Even if you're going to manage your registry online, seeing your registry items in person first is a good idea. Make an appointment with a wedding consultant at each shop and ask that person to help you with ideas for mixing and matching china patterns or to give you advice on the number of coffee cups you should own – personalised tips can be very helpful. We recommend hitting the shops during the week, when they're likely to be less crowded than on weekends.

Register for a variety of items in different price ranges. Although your eyes may widen at the thought of owning the most elegant designer china and golden flatware, be realistic. Unless your friends and family have collectively won the lottery, you may find yourselves owning no more than a single tea-spoon and a gravy boat in those pricey patterns. If your needs are limited to a state-of-the-art sound or video system, or something equally unaffordable for one person or a couple to bestow upon you, hint broadly to a close buddy for a group of friends to chip in for a large item.

Don't get carried away by the thought of choosing all sorts of free loot. Whether you're just starting out, are merging two households or have dreams of trading in the wine crate you've been using for a dining-room table, approach registering methodically. Take a careful inventory of what's missing from your lives and use that list to begin selecting items for your registry.

Before you show up at your favourite department store wearing comfortable shoes and clutching a wish list, call the shop to find out whether you need to make an appointment. A few other questions worth asking:

> ✔ In what format does the shop keep your registry – computer, online, a sales assistant's little black book? Do other store locations use the same format? How easily can other branches access your list?

✔ What is the shop's privacy policy? How do they ensure that only the people you want to see your registry list will?

✔ Does the shop allow you to opt out of promotional emails and other 'special offers'?

✔ How does the shop use your personal information? Do they promise not to share or sell it with marketing partners or anyone else?

✔ Are you assigned a customer-service representative who oversees your particular registry?

✔ How quickly after you fill out the paperwork is your registry up and running for people to order from?

✔ Does the shop have a freephone number? Try the number at different times of day to see whether your guests may have to endure rude operators or being put on hold interminably.

✔ How quickly does the shop update your list when someone buys something? (Instantaneously is best to avoid duplicate gifts.) How does the shop avoid sending duplicates?

✔ Does the shop actually put aside items on your list after guests purchase them? (Doing so is the only way to ensure you get the exact items you want, at the price currently charged. See the nearby sidebar, 'Check what service you're getting'.)

✔ How can you add items to your registry?

✔ How long is your registry active after your wedding date? (Up to a year is a good idea because etiquette dictates that guests have that long to send a gift.)

✔ What are the shop's return policies?

Check what service you're getting

We recently came across a well-known UK department store that offers a service where you select items to add on to your list and, as the items are purchased, the monetary value of these items is stored in an account for you. When the list closes, the store presents you with a gift card that contains all the money that your guests spent on the items you listed. The store does not put on hold the items you selected or those that have been 'nominally purchased' for you by your guests for you or reserved in the department. Therefore, they cannot guarantee the price of these items; in some instances, prices may increase and in others they will decrease, be on special offer, or on sale. When your list closes, you can then purchase the items that were purchased for you by your guests, or purchase entirely different items.

Here are some other pointers:

✔ Collect lots of brochures and magazine ads to assist in those late-night discussions about non-stick cookware and satin sheets.

✔ If you just can't agree on the items to have on the list before your wedding, find a shop that offers a 'gift voucher' service: you just have vouchers on your list and your guests contribute any amount of money they like. After your wedding, when the dust settles, you can then shop at the shop and spend your vouchers.

✔ If you already own a set of china, crystal, or flatware, but it's incomplete, consider registering for the missing pieces rather than a whole new set.

✔ Ask the shop if you can get a discount on any items left on your registry after it expires.

Going Beyond Department Stores

Despite the variety and audaciousness of registries these days, finding one shop that sells everything you need for your new life together is difficult. Many couples find it useful to divide their registry between two or three retailers – for example, a home-furnishings shop for decorative items and everyday glassware and china; a department store for linens, formal china, stemware, crystal and kitchen appliances; and a home-improvement centre for house and garden supplies. And don't forget boutiques, artisan crafts shops and galleries, many of which now offer registries as well.

Asking for non-essentials for wedding gifts seems a trifle self-indulgent, but it's not out of the question. After all, who's to say that an annual membership to the National Theatre or a new set of golf clubs isn't exactly what you need to get your marriage off on the right foot?

Non-traditional registry concepts include:

✔ **Artwork:** We had a client who asked for money to be sent to a local art gallery, and after the wedding they used the money to choose a sculpture for their home.

✔ **Charity:** For non-materialist types and previously married couples. You ask guests to make a tax-deductible contribution in your names to one or more charities of your choice. (Rumour has it that guests at the wedding of Prince William and Kate Middleton were asked to give to charity rather than purchasing gifts for the couple.) A number of websites can assist you with this process; just type 'charity donations for wedding gifts' into your web browser and many sites come up. Alternatively, try Just Giving (www.justgiving.com), Just Give (www.justgive.org) or the Alternative Wedding List at www.thealternativeweddinglist.co.uk. The Oxfam Unwrapped website (www.oxfam.org.uk/shop/oxfam-unwrapped) enables you to create donation registries.

✔ **Hobby/experience:** For the couple who either have everything or care more about keeping their inner-child happy than having matching sets of towels. Gifts range from sporting goods to wine to CDs to racing around the track at Silverstone. Look for these in speciality shops and travel agencies, and on experience websites.

✔ **Home improvement:** This category includes tools, lawn mowers, gardening paraphernalia, Jacuzzis – anything a couple of fledgling home-owners may need. Check out hardware shops, large home-improvement centres and garden shops.

✔ **Services:** These can include spas, massages, steak-of-the-month dinner clubs, housecleaning – use your imagination.

✔ **Travel:** Many websites allow your guests to pay for parts of your honeymoon, including airfare, hotel, restaurants, snorkelling, tennis lessons, horse riding, parasailing or whatever else you've planned – plus spending money.

Grandiose gifting

In recent years, there's been a lot of talk about registries for extremely unconventional and high-ticket wedding-gift items, such as mortgages, cars and personal debt relief. However, the idea hasn't really caught on. Few, if any, companies know how to market the concept without appearing crass, and much of the wedding-going public isn't ready to give up the box tied with a bow. If you can pull it off tastefully, more power to you.

Not everyone appreciates a non-traditional registry. As with cash gifts (see the later section on these), drop the hint to only your closest friends and relatives – and only if they ask.

Surfing for Gifts

Registries are increasingly moving online, which has numerous advantages:

- ✔ You can sign up from home (although some shops, such as Tiffany's and Harrods, require you to register in person first).

- ✔ Gift givers who live anywhere in the world can shop at your favourite shop, and at an hour that suits their time zone.

- ✔ You can check on the status of your registry or edit your gift list at any time from your personal computer.

- ✔ Many registries are affiliated with websites that offer other planning tools, tips and information.

- ✔ You and the people buying can see the goods displayed on-screen along with descriptions, availability and prices.

- ✔ You can email your registry to close family members or intimate friends, even if they live far away.

Hinting and Hoping

After you sign up for all those goodies, you may have to keep reminding yourself that you only registered for them – they're not yours until people purchase them for you. As tempted as you may be, restrain yourself from shouting the shop's free-phone number or Web address from the rooftops, renting out a billboard or ticking off the places you've registered on your answering machine.

 If you're wondering whether you should discreetly print the shop name at the bottom of your wedding invitation, the answer is an unequivocal 'no'. The information should appear on your information sheet (see Chapter 8). Some people will even tell you that you shouldn't mention your registry at all and only mention it if someone asks you about gifts, but most couples do.

Many shops provide a card with details and your registry number, which you put in the envelope with the invitation. You can then place info on the registry on an 'additional information' sheet of paper. Some guests are sensitive about requests for gifts, so choose your wording carefully. We suggest something along these lines:

Is once enough?

If you or your future spouse have already been married (and presumably got what you need the first time around), you may feel uncomfortable registering again. If so, trust your instincts. But, in our opinion, just as a previously married bride may wear white if she chooses, so may an experienced couple register. You can't stop people giving you gifts, and they may appreciate your guidance all the more because they don't know whether you or your ex got custody of the crystal decanter.

The only exception may be if your last marriage was extremely short-lived and you're inviting many of the same people to your second-time-around wedding.

We do not want our guests to feel obliged to give wedding presents. However, if you were planning to give a gift then you may like to know we have registered a gift list at xxx. A card with further details is enclosed.

If you don't want to include information about your registry with your wedding invitation then the only other way to get the message out is by word of mouth. Guests may enquire, 'Where are you registered?' Then you or your mother or your attendants can respond, 'My, that's so kind of you to ask,' while whipping out a card with the shop's name and phone number. For those who phrase the magic question as 'What do you need?' or 'What do you want?' don't be coy. Give them some general parameters and then direct them to your registry.

Although your intentions are certainly the best, be aware that to many guests writing something like 'No gifts, please' on an invitation is both presumptuous and offensive. Doing so is actually likely to backfire because people who feel they must give you something have to rely on their own devices and taste.

What We Really Want? Well, It Rhymes with Honey . . .

The very idea of the gift of a cheque winds up some etiquette stalwarts, but we think money can be a very thoughtful gift. Usually, only close relatives are likely to give you money, and, depending on your family, you may have to have a little bird (of the close-friend species) mention your wishes. However, providing your account number on your information sheet is considered quite pushy and, for some guests, rude. Try using the wording in Figure 9-1, which has worked successfully for a lot of couples.

Because we are lucky enough to have a home together and we already own many of the items that we need, we have decided not to request wedding gifts. We know, however, that some of you have been enquiring about a registry. If you are interested in marking the occasion of our marriage with a gift then we would be more than grateful to receive a small contribution towards our honeymoon.

Should you wish to make such a gift you can contribute as follows:

1. You can bring along the gift personally to the wedding, placing it inside a card and envelope, and post it directly into our 'wedding post box', which will be at the venue.

2. If you prefer, you can make your contribution directly to our honeymoon fund. In this instance, please contact our wedding planner / our maid of honour [insert contact details], who will be able to send you the details.

More than anything, we hope that you can make it on the day. So please do not feel obliged to give in any way. We value your company more than anything else.

All our love,

Sophie and Henry

Figure 9-1:
An example
request for
money.

Many couples have a wedding post box at their wedding, which can range from a pretty box that you decorate yourself to a replica Victorian post box in traditional red or a cream colour that you hire. Type 'hire a wedding post box' into your browser to see what you can find. For a more rustic or country theme you may prefer a wishing well. You can buy or hire these wishing wells from wedding hire companies.

Finding inspiration in foreign money-giving customs

In some cultures, giving money for weddings is a revered custom:

✔ A Nigerian tradition is showering the bride with money during the reception. The bride carries a specially decorated moneybag into which guests slip envelopes with cheques.

✔ The parents of Japanese grooms present a cash gift (about three months of the groom's salary) to the bride's family in a special envelope. Knotted gold and silver strings, which are supposed to be impossible to undo, adorn the envelope, which is called a *shugi-bukero*. The amount and giver's name is written on the back of the envelope.

✔ Chinese brides serve a ritual tea to their new in-laws, who then give them money in lucky red envelopes called *hung boas*.

✔ At a Polish wedding, to secure a dance with the bride, guests pin money to her dress.

✔ A Turkish custom is for the bride to wear a white sash and carry a basket, and she and her female family members visit each guest, who offers a kiss and puts money or gold in her basket, tacks a coin to her sash or gives her a gold bracelet or necklace to wear.

If you want to follow a family or cultural tradition, we recommend that you warn your guests, who may not be familiar with the tradition, so they're not caught out on the day. Add to your information sheet or website some wording such as: 'We do not have a wedding list. However, if you were thinking about giving a gift, we would very much like to honour Sophie's heritage and follow the Polish tradition of xxx.'

Keeping Track

The minute you receive a present, write down what it is, who gave it to you and the date. This information can go on an index card with the guest's other vital information, or in a spreadsheet. Also record when you send a thank-you note (see the following section). Many shops send an email that notifies you of the gift, the giver and any message, but they hold the gifts for you until they're amassed. This enables you to write prompt thank-you notes but not have to contend with receiving one set of silver at a time.

Also save the paperwork (such as a receipt, which probably doesn't list the price). You may need this to prove an item's origin if you return or exchange it. Receipts are also helpful if the shop sends duplicates or fails to send out the gift because of some oversight.

Displaying the gifts has been an integral part of wedding tradition in some cultures. In 1893, for example, when Princess May and the Duke of York married, their wedding presents were displayed at Marlborough House – all 3,500 of them! You may want to have a gift table at the wedding or reception, but don't open any presents on the day and don't display envelopes containing money. Appoint someone to whisk away your presents to a safe spot at the end of the evening.

Giving Thanks

People may give you a gift at any time from the moment you announce your engagement until one year after your marriage. Even if you're the busiest person in the world, keeping up with your thank-you notes is imperative.

Although opinions vary, we feel that you have a month to send a thank-you note. (Honeymooners are cut some slack, but only a few weeks' worth.) If you fall behind, triage the situation: send notes first to people such as dear, neurotic Aunt Betty, who's probably losing sleep wondering whether her vase arrived intact; send the next batch to folks whose cheques you've already deposited; and then take care of the rest.

A well-written thank-you note mentions the gift, how much you like it and how you intend to use it. You may also add a few words to the recipients regarding how much you enjoyed (or missed) them at your wedding. For example:

> *11 August*
>
> *Dear Aunt Betty and Uncle Howard,*
>
> *Thank you so much for the exquisite hand-painted vase. It looks like it was made for our mantelpiece, and we have already put it to use holding a bouquet of daffodils. We were thrilled that you came all the way from Edinburgh for our wedding – your presence made it an even more memorable family event.*
>
> *Again, our deepest thanks.*
>
> *With love and affection,*
> *Sophie and Henry*

Both of you may sign the note. A sweet touch is for the other spouse to append a brief postscript: 'P.S. I so enjoyed meeting you after hearing Sophie say such nice things about you for so long. Thank you again. We hope to see you soon. Henry'.

If the gift is actually quite hideous and destined to be exchanged or donated to charity, brush up on your euphemisms – *unusual, unique, bold, conversation piece* – and focus on the thought behind the gift.

Thank-you notes for money gifts are exercises in the oblique. Don't mention the words cash or cheque – refer to it as *your gift* or *your generous gift* – and never mention the exact amount. You may, however, indicate how you intend to use the money: 'We have earmarked it for our house fund . . . .'

Thank-yous in general should be short, sweet and uncomplicated. You should write them yourselves, and by hand rather than via email.

Send thank-you notes to all those people who got you through your day – the hairdresser, caterer, photographer, florist, wedding planner and so on. Service professionals rely on letters of reference for their business, and a laudatory letter often means more to them than a monetary tip or gift does.

Dealing with Problem Presents

Sometimes, hiccups occur in the land of gifting. Here are some pitfalls to watch for, and how to overcome them:

- **The missing gift:** Some gifts never make it to their destination. Weeks after you receive a notice from the shop or a friend has mentioned that a present is on its way, you realise that something has gone awry. First, call the shop. Then notify the giver, who's no doubt wondering whether you just hated the gift or are too inconsiderate to write a thank-you note.

- **The damaged gift:** If a gift arrives damaged, take or send it back to the shop from which it came. (Returns and exchanges shouldn't be a problem with reputable shops, which want to keep you happy.) If the giver personally shipped the present, check the wrapping to see whether it was insured so that the person can collect the insurance and send a replacement.

- **The unmerited gift:** The only time you return items to the giver is if the wedding is cancelled. No big explanation is necessary, but you may ease any awkwardness with a simple note along the lines of 'Thank you, but under the circumstances we cannot accept your wonderful gift. We greatly appreciate your thoughtfulness . . . .'

If you've already used the gift, you must send the giver an identical replacement. Of course, some couples decide to use a gift before the wedding actually takes place. Many superstitions state that this should never happen, and we agree that an element of bad luck may be involved. However, for some couples, it won't bother them in the slightest that they've already slept on the sheets from Aunt Alice before their wedding day – we leave it up to you to decide what you're comfortable with.

✔ **The unwanted gift:** Sometimes you receive perfectly nice gifts for which you have no use, but exchanging them is more trouble than it's worth. You put the present in a drawer, with the idea that one day you'll find someone who can truly appreciate it. However, be aware of giving a gift away to the very person who gave it to you, so make a note who you received the gift from.

Regifting, as it's known, seems like a harmless way to recycle, but we've noticed that these gifts tend to have a vibe (perhaps it's guilt) that can come back to haunt you. And you have to remember who gave it to you and whether that person would ever come across it in the secondary recipient's home or notice its absence from yours. In a world where everyone nods when you say 'six degrees of separation', regift at your own risk.

Returning gifts for exchange, however, carries with it no guilt penalty. You don't need to inform the sender of the switch. Just thank the giver of the original gift – lie a little if you must – and let the matter rest.

Chapter 10

Rings That Rock

*U*ndoubtedly, engagement and wedding rings qualify as a major purchase for most couples. Finding the right ones is crucial – you'll wear them forever and they symbolise the start of your lives together.

Despite the cliché of the man proposing on one knee and springing open a jewellery box or surreptitiously sinking a ring in her Champagne glass, many brides and grooms prefer to shop for the engagement and wedding rings together – or at least pre-shop together so the groom doesn't buy something that is his taste, not hers. When you do go looking, consider your lifestyle. For a woman who runs her tights by just looking at them, a pointy pear or marquise shape would be a disaster. We suggest trying on many different rings before you buy anything. Using the guidelines in this chapter, you may develop an eye for quality stones and craftsmanship, but your final choice is extremely personal and should reflect your taste, feelings for each other and, as unromantic as it sounds, your budget.

Understanding Diamonds

A diamond is nothing more than a hunk of carbon, yet in its pure, crystallised form, it is the hardest transparent substance known to man, four times harder than ruby or sapphire. Only another diamond can cut a diamond. This durability, along with its light, has made the diamond an enduring marriage symbol. Today, most engagement rings (about 80 per cent) in the UK feature diamonds, so you probably haven't got this far in your engagement without having heard about the *four Cs* – cut, colour, clarity and carat weight – by which all diamonds are judged.

Cut

A diamond's *cut* and proportion determine its brilliance and fire, making the cut perhaps the most important factor in a diamond's beauty. Because each facet acts as a light-dispersing mirror, more facets generally mean greater beauty. To appreciate a stone's cut, you should be familiar with the anatomy of a well-proportioned diamond, as shown in Figure 10-1.

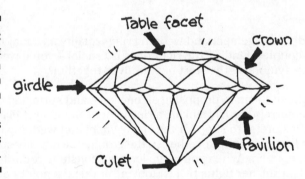

Figure 10-1:
The different parts of a stone can vary in proportion and thus affect its brilliance.

A modern, round-brilliant-cut diamond has 58 facets (including the culet, or 57 facets if you exclude the culet), which makes it more brilliant than other shapes. When light enters an ideally proportioned diamond, it reflects from facet to facet and back up through the top, maximising the diamond's fire and sparkle. In a well-proportioned diamond, the crown appears to be roughly one-third of the pavilion depth. In a diamond that's cut too deep, light is lost through the sides and the centre appears dark. A diamond that's cut too shallow in order to make it look larger appears dull.

Don't confuse *cut* with *shape*. Figure 10-2 shows various shapes: oval, pear, round brilliant, emerald, baguette, princess and marquise. (However, just to confuse you, a diamond may be emerald cut, and an emerald may be cut like a round brilliant, typical of diamond solitaires.) Note that straight and tapered baguettes are often used to surround and complement centre stones.

There are many new and unusual cuts appearing all the time – such as the JC Millennium, which is basically a round-cut stone similar to the round brilliant, and the radiant cut, which is an octagonal stone similar to an emerald with upper girdle facets similar to the princess cut.

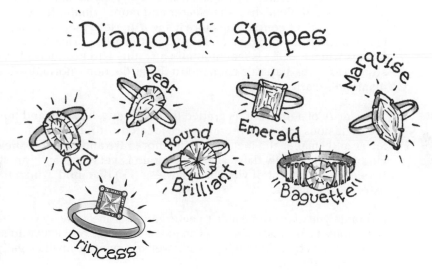

Figure 10-2:
A few
traditional
diamond
shapes.

Colour

For some people, a diamond can never be too white. Different organisations use many differing scales to rate colour, but the most common is an alpha-numeric scale starting at the colour D (pure white and the most prized colour) and ranging to Z (yellow/tinted colour). A typical commercial colour you see in jewellery shops in the UK is probably around J to K – which is lovely, but doesn't cost anywhere near a D diamond.

Some diamonds possess natural *fluorescence,* which produces a yellowish, bluish or whitish glow when viewed in daylight or under fluorescent lights. Professional gemologists test for fluorescence to ensure that the diamond colour is graded properly, otherwise, a strong fluorescence may throw off the colour. A stone that fluoresces blue can mask a yellow tint or make a white diamond look blue-white – a kind of bonus, actually. A white diamond that fluoresces yellow, however, can make the stone look less white, decreasing its value.

In nature, diamonds occur in virtually every colour and shade – blue, pink, lavender, yellow, green, red and even black. Known as *fancies* in the trade, coloured diamonds are increasingly popular for engagement rings. In fact, many celebrities wear pink diamond engagement rings and therefore they've grown in popularity – be aware, though: some rare colours can be pricey.

Clarity

Internal imperfections, such as small cracks, whitish dots or dark spots, are called *inclusions*. External flaws, such as naturals (unpolished portions), nicks, pits and scratches, are *blemishes*. Generally speaking, the fewer the inclusions and blemishes, the clearer and more brilliant the diamond, the rarer it is and, of course, the more it's worth. Note that cutters sometimes leave naturals along a diamond's girdle – the area normally grasped by prongs when a stone is mounted into a setting – to produce a larger-cut stone. However, naturals confined to the girdle don't normally impact the diamond's clarity grade.

The clarity of a diamond is graded by how many, how big and how visible the inclusions are, and where they're located within the diamond. The fewer and smaller the inclusions, the more rare and valuable the diamond. Finding an internally flawless (IF) diamond is very rare and rarest of all (from a clarity point of view) is a flawless (FL) diamond, which has no external blemishes.

Although you may not be able to determine a stone's clarity with the same precision as a professional, you can judge brilliance and light and see certain imperfections by using a ten-power jeweller's *loupe*, a small magnifying glass that covers the eye.

Most jewellers in the UK grade clarity according to the GIA London system, which has 6 categories, some of which are divided, for a total of 11 specific grades:

- **Flawless (FL):** No inclusions and no blemishes visible under 10x magnification.

- **Internally Flawless (IF):** No inclusions visible under 10x magnification.

- **Very, Very Slightly Included (VVS1 and VVS2):** Inclusions so slight they are difficult for a skilled grader to see under 10x magnification.

- **Very Slightly Included (VS1 and VS2):** Inclusions are observed with effort under 10x magnification, but can be characterised as minor.

- **Slightly Included (SI1 and SI2):** Inclusions are noticeable under 10x magnification.

- **Included (I1, I2, and I3):** Inclusions are obvious under 10x magnification which may affect transparency and brilliance.

Many inclusions and blemishes are too tiny to be seen by anyone other than a trained diamond grader. To the naked eye, a VS1 and an SI2 diamond may look exactly the same, but these diamonds are quite different in terms of overall quality. This is why expert and accurate assessment of diamond clarity is extremely important.

Carat weight

The weight of a diamond is measured in carats. One carat equals 0.2 grams and you get 100 points to a carat. Thus a 50-point diamond is half a carat (0.50ct) and weights 0.1 grams.

If you ask a jeweller *how large* a stone is and she tells you it has, say, 'a 2-carat spread', watch out. Many diamonds are 'spread', or cut, with thin proportions, to maximise weight rather than brilliance. Therefore, a diamond that *spreads* 1 carat isn't the same as a stone that *weighs* 1 carat. The correct way to phrase the question is, 'What is the stone's exact actual weight?' The jeweller should then give you the number of carats – with no mention of the word *spread*.

Where a laboratory team has assessed a diamond it's termed a *certificated* or *certified* stone. A good stone, bought at a reputable jewellery shop, should have a certificate.

We won't go so far as to say that size doesn't matter, but size is virtually meaningless outside the context of cut, clarity and colour. A large stone that's dull, flawed or improperly cut is worth less money than a perfect little diamond. The larger a good-quality diamond, however, the more it's worth.

The fifth C – cost

The jewellery industry has very thoughtfully devised a formula to determine how much you should spend on a diamond ring. If you really love her, they say, spending the equivalent of two months' salary is quite reasonable. Although that doesn't seem outrageous to us, it does seem rather arbitrary. You surely have your own priorities and can figure out for yourselves what's appropriate.

We spoke to diamond expert Vashi Dominguez, who said, 'Gone are the days when you need to spend two months' salary on an engagement ring. Buy the highest quality diamonds to your budget, and beware of flashy surroundings and designer shops as you'll be paying for those too!'

A 'C' change of sorts

In the past few years, concern has grown over *conflict* diamonds – diamonds used to finance conflict and civil wars, particularly in Africa. The Kimberly Process certification scheme, launched in January 2003, is an international agreement to eliminate the trade in what are also known as 'blood diamonds'. To ensure legitimacy, industry leaders and about 70 participating countries have instituted self-regulatory measures that involve tamper-proof containers for transporting uncut gems, counterfeit-proof warranties and electronic recordkeeping. Although participants aren't allowed to trade in diamonds with non-participants, at the time of writing human rights groups are pushing for more stringent monitoring, without which making sure that diamonds aren't sourced from areas held by rebels opposing legitimate governments is impossible.

If Diamonds Aren't Your Best Friend

Although the majority of brides opt for a diamond engagement ring, coloured gemstones, such as emerald, ruby and sapphire, have become increasingly popular. In fact, since ancient times, people have prized coloured gems, believing they endow their owners with power, status, luck and good health. You can find many kinds of meanings attributed to stones through the ages, but ultimately you should choose your stone because you like it.

Judging gemstones

Although clarity is an important factor in buying a gemstone, flawlessness is a harder characteristic to find than in diamonds. A far more important consideration is the colour. The closer a stone comes to a pure spectral hue, the higher the quality. In other words, in a red stone, the purer the red, the better.

To accurately assess a stone's true colour, look at it in several types of light. After examining many ruby rings, for example, you may notice they range in hue from bluish-red to brownish-red to pink, with several gradations in between. In fact, while a true ruby is corundum, some of those 'rubies' may actually be from other gemstone families – beryl, garnet, spinel, tourmaline or zircon – and (should be) priced accordingly. Certification for gemstones isn't as institutionalised as with diamonds, but a jeweller should be able to verify the stone's colour grade and whether the stone is natural or synthetic.

Real or not real? That is the question

If you want more diamond than your budget allows, synthetic or simulated diamonds, which are grown in a lab rather than in nature, are a good alternative. Many imitation diamonds have appeared over the years, and some have gained a large following. The most popular imitation has been *cubic zirconi* (known as CZ) because it's durable and less prone to scratches and cracks than other synthetic and imitation stones.

Now, however, that CZ has competition from a new substance called *synthetic moissanite*, which is the second hardest gemstone next to – and more brilliant than – diamond. Synthetic moissanite has even fooled thermal testers, the standard way jewellers detect CZ.

Synthetic moissanite costs only 10 to 20 per cent less than real diamonds, making it significantly more expensive than CZ. So if wearing several thousand pounds on one little finger makes you nervous, CZ is a good alternative – at least as a backup for day-to-day use. It is not unheard of for many high-society women to wear copies of their most expensive jewels while the real thing sits in a safe, and no one is the wiser.

The next generation of synthetics has succeeded in growing cultured diamonds that are literally perfect and significantly less expensive than natural ones or moissanite. The high-quality stones have been so impressive that De Beers Diamond Trading Company, the London-based cartel that controls the diamond business, has launched a programme to help international gem labs distinguish between man-made and mined stones by using high-tech equipment. It remains to be seen whether consumers will care about the difference between a test-tube diamond and a hand-mined one, as long as they're getting more rock for their buck.

If you're thinking about going for a simulated diamond, find one that's set in a precious metal – such as 18-carat gold, or platinum. A fine setting ensures you get a fine look.

Setting Pretty

A ring's setting is like the right picture frame that sets off a masterpiece to its best advantage. The ring must also be in proportion to your hand. An elaborate setting may camouflage flaws in a stone. In fact, an *illusion setting*, which looks like a little box in which the stone sits (see Figure 10-3), is almost certainly a sign that the stone has something to hide. Particularly distinctive settings, however, may bear the designer's insignia inside the ring, whether the design is elaborate or minimalist.

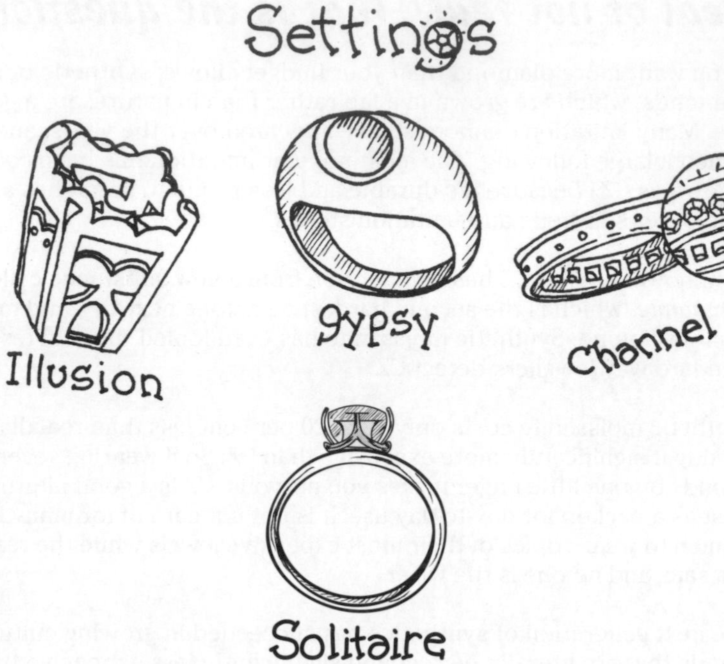

Settings

Illusion

Gypsy

Channel

Solitaire

Figure 10-3:
A stone can look vastly different depending on what kind of setting it sits in.

Other classic settings include:

- **Bezel:** Streamlined setting with no prongs. The stone sits close to the finger. May reduce appearance of brilliance because light can't enter from the sides. Works well with two different metals such as yellow gold and platinum.

- **Carved scroll:** Victorian setting that became an international trend. Elaborate scrollwork surrounds the stone.

- **Channel:** Used in mounting a number of smaller stones of uniform size in a row. (See Figure 10-3.)

- **Cluster:** A large stone surrounded by smaller stones.

- **Gypsy:** Stone lies flush with the band. Metal around the stone is much heavier than around the shank. (See Figure 10-3.)

- **Invisible:** No visible metal prongs or channels. Stones are cut and fit so precisely that no gaps exist between them. These settings cost more because stones must match very closely.

- **Pavé:** Small stones set together in a cluster with no metal showing through.

- ✔ **Prong:** Four or six metal claws grasp on to the gemstone. A six-prong setting is often called a Tiffany setting.

- ✔ **Silver cups:** Edges crimped beneath the stones to reflect light. This design originated in the late 1700s.

- ✔ **Solitaire:** A single gemstone mounted without ornamental side stones, usually with four or six prongs. The classic engagement ring!

- ✔ **Tension:** Diamond appears to be almost floating, barely held in place at the girdle.

Metal Matters

The metal of your ring should flatter both your skin tone and the colour of the stone. You may need to weigh aesthetics against practicality. For example, 18-carat gold is a brighter yellow than 14 or 9 carat, but more expensive and not as hard. On the other hand (so to speak), 18-carat white gold is white, less likely to cause allergic reactions and more affordable than 14-carat white. Platinum is the most expensive, but beautiful, and both hard and resilient. If you want to go the gold route and can't decide whether you like yellow, white or pink (also known as rose) gold best, tricolour rolling rings feature all three.

Whatever metal you choose, you may have a ring designed with a matte or satin finish, patterns such as delicate flowers or swirling paisleys, or detailed edgings such as *milgrain* (like tiny beads) or a soft bevel known as *comfort fit*.

Orthodox Jews believe that wedding rings should be plain with no jewels or stones that may impede the eternal, heavenly circle of life and happiness.

Equal Rights – Don't Leave Out the Groom

Despite the invention of *gimmel rings* (a ring with two or three hoops or links that fit together to form one complete ring), men rarely wore wedding rings until after World War II. Even the romance-obsessed Victorians preferred a plain gold band for women and no ring for men. Today, the majority of weddings are double-ring ceremonies.

The groom's ring is usually a larger, wider version of the bride's. Although his ring may be a completely different style, like hers, his ring should slip easily over the knuckle and hug the base of the finger, leaving just enough room to slip a toothpick through to account for fingers swelling when the temperature changes.

Finding the Right Ring

Whether you decide to buy a brand-new, never-worn wedding set or opt for a set with some history, searching for a ring can be an exciting experience. Like the wedding gown and the groom's ensemble, the rings you choose should be distinctly you.

Buying new

As with so many things, you now have the option of shopping for engagement and wedding rings at a local jeweller or online. An in-person purchase lets you see what you're getting and you're likely to get the offer of lifetime cleaning and maintenance of your ring. But shopping online allows for easy comparison, can save you money and is getting ever more sophisticated.

In the loop

Many couples have a special message engraved on the inside of their engagement or wedding rings. This inscription may be their initials or wedding date. Others are downright tomes requiring a fairly wide and large band. Here are some classics:

✔ *DODI LI V' ANI LO* (Hebrew for 'I am my beloved's and my beloved is mine')

✔ LOVE ~ HONOUR ~ CHERISH

✔ CONSTANCY AND HEAVEN ARE ROUND AND IN THIS EMBLEM FOUND

✔ I DOE RECEIVE IN THEE MY CHOYCE (from a 17th-century ring)

✔ MAY THIS CIRCLE BE UNBROKEN

✔ WHOM GOD HAS JOINED TOGETHER LET NO MAN PUT ASUNDER

✔ PUT IT BACK ON

Left hand, fourth finger?

Through the ages, people have used every digit of the hand – including the thumb, in the 17th century – as the wedding-ring finger. The Egyptians used the fourth finger of the left hand, believing that the *vena amoris* ran straight from that finger to the heart. That no such vein exists hasn't deterred people from favouring that finger for wedding rings. In fact, the English Prayer Book of 1549 specifies the left hand. Perhaps that explains why Roman Catholics used the right hand until the 18th century.

When it comes to buying a diamond, beware of deals. If a price sounds too good to be true, it probably is. Although you're usually safe when buying from a reputable retailer, scams do abound. These range from counterfeit or altered certificates to bait-and-switch advertising to deceptive pricing schemes. A legitimate jeweller should have no problem with having a ring checked out by a reputable, certified appraiser of your choosing.

Whether based on an hourly rate or per carat for diamonds, appraisal fees should be clear. The appraisal should be conducted in your presence and provide:

- ✔ The millimetre dimensions, quality, weight and identification of each stone
- ✔ The cut, colour, clarity and carat weight of the diamonds
- ✔ The hue, tone, intensity, transparency and clarity of coloured stones
- ✔ An identification and assessment of metals used in mounting
- ✔ A thorough description or photograph of the item
- ✔ The estimated value of the piece

You need an appraisal for insurance. Home insurance policies usually include cover for valuable items such as jewellery, but may require you to specify items if they're worth over a certain amount. Check the small print because some companies may have limits as low as £1,000 per single item. In addition, take photos of all your precious jewellery and store them in a photo-quality fireproof box. (Colour photocopies of your ring are also a good record with the added bonus that you can write on them.) Keep your certificate in the fireproof box too.

Analysing antique pieces

If you're interested in finding an antique wedding ring, watch for upcoming jewellery sales at reputable auction houses and antiques shows. Attend previews and inspect the goods. In many cases, the auction house has an expert on hand to answer questions and give you a tutorial in evaluating a ring's attributes. Be sure to also ask about the ring's *provenance* – previous owner(s) – because that may imbue the ring with more meaning for you.

Recognising the appeal and value of antique jewelry, many jewellers have introduced *estate jewellery* departments. Bear in mind, however, that estate jewellery isn't necessarily the same as *antique* (at least 100 years old); jewellery that once belonged to someone else may actually be only a few years old. The easiest and surest way to know is to check a diamond or coloured gemstone certification.

If no certificate is available, the cut may date a stone. Developed in the 16th century, the *rose cut* was characterised by a flat base and facets in multiples of six. In the 18th century, the *old mine cut*, which had unprecedented brilliance and fire, was popular, and by the mid-19th century, the *old European cut* proved even more brilliant. Like today's modern brilliant cut, old mine and old European cuts (see Figure 10-4) have 58 facets. But they aren't as brilliant as stones cut after the '20s and therefore are typically appraised for less.

Figure 10-4:
From the side, old mine and old European cuts have a deep pavilion and high crown.

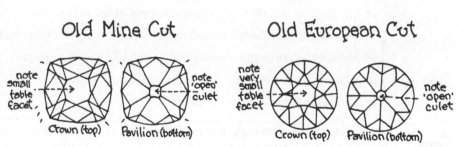

Dirt and grease deposits can collect in and around a diamond setting, making the stone appear yellower than it is. An old diamond ring may clean up whiter than you expect.

An antique diamond ring may be an antique all right, but not a diamond. It was common in Victorian times to use paste or leaded glass gems in precious metal settings, so you may need an expert to determine a stone's true identity.

Although an heirloom ring may hold great sentimental value, it isn't necessarily a paradigm of great taste. If the style looks dowdy, you may be able to strike a compromise by having the stones reset in a more contemporary or flattering setting. First have the stones appraised; you not only want to make sure the stones are legitimate, but you also want to check for any damage that may affect what you can do with them.

If you opt to have a new setting designed, choose a jeweller who specialises in styles you like. Unless you're absolutely sure of what you want and can provide detailed sketches of the top and side views, try on many rings of various weights and styles, and clip magazine photos of rings you like. As you work with the jeweller, request a wax model so that you can make any last-minute changes before the jeweller casts your ring.

Chapter 11

And the Bride Wore . . .

In This Chapter

▶ Evaluating wedding dress styles

▶ Determining which white is right for you

▶ Deciding what to wear underneath it all

▶ Dressing the bride from head to toe

*P*rincess, queen, siren, vixen/maiden – fashion designers are immensely creative in imagining what roles women want to play. As frivolous as some designers' visions seem, buying into a fantasy is easy because the garment known simply as a *wedding dress* is so loaded with meaning that it can throw even the most confident women for a loop. Perhaps the costliest item of clothing you'll ever buy, this dress symbolises the start of a new phase in your life. It must also endure several nerve-wracking hours of being inspected by umpteen pairs of eyes and being photographed relentlessly. Thinking about it, shopping for it and purchasing it can induce nothing short of sheer panic.

It doesn't have to be that way. For starters, bear in mind that the dress that ultimately makes you happiest is the one that reflects your inner self – the woman you're most content with. If you're not a slave to fashion in everyday life, why start now? Even though most wedding dresses are inevitably long, some shade of white and quite possibly bejewelled, you don't have to feel like a carbon-copy bride. And although dresses tend to be a major factor in any wedding budget, by shopping smartly, you *can* find a stunning dress without breaking the bank.

In this chapter, we take you through all the considerations for wedding outfits, from the all-important dress – style, fit, quality and places to purchase – to undergarments, shoes, headwear, hair style, make-up and accessorising. Then we round off by outlining your options for your dress after the event: preserve or pass on? By the end of this chapter, you can sail into a wedding boutique in full confidence that you know your Juliet cap from your watteau.

Sizing Up Your Style

The most important thing to remember when choosing your wedding dress style is that you're the central character in the show being cast, and all the players' costuming revolves around your ensemble. Don't worry about what dress code you've noted on your invitations (see Chapter 8); concentrate on *you* and what you want to wear.

When dress hunting you need to focus on three aspects of your wedding:

- ✔ **When:** As in the season and time of day. Heavy fabrics such as brocades, velvets and satins are most comfortable in late autumn and winter. A spaghetti-strap crepe dress works better in hot weather. A simple suit with a beaded bustier or a lavender sundress is intrinsically more appropriate for a casual daytime wedding, but you may prefer full-on glamour if you're having a formal evening reception. If you're having a beach wedding then light, soft and floaty works well.

- ✔ **Where:** Will you be getting married in a place of worship, where bare shoulders may seem disrespectful (or be prohibited)? Consider where you'll say your vows as well as where your reception will take place. If, for example, your ceremony is in a church and your reception is in a garden, keep those locales in mind when determining the length of your train or the height of your shoes.

- ✔ **Price:** How much are you willing to spend? And how likely are you to change your mind? Be realistic with yourself and upfront with salespeople about your dress budget. You can save a lot of time if everyone isn't playing cat and mouse. Being upfront also saves you from the depressing scenario of falling in love with a dress that you couldn't possibly afford.

The following sections help you think about all the different aspects that make up a wedding dress style, and choose which most appeal to you.

Selecting the right silhouette

Those brave souls who sell bridal apparel for a living all agree that you need to begin your dress quest with the *silhouette*, or overall shape of the dress, in mind:

- ✔ **A-line:** Flared from either under the bust or the waist, often with a fitted waist. Looks like an upright letter A, and is also called a *princess line*. An A-line is a flattering silhouette for just about everyone. Many silhouettes feature variations of the A-line, as shown in Figure 11-1 (dresses C, D, E and F).

Figure 11-1:
Wedding dresses come with a range of silhouettes, necklines and sleeve styles.

✔ **Ball gown:** A fitted corset with a very full skirt that brushes the floor. The waist may be nipped in at your natural waist, be shaped in an elongated triangle (called a *basque waistline*) or be dropped to hug your hips. This is the classic fairy-tale wedding-dress silhouette, and when the dress is highly embellished with sequins, lace or crystals, you've got your very own Cinderella fantasy costume. Figure 11-1F shows this dress all ready for the ball. The ball-gown silhouette looks particularly good on women with small waists and is most flattering for the less-buxom bride.

✔ **Empire:** The bodice is cropped and the waist seam ends just below the bust line to create a flattering elongated effect (check out Figure 11-1E). It can have short sleeves or be sleeveless and may have various necklines. Works particularly well on women with medium to large breasts and less-than-tiny waistlines.

✔ **Mermaid:** Narrow, body-hugging dress that flares dramatically at or below the knee like a mermaid's tail, as shown in Figure 11-1G. Also known as a *fish tail*. Good for showing off your curves, especially if you're tall. Some women find the cut constricting, but others like the shimmy effect.

✔ **Sheath:** A narrow, close-fitting dress that goes to the floor in an unbroken line. This shape is more reminiscent of an evening gown than a wedding dress and is currently very popular with slim, toned brides. Particularly revealing when cut *on the bias* (diagonally to the grain of the fabric). Not suitable for kneeling. Basically, a sheath is the mermaid style without the flared bottom.

✔ **Slip:** Like a long tank top. May be backless or bias-cut (see the preceding bullet), but usually without ornamentation. Most elegant on someone tall and slender. Check out a version in Figure 11-1B.

The recent popularity of vintage-styled weddings has inspired many designers to recreate vintage silhouettes. *Vintage* can mean anything from the 1920s to the 1970s, so the silhouettes and styles can be very different – from drops waists á la flapper style to 1960s prom dresses. Usually made with the most wonderfully delicate fabrics (think silk, satin, silk crepe, taffeta and delicate lace lined in silk), vintage styles can be suitable for all brides. They come in all lengths, so can work for you whether you're looking for a full-length gown or mid-length prom dress. (See further on in this chapter for tips on reusing an original vintage dress rather than buying a new dress in a vintage style.)

Preparing to shop

For a successful and less-stressful dress-hunting expedition, it helps to have a plan:

- **In preparing to shop, get a handle on wedding-dress language.** You don't have to know every term in the book, but having some basic knowledge may help you from feeling intimidated or exasperated when dealing with salespeople.

- **Bring along pictures and fabric swatches.** Take a trip to a fabric store and gather some swatches that appeal to you. Clip pictures from both bridal and general-interest magazines and download images from the Internet that convey the style or mood you want for your wedding. Then narrow the looks down to four or five. Be realistic and always keep your shape and size in mind. A picture in a magazine of a tall model wearing a sheath may not look the same on you if you are short and have womanly curves!

- **Skip the plastic and entourage.** The first time you venture out to try on dresses, leave the credit cards at home – even if you love a dress, come back and try it on again to be sure it's 'The One' before making a purchase. Bring only one trusted friend with you (someone who'll give you an honest, but not hurtful, opinion); a chorus of different opinions only confuses you.

- **Wear appropriate underwear.** That is, tights, a thong, a strapless bra or whatever foundation feels comfortable, looks pretty and is what you may wear under an evening dresses. Nude underwear is probably best to take along rather than a colour as it goes under most fabrics. Keep in mind that you'll be in a dressing room with a sales consultant as well as the friend you've brought with you, and you don't want to be trying to hide in a corner as you undress.

- **Take notes and pay attention to first impressions.** If the bridal shop will allow you to take a photograph, try to resist the temptation of sending the photos to your friends and keep the 'dress committee' down to one or two trusted people.

- **Take along a pair of neutral heeled shoes.** Make sure they're of a height that you feel comfortable in and are a pair that you would consider wearing on your wedding day.

Figuring out the neckline

The neckline is next in the style triumvirate (along with the waistline and sleeves) that determines the *bodice*, or part of your dress that covers from your waist up. Possibilities include:

- **Audrey:** A nearly horizontal line from shoulder blade to shoulder blade. Like a bateau neck (see the next bullet), but starts two inches in from each shoulder, so the neck opening is narrower. Lovely on brides with long necks.

- **Bateau neck:** Follows the line of the collar bone straight across, is high in front and back, and usually skims both shoulder blades and may drape beautifully from the bust line. Also known as a 'boat neck'. Refer to Figure 11-1E.

- **Cowl neck:** Similar to the portrait (see the later bullet), but has more material and a softer flow across the neckline. Very nice if you have broad shoulders and want to soften the look of your dress.

- **Halter:** One or two straps go around the neck or across the back to hold up the bodice. Refer to Figure 11-1G. Backless (or keyhole backed), it's revealing but, when worn with a strapless/backless bra, surprisingly comfortable and sexy on women of most sizes.

- **Jewel:** A simple curve at the base of the neck, like a necklace around the collarbones.

- **Keyhole:** A keyhole or teardrop-shaped opening either at the neckline or in the back of the dress.

- **One shoulder:** An asymmetrical dress where one arm is bare and the other may be long sleeved, short sleeved, sleeveless or anywhere in between. Very dramatic.

- **Portrait:** A fold of fabric creates a shawl-like collar, framing the face. Usually worn off the shoulder. Can be flattering on angular bodies, but matronly if not cut low enough.

- **Scoop:** Rounded but lower than a jewel neck, perhaps even revealing a hint of cleavage. When the dress is sleeveless with deeply cut armholes, this neckline resembles a tank top.

- **Strapless:** When the neck and shoulders of the dresses are completely bare, usually with a tightly fitted bustier or corset-type bodice. Strapless dresses, like the one shown in Figure 11-1F, are the most popular dresses and you generally find a wide range in the bridal shops.

- **Sweetheart:** Open, somewhat revealing, sweeping down, dipping to a point in the middle of the bust and forming a heart shape. Refer to Figure 11-1D.

- **V-neck:** Forms a point, making the neck look longer and slimmer. Figure 11-1C shows a deep V-neck.

- **Wedding-band collar:** A band high on the neck usually in a contrasting fabric to the rest of the bodice; often made of lace. Emphasises a long, slender neck.

Negotiating arms

In bridal and other fashion, you can no longer determine the season by the length of the sleeves you see people wearing. After countless hours at the gym, many toned brides are going sleeveless no matter how chilly the weather, and women who either don't love their arms or never feel completely dressed in anything but full-length sleeves are wearing sheer sleeves to their wrists even during the dog days of summer. One word of warning: a tightly fitted long-sleeved dress can be very restricting. Think twice about choosing one if you intend on dancing, hugging anyone taller than you or tossing your bouquet with more than a wrist-flip.

The most popular dress in the UK in recent years has been strapless, and for the most part designers haven't given many alternatives. However, since a certain royal wedding in 2011, many women have realised that, no matter what their dress size, sleeves can be elegant, demure and even sexy. Designers are now beginning to catch on and the range of 'with-sleeves' dresses is increasing every year.

The most common sleeve styles include the following:

- ✔ **Balloon:** Wide, puffy, wrist-length sleeves. Pouf sleeves are a variation with a short, gathered sleeve sometimes worn off the shoulder *à la* Princess Diana. Perhaps a little '80s now, but it may be your dream dress.

- ✔ **Bell:** Narrow at the top and widely flared at the bottom, as Figures 11-1A and 11-1C show. The look can be very elegant and make you seem a little taller if the proportions are correct.

- ✔ **Cap:** A short, fitted, set-in sleeve that barely covers the shoulders.

- ✔ **Dolman:** Wide armholes extending out from the waist of the dress and tightening at the wrist. Also called bat wings. A bit of Morticia from *The Addams Family*, but heavy drama with the right dress – a tight and slinky one.

- ✔ **Fitted:** Long and tapered, these sleeves are sometimes designed to come to a V-shaped point at the top of the hand – that type is cleverly called *fitted-point* sleeves.

- ✔ **Juliet:** A long sleeve with a short pouf at the shoulder and the rest tapered. A period look in the style of the Shakespearean heroine.

- ✔ **Three-quarters:** Ends just below the elbow and is finished with a small cuff or band. Very '50s, and lovely if you want to show off a beautiful bracelet on your wrist.

- ✔ **T-shirt:** As the name implies, sleeves are closely fitted to the shoulder, and slightly fuller and longer than a cap sleeve.

Looking behind you

Take into account that guests will be gazing at you from behind during the entire ceremony, so the back of your dress should have at least some detailing. With the trend toward sleeker dresses, the lines of the dress, particularly the back, have become more important. In fact, some dresses are virtually plain in the front with all the ornamentation on the rear. (Of course, women who are larger on the bottom than the top may think twice before plastering a dramatic butterfly bow across their *derrière*.)

If you have a lovely back and are quite toned, you may want to consider a dress that shows it off. But be careful with a strapless dress from behind – squishy bits coming over the top of your dress isn't the most flattering look. The dress must suit you, rather than the model in the magazine in which you first saw it.

Among the possibilities:

- A dress that dips *below* the small of the back, as shown in Figure 11-1B
- A halter neckline as in Figure 11-1G
- A scooped back edged with silk flowers or composed of *illusion* (a fine, almost transparent, mesh-like netting usually made of silk)
- A strapless dress that's completely backless (take a good look from behind, though)

Deciding what lengths you'll go to

The length of the wedding dress you choose largely depends on the silhouette, your height and what height heel you feel comfortable wearing. Typically, wedding dresses come in these lengths:

- **Ballerina:** Usually associated with full skirts; just graces the tops of your ankles.
- **Full length or floor length:** The toes of your shoes should just show. The back hem should be short enough to dance in without you or your partner stepping on your dress and tripping you. All the dresses in Figure 11-1 are this length.
- **High-low or intermission:** The skirt is cut shorter in front, usually to mid-calf, and goes to floor length in back, giving a Latin flavour.
- **Mid length:** The hemline covers the knees.
- **Mini:** Ends right above the knee or shorter.
- **Tea length:** Ends at the lower calf or right above the ankle.

Considering a train

Perhaps more than any other aspect of your dress, the bridal train has transformative powers. This extended length of fabric forces you to walk a little differently, swishes around luxuriously and makes you feel positively regal. The longer the train, the more you may want to decorate it with bands, bows, pearls or sequins. Even an embroidered monogram is exquisite on the right dress.

A long train may suit a large church wedding, but consider how it will look at your local register office.

Possible train lengths include:

- **Chapel:** Extends 3½ to 4½ feet (approximately 1 metre to 1.5 metres) from the hemline.

- **Cathedral:** Extends nine feet (2.75 metres) from the waist, which is roughly 5–6 feet (1.2 or 1.8 metres) behind the bride.

- **Royal cathedral or monarch:** A train that extends longer than 9 feet. From the waist, can actually be upwards of 25 feet (7.62 metres) long.

- **Sweep:** The shortest train, just brushing the floor or the tops of your shoes. Also called *brush*. Looks great as is, but isn't a wonderful choice for someone who plans to dance a lot because it doesn't bustle well (read on to find out about bustles).

The shape of your train is determined as much by its length as the way the fabric is attached to your dress. Usually, the train is the same piece of material that makes up the back of your dress, but if it's a separate piece of fabric, you may choose one of these styles:

- **Court:** Attaches at the shoulders and falls to the floor.

- **Detachable:** Attaches with hooks and loops either around the waist, like a long skirt over a short dress, or just to one point at the back of the dress.

- **Watteau:** Attaches at the shoulders, forming box pleats, falling loosely to the hem and sweeping into a train.

More common in the UK than a detachable train is a train that you can gather up into carefully orchestrated folds and layers to form a *bustle*. Bustles come in several styles:

- **Traditional:** You bring up the hem and attach it to loops at the back of the dress, creating symmetrical layers. See Figure 11-2.

Figure 11-2:
Bustling
your dress
makes those
oodles of
fabric more
manageable.

✔ **French:** You pick up the train and attach it with a series of numbered ties, creating a two-layered scalloped effect near the hem.

✔ **Floor length:** You bustle the dress underneath to create an even hem. The train essentially disappears under the dress.

✔ **Wristband:** You pick up the train and hold it by a loop at the bottom that attaches like a bracelet around the wrist. Although this look can be very glamorous and perhaps even impart some drama to the first dance, it's an impractical and uncomfortable choice for an entire reception.

Often overlooked until the last fitting, the way you bustle the dress is extremely important. If, for example, the train is long and the fabric quite heavy, efficient bustling is difficult. And having a yard of heavy material attached to your rear end can seriously cramp your style on the dance floor.

Bring the person who'll be bustling your dress to your last fitting for an instructional session – you want to avoid being away from the party for hours while someone figures the darn thing out.

Choosing the right white

By the late 1800s, when white became the standard in bridal gowns, *Ladies Home Journal* advised readers:

> *Thought must be given to the becomingness of the shade, for after all, there are as many tints in white as in other colours; the one that may suit the pale blonde is absolutely unbecoming to the rosy brunette. Dead white, which has the glint of blue about it, is seldom becoming to anyone. It brings out the imperfections of the complexion, tends to deaden the gloss of the hair, and dulls the brightness of the eyes. The white that touches on the cream or coffee shade is undoubtedly the most artistic.*

Although the terminology has changed, the advice remains important. Lots of different whites exist, and some will look better on you than others:

- What the bridal shops call *diamond white*, *silk white* or *natural white* is soft white, found only in natural (more expensive) fibres like silk, cotton or linen. These tones are usually flattering for fairer brides.

- *Blue-white* or *stark white* is generally polyester and, though unflattering to most blondes, can be stunning on dark-skinned women.

- *Ivory*, *eggshell* or *candlelight* is a creamier shade of white with golden or yellow undertones. It generally looks good on fair brides, but don't take it for granted because a huge disparity lies between what different designers call ivory.

- *Champagne* is off-white with pink or soft yellow undertones. This shade looks particularly nice on olive or darker skin tones.

Ah, but you've probably already realised that things in Bride Land are never simple. Thanks to designers such as Vera Wang, Monique Lhuillier, Badgley Mischka, and Reem Acra, bridal dresses are taking increasingly more cues from mainstream fashion, which means that white is just the beginning. Consider trimming your dress in brilliant yellow satin or opt for the surprise of a dainty row of black velvet ribbons running down the back of a full skirt. For some women, a peach or blue sash or under-layer adds oomph to a traditional dress. A small percentage of others do away with white completely and walk down the aisle wearing a gold brocade ball gown or even a burgundy sheath. In 2011, we even saw black wedding dresses coming down the runway of Vera Wang.

Coloured dresses are often popular if this isn't your first wedding – perhaps you've already done the white dress thing? Then choose a colour that suits you; you'll still look very much like the bride on the day.

Feeling your way through fabrics

Several fabrics are popular in the design of bridal dresses and each imparts a different feeling to the wearer. Here, we list the most common. With the exception of silk, all the other fabrics we list are available in less-expensive synthetic versions.

- **Charmeuse:** A lightweight satin that clings to the wearer and is less shiny than regular satin.

- **Chiffon:** Semi-transparent fabric with a very soft finish. The fabric moves with the wearer and drapes well. In addition to being used for dresses, this material is used for veils, sleeves or layers over other fabrics.

- **Organza:** Flowing but stiffer than chiffon, this fabric is often used for multi-tiered skirts.

- **Satin:** Heavier fabric that's glossy on the front side and dull on the other side. *Duchesse satin*, a blend of silk and rayon, is lighter and less expensive than silk satin.

- **Silk:** This fibre, made from the cocoon of silkworms, is luxurious, resilient and strong. *Traditional silk* has a 'silky' feel (referred to as a *hand*), and an almost iridescent sheen that makes you think of luxury. However, many other types of silk are also popular for wedding dresses, including *jacquard* (generally heavier and more densely woven with patterns in florals and paisleys, using matte and reflective threads to create a light and dark effect in the fabric. This effect is similar to brocade, although the jacquard is originally created in one colour), *raw silk* (any silk yarn or fabric that hasn't had the *sericin* – the natural gum that protects the fibre – removed. The fabric is stiffer and duller in colour) and *shantung* (which has a knobbly texture similar to raw silk made from combining thick and thin yarns; depending on the yarns used, shantung may be lustrous or dull).

- **Taffeta:** Crisp and almost papery feeling, this fabric can be slightly shiny or have a matte finish.

Getting a taste of the icing on the dress

A dress gets much of its sparkle and individuality from *the finishing touches*, which are trims and ornaments that usually work best when applied with masterful restraint as opposed to with a shovel. These elements may include one or more of the following:

- **Appliqués:** Additions either re-embroidered or sewn on to the fabric of the dress.

- **Border trims:** Braids, ribbon, ruffles or scalloped edges.

- **Bugle beads:** Small, cylindrical glass or plastic beads used for ornamentation. Beads are hand-sewn on expensive dresses, hand-glued on less-expensive ones.

- **Edging:** Lace, cord, embroidered band or silk satin that outlines a section of fabric. For example, a bodice with alternating bands of lace and satin.

- **Embroidery:** Can be sewn over *illusion* (a fine, almost transparent, mesh-like netting, usually made of silk) or other bridal fabrics in either the same or contrasting colours. Some designers use metallic thread in gold or silver.

- **Fringe:** Used as an embellishment or all over for a flapper look. Some designers bead the fringe.

- **Jewels:** Crystals are often used to embellish dresses or veils.

- **Ribbons and bows:** Used in various sizes and lengths, from one giant butterfly bow in back to many tiny bows sprinkled over a tulle skirt, and from silk ribbon closures on a corseted dress to floor-length streamers.

- **Seed pearls:** Very small and often irregular pearls used to adorn garments, headpieces and shoes.

- **Sequins and paillettes:** Flat, disc-shaped, plastic beads sewn on to give dresses a twinkly, modern look. Unlike sequins, paillettes jiggle.

- **Silk flowers:** Either the same colour as the dress or in contrasting colours. Used to highlight a specific area, such as the back or neckline, or as an all-over embellishment.

Getting the Goods

When it comes to buying a wedding dress, the lay of the land usually goes one of three ways:

- **Bespoke** is often the most expensive option, but opting for a *bespoke dress* will ensure that the dress is exclusive to you. Even though the designer may have a sample in their showroom, you'll be able to make the dress yours by making changes, such as shortening the hemline or adding in sleeves.

  When buying a bespoke dress, you try on samples at a designer's showroom, usually by appointment. When you find one you like, the designer will note your measurements and any other custom-order information (such as, 'substitute jewel neckline for sweetheart') and send your order to the seamstress. Your *toile* (a mock-up of the dress made of a cotton or calico fabric) is then made for your first fitting, after which adjustments are made to it and then the actual dress is made for your next fitting. It may take two or three fittings before your dress is complete. For most brides, this dress is the only piece of clothing created solely for them that they'll ever own.

✔ **Off-the-peg** dresses are stocked by bridal shops (sometimes called *salons* or *boutiques*) that have many designs available. You visit, and select a dress in the nearest size to your measurements. The dress is then altered to fit you, but a new dress is not made. Buying off the peg is usually the most economical option.

Note: some bridal shops do make the dress from scratch for you, but make an additional charge for this. Ask about this service when you make your appointment with the shop.

✔ **Handmade dresses** are made by a dressmaker after being designed from scratch specifically for you, with your full input. Weirdly, handmade dresses can be the cheapest option. You do, however, need to know your stuff when you come to choose material, styles that suit you and so on, as you have nothing to try on beforehand to 'check' before ordering.

The perfect dress for you is out there, even if it has yet to be designed and sewn. Read on to discover where you'll find it, how to check that it's perfect and how to get the ideal fit for you.

Tracking down the dress

Here's where you may find your dress:

✔ **Bridal shops/salons/boutiques:** Most brides purchase their dresses at these places, which range from famous wedding-dress emporiums to suburban bridal boutiques and bridal departments located in large department stores. Many bridal boutiques offer everything for the bridal ensemble including headpieces, shoes and accessories. These shops almost always operate by appointment only and you can save tons of time and undue teeth clenching by scheduling your appointment during off-peak hours. You'll be seated in a private dressing room and the sales consultant will bring you dresses to try on. Generally, the larger the store, the better the prices because of the store's buying power. Some couture bridal designers allow you to order your dress with myriad changes, from the neckline to the entire bodice, but others allow only specific changes. In any case, ask whether they do their alterations in-house.

✔ **Designer, couture and bespoke:** Some well-known private designers work with brides personally to create one-of-a-kind dresses. Starting with the bride's vision, they work together to choose fabrics, create the style and decide the detailing. The designer oversees each fitting as well as the hand-sewing and finishing. The first step is to make the toile. After a few fittings with this, the designer then cuts the dress using the expensive fabrics. Many bridal salons may refer you to capable designers willing to create a dress from scratch. These one-of-a-kind dresses vary greatly in price depending on the designer, the fabrics and the embellishments. Aside from the obvious advantages, these dresses generally take less time to make than those from manufacturers, which produce in much greater volume per season.

✔ **Discount bridal shops:** These shops have a large variety of mass-produced dresses in all sizes. Although substantially less expensive than a full-service store, the atmosphere is definitely for those on a mission to shop, not to be pampered. One plus: these off-the-rack dresses are usually ready to take home when you buy them, although we recommend that you find a local seamstress to ensure the dress becomes a perfect fit for you.

✔ **Internet:** Many salons and designers have websites where you can browse the collection or order catalogues. Some shops also let you place orders online, but be careful. In many cases, sales are *final*. If they do offer refunds or exchanges, they may charge a restocking fee. Before ordering online, try on dresses at a store to become familiar with the way different styles and sizes fit you and the way various fabrics feel. You may be able to save money, but, as with almost any dress, be prepared to have alterations made.

Thousands of dresses are for sale every day on eBay or other Internet auction sites – some new, some used – and you can find incredible bargains if you shop and bid carefully. To ensure a positive transaction, check the seller's feedback, shipping fees and return policy. And don't hesitate to email the seller with questions (What's the fabric? Has the dress been worn or altered? Are there any stains? Why are you selling it?).

✔ **Rentals:** The idea of renting a dress you'll wear only once may sound good, but it requires extensive research because rental stores are few and far between. The rental companies claim that bridal magazines discriminate against them, refusing to cover them or let them advertise for fear of alienating the retail trade. The magazines contend that people simply don't want to rent wedding dresses. In any case, consider what a psychic friend of ours says on the subject: 'The confluence of vibes from who-knows-how-many previous wearers could send you over the edge on your wedding day.'

✔ **Sample sales:** Stores and designers regularly hold sample sales where dresses that have been tried on often as samples or ordered especially and cancelled are sold to the general public at huge reductions (usually 20 to 50 per cent off the original price). On the downside, sizes are limited (that's what alterations are for) and the dresses may be slightly shopworn. But many brides have hit the jackpot at these sales.

✔ **Sew your own:** Making your own dress is definitely not for novices. The fabrics are delicate (and expensive), so if you're not a skilled seamstress, consider carefully before undertaking a project that could make you unravel.

✔ **Tailors:** A talented tailor or seamstress may be a frustrated designer or at least skilled enough to create a pattern from a magazine photo. Alternatively, you may already own a dress that you love and know you look good in; if it were re-made in a different colour and fabric then it would make the perfect wedding dress. The tailor makes a pattern and then cuts the actual fabric precisely to your measurements. Creating a bridal dress is a specialty – you don't want to be the bridal guinea pig. Get references, look at photos of other dresses the tailor's done and be very specific about what you want.

✔ **Vintage:** If you can fit into your mother's or grandmother's dress, you may want to complement it with vintage jewellery or accessories. If the moths have turned the dress into a large lace hankie, however, you may want to find a dressmaker who can incorporate the remnants into a contemporary design. You can find some wonderful vintage stores that stock amazing dresses in many major cities. To find one near you, just type 'vintage wedding dresses' into your web browser.

Fitting into an antique/vintage dress can be tricky. Depending on the era, you may need a girdle or corset. Alterations are virtually impossible depending on the fabric's fragility. For this reason, many designers actually design new dresses in a vintage style, which may work better.

✔ **Wedding showcases or exhibitions:** These showcases are held at bridal salons and occasionally at hotels and many major wedding exhibitions are held around the country each year. These shows enable you to see a designer's dresses (a larger selection than the store ordinarily carries) on live models. If you purchase a dress at that time, the designers may advise and fit you personally.

Pregnant and postnatal brides are hardly novelties these days, but the bridal industry doesn't cater to them as much as it should. Fortunately, a growing number of maternity stores carry elegant eveningwear that you can sometimes adapt for weddings. And more and more major bridal ranges are adding a few maternity dresses, but do call before you visit to check first. Custom-made dresses are the other option. Just be sure to put off the final fitting until as close to your wedding as possible (see the section 'Getting the right fit' for the scoop on dress fittings).

Thinking about quality control

For most people, deciphering whether a dress is *mass-produced* – cut en masse by laser and sewn with machines – or individually cut and sewn is virtually impossible. But don't get hung up on that point. When shopping, inspect the sample dress carefully, checking the quality of the workmanship.

Don't expect the quality of the dress you order to be much better than that of the sample. If the sample doesn't have, say, covered buttons then neither will the one you order.

When trying on dresses, your inspection checklist should cover:

- ✔ **Aesthetics:** If a long row of buttons goes down the back, do they have a zipper underneath? Are cloth-covered buttons the same fabric as the dress? Is the *interfacing* (a material used on the unseen or 'wrong' side of fabrics to make an area of a garment more rigid) fused to the outer layer? (It shouldn't be!) Check for loose threads on beading – one tug may undo an entire row.

- ✔ **Fabrication:** Do *naps* (the surfaces of the material) on separate fabric panels run the same way? (You don't want one panel to look shiny and another matte.) Is the lace free of snags? Is the fabric in good shape (as opposed to being pilled or worn)? Does the dress have a lining? Can you tell exactly what the fabric is? Does the style take advantage of patterns in the lace?

- ✔ **Security:** Are beads, loops and appliqués sewn on well? Does the dress have extra hooks and eyes or stitching at crucial stress points of the dress? Does the zipper extend to the widest point of your hips to prevent tears? If the dress is strapless, does the bodice have boning for support?

- ✔ **Sewing:** Are seams sewn straight and smooth? Is the fabric free of tiny telltale holes from ripped-out stitches? Are lace patterns matched up or laid out evenly? Are the lace seams invisible? Are the hems of heavy fabrics stitched with horsehair to make them stand out? Are seams finished with overlock stitching so the inside edges won't fray? Is the seam allowance generous? Do illusion panels lie flat? Are all layers sewn separately rather than stitched together as one piece? (If sewn all together, they may pucker.)

- ✔ **Stains:** If the dress is off the rack, hired or on consignment, does it have any perspiration, food or lipstick stains? Can they be removed? Is it free of glue marks?

Getting the right fit

When it comes to sizing, don't get obsessed with the size. (It's just a number, after all.) Put your ego aside and order a dress that fits you now, not the size you want to be one day. Don't buy a smaller dress thinking you're going to lose weight before the wedding. If you've been known to go up and down when under stress (due to nerves, many brides gain or shed up to 10 or 15 pounds before a wedding), go with a larger size and have your final fitting close to your wedding day. Making the dress smaller with tucks and darts generally works better than letting out seams, especially if the seam allowance is minimal.

Keep in mind, however, that when a dress fits very poorly as a sample, it most likely can never be made to feel right. When you try on a sample dress, it should curve in where you want it to, the waist should sit where it feels comfortable and the neckline should be flattering. Often, if the sample size in a bridal salon is way off, they use giant clips to show how the dress may fit you after it's altered.

After you get your dress, plan on between two and four fittings. From your second fitting on, bring the right undergarments and shoes (see the upcoming section for more information). Your dress may need minor or major alterations. Minor alterations include tweaking to make the bodice lie flat and adjusting the length of shoulder straps. Major alterations involve such things as shortening sleeves with buttons or detail trim on the wrist from the shoulder (rather than turning them under at the wrist), and shortening a hem with a special finish such as detail scalloping from the waist, not the bottom.

Remember that you have to move in the dress, so sit, kneel, do the Twist. Can you rotate your arms like a windmill? Does the fabric pull across your hips or bust? Will you be able to hug your new husband on your wedding day?

When buying your dress and setting up your fitting schedule, find out about the shop's policies ahead of time. Specifically, you want to check:

- Whether you've incurred any additional charges such as for a plus size, rush order, design change, special colour or custom bustle.

- Whether design specs, exact colour and wedding date are all on the sales slip. In other words, you want proof that the shop has a tracking system so your order doesn't get lost in the shuffle.

- How many fittings they think you'll need and approximately when the first one will be.

- How much the shop charges for alterations or are they included?

- How much it costs to add extra beading or ornamentation to the headpiece.

- The cancellation policy and how much of the deposit is non-refundable. (Typically, you forfeit the deposit if the dress has been cut.) Oh, and get that policy in writing.

Delving Underneath the Dress

What you put on before you get into your dress makes a big difference in the overall effect. Many dresses require elaborate foundations to enhance the silhouette. As you search for these important but unseen things, go to lingerie shops where you'll get personal attention.

By the second fitting, have all the correct undergarments and your shoes. It also helps to have any other accessories you intend to wear, such as gloves, tiaras or fascinators, so you can decide whether to edit your look. At this point, you can bring a camera to the salon and take a picture to help you obsess after the appointment.

A little bra-vado

The most important part of your under attire is the bra. If your dress doesn't have a custom-made or built-in bra, you need to find an off-the-shelf number that packages your assets in the best possible way.

Different dresses require specific bras:

- **Strapless or spaghetti straps:** Go for a bustier, preferably a seamless one, to keep the look of the torso smooth.
- **Low-cut back:** A backless bra that hooks at the waist is a good bet.
- **Low-cut front:** Push-up or semi-cup bras are the way to go.

Even totally fit babes may find that their fantasy wedding dress needs some filling out. If you need to give Mother Nature a non-surgical boost, invest in a pair of silicone bra inserts, available at fine lingerie stores and via the Internet.

To keep your bra from playing peek-a-boo in a low-cut dress, sew a few snaps on the front and back of the bra to attach it to the dress. On a sleeveless dress, sew little catches with snaps in the straps through which you thread your bra straps. Or have a seamstress tack your bra into your dress. If you want to show some skin and do it with nonchalance (that is, without tugging at your dress all night), buy a roll of Hollywood Fashion Tape, a special double-sided tape – the 'stars' secret' – that holds bra straps in place, strapless dresses up and revealing necklines in situ. This tape is also good to have for last-minute disasters like a hem that has come down. In the UK the tape costs around £10; check the Internet for suppliers.

Perfecting your proportions

With some wedding dresses, you may need specialised undergarments to fill out and tuck in. Here's what else may be going on beneath your dress:

- **Body shaper:** These used to be called girdles, but today's versions do the job better and don't make you feel like you're wearing a body cast. You can find them in a variety of styles – slimming shorts, bottom boosters, full-body smoothers, thong-cut bodysuits, full-support slips, long-waist panty-girdles – and in comfy fabrics such as spandex, Lycra and microfibre.

- **Garter:** Either in the form of straps suspended from a wide elastic belt (called a garter belt) or an elastic band wrapped around the thigh, a garter helps hold up your stockings. Although you may feel personally titillated by wearing a garter belt and thigh-high stockings, they won't give you the smoothest line in a sheath dress or even under a ball gown, and they can come unsnapped during a strenuous session on the dance floor!

- **Petticoats:** Many dresses have built-in petticoats, which are underskirts usually made of tulle, lace or *crinoline* (a stiff, open-weave fabric made of horsehair or cotton) to give fullness to the silhouette, especially on ball gowns. Or you can buy them separately in the same silhouette as your bridal dress. Experiment with the number of crinolines; even if two look perfect, add one more just to be sure. Big dresses need fuller and stiffer petticoats. Wear them for all your fittings.

- **Slip:** For a long sheath dress, you probably want to wear a slip. New body-hugging slips act as gentle, long-line girdles, extending from waist to mid-calf. Just make sure yours doesn't ride up when you walk.

- **Stockings:** Bare legs don't look finished unless you're wearing strappy sandals. Avoid patterned stockings. Your mother may want you to wear stockings with reinforced toes, but that's a no-no with open-toed shoes. If you plan to wear open-toed shoes but want the smoothing effect of control-top tights, go with a sheer footless style such as Spanx Power Panties. To avoid panty lines, buy either invisible seams underwear or stockings with built-in underwear.

Dressing Your Tippy-Toes

Don't think that because your dress is long, your shoes are invisible. They aren't. Your feet are actually seen again and again: getting in and out of the car, walking down the aisle, during the first dance. An ill-chosen pair can sabotage your look just as easily as a well-chosen pair can complete it.

You have many options when it comes to bridal footwear, because shoe designers have become keenly interested in the bridal market. Even top couture designers make shoes specifically for brides to wear with wedding dresses.

When shopping, keep these guidelines in mind:

- **Plain skirts call for beautifully detailed shoes.** Try some trimmed with bows, beading, lace or jewelled clip-ons.

- **Ornate shoes with an ornate dress may be overkill.** A subtle embellishment on the heel, toe or *throat* (the opening in the vamp of a shoe at the instep) may be enough.

- **A shoe's fabric doesn't have to match that of the dress.** In fact, mixing textures often looks better. The same goes for colour; a pair of hot pink satin heels can look very sexy peeking out from the hem of a white dress.

- **Comfort is key.** Some brides have different shoes for different parts of the day – a pair to walk down the aisle, a pair for dinner, a pair for dancing and a really comfy pair to go home in. Feet heaven. (If you're feeling generous, you may even supply some flip-flops or ballet shoes on the day for other foot-weary revellers.)

    If you plan to dance all night, try buying professional dance shoes, which are extremely light and flexible. With padded, textured insoles, they're built to perform. Another dancing option is ballet slippers dolled up with bows and *grosgrain* (patterned) ribbon or covered in lace or eyelet fabric.

    For dress shoes, try self-adhesive shoe inserts – they keep the balls of your feet padded and your toes from scrunching forward. Some pads are virtually invisible, even in strappy, open-toed styles.

- **Shoes with back straps must fit perfectly.** Make sure they're neither too tight nor a smidgen too loose. Manoeuvring in your dress may be tricky enough without having to mess with slipping heels or painful straps.

- **Get height while still walking gracefully.** If you want extra height without losing your balance, platforms or wedges are chic.

You can dye an inexpensive pair of shoes in satin or *peau de soie* (a soft silk fabric of satin weave with a dull finish) to match your dress or a subtly coloured underlay of silk on your dress (type 'dyeing my wedding shoes' into your web browser and a number of useful companies will show up). Unfortunately, cheap shoes usually aren't very comfortable. Bring a pair of ballet shoes or a comfortable, yet still lovely, lower-heeled pair of shoes as a backup for the reception – just make sure the dress is short enough to accommodate the difference in height between the two.

To avoid a wedding-day tumble, gently roughen up the soles of your shoes with sandpaper and, if necessary, a sharp kitchen knife. Also, practice walking and dancing in your wedding shoes (on a clean floor, of course) until you feel completely comfortable in them.

Getting a Heads-Up on Headwear

In ancient Rome, brides appeared enveloped in a saffron-coloured haze that symbolised the flame of Vesta, the goddess of home and the provider of life. Today, putting on a headpiece and veil completes the transformation from your daily persona to (hear the cymbals?) your alter ego: THE BRIDE!

Comparing types of veil

The veil is definitely on something of a comeback and brides are starting to move away from the recent trends in headpieces (tiaras, jewelled hairclips and so on). Some designers and celebrities are now championing its return and it can look very elegant on the right bride.

For most brides today, the veil functions more as a fashion accessory than a religious necessity. Among your options for veils are:

- **Angel:** This veil may be any length, but the cut is the distinctive part. It comes to a gentle point in the back from wide sides, giving the look of angels' wings.

- **Ballerina:** Ends at the ankles. Also called *waltz*.

- **Birdcage:** Falls to just below the chin, covering the face. Often worn attached to a small hat or fascinator.

- **Blusher:** A short, single-layer veil that covers the bride's face as she enters the ceremony, and then she pushes it back over her head. Usually worn layered over a longer back veil.

- **Cathedral:** Falls 10 feet (3 metres) from the headpiece.

- **Chapel:** Approximately 3 feet (1 metre) shorter than a cathedral veil. Often worn with a sweep train to give the illusion of a longer train.

- **Circular:** Can be any length and attaches to the head with a flat comb just to keep it in place. If worn long, it creates a very ethereal look with the bride swathed in a pouf of tulle.

- **Elbow:** A veil that goes to your elbows.

- **Fingertip:** The veil touches the tips of your fingers, a length that often works with ball gowns and is therefore one of the most popular veils in the UK. This is the veil famously worn by the Duchess of Cambridge at her wedding.

- **Flyaway or two tiered:** A multilayered veil that just touches your shoulders. Sometimes called a *Madonna* veil.

- **Juliet cap:** Making a comeback from the '50s, you wear the cap on the crown and the veil comes to about elbow length. Think Grace Kelly.

- **Mantilla:** A long, Spanish-style, circular piece of lace that frames the face. It usually isn't worn with a headpiece, but rather is draped over a comb. The fabric is either lace or lace-edged tulle. Sew clear plastic snaps on both your mantilla and the shoulders of your dress to keep the fabric draped gracefully.

- **Pouf:** A short, gathered piece of veiling that fastens to a headpiece or comb at the top of the head to add height to the veil.

Some etiquette sticklers consider veils, particularly blushers, inappropriate for second-time or pregnant brides. Some brides, on the other hand, object to a veil's other connotation: the handing over of the woman to a man. Besides, they want to see where they're going. If you have stage fright, a veil can certainly help to calm your nerves. Either way, unless religious considerations are in order, these days it's your call.

Take a few tips to heart when veil shopping, and you'll be sure to find a look you love:

- **If your dress is ornate, wear a plain veil.** A simple dress, however, can take either a plain or ornate veil.

- **Any ornamentation on the veil should start below where your dress ornamentation ends.** Decoration (such as flowers or crystals) on a cathedral veil, for example, should cover only the bottom third.

- **Opt for crystals in lieu of rhinestones.** Crystals reflect light and usually photograph better than rhinestones, which can look like black dots.

- **The adornments on your veil don't need to match those on your dress.** All the elements, such as seed pearls, sequins or other adornments, should merely complement each other.

- **A ribbon trim may not be your best bet.** Ribbon trim may look better to you than unfinished tulle, but depending on the length of your veil, a ribbon can create a horizontal line across your middle, effectively stopping the eye and making you look shorter. We suggest considering trim only for veils that fall above or below your waist.

A poufy veil or headpiece doesn't necessarily make you look taller. In fact, if you're short, a voluminous veil can make you look like a mushroom. Many women opt for narrow-cut veils, which create a vertical line. Remember, your head isn't flat. (At least we hope not.) Examine a veil from all angles and, if possible, try it on with your dress. A veil that suits you from the back may not flatter your face, or vice versa.

Make sure the veil matches your hair – a big hairdo, for example, looks best with a veil that attaches at the back of your scalp. Generally speaking, the headpiece should align with your ears, as with a headband, for the most flattering look.

If you're lucky enough to have lace from your mother and/or grandmother's wedding dress, you can use it to create a veil. Avoid making the mistake of trying to dye an antique veil, however. Its appeal lies in its uniqueness, so it shouldn't match the dress exactly.

Hats, headpieces, crowns and trinkets

Although your fantasy may be to look 'bridal' by wearing your veil during the reception, it may not be the best idea for photos, particularly profiles where the pouf of the veil obscures your face. Many brides opt for the best of both worlds – detachable veils that they can remove after the ceremony, leaving a headpiece to maintain the bridal aura.

A *headpiece*, another of those great wedding-speak terms, is what a bride wears on her head. Worn either alone or as an anchor for the veil(s), it's an integral part of the ensemble.

The key to finding the headpiece that works best with your hair style, veil and dress is to try on many variations of the basic styles, which include:

- **Cloche:** A small, helmet-like cap, usually with a deep rounded crown and narrow brim. You can have netting attached to create a pouf, a cloud or an eye veil. It's slightly more substantial than a fascinator.

- **Hair jewellery:** Often used in lieu of a classic headpiece; many types of hair clips/clasps, jewelled hair (or bobby) pins and brooches, and wired crystals are available. These look lovely embellishing an updo or keeping hair away from the face, particularly after the ceremony when you remove the veil.

- **Hat:** Can be in any variety of styles and sizes – large-brimmed hats trimmed with lace, flowers and/or pearls; pillboxes; or wispy little cocktail concoctions.

- ✔ **Headband:** Come in various widths that follow the shape of the skull and are decorated with fabric, seed pearls and flowers. They can serve as the base for saucer-styled tulle instead of a veil.

- ✔ **Juliet cap:** Often made of elaborately decorated mesh. A larger version is called a *skullcap*. This may also have a veil attached (see the preceding section, which looks at veils).

- ✔ **Nefertiti headdress:** An African headpiece; the bride wraps ethnic fabric around her head.

- ✔ **Profile:** A comb decorated with sprays, pearls or sequins and worn on one side of the head or at the nape of the neck.

- ✔ **Tiara:** The key accessory for playing queen for a day. Extremely popular of late. In Eastern Orthodox and Byzantine Catholic ceremonies, the most solemn moment is the crowning of the bride and groom, when metal crowns or floral wreaths are held over their heads. This part of the ceremony symbolises that they're king and queen of a heavenly kingdom on earth.

- ✔ **Wreaths, garlands and circlets:** Composed of flowers, twigs and/or ribbon. The maker needs your exact cranium measurement. A romantic, organic look with a couple of drawbacks: by the end of the day, a flower wreath can feel like the world's heaviest doughnut on your head, and in photographs, twig wreaths can make you look like you've sprouted antennae.

When shopping for a headpiece, imagine a picture frame extending from the neckline of your dress to several inches above your head. A big, elaborate headpiece on top of a big, elaborate hairdo may look like you're modelling the wedding cake. Less, in this case, can be very much more.

Resist if a salesperson pushes you to purchase the veil and/or headpiece at the same time you purchase your dress. You should have time to do this after your dress comes in. You'll be much happier choosing the veil and headpiece based on how you want to wear your hair, rather than trying to design a hairstyle that accommodates a headpiece you chose in a frenzy.

From Hair to Eternity

Your hairstyle should complete the image of yourself that you've been creating for your wedding. If your dress is very formal and romantic, you may want an elaborate updo, but brides wearing a sexy sheath opt for something sleeker and edgier.

When deciding on a style, take into consideration how it looks from all sides (particularly how it looks with the back of your dress), because you'll be photographed from many angles, not just head on.

To get a look that's perfectly suited for you, make an appointment with a trusted hair salon for a run-through and get the stylist's opinion on how you should wear your hair and what sort of headpiece would best accommodate that style. Experiment with some possibilities and take a photo to help you when you shop for a headpiece. Perhaps you'll decide on two slightly different hairdos – one for the ceremony and another for the reception. You may take some of your hair down for a modified updo after the ceremony, or you may add hair jewels or fresh flowers after you remove your veil.

If you have fine hair and plan on wearing it in a *chignon* (a knot at the back of the neck), you may want to wash your hair the day before the wedding, rather than the day of, to give it more oomph. Otherwise, your sleek knot may slip out.

The fact of the matter is that brides wilt, even in subzero temperatures. Start the day with your hair a little higher, wider and more done than you're accustomed to. By the time you get to the reception, you'll be lucky if it looks teased at all. But remember that people are less interested in seeing your new cutting-edge hairdo than your face.

Insist on smelling and feeling anything that's put in your hair. You don't want products that clash with your perfume or stick to anyone's face while you're dancing.

Remember that the wonders of modern hairdressing mean you can do more with less. Your classic pageboy cut is fine for business, but your wedding vision features you with flowing tresses that rival Rapunzel's. So if you don't have time (or patience) to grow your locks, fake it. Many salons specialise in temporary, clip-on hair extensions, often made with real hair and dyed to match your hair colour, that can also give subtle extra fullness to an updo.

Keep in mind hair elsewhere on your body than your head. If your dress is sleeveless and you have dark hair on your arms, you may consider waxing, which many women find more satisfactory than depilatories or shaving. Although the process doesn't tickle, it's not torture either. Many salons offer cold waxing, which is less painful than the traditional wax. Other areas that may benefit from a treatment are your underarms, legs, bikini line, upper lip and eyebrows (make sure you use a trusted person or salon for this or have a run-through with someone a few months before the day – you want to ensure you're happy and confident on your day).

Making Your Face Wedding Proof

Although you want to look special on your wedding day, deviating too much from your routine is asking for trouble. Your groom wants to vaguely recognise the person walking towards him down the aisle.

If you want a slightly different look, rehearse your make-up as you would the ceremony, but do so well in advance, not the day before. Your wedding day isn't the time to try out anything new such as contact lenses, acrylic nail tips or perfumes. Because of the healing time required, schedule procedures such as chemical peels at least two months before your wedding, and facials, fake tans and vigorous loofah scrubs least a week before. Unless you want to look in your photos like you just stepped out of Madame Tussauds, avoid trendy make-up techniques such as heavy black eyeliner or white lipstick. Stick with timeless, neutral colours, but be careful about using colours that are too subtle because you may look washed out. A run-through with a make-up artist, preferably on the same day as your hair run-through, helps you make your final decision.

We asked several top make-up artists for their tips in putting your best wedding-day face forward. Their advice:

- **Blemishes:** If you get a blemish right before the wedding, try to get a last-minute facial appointment at a reputable salon. If one isn't available, paint the area with concealer by using a thin eyeliner brush before applying foundation. We know your mother told you this, but it bears repeating: attempting to pick or squeeze the problem away only makes it worse! A number of 24-hour serums may also help.

- **Brushes:** A good set of make-up brushes is the number-one tool for achieving wonderful results when applying make-up.

- **Cheeks:** For the blushing bride look, use rosy hues and blend well. If the wedding is in the evening, you can use darker shades of contouring blush to get the sculpted-cheekbone look.

- **Eyes:** To make the whites of your eyes crystal clear, use white or blue pencil on the inner rim of the lower lid. (If your eyes are sensitive, however, they may try to flush out the liner, making for unsightly globs in your tear ducts.) Greys, taupes and smoky colours, as well as charcoal liners on the eyelids, usually photograph well.

- **Face:** Use a primer on your entire face to provide an especially smooth skin surface and stabilise your base foundation. Many major brands now have great primers, but try them well before the big day to ensure they suit you. Blend well for a minimum make-up look. Use feather strokes towards the bottom of the face to avoid showing a line along your jaw.

- **Lips:** Use a lip liner and lip sealer so colour doesn't bleed, cake or peel. Red lipstick works best for dark skin and olive complexions. Otherwise, unless it's your signature look, use soft pastels. Matte lipsticks last longer than glossy ones, and you can now buy some excellent lip stains that don't come off when you take your first sip of champagne. To apply, either use a silicone-based lipstick or apply your normal lipstick, blot it thoroughly and colour over your lips with a pencil. *Warning:* Lip gloss is a magnet for hair, veils, gnats and other people. Save it for after the ceremony and before photographs.

- **Skin tone:** To get an even skin tone all over your body, avoid tanning beds, sunless tanning lotions (which can turn your skin, eyebrows and hair orange) and body make-up. For problem spots – scars, brown spots, discolourations – enquire at a good make-up counter about waterproof camouflage creams. (Or even better, try airbrushing.) If you tend to get blotchy or break out in hives, use an antihistamine cream on the affected area.

For the closest thing to permanent perfection, try *airbrushing*, an amazing technique that until recently was used only for theatrical special effects or cover girls. A trained professional sprays the makeup on in a very fine coat, and it dries almost immediately on contact. No brush marks or imperfections to deal with, only excellent colour and coverage. Having this done is a bit pricey, but the result is a sheer finish that miraculously minimises pores and stays on until you wash it off. You can use airbrushing to cover scars, tattoos and freckles, apply nail varnish and provide an all-over, even tan. (The latter isn't for the modest because the technician essentially paints every part of you.) Look for a salon or studio that offers airbrushing near you.

Accessorising: The Finishing Touches

After devoting so much time and energy to getting your dress and headgear under control, accessories may seem like an afterthought, but they shouldn't look like it. Try different combinations of jewellery and/or gloves until you get the right balance.

Covering up

Getting to and from the ceremony may require protection from the elements. Your woolly winter coat simply won't do, nor will your best white jumper. Some options to consider co-ordinating with your dress:

- **Bolero:** A cropped jacket, ending at or above the waistline. Can match the dress to give a tailored look or be beaded to enhance the dress. Works well with long, draped skirts.

- ✔ **Capes and cloaks:** A dramatic statement in either a complementary shade of white or, for real flare, an intense shade of red.

- ✔ **Muffs:** The Dr Zhivago look is perfect for winter weddings, especially in a vibrant colour in faux fur.

- ✔ **Shawls:** In matching or contrasting fabric or colour; something simple to drape over your shoulders. Worn threaded through arms and tied in the back, leaving long streamers to look more glam than granny. Lace, chiffon, raw silk or appliquéd velvet may be sheer enough to wear over your dress at the ceremony and heavy enough to wear as a cover-up in early spring or autumn.

- ✔ **Shrug:** Basically, two sleeves that meet in the back and cover the very top of the shoulders. (Refer to Figure 11-1A.)

Going for hand-some gloves

If you feel perplexed when you look in the mirror, like something is missing, the right pair of gloves may do the trick. Generally, you wear over-the-elbow (*opera*) gloves with strapless or sleeveless dresses, short gloves (considered less formal) with either short-sleeved or long-sleeved dresses, and elbow-length gloves with cap-sleeved dresses. The style, fabric and texture should complement the dress. Kid leather is considered the dressiest, but satin spandex, crushed velvet and sheer organza can look ultra-elegant. The fabric should be matte; shiny looks chintzy and brings undue attention to your hands and arms. Gloves can also have jewelled cuffs or iridescent sequins, tiny pearls or beads down the length of the arm.

Glove lengths are expressed by the number of buttons they have (or would have). A one-button glove is wrist length. Two-, four-, six- and eight-button gloves all end between the wrist and elbow. The longest is a 16-button glove, which ends above the elbow. In addition to knowing the glove length, you must know your glove size, which generally corresponds to your dress size. Stretchy gloves come in small, medium and large sizes.

Somehow, your ring finger needs to be exposed during the ceremony. Although you have various ways to manoeuvre gloves at the altar (a slit at the ring finger or at the wrist), these are usually clumsy and distracting. Your best option is to remove the gloves altogether. This procedure should look like neither a strip tease nor a tug-of-war. Practice removing your gloves before the ceremony by gently tugging on each left-hand finger and sliding the glove off, right side out. (If you remove only one glove, you'll want to put it back on before the recessional). Hand the gloves to your maid of honour when you hand her your bouquet – she'll return the gloves to you after the recessional. And when you eat, daintily remove your gloves. You don't want to turn them into five-fingered napkins.

Gloves or no gloves, get your nails in tiptop shape. Get regular manicures (and pedicures) for several weeks before the wedding. On your wedding day, consider springing for a manicurist to make a house call. Painting your nails the night before can result in *sheet prints* (marks on the nails from your bed sheets) and gives you all the more time to mar the lacquer.

Selecting your jewellery

Opinions about jewellery are as varied as wedding dresses themselves. An off-the-shoulder dress may look best with no embellishment around your neck and only some *wow* earrings. Pearls are the bridal favourite, and it may be touching to wear your mother's, but unless they're the perfect length for the neckline of your dress, they may take away from, not add to, the effect.

Many brides are now choosing to wear funkier jewellery than in the past. Beautiful faux jewel earrings or a chunky necklace may set off a dress perfectly, particularly in white gold or silver. Proportion is the key. Bracelets are overkill with gloves and not only may detract from your hands but also may catch on a tulle dress or veil, so put them on last and carefully.

Notice when you're perusing dress ads that a vast majority of dress designers show their dresses without any necklaces and with dainty earrings. They do that for a reason: with rare exceptions, brides look most beautiful with a clean line from the bodice up to the headpiece, emphasising their radiant faces.

Bagging it

When it comes to bags, the best advice is to get a good night's sleep – oops, wrong page! Seriously, even if you normally need a tractor-trailer to transport your daily necessities, the exquisite handbag that accompanies your attire can accommodate only a minimum of survival tools – lipstick, powder, breath mints, mascara, handkerchief. Stow bigger, bulkier items (hairbrushes, hairspray, hair dryers) in the bathroom or your dressing room.

This miniature bag doesn't make the trip with you down the aisle. In fact, you don't wear it at all. Arrange for someone to hang on to it during the ceremony and leave it on your seat at the reception.

Getting into the Dress

Getting dressed on your wedding day is a two-person job. Check on the cost of hiring an alterations person from your dress shop to assist you in getting dressed if you're really worried about it. This may sound ridiculous but, believe us, they can be very helpful both in getting the dress ready (if last-minute steaming or minor alterations are necessary) and in cinching up a complicated bustle after the ceremony.

Another life-saving tip (albeit a tad indelicate): visit the loo before you get into your dress (for reasons that should be obvious).

Now you're ready to get dressed.

1. **Unzip the dress all the way down.**

2. **If you have a separate petticoat, put it into the dress.**

   Make sure the waists match up.

3. **Have your designated lady-in-waiting hold up the dress for you with the bodice falling forward.**

   Put your hands on your waist, arms akimbo, and step into your dress instead of pulling it over your head. If you must do the latter, cover your head with a head netting or a silk scarf so your make-up doesn't ruin your dress or vice versa.

4. **Fasten any buttons, zip up any zips and so on.**

   To pull the loops over a parade of covered buttons marching from neck to hip, a crochet hook may seem like the eighth wonder of the world as you try to get dressed in less than three hours.

5. **Put on your headpiece.**

6. **Sit on a backless stool to finish your make-up with the dress fluffed out around, not under, you.**

Caring for Your Dress After the Party

After all you spent in terms of time, money and emotional reserve, it doesn't seem fair that you get to wear your wedding dress for only one day. Whether you decide to recycle your dress or store it in your wardrobe, the first step is to have it professionally cleaned, and then you can consider whether to keep it or pass it on.

Preserving for posterity

While you're away on your honeymoon, have someone take your dress to the cleaners and point out all the spots, such as mud stains at the bottom, needing special treatment. Some people suggest waiting a week because some stains, such as champagne, don't show up for a few days. Use a cleaner that specialises in wedding dresses and make sure the cleaner uses clean fluid and does each dress individually.

Specify how you want the dress packed and inspect it when you get it back. The dress should be wrapped in acid-free tissue and stored in an acid-free box that isn't airtight because natural fibres need to breathe. If the box has a window, it should be acetate (which is acid free), not plastic. Store the headpiece separately; metal parts can rust or turn a dress brown. You may store both the dress and veil without a box in a clean, white muslin sheet in a dry, dark place. *Warning:* A basement may be too damp and an attic too hot. Wherever you store the dress, check it every year in case stains such as mildew start to develop.

Cleaning and preserving your wedding dress can be very expensive (often several hundred pounds), so get an estimate based on the condition and material of your dress before you leave it with the cleaner.

Recouping your investment

If spending a lot of money on a dress you wear only once makes you crazy, consider getting a bit more mileage out of the dress by recycling it. You can do this in one of several ways:

- ✔ **Restyle:** Take your dress to a good tailor and have it reconfigured into a ball dress for you or a christening or party dress for a child.

- ✔ **Sell:** Put the dress up for sale at a consignment shop. You may find one that specialises in wedding attire or, if you have a creation by Vera Wang, for example, designer apparel. Another option is to sell it yourself on an auction site, which does a brisk business in bridal paraphernalia (see Chapter 2 for more auction site details).

- ✔ **Donate:** Find a charity shop in your area that's clean and well run (it's heartbreaking to see wedding dresses dumped in a pile in some smelly shop). Better yet, seek out an organisation that caters to brides or other needy formalwear clients.

Transporting the dress

One of the hairiest feats of planning a faraway wedding is getting your wedding dress from A to B with a minimum of wrinkles (to either you or it) or other damage, especially if you have a poufy ball gown the size of Wales that can stand up by itself. After the final fitting, have the shop pack it in acid-free tissue paper – lots of it – and a special hanging bag. If you're flying, try to take an off-peak flight when you have a better chance of getting an empty seat for your companion. Most airlines charge you, but others may give you a break because you're a bride.

Another option is to pack the garment bag in reams of bubble wrap in a large box and have it couriered to your wedding destination. We don't suggest that you check the dress with your baggage. Ditto with your headpiece and veil(s) – despite its airiness, tulle can actually crease, so don't scrunch it into a suitcase. To be totally safe, bring a portable steamer or find out whether the hotel has one. Even better, try to find a professional cleaner or tailor who can steam your dress – as you watch. Never, ever let anyone with an iron near your dress unless you've ordered the special asbestos model. Also, if your dress is heavy, avoid hanging it for more than a day or two; the weight may stretch it out. Pack other clothes in plastic dry-cleaning bags, leaving them on the hangers.

Chapter 12

Attending to the Bridal Party

The wedding starts in one hour. As the bride struggles into her dress, she puts the heel of her shoe through the lace overlay and topples over. Lying there helplessly in a heap, she gazes up to see two sour-faced women with their arms crossed glaring at each other. 'When is someone coming to do my hair?' one of them wails. 'Well,' the other fumes, 'if Daisy would get out of the bathroom I could at least pluck my eyebrows.' The bride looks about for her maid of honour to act as referee. She's glued to the mirror in a fit of self-loathing. 'I want to burn this dress,' she snarls.

Across town in his apartment, the groom and his best man pace, looking at their watches. The doorbell rings; one of the ushers has arrived. 'Sorry about the suit, man,' he mutters as he sees the groom's eyes cross. 'It looked really cool at the shop.' As the other gentlemen arrive, one later than the next, a somewhat pathetic display of men's formal fashion parades across the living room. The best man is bewildered – he had, after all, painstakingly briefed the group on the proper uniform. Is this a case of subliminal sabotage or mere apathy?

The key, as always, is proper preparation – making sure that everyone knows what their duties are and what is expected of them and involving your attendants in the wedding process by taking them shopping and dressing them according to their shape and colouring. To that end, through this chapter we guide you through what to expect of your attendants and how to make them – and the groom – look gorgeous in your wedding photos!

Choosing Your Entourage

They may be your siblings or cousins or best friends, but that doesn't automatically qualify them for wedding duty. To prevent major tantrums, screen your attendants with care and, after you choose them, brief them clearly on your expectations.

When it comes to those who you want to honour in some way, but not as an attendant, be thoughtful. Asking someone to deliver a poem, sing a song or be a witness is truly an honour. But asking someone to hold the guest book, hand out escort cards, double-check the seating chart or some other plum assignment feels like busy work.

Traditionally at weddings, you see one usher for every 50 guests. (Having a wedding planner present on the day means that you can get away with fewer ushers, as the planner invariably manages some of their duties.) It can be nice to mirror the number of ushers you have with the number of bridesmaids, which looks symmetrical in photographs, but unless you're choreographing your wedding to look like a West End musical, you don't need a cast of thousands fanning out from the altar. Many people have trouble narrowing down the field, feeling that if they ask one friend, they must ask another, and so on. Don't feel that because you were an usher or a bridesmaid at someone's wedding ten years ago, you need to reciprocate the honour. People understand that relationships change. In a seemingly impossible dilemma, here are some possible solutions: ask only family to form part of the wedding party or choose only children.

As you decide how many and what kind of attendants to have in your wedding party, think through what you expect them to do. (To figure out where they all go in the processional, see Chapter 16.) Ideally, attendants perform duties to get the wedding off the ground and keep *you* grounded.

Maid to order

Remember that not every married woman loves the connotations of the word *matron*. Many brides have dubbed their honour attendants 'best woman' or 'best person'. Which brings us to another point: the person who stands up for you doesn't have to be the same sex as you. If you're a bride whose best friend is a guy, make him your best person. Likewise, if you're a groom whose best friend is a woman, appoint her to the job.

✔ **Maid (or matron, if married) of honour:** Head cheerleader, sounding board, therapist, saint, gofer (on occasion) and actress, pretending to care about the marital minutiae as much as the bride does. May serve as a fashion consultant for the bride's and attendants' outfits and as the school mistress, keeping other attendants in line. Sees to it that the bride is properly corseted, zipped, buttoned, powdered and primped on her wedding day. May throw a wedding shower (see Chapter 13) and/or dream up a special group gift for the bride (in addition to her own gift to the couple). May also spearhead the hen party.

✔ **Best man:** A master at strong yet subtle emotional support because most men aren't skilled at asking for it. Telepathy is a good quality. So is punctuality: if the groom arrives late with a crooked tie, the best man takes the heat. Arranges the stag night/weekend. (Also buys his own gift for the couple.) Oversees the ushers, making sure they're appropriately dressed as per the groom (and most probably the bride) instructions. Holds the bride's ring at the ceremony. Quietly slips the church, organist and/or choir fee into the vicar's hand after the ceremony. Keeps the marriage licence safe. Makes a stirring toast at the reception.

✔ **Bridesmaid:** Is the epitome of charm at the wedding and pre-wedding events. May collaborate with the maid of honour and other bridesmaids in planning a hen night/weekend. May not apply lipstick at the altar. In theory, is on call for anything the bride needs, particularly in the realm of emotional support. In reality, may be too far out of the loop to be effective.

✔ **Usher:** Acts jovial and comedic but not raunchy at the stag party. Takes ushering duties seriously enough to refrain from downing scotches until after the photographs. Possesses a photographic memory, able to match names, or at least ceremony seat assignments, with people he's met only once before. A human compass, escorting guests to their seats and directing them to car parks, bathrooms, dining rooms and so on. A good ratio is one usher per fifty guests.

Ushers arrive 45 minutes before the ceremony, assist in seating guests and handing out order of services (and, if you like, tissues for guests who feel they may get emotional, and fans if the weather is hot). Each usher is assigned a particular duty and ushers are the last to sit down before the bride arrives (so ask an usher to escort the mother of the bride down the aisle when she arrives right before the ceremony).

✔ **Flower girl:** Looks adorable. Old enough to make it to the end of the aisle without Mummy or Daddy on their knees pleading in a stage whisper for her to keep moving. Chosen because the couple is inordinately fond of her and/or her parents, not because she looks like a Laura Ashley model. Scatters petals or carries a basket, or wreath (see Chapter 6 for floral details). Smiles sweetly all the way.

✔ **Ring bearer:** Traditionally goes to an adorable young boy (although some couples have trained their pet dog to undertake this role!). Like the flower girl, must look precious but be mature enough to complete his journey down the aisle without bursting into tears or taking a detour mid-procession. Carries a pillow with rings (usually fake) tied on. Looks adorable wearing a mini version of the usher suits including waistcoat, tie and buttonhole.

✔ **Junior bridesmaids and ushers:** The default category for youngsters (meaning anywhere between 7 and 15) who are no longer cute enough to serve as flower girls and ring bearers but not yet grown-up enough to be fully fledged attendants. Like their adult counterparts, they walk down the aisle and act charming. However, girls wear dresses that are similar to but less sophisticated than those of older bridesmaids, and boys wear suits.

Just as the attendants exist to make your life easier, you must behave with all the grace and magnanimity towards them that you can muster during this anxious time. In the same way you and your intended wisely chose each other for your wondrous points and in spite of the downsides, don't choose your attendants thinking you can change them. Remember that they're not indentured servants or workers for hire who can be dismissed because they fail to love (or look stunning in) the baby-pink chiffon dress or traditional Scottish kilt you've picked out for them. Compromising on the attendant's outfit is just one example of a gracious pre-wedding manner.

Next Stop: Wardrobe

The wedding clone concept dates back to fifth-century Britain, when bridesmaids and ushers, exhibiting amazing loyalty, dressed identically to the bride and groom to fool evil spirits that may harass the happy couple on their way to be joined. (Evil spirits being rather near-sighted, apparently.) Somehow, over 17 centuries, the original concept has become a little mixed up. Female attendants now dress to look like each other (yet not enough like the bride to fool even the dimmest evil spirit), and the male attendants dress to approximate the groom.

Choosing bridesmaid dresses to please all

When selecting a colour for the bridesmaids' dresses, think carefully about skin tone and hair colour. Just because the wedding theme has pastel colours doesn't mean those colours look good on your bridesmaids. Generally speaking, brighter colours suit most complexions whereas pastel hues suit fair complexions. If your bridesmaids have an array of skin tones then select tones of colours that suit them and the wedding design.

'I thought you were paying for this?'

When you ask people to be in your wedding, they're often flattered and honoured – until they find out what it's costing them. Admittedly, some tours of duty are more expensive than others, so either be sensitive about asking those who can't afford to be an attendant or be prepared to defray (or pick up entirely) the cost for them. Whatever you decide, the time to explain the expenses and who's responsible for them is when you do the asking. The items that most often produce misunderstandings are:

✔ **Appropriate clothing:** Traditionally, you're responsible for buying their clothes, and sometimes you may buy a particular item as a gift, such as earrings for the bridesmaids or cufflinks for the ushers.

✔ **Bridesmaids' hair and make-up:** Clarify whether attendants are responsible for getting and/or paying for their own hair and make-up. If you do pay for any of it, set parameters so you don't end up paying for manicures, applying false eyelashes or other extra-charge items.

✔ **Long-distance transportation:** Out-of-town weddings may require a serious financial investment by guests, but at least guests have the option of simply not attending. If your wedding party, however, is expected to pay for plane fares on top of all their other expenses, make sure that your relationship and their wallets can take it.

✔ **Local transportation:** You should provide transportation for attendants to the ceremony (and reception, if it's not in the same venue). If, as is common, bridesmaids have got dressed in what will later be the honeymoon suite, they need to take their things with them when they leave for the reception. As for ushers, they usually don't get dressed all in the same place, so they get themselves to the ceremony site. If you want them to be at a certain place, for photographs either before or after the ceremony, consider transporting them en masse. After the reception, transporting attendants to where they're staying isn't necessarily your responsibility, because often they neither leave at the same time nor are bound for the same destination.

Of course, finding a dress shape that looks good on several different women is another issue. Even if you manage to pull this one off, you can be sure not all the women will be convinced that they look terrific. The effort you devote to this search depends on how desperately you want your attendants to look like a bridal *party*. Consider, more importantly, who these women are. If your friends are your friends because they're individualists, don't try to turn them into a matched set of septuplets. They'll feel uncomfortable and look it. Many bridesmaids' dresses now come in various styles of the same colour and fabric so that your attendants may choose between a few of these styles and still look like a bridal party. If you simply must have them all in the same dress, keep it simple and choose a style that flatters the largest size among them. (See Figure 12-1 for silhouette ideas.)

v-neck   high neck   strapless

Bridesmaid Dresses

Figure 12-1:
Tweak a simple silhouette to suit the various shapes of your bridesmaids.

If one of your dear friends is expecting, she can still be a bridesmaid. Just take her dress-hunting first, because she'll be the hardest to fit. Go for softer, flowing materials that glide over – and can be let out to accommodate – an expanding tummy. And skip the stiletto sandals. Opt instead for a thick heel with plenty of support, or wedges.

Outfitting the guys

The groom and his attendants are as much a part of this set piece as the bride and hers. Both the groom and his ushers should look and feel the epitome of debonair. A heavy wool morning suit for a mid-afternoon garden wedding in August doesn't make a guy feel as crisp and confident as a light lounge suit. This insight is common sense, but it's easy to get flummoxed in figuring out what *is* appropriate and stylish. We suggest you choose something that makes the men feel comfortable, dashing, sexy and in command.

Nonetheless, ushers should be either smartly dressed to match each other or purposely diverse. You especially don't want three ushers who have the same suit, tie and waistcoat but one with a different tie. The poor guy will look like the casting department made a dreadful mistake. If budget is an issue, simply ask ushers to wear their best dark suit and then provide them with matching ties, handkerchiefs and socks (that may sound bizarre, but lines of funky socks look fabulous in your usher photos).

Suits and tuxedos

When it comes to suits, the fit is key. Guys, place your arms at your sides, fingers extended. The hem of the jacket should be no longer than your thumb knuckle and should cover your derriere. The sleeve should grace the top of your hand, and your shirt cuff should peek out from the jacket sleeve no more than half an inch. Your trousers should skim the heel of your shoe in back and break slightly over the tops of your shoes in front. Because the extra buttons on a double-breasted jacket draw the eye toward your midsection, that style looks best on someone who's tall and slender. To create a more elegant silhouette, consider having some extra padding put in the shoulders and the waist taken in a bit.

The options include

- **Dinner suit:** In classic white or ivory or a subtle pattern of the same, with peaked lapels or shawl collar. Works well in summer months or in warm climates, and is considered an appropriate substitute for a standard tuxedo. Looks particularly smart with formal black trousers with a side satin stripe – think Humphrey Bogart in *Casablanca*. You may wear a white dinner jacket even if your ushers are in black tuxedo jackets.

- **Formal suit:** Among the most popular suits for weddings, a three-piece versatile suit in navy, beige, charcoal or pale grey for the summer months. Worn with a tie or cravat. Many men choose to have a suit made for them that they can wear again in the future.

- **Lounge suit:** Smart jacket and trousers but each using different fabrics. Ideal for weddings with a more informal feel to the proceedings.

- **Morning coat:** In its traditional design, this coat is for the most formal morning weddings. A novel experience in dressing up for men used to wearing jeans and T-shirts. Coats are black or grey with a single button at the waist and one broad tail at the back. Worn with a winged-collared dress shirt, cravat, and grey or black trousers. Can be made a bit less formal with a tie in lieu of the cravat.

- **Tails:** A jacket that's short in front with two longer tails hanging in the back. Worn with braces and a white formal shirt, waistcoat and bow tie (as in 'white tie and tails'). Very formal.

- **Traditional tuxedo or black tie:** More popular in the US and usually more suitable for later-in-the-day weddings. A black or grey jacket with a single button is classic, but navy has been making a big impact in recent years. Has shawl, peak or notched lapels (two of which are featured in Figure 12-2). Worn with matching flat-front (or one-pleat) trousers, bow tie (no clip-ons or glitzy colours) and braces, waistcoat or cummerbund. For some of the elegance of tails without the full grandeur, you can wear a tux with a white waistcoat and white tie.

Tuxedo Junction

Notch Lapel   Shawl Collar

or

Figure 12-2:
Tuxedos
come in
several
styles and
are easily
updated
with dif-
ferent
accessories.

Note: Wear either a cummerbund or waistcoat,
but never both!

Tip: Waistcoats look 'HOT' with suits too!

Check the lapel

One of the most important aspects of a jacket's cut is the lapel, especially with a buttonhole pinned to it. Here are the main choices:

✓ **Notch lapel:** This jacket lapel boasts V-shaped cuts pointing inward where the collar and lapel meet the jacket (as in Figure 12-2). Accentuates the horizontal, so not a good choice if you're on the heavy side.

✓ **Peaked lapel:** A jacket lapel that includes two points of fabric on either side that

project upwards, with narrow spacing between the lapel and collar.

✓ **Shawl collar:** A rounded jacket lapel (as in Figure 12-2) that rolls back in a continuous tapering line. Double-shawl collars roll to reveal satin lining. Looks very elegant trimmed with satin stripe or contrasting piping. A great choice whether you're tall and husky, short and stocky, or generally super-buff and want to create a more vertical line.

Shirts

You probably haven't got this far in life without figuring out what kind of shirts you prefer. But if formalwear is an alien concept to you, you may find that one style of collar (or cuff) doesn't fit all.

- ✔ **Double cuff:** Roll-back shirt cuffs fastened with cufflinks. Spend some time shopping for interesting cufflinks for both you and your ushers. Attention to this detail attests to your impeccable taste.

- ✔ **Mandarin collar:** Flashback to the Nehru jacket of the '60s. High-necked band collar that has become fashionable for both shirts and jackets. A Mandarin collar looks good with high-neck waistcoats. (See Figure 12-3.)

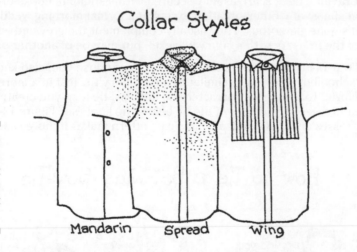

Collar Styles

Mandarin   Spread   Wing

Figure 12-3: Choose a collar that flatters your jacket and you.

- ✔ **Spread collar:** Dressy shirt collar with a high band that sits slightly up on the neck. Also called the English spread, because it was invented by the Duke of Kent.

- ✔ **Winged collar:** Very dressy. Collar band stands up, but the tips fold down. Front panels of a shirt with a winged collar may be pleated. (See Figure 12-3.) Looks best on men with long, slender necks.

Neckwear

What you wear around your neck to accessorise a suit can let your personality shine:

- ✔ **Bow tie:** Worn with tuxedos and dinner jackets. May be the ubiquitous black, but consider wedding-like silver, or an elegant black-on-black damask. Should match the lapels on a tuxedo (satin with satin, grosgrain with grosgrain) and co-ordinate with, but not necessarily be identical to, the cummerbund or waistcoat. Hand-tied looks rather dapper, either bat wing or butterfly style (see Figure 12-4 for instructions on tying the bat wing). Leave shiny materials and garish colours for magicians. Some men simply untie in the evening and leave hanging for a sexy look.

- ✔ **Cravat:** A neck scarf, usually secured with a stickpin. Looks pretentious in almost any other situation except at a formal morning wedding, where it's quite glamorous. They usually complement the grey-and-white stripe of the trousers with a cutaway jacket, but may be of another pattern.

- ✔ **Four-in-hand tie:** A clever term meant to confuse you, also known as the 'schoolboy knot'. Very similar to an ordinary tie, just in a more-formal fabric. To ensure its characteristic fullness, tie it so you create a dimple or crease in the centre of the tie below the knot (see Figure 12-5). Silver dresses up a navy suit; a whimsical pattern makes it more casual.

How to Tie a Bat-Wing Bow-Tie

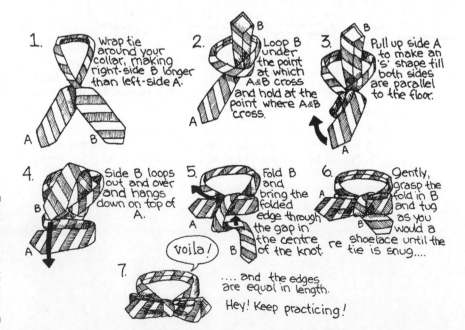

Figure 12-4:
After you learn to tie a bow tie, throw out all your clip-ons.

1. Wrap tie around your collar, making right-side B longer than left-side A.

2. Loop B under the point at which A&B cross and hold at the point where A&B cross.

3. Pull up side A to make an 'S' shape till both sides are parallel to the floor.

4. Side B loops out and over and hangs down on top of A.

5. Fold B and bring the folded edge through the gap in the centre of the knot.

voila!

6. Gently, grasp the fold in B and tug as you would a shoelace until the tie is snug....

7. .... and the edges are equal in length.

Hey! Keep practicing!

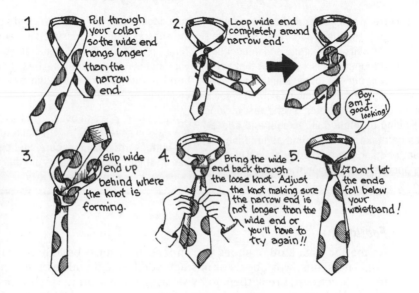

Figure 12-5:
Tying a
four-in-hand
tie comes
naturally
after a little
practice.

Accessories

Even if the ushers all wear different styles of tuxedos, they can create a co-ordinated, unified look through a single accessory in matching or similar fabrications:

- ✔ **Cufflinks:** For those wearing a double-cuff shirt, don't forget some smart cufflinks. Some men buy engraved versions for their wedding party.

- ✔ **Cummerbund:** A satin sash with pleats that face up. (Refer to Figure 12-2.) Worn in lieu of braces or a waistcoat. Should co-ordinate with the bow tie.

- ✔ **Pocket square/handkerchief:** Perfect for continuing a wedding colour theme, matching the shirt or tie and folded in the breast pocket. You can do a number of different folds; whatever you finally decide upon, use your forefinger and thumb to insert into the pocket.

- ✔ **Waistcoat:** A waistcoat that covers the trouser waistband (refer to Figure 12-2), which means you don't need a cummerbund. May match or contrast with the fabric of the jacket. Has become a fashion statement for men's formalwear and is less constricting than a cummerbund. Designers are turning out custom and off-the-rack waistcoats that are as beautiful as tapestries.

  Many couples choose a waistcoat colour that blends with the wedding theme, but the groom's is a different shade altogether so that he stands out among his ushers.

Renting versus buying a tux

Buying a tuxedo or a good suit is a better investment than hiring a cheap suit. Hired suits often look like hired suits, as ill-fitting and uncomfortable as bad toupees. It is a safe bet that you'll get more wear out of a formal suit that you own than you may think. Remember, also, that you'll be looking at these photos for the rest of your life. Finding the right suit, tuxedo, and accessories can take as much time as locating the perfect wedding gown. If you're getting married in a popular wedding month and are planning on hiring for yourself and/or the ushers, reserve the suits as soon as possible so that you don't wind up with the dregs. Because you'll be on your honeymoon, have the best man return hired outfits the first working day after the wedding.

If you do hire, you can usually pick up the suit a few days in advance. Check to make sure that all the buttons are on and secure, and that the tux has no stains, cigarette burns or other extras.

Footwear

No matter what kind of shoes you choose, they must be in excellent condition – no scuffs, worn heels or mismatched laces. If you're buying new shoes for the occasion, break them in by wearing them around the house a few times. And don't forget to take the labels off the soles –otherwise everyone will see them if you're kneeling in church!

Consider slipping on a pair of the following:

- **Socks:** If you buy only one pair of fine-gauge socks in your life, do it for your wedding day. However, do bring a slightly heavier pair as a backup if you plan to do a lot of dancing.
- **Patent shoes:** Low-cut slip-on shoes with a ribbed ribbon bow in front have traditionally gone with very formal attire. Many grooms are choosing to wear the more-comfortable plain-toe patent Oxfords.

Making Mum look good

Traditionally, the bride's mother (hopefully in tandem with the bride) chooses the style and colour of her outfit first and lets the groom's mother know what she's picked. The idea is that the groom's mother then purchases something similar (not identical) in both colour and degree of formality. Neither mother needs to match your attendants – they'll just look like ancient bridesmaids.

If your mother is a tailored, sporty dresser, don't insist on draping her in sequins; if she's a drama queen, let her go for it. Arguing because you have some strict vision of your day that allows for no variations is more trouble than it's worth. Remember, your mother may very well have been obsessing about this day for far longer than you have.

Dapper dads

When the ushers and groom are going suit hunting, think about inviting the fathers so they can be a part of the process. Make sure you costume your father similarly to the ushers. Consider his personal style in the same way you would that of your attendants and mother. Similarly, the groom's father looks best and feels most comfortable if he, too, is dressed in the same manner as the ushers.

Showing Your Appreciation

So, enough about you. What are you going to do for all those selfless souls who've stood by you during the creation of your masterpiece and are now prepared to deliver a flawless performance at the wedding? You need to give them something that's both a memento of the wedding and personally meaningful to them.

Just because you're on a budget doesn't mean that you're stuck giving tie clips and fake pearls. Nor do you have to give each person the same thing. Here are some creative ways to say thank you to your female attendants:

- A charm bracelet with a starter charm chosen for each bridesmaid.
- A chiffon scarf and/or a handbag to match their wedding attire.

For the male attendants, some tried-and-tested gifts include:

- A set of monogrammed glasses, such as tumblers or beer tankards.
- A leather shaving kit for travelling.
- A portable mini-golf set.

You may also consider tokens of appreciation that aren't gender specific:

- A silver picture frame inscribed with the date and your names. After the wedding, send a photo that fits the frame of them walking down the aisle at your ceremony or otherwise enjoying themselves at the reception.
- Antique glass, watches or silver serving pieces with a hand-written card describing the item's provenance and vintage.
- Monogrammed bathrobes.

Search eBay for fun, meaningful – and often inexpensive – mementos, such as souvenir postcards (and frames) of your hometown or wedding location, monogrammed jewellery or utensils, or goofy vintage books that fit each attendant's personality. Such gifts could include pulp-fiction novels, arcane etiquette books, sports biographies and cookbooks.

Thank the little ones in your wedding party with gifts that are appropriate for their ages. Some possibilities are birthstone necklaces, initial key rings and faux-jewelled hair clips. A lovely gesture is to send their parents a framed photo of them during their grand entrance.

Show your parents how much you appreciate their support during the wedding-planning process by presenting them with something they'll enjoy. Theatre tickets, a weekend away or even arranging to have a hamper with a note delivered while you're on your honeymoon are ways to show how grateful you are.

For your beloved

In ancient Danish and Germanic tribes, husbands traditionally presented their new wives with a special piece of jewellery the morning after the wedding night as a symbol of their love. Today, many couples send something to each other just before the wedding, asking a bridesmaid or best man to deliver said gift the morning of the wedding. These gifts needn't be extravagant – in fact, they may be as simple as a handsomely bound edition of love sonnets inscribed with a heartfelt message, a small keepsake box or a watch, perhaps engraved with your wedding date. Popular in recent years are bridal boudoir shoots by the bride. This is the perfect time when brides feel and look their best, and grooms do appreciate this unexpected gift!

Chapter 13

Partying Before and After the Wedding

Brides and grooms can find themselves being honoured at several events, including engagement parties, showers, stag/hen parties and the morning-after brunch. In this chapter, we help you figure out the customs for these occasions and invite you to invent traditions of your own.

Do send a note and a gift thanking anyone who hosts a party for you.

Surprising Your Spouse-to-Be with a Special Proposal

Often the first questions people ask a recently engaged couple are when, where and how they got engaged. You'll be asked those same questions again and again both before and after the wedding, and for the rest of your life. You want to ensure the story is told with utmost positivity – no pressure, right!

The proposal is your chance to express your love. By proposing in a thoughtful and unique way, you show your future spouse you are a romantic at heart.

Knowing the traditions

Traditionally, it is the man that asks his girlfriend to marry him by getting down on one knee and saying 'Will you marry me?'. Sometimes, he may have the engagement ring ready to place on her ring finger (which is on the left hand, next to little finger). Ancient tradition however dictates that women can propose on a leap year, and many women take advantage of this break in tradition. No one is completely clear about where the tradition came from; opinions range from this being a law passed by Queen Margaret of Scotland in 1288 to it being introduced by St Patrick in the fifth century. However, you live in the modern world so if a woman wants to propose to her partner, then we see no reason to wait until a leap year!

Guys, if tradition is important to you, we advise you ask your girlfriend's father his permission to marry her first. Do this in person if possible. Assuming he says yes, brief him on when you hope to propose and ask him to keep the proposal confidential for now.

Preparing for the big day

You wouldn't dream of doing a company presentation without preparing beforehand, and you need to give the same attention to the proposal. Create a plan that includes all the following aspects:

Where to propose

One of the first decisions to make is *where* to propose. Think about whether you plan to take your partner away for the weekend or propose closer to home. One factor in your decision could be whether you do the proposal in private or public. Consider whether your partner would be happy with a public proposal with friends and family or prefer something more private? It's important to ensure your partner is within their comfort zone.

You're trying to create a beautiful memory for years to come, so make sure you know what your partner likes. Have they ever mentioned a place they would like to go? Maybe there is a place you go as a couple: the beach, woods, a restaurant – is this a suitable setting for the proposal?

What to say and do

How will you deliver, 'Will you marry me?'? Be honest about your feelings – why do you want to marry your partner? Don't just say 'you mean so much to me', but go into why you're entrusting your heart into their hands and hoping he or she will do likewise. Use words that are positive and confirm your love. For example, don't say 'I believe we should get married' or 'I think I love you'. If you're not sure, then leave the proposal to a time when you *are* sure.

Here are some ideas for good phrases to use:

- ✔ 'You mean everything to me, and I cannot imagine my life without you in it. I love you so deeply, I want to grow old with you. Please will you marry me?'

- ✔ 'I love watching you go to sleep at night and seeing you wake up in the morning. I love that you laugh at my jokes and cry at sad movies. I love that you look at me as if I'm your knight in shining armour, as if I've already rescued you. I want to grow old with you and raise children together. Please say "yes", please say you'll marry me.'

- ✔ 'When I first saw you at work/the club/on holiday, I was awestruck. I knew we were destined to be together. I was so nervous on our first date but we had such a connection that you put me at ease. Before I met you, I was merely existing in life, you have taught me to live life to its fullest. I look forward to every moment we spend together and can't imagine a life without you in it. I'm hoping you'll consider spending the rest of your life as my husband/wife. Please marry me.'

Immortalise the moment! You can ask a videographer or photographer to record the moment, especially the surprise and hopefully a delighted YES! Or if your budget is tight, ask a trusted friend or family member to record the moment for you, ensuring they are sworn to secrecy.

Five simple ideas

Here are ideas to hopefully inspire you:

- ✔ **Photo proposal:** Arrange a photo shoot. Ask the photographer to take some natural shots that emphasise why you love your boyfriend/girlfriend, perhaps in locations that have meaning to you both. You could either have them enlarged or combine some shots in a small album. Then the last shot could be of you holding a sign saying, 'Will you marry me?'

- ✔ **Treasure hunt:** If there is a remote spot you like to go to, perhaps for country walks or picnics, think about arranging a treasure hunt. Organise a day out in the country with your partner and when you arrive at the location hand your partner an envelope giving a clue as to where he/she goes next. Make sure the instruction has been beautifully printed or written in calligraphy. Keep leaving clues, perhaps some items from home or pictures of you together highlighting your history. The last clue leads your partner to you standing by a picnic rug and a Champagne picnic where you can either hold a sign asking 'will you marry me?' or you can be down on one knee before asking the question.

✔ **Involve friends and family:** They could help you with a mini flash-mob proposal by miming and dancing to a particular song that's meaningful to you both. This can either be in a public place like your local park, or recorded and shown privately, maybe at a family party. Normally, a song would begin playing and people suddenly start singing or dancing. At the end of the surprise performance you would kneel before proposing. Don't forget to rehearse before the actual day, though, and organise a sound system if you plan to play music though an iPod.

✔ **Anagram it:** Arrange a night in with friends and family and ask them to wear plain t-shirts with a letter printed on each. Ask your partner to try to solve the jumbled up anagram until the letters eventually spell out, '*Will you marry me?*'

✔ **Say it with chocolate:** Have candles and petals lining the hallway and leading into the bedroom or garden, where a candlelit dinner for two is waiting. When it's time for dessert, write '*Will you marry me?*' in chocolate sauce around the rim of your partner's dessert plate.

✔ **The silent proposal:** For the man proposing to his girlfriend, this idea lets you be a little sneaky. While your girlfriend is sleeping, slip the ring on to her finger, and in the morning await her shrieks. Then simply kneel and say 'Please say "yes", please marry me'.

✔ **Love Actually:** Re-enact the scene from the film, *Love Actually,* ideally on a cold winter night, by knocking on your partner's door and holding placards which have short personal messages. Some could be the same as in *Love Actually,* like 'to me you are perfect'. To be very realistic, you could even have *Silent Night* playing on your phone or, like the film, via a portable sound system. The last placard should say 'will you marry me?'

✔ **Word search:** Create your own word-search puzzle and ask your partner to solve the clues with you. Keep it love- and marriage-themed. The only letters left at the end should spell out 'will you marry me?'

✔ **The frozen ring:** Freeze the engagement ring in an ice cube and then make her a drink one evening with the ice cube in the glass. This idea works best if the drink in question is a clear one so the ring can be seen as the ice cube melts.

✔ **Glowing:** Either use glow-in-the-dark stickers on the ceiling or glow sticks on the bed to spell out 'will you marry me?'. Turn the lights off for the full effect.

Pop on to YouTube.com and type in 'marriage proposals' or 'flash-mob proposals' and you'll see some amazing past public proposals to inspire you.

Throwing an Engagement Party

An engagement party may be as simple as an at-home dinner with your families followed by a round of toasts. Or it may be a major do, complete with themed entertainment and foods. The most common scenario is a reserved area at a bar or restaurant with drinks and nibbles.

Traditionally, the bride's parents held the engagement party. If that wasn't feasible, the duty fell to the groom's parents. Nowadays, friends of the couple often honour the couple with a shindig, particularly if the couple lives far away from their parents or if complicated family relationships make it awkward for the parents to throw a party. But if you're the type who likes to be in control then there's no reason why you can't organise the engagement party yourself.

Normally, the engagement party would be held within a few months of getting engaged but no later then six months prior to the wedding. Send a simple invitation to guests, even if this is via email.

Although you (or your parents) may announce your engagement in a newspaper, mailing printed engagement announcements may be seen as a 'send gifts' alert, and neither engagements nor engagement parties are occasions for gifts. Writing personal notes or emails or calling friends and relatives you want to inform personally, however, qualifies as a sign of affection.

Everyone who is invited to the engagement party should be invited to the wedding, if the same people are hosting both. (Otherwise, guests may wonder what they did at the first party to keep them from being invited to the wedding.) You can make exceptions in two circumstances: when the engagement party is significantly larger than the wedding, and when friends or relatives who have no control over the wedding guest list host the engagement party. Sometimes, couples may opt to have a large engagement party and invite all their family and friends but keep the wedding itself more intimate. Having a large engagement party gives you the chance to still celebrate with guests perhaps not invited to the smaller wedding.

Engagement party hosts aren't normally expected to provide all the drink at the party although you may want to welcome guests with a drink or put a tab behind the bar. Remember – the engagement party is normally far more relaxed then the wedding, with no formalities or etiquette to follow. The bride and groom or the father of the bride may get up for an impromptu speech but there are no official thank yous like you'd have at the wedding. Presents aren't normally given but, of course, if someone does send you a present be sure to send a thank-you note.

Showering the Bride

Until very recently *bridal showers* – where people come together to give gifts to brides-to-be – were events you read about in American magazines and blogs. (Don't confuse them with the larger hen night or weekend, which we discuss later in this chapter.) However, the past few years has seen a steady if slow increase in UK bridal showers due to the accessibility of American wedding blogs, magazines and even movies like *Bridesmaids*.

The best showers are those that are kept low key and relaxed, and as something hosted by your maid of honour at her house, perhaps. The guest list for the event should be small and include just females in your immediate family and your closest friends, although you may decide to have a family shower one weekend and friends another. Normally, bridal showers are held on an afternoon; think afternoon tea with dainty sandwiches and pastries.

Bridal shower guests normally bring a gift that is fun, rather than the more serious wedding gift. It could be tickets to see a show, a lovers' hamper, scented candles, books on a favourite hobby, a cocktail shaker and ingredients for the bride's favourite tipple, Champagne with a personalised label or a spa voucher, to give just a few examples.

According to tradition, the maid of honour throws the bridal shower. (We like to see the other attendants chip in, but the bride should keep her nose out of such matters.) For a relative to host this party is way uncool; it looks as if your family is conspiring with you to amass booty. Consequently, if a relative such as your sister or mother is your maid of honour, someone else needs to throw the shower. (Your family may have other opportunities to host events closer to the wedding.)

The shower dowry

The bridal shower is a tradition that apparently started a few centuries ago in Holland with a poor yet beautiful girl whose father had betrothed her to a prosperous pig farmer. Her father, the miser that he was, refused to give the girl a dowry if she married the honourable but penniless miller she was in love with. Although the community wasn't exactly loaded, people were so touched by the couple's obvious love for each other that they took matters into their own hands. They 'showered' the bride with small, useful gifts, adding up to even more than her dowry would have been, so that she and her beloved could marry and set up house.

Unless a surprise shower appeals to you, make it clear from the outset that you're not being coy – you really prefer not to be surprised. After the hostess tells you of her plans, be as helpful as possible, supplying a typed guest list with correct names, addresses and phone numbers. If you're going to be 'showered' more than once, cross-check the lists so the same people aren't invited and aren't overburdened with buying too many gifts.

Unlike engagement parties, showers do call for gifts, so invitations should go only to people who are invited to the wedding. The exception is when people from your work, school, club or other part of your life throw a shower. In these cases, the groom may also be a guest of honour. Many women who boycott girls-only showers are happy to attend co-ed ones.

Reinventing the Stag Party

> *Drink, my buddies, drink with discerning*
> *Wedlock's a lane where there is no turning;*
> *Never was owl more blind than lover;*
> *Drink and be merry, lads; and think it over.*
>
> – Stag party toast

The original stag (bachelor in the USA) parties were thrown by a group of unmarried friends to give the poor soul about to be incarcerated a stipend of drinking money for the future, when his new wife would make him account for every penny. Before the party ended, they nonetheless offered a toast in honour of the bride, and smashed their glasses so they would never be used for a toast of less importance.

The best man is responsible for throwing the stag party (usually with the ushers), but it does fall to the groom to dictate the sort of event he feels comfortable attending. Clichés abound that you're supposed to take this one last shot at freedom to the extreme, making crude jokes about the female gender, playing air guitar in your pants, mooning passing cars, ogling strippers, swigging beer or doing things your buddies may blackmail you with for the rest of your married life. Perhaps because women have made good on their threats to have equally raunchy hen weekends, or because many men today have reached a higher state of consciousness, this kind of primal exhibition is becoming less popular. Grooms are wanting something more imaginative then a boozy pub crawl and strip club.

Men have many options for sending off one of their own – options that can actually be fun. You may even have two stag dos: a PG-rated one with your father and future father-in-law in attendance, and a raunchy one reminiscent of the movie *The Hangover*.

Stag dos of the past would literally last one night and would normally take place the night before the wedding. Times have changed, and frequently the stag do takes the form of a weekend away. You should invite all male members of the wedding party, close friends, brothers and fathers on yours and the bride's side. The stag do is for men only; no girls are allowed, and especially not the bride.

In case of pranks going wrong (think shaven eyebrows and the like), hold the stag do a few weeks prior to the wedding so the groom has a chance to look his very best, totally recovered from any wild stag do partying.

Here are some popular ideas:

- ✔ **Get active.** Organise an outdoor activity like SAS training, tank driving or paintballing. It gives you the chance to be competitive, use 'boys' toys' and let off some steam. Also, such activities are ideal for breaking the ice between people who don't know each other.

- ✔ **Motor away.** Try a day at a test centre driving fast cars or keep it more affordable with go-karting.

- ✔ **Be a gent.** Dress in your best suit and flutter your money away with a day at the races. You get the chance to become a millionaire before the wedding and enjoy the buzz of wondering whether your horse is going to win.

- ✔ **Get on a plane.** Popular options for a weekend away include Amsterdam, Dublin, Edinburgh, Prague and Barcelona. All have plenty of bars and nightlife, and if you're lucky, you may catch a little sun as well.

- ✔ **Go for the adrenaline rush.** For those daredevil stags, arrange white-water rafting or bungee jumping or *coasteering* (swimming and climbing around the coast).

- ✔ **Hold a mini Highland Games.** Hire some kilts and head to Scotland for your own version of the Highland Games. Try your hand at tossing the caber, hurling willies and good old tug-of-war.

- ✔ **Find out if your luck's in.** Arrange a night out at a casino, horse racing or the dog track and see if lady luck is on your side.

Some great stag and hen organisers out there can do the legwork for you, recommending options within your budget at the location you've chosen. The world is your oyster. Simply type 'stag organiser' into your search engine and compare the activities they offer. Remember to check how long they've been in business, and ask for references.

Planning the Hen Bash

In comparison to stag dos, the girls' hen celebration is a newer phenomenon. It was in the '80s that women first started gathering together for a pre-wedding celebration. The term *hen party* (or *bachelorette party* in the USA) derives from the 1800s when it simply meant a *gathering of females,* but this had no relation to weddings.

The task of organising a hen celebration is normally given to the chief brides-maid. However, if that person isn't good with lists and spreadsheets, you may want to delegate to someone who is, because organising a group of women with varying personalities is not easy. The bride should give a list of hens to invite, along with their contact details, to the chief organiser.

Normally, the organiser will gather ideas of what the bride likes before investigating the options and keeping all plans a surprise from the bride. Remember to be sensitive of budgets when organising the celebration and give the hens the opportunity to opt in and out of activities.

Hens are normally asked to buy a small gift, under a certain value, for the bride – you could say, for example, to spend no more then £10. Frequently, these gifts will be risqué with the aim of embarrassing the bride on the night.

In our opinion, hen parties where the main event is getting as wasted as possible in a stretch limo and stumbling into every club that features male dancers is as unattractive as the guy version. If you want to have a more intimate time with your very closest friends, other possibilities may leave you feeling much better:

- ✔ **Have a pamper.** Take a weekend outing to a spa with treatments, sauna, Jacuzzi and a lunch to relax after all your wedding planning.

- ✔ **Get busy.** Combine a few activities in one day like pole-dancing lessons followed by cocktail making. End the night with dinner and dancing.

- ✔ **Veg out.** Rent a slew of wedding films such as *Father of the Bride* (both the original and the remake), *Monsoon Weddings* and *My Best Friend's Wedding*, and have a movie marathon.

- ✔ **Have a pyjama party.** One of the most fun bonding experiences known to females! If budget allows, hire a chef to cook for you and have a local wine merchant put on a wine-tasting session.

- ✔ **Get on a plane.** Have a weekend city break somewhere hot and keep it simple with sun, sea and serious dancing at night.

- ✔ **Sit back and chill.** Go on a river party boat or city party bus so you never have to walk far in those stunning but treacherous high heels.

✔ **Learn a new skill.** Many companies arrange half-day sessions so that you can all learn a skill and have fun at the same time: pasta making, blending your own perfume, wine tasting, flower arranging – choose something the bride has an interest in.

✔ **Take afternoon tea.** A simple and refined idea that allows all generations to join in with the hen party (grandmothers included). Choose a special hotel – in London, The Ritz, Claridge's or The Wallace Collection, for example, but there are many other places up and down the country that specialise in afternoon teas, too.

✔ **Get dancing.** Book a chorographer for a special hen lesson and either learn some new moves for a nightclub outing that evening or perhaps a routine that you and the girls can perform at the wedding.

Gathering for Pre-Wedding Celebrations

Some couples are making the most of having their family and friends all together by holding additional events in the days leading up to the wedding. Generally speaking, these events are hosted and paid for by a close family member – normally a parent. Guest lists are smaller and etiquette dictates that if you're inviting people to a pre-wedding celebration, you also invite them to the actual wedding itself.

Revving up: The rehearsal dinner

The rehearsal dinner is an American tradition that's becoming popular in the UK. We think this pre-wedding event is lovely as it gives key people a chance to have a dinner in a more relaxed atmosphere before the subsequent wedding, and we anticipate it will become the norm before much longer.

Held a day or two before the wedding, the rehearsal dinner is more intimate than the actual wedding reception. As the name suggests, it's usually held after the wedding rehearsal, but it is often held whether you're having a rehearsal or not (see Chapter 16). Because everyone is buzzing with anticipation, this meal can be an emotional tour de force, with both teary toasts to the memory of loved ones who are no longer living and slightly ribald anecdotes not suitable for more public consumption.

Take this opportunity to express your deepest gratitude and affection to anyone in the room who helped get you to this point. Thank your parents and family, and toast each *individual* in your wedding party. (See Chapter 18 for a few words about toasts.) Many couples present the attendants' gifts at this time and sometimes also give something to their parents. Sometimes the bride and groom present these gifts in tandem, to make clear that they are from both of them.

The guest list for the rehearsal dinner can be as complicated as that for the wedding. This gathering may be limited to just the wedding party and very close family members, or it may comprise all the out-of-town guests. Because the guest list – and the expense – for the rehearsal dinner can balloon out of proportion, and because you don't want this event to compete with the wedding itself, you may want to keep the rehearsal dinner very informal. The local Mexican, Chinese or Italian restaurant can be an economical venue at which to feed a lot of people in a festive atmosphere. The dinner may also be a simple barbecue or picnic.

If you have a number of guests staying in one hotel, you may be able to negotiate a better price there for both your rehearsal dinner and next-day brunch.

Keep the invitation simple and verbally invite guests or send a personal note or a short email. There's no need to theme the dinner or go all out with the decor.

Don't think you have to close down the joint at your rehearsal dinner – everyone will understand if you bow out early to get a good night's sleep.

Coming together the evening before

Even if you don't hold a formal rehearsal dinner many families arrange informal gatherings the night before the wedding. This dinner may take place at a local restaurant, the wedding hotel/venue or the parents' home. In fact, the gathering needn't involve dinner at all – it could be just a casual invite that says 'meet us in the hotel bar at 8 p.m.'. This gives out-of-town guests a wonderful opportunity to unwind and feel welcomed prior to the formalities of the following day.

Frequently, parents of the bride and groom each host an event with relatives or friends attending either bash, as deemed appropriate. There are no formalities to these events. You may decide to slip a note detailing the gathering in with wedding invites or simply by telling guests, verbally, when you speak with them.

Don't forget that the main event is the wedding on the following day, so limit your drink intake. You don't want to have bloodshot eyes on your wedding day as no amount of make-up can diminish this.

Wrapping Up the Day After

Often, the bride and groom will arrange a farewell breakfast or brunch the day after the wedding and offer casual invites particularly to their out-of-town guests before they begin their long drives home. In terms of the venue, farewell breakfasts and brunches are either hosted at the wedding venue itself if guests have stayed there, the parents' home if it was a marquee wedding, or a local restaurant.

Everyone loves to chat about 'the night before', and a wedding is no exception. Farewell meals are also a wonderful opportunity for guests to relay their thanks for being invited but they also give you the chance to talk to guests you were unable speak with the day before.

Breakfasts or brunches are best planned as buffet-style, either *full English* (that is, eggs, bacon, sausages, toast and so on) or *continental*, with breads, cheeses, fruits, juices, cereals, croissants and the like. Alternatively, you may decide to have a casual family barbeque from about midday onwards, and have a mini party all over again.

The invitation may be included with your main wedding invitation if the same guests are invited, or may simply be extended via phone call. Because people are on different schedules (and you may drop by for only a short time, if at all), schedule these events over a few hours – 'Drop in and have a bite from 9:30–1:00', for example. Obviously, seating is not assigned, and tables should be constantly cleared and reset.

Part III
Ceremony Survival Guide

FRONT COVER

ORDER OF CEREMONY

The Marriage of

Sophie Smith-Jones
and
Henry Featherstone

11th August 2014

St Mary's Church, Mayfair

Pick up some essential tips for a faultless wedding ceremony reading at www.dummies.com/extras/weddingplanninguk.

In this part...

- Get busy with the spreadsheets and create a schedule for a seamless and worry-free wedding day.

- Know your options and choose the type of wedding ceremony that means most to you.

- Mull over the minutiae; determine the detail. Think about vows, music, readings, rehearsals and everything else that you need to consider.

Chapter 14

Creating a Foolproof Wedding-Day Schedule

In This Chapter

▶ Figuring out the flow of events

▶ Transporting the players

▶ Co-ordinating the receiving line

*W*hether you've hired a wedding planner, are arranging things yourself or have placed yourself totally in the hands of a venue co-ordinator or caterer, you'll find it helpful to compose a wedding-day schedule.

The schedule tells all the players – members of the wedding party, suppliers and staff – what they're to do and when they're to do it. More importantly, the schedule serves as your personal prompter and helps you to envision how you want the day to flow. Granted, you're not masterminding D-Day, but a little organisational wizardry in advance never hurt any wedding. Realise that scheduling your wedding on paper is a tool that helps get everyone – namely, your wedding party and your suppliers – on the same page. The schedule isn't meant to be treated as gospel or followed to the letter with blind obedience. In other words, leave room for the day to evolve naturally.

Putting Everyone on the Same Page

Every wedding is unique, which makes creating a one-size-fits-all wedding-day schedule impossible. However, here's a generic prototype to give you an idea of how to create your own version. (If you hire a wedding planner they will produce the schedule on your behalf and send it out to the key players.) The best approach is to create three versions of your wedding-day schedule:

✔ **Master:** The big daddy. See 'Creating the Master Schedule', further on in this chapter.

✔ **Topline schedule:** Send this streamlined version of your schedule to your suppliers – caterer, band, florist, cake maker and anyone else who needs to know all the players and how they interconnect.

✔ **Ceremony only:** The abridged version of the master schedule focuses exclusively on the ceremony. Give this information to the attendants, your priest, parents and other ceremony participants. Distribute this schedule at the rehearsal and go over it carefully. Ask someone to bring copies to the actual ceremony, unless your attendants are all able to memorise a script in one reading.

The rehearsal shouldn't be the first time you tell everyone of the way you want your wedding day to flow. Create a preliminary order of events and have key people give it a once-over, offering suggestions for improving the flow and timing. You may revise it up to the last minute, but make sure that everyone keeps up with the latest version. Put the date of the schedule in the footer, making it easier to spot the latest version.

The biggest tip we can give you when thinking about your wedding schedule is to put yourself in your guests' mindset. Think about what they will be doing from the minute they arrive until they stagger home. If you were a guest, when would you expect to be able to drink, eat and relax? Take into consideration any guests who require special assistance – perhaps you have some breast-feeding mums who may appreciate a private room in which to feed or change their baby? If you have elderly guests and a long drinks reception, ensure you have chairs for them to sit on and rest their legs.

Working Out Transportation Timings

If you've hired a lot of transport for your wedding you may want to produce a *transportation schedule* (see Table 14-1) so that you can organise the movements of key members of the wedding party. Give this sheet to anyone whose name appears on it, and to the drivers.

Table 14-1	Co-ordinating Pick-Ups and Drop-Offs			
Pick-Up Time and Location	*Drop-Off Time and Location*	*Driver to Wait?*	*Passenger(s)*	*Car Number and Type*
1 p.m. Bride and groom's home	1:30 p.m. St Mary's Church	No	(Groom) Henry Featherstone; (best man) Steve Lawrence	#1 Mercedes

Pick-Up Time and Location	Drop-Off Time and Location	Driver to Wait?	Passenger(s)	Car Number and Type
1:45 p.m. Bride's parents' house	2 p.m. St Mary's Church	Yes	(Bride) Sophie Smith-Jones; (father) Charles Smith-Jones	#2 Rolls-Royce Silver Wraith
1:45 p.m. Bride's parents' house	2 p.m. St Mary's Church	Yes	(Mother of the bride) Catherine Smith-Jones; (bridesmaids) Kerry Smith-Jones, Lindsey Featherstone, Sally Jones, Lucy Lyons	#3 Vanden Plas Princess
2:40 p.m. St Mary's Church	3:10 p.m. The Wedding Society	No	(Parents of the bride) Charles & Catherine Smith-Jones; (bridesmaids) Kerry Smith-Jones, Lindsey Featherstone, Sally Jones and Lucy Lyons	#3 Vanden Plas Princess
2:40 p.m. St Mary's Church	3:10 p.m. The Wedding Society	No	Bride and groom	#2 Rolls-Royce Silver Wraith

On the wedding day, you may want to arrange separate transportation to the ceremony for just your wedding party and your parents, to have them all in one place at the same time.

Unless you're holding your ceremony and reception at the same venue, consider arranging transport from the local hotels where guests are staying to the ceremony and reception. Although this may seem an unnecessary expense, it'll be worth every penny to ensure guests arrive at the venue(s) in time. Guests will also appreciate only needing to arrange transport at night back to their hotel, meaning they don't need a designated driver. And booking transport in advance can also be very beneficial if your reception is in a marquee at home, because finding parking for circa 50 cars can be difficult.

You also need to provide an addendum in your schedule in case someone isn't familiar with the town or venues. Include the address of and directions to the ceremony and reception, as well as for such intermediate stops such as the location where the bridal party is dressing.

Also consider end-of-the-evening transportation. If guests are going to require taxis, rather than leave them to sort this for themselves (cue chaos and queues), why not contact a local cab firm and ask it to supply taxis to wait outside your venue for the last hour? You should only have to pay an hourly rate, which usually includes taking guests within a certain radius of your venue.

Creating the Master Schedule

The comprehensive, master version of your wedding-day schedule needs to include *every* detail of the day with minute-by-minute precision, starting a few hours before the ceremony to after the last song. Give this list to those key people involved in the organisation of the day: wedding planner, banquet manager/venue co-ordinator, photographer and your best man and/or maid of honour.

Your master schedule should include:

- A list of all the suppliers, including email addresses and numbers for office and mobile. (See Chapter 1 for information on assembling everyone's pertinent stats.)
- Transportation logistics, including names and times of arrival for everyone involved.
- Directions to sites.
- Outline of steps before, during and after the ceremony.
- Specifics for ceremony.
- Estimated timing for each activity, including speeches.
- Specific notes or addendums for each supplier, as applicable.
- Highlighted list of important details.

Develop the master schedule in tandem with your suppliers and with your wedding planner, if you have one. The banquet manager can tell you how long it takes to serve and clear each course, the band leader can give you the timing for a dance set, and so on. Send the first draft to all your suppliers to get their input. Let them make notes on it and return it to you so you can incorporate any changes in the finished schedule.

Devising your schedule

Your master schedule (even if it's for your eyes only) begins with the pre-ceremony rituals of getting dressed and – if you're not waiting until after the ceremony – taking photographs (see Table 14-2). The timing of what has to happen before the ceremony is crucial. Make sure you take into account even seemingly little things, such as when you'll have time to eat before the ceremony. Putting these items on your master schedule acts as a reminder on a day when time can be on warp speed.

Table 14-2	A Sample Pre-Ceremony Schedule	
Time	**Event**	**Notes**
8 a.m.	Hair and make-up artist arrives at bride's parents' house	5 The Mews, Mayfair Bridesmaids, mother of the bride and bride
9:30 a.m.	The florist arrives at St Mary's Church to set out flowers	
10:30 a.m.	Danish pastries, sandwiches and fruit delivered to 5 The Mews for easy snacking throughout the morning	To be delivered between 10:30 and 11 a.m. by The Deli, The Town
11:15 a.m.	Photographer arrives for getting-ready images	
11:30 a.m.	Bouquets and father of the bride buttonhole delivered to 5 The Mews	Buttonholes for the groom, ushers, best man and father of the groom to be delivered direct to the ceremony
12:15 p.m.	Bride and bridesmaids get dressed	Maid of honour to assist with the bride's corset
12:30 p.m.	Bride gets dressed	
1 p.m.	Groom and best man depart for ceremony	Refer to transport schedule
1:15 p.m.	Formal photos in the garden	
1:20 p.m.	Groom and ushers arrive at St Mary's Church	
1:25 p.m.	Wedding cars arrive at 5 The Mews	Photographer to take a photo of the cars before heading to ceremony location
1:45 p.m.	Bride and bridesmaids depart for the ceremony	Refer to transport schedule

Whether the attendants are getting dressed in a hotel or at someone's home, always arrange for lunch or tea. They won't be eating for hours, and the combination of starvation and the first glass of Champagne can be explosive. Also, the bride should usually be the last to have her hair and make-up done so that she waits the least amount of time 'done up' before the ceremony.

If you're staying in a hotel, check-in is at 2 or 3 p.m., so the bride should either stay in this room (perhaps with her maid of honor) the night before the wedding or try to negotiate with the hotel for an early check-in so that there is time to get ready there. If you've chosen a wedding venue like a country manor house then a bridal room is usually included within the price, so you can head there the night before or early in the morning to get ready.

After you've planned the pre-ceremony hours, you have the ceremony itself to work out (Table 14-3). In Chapter 15, we cover the elements of major religious ceremonies, chapter and verse, so to speak. That's where we help you create a specific schedule and script, complete with music cues, readings and other details. For the master schedule, you're interested in the broad strokes.

Table 14-3	A Sample Ceremony Schedule	
Time	*Event*	*Notes*
1:20 p.m.	Groom, best man and ushers arrive at St Mary's Church	Ushers to hand out orders of service and escort single ladies to their seats
1:30 p.m.	Guests start arriving; harpist plays background music	
2 p.m.	Ceremony	Refer to the order of service for music and reading cues
2:30 p.m.	Recessional, followed by confetti photo outside the church doors	Bridesmaids and ushers to pair up and walk out together
2:45 p.m.	Bride and groom, wedding party and guests depart for the wedding reception	Refer to transport schedule

Finally, the master schedule leads into the reception, where you want your caterer, band, bartender and other suppliers to know exactly when (at least in theory) you want to eat, dance and toast (see Table 14-4). We recommend sending the suppliers the details of their duties a month before. This gives you time to tweak the schedule, if needed, after you receive supplier feedback.

Table 14-4	A Sequence of Events for a Happy Party	
Time	*Event*	*Notes*
3:15 p.m.	Drinks reception commences; jazz trio plays under the pagoda	Bellini cocktail/ champagne/ elderflower presse
3:30 p.m.	Canapés served; garden games available on the lawn	During this time the photographer will work through the required shot list
4:30 p.m.	Candles are lit on guest tables	Venue co-ordinator/ banquet manager
4:45 p.m.	Guests called into dinner	Top table to enter last, to be announced by the venue co-ordinator/banquet manager
5 p.m.	Wedding breakfast	Wine to be poured, then bottles left on tables
6:45 p.m.	Champagne is served ready for the speeches	
7 p.m.	Speeches announced	Order: Father of the bride Groom Best man *Ensure wireless mic is ready*
7:30 p.m.	Teas and coffee served in the lounge	Venue staff turn the room around ready for the evening
8:15 p.m.	Evening bar opens/evening guests arrive; background music played via venue sound system	Evening guests to be welcomed with a glass of wine
8:30 p.m.	Cutting of the cake followed by the first dance	Top tier to be saved, the rest to be sliced and bought around on trays
8:45 p.m.	DJ commences; cheese table set out	Any cake left over to be set out next to the cheese
9:30 p.m.	Band's first set	
10:15 p.m.	Band break/DJ commences; hog roast opens	Served in the courtyard
11:15 p.m.	Band's final set	
Midnight	Final song Carriages home	

Tossing the bouquet

Gone are the days of a formal bouquet toss where all the single ladies would try to catch the bouquet as a sign that she'll be the next to marry. Many brides are either foregoing this tradition altogether or using a cheaper version of their bouquet to toss instead. If you don't have a critical mass of single friends at the wedding, you may want to simply present the bouquet as a memento to a favourite aunt or other person you want to honour.

When you're eating the wedding breakfast is the perfect time for suppliers to take their break. Depending on the suppliers' contracts, you may be required to provide a hot meal for them, but this doesn't need to be the same as what you're eating. You can simply provide a large lasagna with salad to share among the suppliers, for example, in a designated staff room somewhere. The cost of the supplier meal will normally be cheaper then the cost of the wedding breakfast.

Managing the schedule on wedding day

On your wedding day itself, someone needs to be in charge of project managing the schedule for you. Ask your maid of honour to do this on the morning of the wedding while you get ready, taking note of when the make-up artist, hairdresser, photographer and wedding cars arrive. During the ceremony, your wedding planner will be on hand, if you have employed one, to look after the schedule; if not, delegate the responsibility of managing it to an usher who will ensure that key suppliers have arrived and been briefed on their duties. Back at the reception venue, either one of the wedding planner's team or the venue co-ordinator will run the schedule for you. They will be in charge of supervising your suppliers and, in some instances, implementing the wedding design. Your wedding planner, if you have one, may have produced a separate design set-up schedule if the wedding incorporates a lot of design elements.

Receiving-Line Logistics

If you have 125 guests and allot each one 30 seconds, you're looking at an hour-long receiving line, which is rather tedious for both your guests and you. Therefore, many modern brides are foregoing the receiving line for more time-suitable alternatives, like simply announcing the bride and groom or the top table in the reception room. A receiving line does ensure that the couple greets all the guests, but you can greet them by making your rounds at the reception, which is more hospitable anyway.

If you feel you must have a receiving line, keep it short. An ample receiving line includes, from left: the mother of the bride, the mother of the groom, and the bride and groom. A longer one has, from left: the mother of the bride, the father of the bride or groom, the mother of the groom and the father of the bride or groom, ending with the bride and groom. If time isn't an issue, you may include the maid of honour and, even though he's not considered part of the standard line-up, the best man. Anything longer is for the cast of *Riverdance* only.

If issues exist with divorced parents, be kind. Don't force people who can't bear each other to stand side by side, smiling through clenched teeth.

The receiving line is like a good game of Chinese whispers. A guest introduces herself to the mother of the bride, who then introduces the person to the mother of the groom, who introduces the person to the bride and so on.

Weather art thou?

Obsessing about the weather is a big part of wedding planning. Several websites are tailored to this compulsion at no charge, including:

✔ The Weather Channel: uk.weather.com

✔ BBC Weather: www.bbc.co.uk/weather

✔ The Met Office: www.metoffice.gov.uk/public/weather

Chapter 15

Sensational Ceremonies Part I: Choosing the Type of Ceremony

. . . .

In This Chapter

▶ Weighing up the pros and cons of different types of ceremony

▶ Choosing a civil ceremony

▶ Marrying before your god

▶ Knowing the rituals for different religions

. . . .

Although the ceremony – the exchange of vows – is the most important part of your wedding, as you bury yourself in prenuptial minutiae, the ceremony (believe it or not) is one aspect that may slip through the cracks. If you and your intended are the same faith, for example, and you belong to a house of worship, the tendency is to assume that everything will fall into place without much thought from you. True, many kinds of ceremonies have a specific structure, but you still need to do your homework. That means investing a good deal of time in thought – deep thought – and soul-searching.

Understanding how you feel about Life's Big Questions prepares you for planning a ceremony that's meaningful to you and those around you. The subsequent chapter, Chapter 16, takes you through all the considerations for the ceremony, from vows to music, the order of service to the rehearsal. In this chapter, then, we focus on the fundamental question 'What type of ceremony do we want?', outlining the options, from civil to religious.

We highly recommend taking a look at Chapter 3 alongside this chapter. There you find lots of information on legal matters so that you understand the rules for various types of ceremonies and how you register to marry.

Going for a Civil Ceremony

A *civil ceremony* is ideal if you're not religious or if you perhaps want to marry in your dream venue. It enables you to tailor your ceremony with readings and music to suit your personalities. Civil ceremonies are open to both heterosexual and same-sex couples, as of 2014.

You can have a civil ceremony at a register office or any venue licensed by the local council, such as a stately home or hotel (see Chapter 4). Many couples choose to have their ceremony at a venue, rather than the register office, which sometimes isn't the most glamorous of venues.

Ask the wedding co-ordinator at your dream venue if they have a licence to conduct weddings there; ensure you ask how many people they're licensed to have at a ceremony, as this varies at every venue. You can check the government's master list of all approved civil marriage venues online, at www.gov.uk/government/publications/civil-marriages-and-partnerships-approved-premises-list.

A civil ceremony may suit you if you want:

- ✓ **No religious content.** If you and your partner have no religious leaning and you don't want to 'pretend' just for one day.

- ✓ **A wedding on a budget.** A small fee is payable to have your ceremony at a register office; each register office charges slightly differently, but you can expect to pay from £35 to £50. A higher fee is payable if you want to have your ceremony at a licensed venue; it can cost anything up to £450 for the registrars to conduct the ceremony for you.

- ✓ **More control of the ceremony content.** Civil ceremonies can include non-religious readings, songs or music of your choice, and you can write your own vows.

- ✓ **A low-key or intimate affair.** You need only two witnesses.

- ✓ **A dream location.** Opting for a civil ceremony enables you to have your wedding at some of the most desirable licensed venues in the UK.

But civil may not be ideal if you want:

- ✓ **Religious content in the ceremony.** Civil ceremonies cannot include anything that's religious, such as hymns or readings from the Bible.

- ✓ **Exclusivity.** A ceremony in a register office can feel like you're on a conveyor belt – they may be conducting a wedding every half an hour and as your guests are leaving the next weddings' guests will be waiting to enter.

- ✓ **A dream location.** If you decide to have your ceremony at a register office bear in mind that they have neutral and, dare we say, boring, decor. By their very nature they have to appeal to everyone so don't expect to be able to personalise the space.

Having the wedding you want after the wedding: Hiring a celebrant

If you want to have a more traditional wedding but don't feel that a religious ceremony is for you, you may opt for a *humanist* or *non-religious celebrant* to conduct your wedding. These ceremonies occur *after* you legally marry at a register office.

Wedding celebrants aren't widely known in the UK, but in fact they've been in existence for over 40 years and are increasingly used by couples who want to design their ceremony the way they want it. Using a non-religious celebrant allows you complete flexibility. You can:

✔ Express your vows to each other in your own words, being as formal or thoroughly informal as you like and including religious content if you so desire (which you can't do at a civil ceremony).

✔ Use any venue or location that is important to you, at any time you want. You could use your home or your parents' garden, a boat on the Norfolk Broads, a beach in Dorset or even a cliff top in Dover!

✔ Choose all the readings and music you want, with no restrictions in place; you can go traditional, religious or even select your favourite children's nursery rhyme.

In other words, you're only restricted by your own imagination – the world is your oyster!

Celebrants cost anything from £300, with travel expenses on top. Here are some tips for hiring a non-religious celebrant:

✔ Choose a celebrant who you connect with – you should like them immediately.

✔ Arrange a face-to-face meeting, which should be free, so you can get to know the celebrant and ask questions. A limited number of professional bodies for celebrants exist in the UK, but you can find trained professionals at www.humanism.org.uk and www.civilceremonies.co.uk.

✔ After you select your celebrant, have at least one more meeting with her to discuss your ceremony in detail, including your vows, readings, speeches, music and timings. Your celebrant then writes down your ceremony plan in detail for you to review and finalise.

✔ Ask your celebrant to attend your ceremony rehearsal.

Opting for a Religious Ceremony

A religious wedding can take place at a church, chapel or other registered religious building. Alternatively, you may choose to have a religious blessing, which can take place after a civil ceremony. (See Chapter 3 for legal requirements on where you can get married.)

Deciding on a religious ceremony is a very personal decision that you both need to make together. Remember though, you can't just decide to have a particular religion's wedding ceremony because you like the sound of it – most religions require you to have an association with that religion and at the

Separate but equal

Sometimes as a compromise or out of respect to the parents or grandparents, couples of different faiths have two separate services (as opposed to having two different clergy members at the same service). A two-ceremony wedding may be a small religious ceremony one day and a larger civil one the next. Alternatively, you may have a small civil ceremony on day one to ensure the couple is legally married and then a large religious event on day two. You may even opt for two religious ceremonies within moments of each other at the same venue.

very least believe in their faith and values. If you're unsure on whether you qualify to get married within a particular religion you need to enquire with your local church, temple or synagogue.

Even devout members of their faith may not be familiar with the wedding rituals, which in some cases can be quite involved. Delineating all the particulars of every religious and ethnic wedding tradition is beyond the scope of this book, but in the following sections we do take a look at some of the major UK religions' wedding customs, should you decide to have a religious ceremony.

Church of England

You don't have to regularly attend church or have been baptised to get married in the Church of England. Currently, the Church of England gives all British citizens, with no former partner still living, the right to get married in the parish church of the town where they're resident or in the church where either of the couple is on the church's electoral roll. You can also get married in a church if you have a strong family connection with it, either now or in the past.

You're welcome to be married in a church in a parish if just one of these applies:

- One of you was baptised or prepared for confirmation in the parish.
- One of you has ever lived in the parish for six months or more.
- One of you has at any time regularly attended public worship in the parish for six months or more.
- One of your parents has lived in the parish for six months or more in his or her child's lifetime.

- ✔ One of your parents has regularly attended public worship there for six months or more in his or her child's lifetime.
- ✔ Your parents or grandparents were married in the parish.

More than a quarter of all marriages in England take place in the Church of England. Churches can get booked a long way in advance, so make contact with the minister in charge of the church at your earliest opportunity, preferably before you book your reception, to ensure both that you can get married there and that the date is available.

Once you've booked your wedding with the vicar, you work together to develop an *order of service,* which determines the sequence of events. Although the basic format of the service cannot be changed too much, you can still personalise a church wedding a great deal through your choice of entrance and exit music, hymns, readings, readers and the way in which the church is decorated.

In most cases, the order of service you agreed gets printed and handed out to your guests, usually by your ushers, as they enter the church. (See Chapter 16 for ideas for your order of service.) The ceremony then begins with the entrance of the bride and a welcome by the celebrant (usually the vicar, rector or priest in charge of the parish), followed by a hymn. The vicar then begins the *preface* (an introduction to the wedding vows), which is followed by the couple's declarations to each other. Next comes the *collect,* where the vicar asks the congregation to pray while he says the collect prayer. Two readings, one of which will be a Bible reading (see Chapter 16 for ideas for readings), usually take place, after which the vicar may give a short talk on the readings and lead another hymn. There then follows the vows (see Chapter 16) and the giving of the rings. The vicar reads the *proclamations* (proclaiming that the couple are now husband and wife) and the couple signs the *register,* the official registration of the marriage, and the wedding certificate. The service concludes with prayers, usually ending with the *Lord's Prayer.* Finally, the vicar gives the blessing and the recessional music plays as the bride, groom and bridal party leave.

Church of England ministers have the legal power to register marriages, which means that if you get married in the Church of England you don't need to have a civil registrar present, nor do you need to have a civil ceremony in order to make the ceremony legal. (Chapter 3 has the details.)

Depending upon the style and location of the building a church wedding can be a beautiful occasion, and 'extras' such as having a choir singing or having church bells ringing as you exit the church can make the day even more special.

North of the border

In Scotland, a religious marriage may take place anywhere and may be solemnised only by a minister, clergyman, pastor, priest or other person entitled to do so under the Marriage (Scotland) Act 1977.

A civil marriage may take place in a register office or at an approved place, and may be solemnised only by a registrar or an assistant registrar who has been authorised by the registrar general for that purpose. You can obtain a list of approved places for the area in which you want to be married from the registrar for that area. Alternatively, you can get a list of approved places to marry in Scotland from the marriage/civil partnership section of the National Records of Scotland website at www.gro-scotland.gov.uk. If you want to apply for temporary approval for a civil marriage to be conducted at a place of your own choice, such as your own home, contact the local authority, which can advise you about the fee and the application procedure.

You can find further details on Church of England weddings online, at www.yourchurchwedding.org.

Hindu

All Hindu weddings are performed by a priest and considered a sacred trust, yet they vary greatly from region to region. Depending on geographic location, family customs, social class and personal taste, weddings may be a few hours to several days long. Hindus believe that many paths lead to the same summit, as it were, so intermarriage is much less of a threat on religious grounds than a potential loss of cultural identity. The wedding rites are prescribed in the holy scripture known as the *Veda,* but ceremonies don't have to take place in a holy temple. The family and priest usually consult astrological charts for an auspicious date.

After invoking all the elements of nature and divine energies to witness and aid the proceedings, the priest sprinkles holy water and chants Sanskrit mantras to purify the bride and groom. The bride wears a traditional red and gold sari and lots of jewellery. The parents of the bride may wash the groom's feet while he sits in a chair behind a cloth curtain, offering him gifts of bananas, coconuts and so on – all the while earnestly asking him to accept their daughter in marriage. The Auspicious Moment occurs when the bride and groom affix a paste of cumin seeds and *jiggery* (an unrefined brown sugar made from palm sap) with their right palms to each other's heads to symbolise their inseparableness. The groom accepts the bride as his wife by tying strings, a pendant or a gold necklace around her neck. The couple place garlands on each other to show their adoration and shower rice on each other's head to symbolise prosperity.

The bride and groom then take seven steps (called *Saptapadi*) around a sacrificial fire to signify their vows. With each step they pray for different blessings such as wealth, happiness and devotion. At some point during the ceremony, the bride may stand on a stone to symbolise loyalty and faithfulness.

Jewish

Four main divisions of Judaism exist: Orthodox and Conservative, which are very religious, and Reform and Reconstructionist, which can be far less stringent. The person who presides over a Jewish wedding may be a cantor, rabbi, community leader or scholar.

If both the bride and groom are Jewish and affiliated with a synagogue, getting married in that synagogue is no problem. Most rabbis are amenable to co-officiating with another rabbi – the other family's rabbi, for example. If, however, you aren't connected to any synagogue or religious organisation, start your search for a rabbi by asking people you know for recommendations.

Weddings may not take place on the Sabbath – from Friday sundown to Saturday sundown. On the Sabbath, work and travel are forbidden, and you may not have two celebrations (the Sabbath being one) at once. If you're planning a religious ceremony, check the dates carefully with your rabbi. Jewish weddings are forbidden on major holidays such as Rosh Hashanah, Yom Kippur, Passover, Shavuot and Sukkot. Three weeks in July and August, and the seven weeks between Passover and Shavuot (usually April and May) are also off-limits.

A Jewish ceremony may take place anywhere – and outdoor spots are very popular – but they must take place under a *chuppah* (huppah), or Jewish wedding canopy. The chuppah carries many symbols of ancestral Judaism. Because the Jews were nomads, their weddings historically took place outside under the stars to make the point that the couple should bear as many children as there are stars in the sky. Today the chuppah is imbued with a variety of meanings: the groom's home into which he brings the bride, a home filled with hospitality (open on all sides) and as a metaphor for the groom covering or taking the bride.

Lighting a few candles

Mystical and awe-inspiring, candlelight ceremonies can take place in late afternoon or early evening.

Unity candles usually consist of three candles at the altar. The bride and groom take the outer two, which are lit, and together light the centre one to symbolise the joining of two hearts and their shared commitment to the marriage. Other guests may also be given candles and the couple walks down the aisle, stopping at each row to light the nearest candle, which in turn is used to light the next and so on. In other cases, only parents or other family members join in the candle lighting.

If you like the idea of using unity candles ask your religious celebrant if they can be included in your ceremony – some religions allow them and others do not. Of course, if you're using a non-religious celebrant you can include anything you want in your ceremony.

Muslim

In Islam, the woman makes the offer of marriage, usually through her father or another male relative. This arrangement is supposed to guarantee that both partners come to the marriage of their own free will. After accepting the proposal, the groom gives the bride a *mahr,* or gift, such as property, jewellery or even education.

Muslim women must marry Muslim men; however, Muslim men may marry non-Muslim women, as long as their children are raised Muslim.

Although marriage is one of the most desirable states for Muslims, the ceremony is simple and takes only about five minutes. The bride and groom are typically in separate rooms, usually in an office as opposed to a mosque, while the *wali,* the bride's representative, answers questions posed by a religious *sheik* (an Islamic magistrate). The groom answers for himself as three male witnesses stand by. When the sheik is satisfied that the groom has provided a suitable mahr, the bride and groom sign the papers and the couple is pronounced man and wife. A week or two later, the couple has a public celebration with a series of parties and rituals, which the groom and his family pay for.

Roman Catholic

Marriage is one of the seven sacraments, so if two Catholics are getting married, the wedding must take place in a Catholic church for the marriage to be sanctified. Only the vicar general's office, in any diocese, can grant permission to wed outside a chapel.

You must provide several documents to prove that you're free to marry in the Catholic Church:

- ✔ **Baptismal certificate**
- ✔ **Letter of freedom** stating that you've never contracted marriage either civilly or in a church service
- ✔ **Letter of permission** from your parents if you're under 21 years old
- ✔ **Premarital investigation** – actually, just a data sheet filled out during an informal interview with your priest
- ✔ **Publication of *banns*** (the publication or public announcement of the engaged couple's intention to marry), usually read at Mass on three consecutive Sundays before the wedding

Ordinarily, the marriage should take place in the bride's parish, so the groom must get a letter of notification from his parish that his banns will be announced three times. If you aren't a member of a particular parish, speak to the pastor regarding the canonical rule and a dispensation.

If you plan to have a Catholic ceremony abroad, you may need a letter from your parish priest confirming that you've been through *pre-Cana* counselling (Catholic course in marriage) and requesting that the wedding be performed in another church. If you want the wedding outdoors or in a secular setting, you need a special dispensation.

When it comes to interfaith marriages, a Catholic can get a dispensation to marry someone from another religion, with very specific guidelines. It may be possible for your partner's religious celebrant to assist at the wedding by reading a Scripture passage, saying a prayer or a few words, or giving a blessing. Only a priest or deacon, however, may perform the actual ceremony if you're getting married in a Catholic church. Most parishes don't publish the banns for an interfaith marriage unless you request it.

A Catholic can also get a 'dispensation from' form to marry in a non-Catholic ceremony.

The liturgical celebration is fairly set, although the couple may – with their priest's approval – amend the vows set forth by the Church, choose to light a wedding candle (see the sidebar 'Lighting a few candles', earlier in this chapter), and offer their own prayer or petition of thanks. Before the recessional, the bride may also place a bouquet on the Blessed Virgin Mary's shrine or statue.

The couple may have a ceremony without a Mass or a ceremony incorporated into a Mass (and called a Nuptial Mass). The couple may enter the ceremony with a traditional processional, or the priest and his assistants may welcome the bride and groom and their families at the door of the church, before they all proceed to the sanctuary. During the ceremony, the bride and groom remain in front of the altar. Throughout the ceremony, they may have to kneel, stand or sit.

The priest recites an opening prayer (usually of the couple's choosing), followed by readings, including a Gospel passage. The couple exchanges vows and rings, which the priest blesses. If the ceremony takes place outside a Mass, the ceremony concludes with the priest saying another prayer and the nuptial blessing.

In the case of a Nuptial Mass, the service continues with the priest calling for the 'Sign of Peace' in which everyone turns and shakes hands with their neighbour, saying, 'Peace be with you' or something similar. A member of the couple's family may then present a gift of bread and wine for Holy Communion to commemorate Christ's Last Supper. The priest consecrates the bread and wine, and the couple takes them as the body and blood of Christ. After Communion, the priest says the concluding prayer and nuptial blessing.

Sikhism

The day before a Sikh wedding, the bride's legs and hands are painted with henna designs. The next morning, her female relatives adorn her with jewels and make-up, and she dons an elaborate, traditional sari in red, pink or white. Whether or not the ceremony is held in a Sikh temple, called a *guardwara,* it takes place in the morning, which is considered the happy time of day.

Before the ceremony begins, the bride's parents welcome the groom and his parents, garlanding them with flowers. The bride enters and garlands the groom with more flowers, and he returns the gesture by garlanding her. Professional singers called *raagis* perform as guests enter and sit around a central platform, upon which the holy book, *Guru Granth Sahib Ji,* is displayed.

The couple sits before the man (a *granthi* or *pathi*) who reads the holy book. Depending on the family's tradition, either the mother or father hands one end of a pink sash to the groom (sometimes placing it on his shoulder) and the other end to the bride. Verses recited from the *Granth* explain the couple's duties in married life. One of the parents, the priest or the g room may tie the sash to the bride's headpiece – literally tying the knot and symbolising the bond that joins the couple.

The couple exchanges vows and then walks around the holy book four times *(lavaans),* the husband leading, to signify their journey together. After each circle, the bride and groom kneel and bow toward the *Granth.* The pathi may address the parents and grandparents regarding their roles in supporting the couple. The *raagis* usually sing a concluding song as the bride and groom exchange a sweet food called a *karah parshad.*

This whole ceremony takes about an hour and a half. When it's over, guests greet the couple, placing a hand on their heads, garlanding them with flowers, throwing petals and often putting a token amount of money into the pink cloth, which the bride and groom still hold.

Useful first questions to ask

After you decide the type of ceremony you want to have, make sure that you're clear on the following points. Usually, the best (and most diplomatic) way to get answers to these questions is by asking the person who's in charge of wedding ceremonies in your chosen faith.

✔ What are the rules and recommendations for ceremony music? For example, do you have to use the house organist or other musicians? If not, must you pay a fee to not use them? (Skip to Chapter 16 for the lowdown on music in the ceremony.)

✔ How long is the ceremony?

✔ How many hours do you schedule between ceremonies?

✔ What are the rules regarding photography and videography?

✔ Are premarital classes/sessions mandatory? Must you attend weekly services in the months before your wedding?

Chapter 16

Sensational Ceremonies Part II: Determining the Details

A s soon as you've chosen what type of ceremony you want to have (and Chapter 15 can help you make this important decision), you need to turn your thoughts to personalising the ceremony so that it reflects you as a couple.

Some types of ceremonies give you more flexibility and room for manoeuvre than others; in this chapter, we go through some of the options for personalising your vows and the sequence of events leading up to the ceremony and for choosing the right music and readings for you both.

All Together, Vow!

Besides having an *officiant* (that is, a registrar or religious minister) declare you legally married, the other key moment of your ceremony is the taking of vows. In a church wedding you make vows to each other with God and friends and family as your witness, and although you have some say over the vows (for example, you may omit the traditional 'obey' promise of a Christian ceremony), you're a little locked in by tradition. In a civil ceremony wedding you make promises to each other with friends and family as your witnesses. In the civil ceremony, you must say the legal vows, but you can choose to add some extra words, if you want. (Remember to have these pre-approved by your registrar.)

There's a lot to be said for the power of history. Many religious services are thousands of years old. Reciting the words that have bound together countless generations before you can give you a feeling of strength and connectivity. You may feel that altering those words will diminish their meaning or insult your forebears. If so, stick with your religious protocol and you'll be happy.

However, it's increasingly popular for couples to personalise standard ceremony rituals, cobble together elements from various religious, ethnic and cultural traditions, and not only write their vows but also script the entire ceremony.

You may feel that conventional vows fall short of expressing what's truly in your heart. And yet, when you try to articulate the numbing joy you feel about your beloved and the great unknowable before you, the words seem banal, lifeless, trite. What can you say that hasn't been said before? After all, haven't poets been writing about love for eons? Yes, but that doesn't mean you can't give it a whirl. Even if the words are already out there, they haven't been said by *you*.

Whether you're creating your own vows or simply looking for ways to personalise your ceremony, consider these ideas:

- ✔ Start by making a list of all the words that describe your spouse to be, why you fell in love with this person and what your hopes are for the future.

- ✔ Think about the people around you. You may want to briefly acknowledge family and friends, thanking God (or whomever) for the dearly departed who were important to you or saying prayers for the good health of elderly relatives and so on.

- ✔ As you start putting together your thoughts, keep your vows upbeat and positive. Avoid anything maudlin.

- ✔ Remember that you want to create a dialogue, not two monologues.

Remember, if you're getting married in a church or synagogue, you probably won't have much leeway as to the creation of your own vows. If, however, you're allowed some creativity, make sure that your officiant approves whatever you're planning in order to avoid inadvertently including anything disrespectful or offensive.

Before you get too creative, keep in mind that although acknowledging the folly of life or the human comedy is fine, this moment is still solemn. In years to come, you want to remember fondly what you said to each other at the altar, not cringe in embarrassment.

Thinking traditional

When in doubt, crib from the standard vows uttered by countless couples through the ages:

- ***The Book of Common Prayer:*** I, [name], take thee, [name], to be my wedded [husband/wife], to have and to hold from this day forward, for better, for worse, for richer, for poorer, in sickness and in health, to love and to cherish, till death do us part, according to God's holy ordinance; and thereto I plight thee my faith.

- **Roman Catholic:** I, [name], take you, [name], to be my [husband/wife]. I promise to be true to you in good times and in bad, in sickness and in health. I will love you and honour you all the days of my life.

- **Civil:** I, [name], take you, [name], to be my lawfully wedded [husband/wife]. Before these witnesses, I promise to love you and care for you as long as we both shall live. I accept you with your faults and strengths, even as I offer myself to you with my faults and strengths. I will support you when you need support, and turn to you when I need support. I choose you as the person with whom I will spend my life.

- **Muslim:** I pledge, in honesty and sincerity, to be for you an obedient and faithful [husband/wife].

Technically, Jewish wedding liturgy doesn't include vows. However, in deference to tradition of saying 'I do', many rabbis have added commitment vows after the ring ceremony.

Going for contemporary

Contemporary vows have as many variations on the theme as there are married couples. The language ranges from the prosaic to the mystical. You can find many sources for contemporary vows in a number of books, and on blogs and Internet sites (try www.myweddingvows.com, for example). Here are examples of modern vows to get your inspirational juices flowing:

- Our miracle lies in the path we have chosen together. I, [name], enter into this marriage knowing that the true magic of love is not to avoid changes, but to navigate them successfully. Let us commit to the miracle of making each day work, together.

- Respecting each other, we commit to live our lives together for all the days to come. I, [name], ask you to share this world with me, for good and ill. Be my partner, and I will be yours.

- Today we move from 'I' to 'we'. [Name], take this ring as a symbol of my decision to join my life with yours until death should part us. I walked to this place to meet you today; we shall walk from it together.

- Today, I, [name], join my life to yours, not merely as your [husband/wife], but as your friend, your lover and your confidant. Let me be the shoulder you lean on, the rock on which you rest, the companion of your life. With you I will walk my path from this day forward.

Pay attention to the promise and ring exchange parts, in which you have lots of scope for romance and commitment:

- ✔ I promise that I will respect you as an individual, support you through difficult times, rejoice with you through happy times, be loyal to you always and, above all, love you as my wife/husband and friend.

- ✔ I promise to love you without smothering you, to encourage your dreams and comfort you in disappointments, to share your adventures and celebrate your achievements, to keep sight of the true values in life, and to be with you, beside you, always.

- ✔ I promise to care for you above all others, to give you my love and friendship, support and comfort, and to respect and cherish you throughout our lives together.

- ✔ I promise that our marriage will always be one of honesty and trust. I will respect you and encourage you, I will laugh with you and be your friend, and I will love you forever.

- ✔ I give you this ring as a token of our love and marriage, as a symbol of all that we share and in recognition of our life together.

- ✔ I give you this ring as a sign of our marriage, and as a symbol of our love. I promise to care for you and to respect and cherish you, throughout our lives together.

- ✔ I give you this ring as a sign of our love, trust and marriage. I promise to care for you above all others, to give you my love, friendship and support, and to respect and cherish you throughout our life together.

- ✔ I give you this ring as a symbol of my love and affection. Wear it with happiness and pride – now and always.

If you've written your own vows, and especially if they include a long poem or passage (see the next section on readings), write them on index cards. Ask someone who'll be at the altar or with you, and who has a pocket, to hang on to them until you need them during the ceremony.

Getting Ideas for Readings

As you script your ceremony, you may want to incorporate poems, scriptures, lyrics, quotations or other readings that are personally meaningful. Here are some pointers:

- ✔ Keep a notebook or journal for jotting down bits of poetry, song lyrics or movie scenes that strike a chord in you or that have been floating around in your subconscious for ages.

- ✔ As obvious as it may seem, look up topics such as love, passion and marriage in encyclopedias, books of quotations, dictionaries and on the Internet. Seeing these ideas distilled to their basic concepts may spark your creativity.

- ✔ Dig for unusual sonnets, poems, songs and the like. Really listen to the words. May a particular piece or a few lines work in your ceremony?

- ✔ Involve your children if you have any, or nieces and nephews. This may be the grandest day of their lives too (at least for a while). And they'll be around longer than anyone else to keep your wedding-day memories alive.

- ✔ Incorporate a ritual or poem from your ethnic heritage or from one you admire.

- ✔ Pay quiet tribute to deceased family members through a reading – or, indeed, certain flowers, musical selections, or a few simple words of acknowledgment.

We could fill hundreds of tomes if we were to reprint actual possibilities here. Instead, we give you some general directions to explore:

- ✔ **Scripture:** Genesis, Song of Solomon, The Talmud, 1 Corinthians, Romans, John, Matthew, Ephesians, Psalms, Confucius, I Ching.

- ✔ **Literature:** *The Little Prince* by Antoine de Saint-Exupéry; *The Velveteen Rabbit* by Margery Williams; *The Prophet* by Kahlil Gibran; *Soul Mates* by Thomas Moore; *The Art of Loving* by Erich Fromm; *The Irrational Season* by Madeleine L'Engle; *The Bridge Across Forever* by Richard Bach.

- ✔ **Poetry:** Louis de Bernières, Adrian Henri, Helen Steiner Rice, Elizabeth Barrett Browning, Shakespeare, Shelley, Marge Piercy, Walt Whitman, Carl Sandburg, EE cummings, TS Eliot, John Donne.

If you intend to honour friends or relatives by asking them to do a reading at your wedding, give them ample time to choose it (if applicable), learn it and practise it. In fact, have them do a run-through at your rehearsal (see the later section 'Places Everyone – Time to Rehearse').

They're Playing Our Song

In this section, we help you get to grips with what music you need, in what format and in what style you prefer.

Music for the ceremony

In general, a wedding ceremony has these facets of music:

- ✔ **Prelude:** Played for 15 minutes to a half hour before the ceremony, this music welcomes the guests and is the background by which they're seated. It should relax your guests and soothe them before the ceremony commences.

Some couples, tired of the usual variety of classical wedding music, opt for pre-recorded music. Jazz favourites from Duke Ellington to Ella Fitzgerald to Nat King Cole put guests in a romantic mood as soon as they arrive, or perhaps a collection of songs from Michael Bublé can keep them amused while they wait for the ceremony to begin.

✔ **Procession:** This music sets the pace for attendants walking down the aisle. The music should be rhythmic enough for them to keep time to (in a natural fashion).

✔ **Ceremony:** At key points in the ceremony music can be played or a choir or soloist can sing. (For a religious ceremony, the officiant will designate at what points a song or musical piece is appropriate and what the choices are.)

Guests need to be able to hear both the music and the words at a ceremony. Make sure that you, your officiant, anyone who's delivering a reading and the musicians are loud enough. Depending on the location of your ceremony, you must either use a stand-up microphone or mic the site or the participants.

✔ **Recession:** This music, at the end of the ceremony, should be powerful and joyous. In any case, it's usually louder and quicker than the processional music. You may feature a rousing live chorus of gospel singers belting out 'Signed, Sealed, Delivered I'm Yours', for example, or a pre-recorded favourite rock song. Anything can work as long as it's celebratory and sends people out of the door feeling uplifted.

A soloist, a choir or something in-between?

Music can be a wonderful way to personalise your ceremony by selecting music that will evoke feeling. Think about what tone you are trying to set for the ceremony. If your ceremony is very traditional then perhaps choose something classical, or if you're going contemporary then more modern songs may be suitable. Also remember that you don't have to book live musicians; many couples now use iPods and MP3 players to create a playlist for the ceremony. You may, for example, decide that you want to enter into the ceremony to the church organist playing but perhaps have something recorded to play when you sign the register. Many venues have inbuilt systems that allow you to plug in your own device.

Going live

Live musicians can create a beautiful ambience to a wedding ceremony, and whether your budget stretches to a solo bagpiper or a string quartet you can normally find a suitable option for you.

Having live musicians at your ceremony creates a talking point with guests, especially as they await your arrival. Sitting there watching and listening to a band perform can be relaxing for them. The downside, of course, is that even if you book just a solo artist the cost can be ₤200 or more, compared with the minimal cost of downloading some pre-recorded music.

Considering configurations

When selecting which pieces to play, think about the number of musicians you can afford to hire and the equipment they'll need. The following are possible musical configurations:

- ✔ **A cappella group:** Generally three or four vocalists who sing without instrumental accompaniment. Can be very upbeat and fun. You can even set up a variety of surprise artists to blend in with the congregation, seated among guests, who then stand up at the agreed time to sing (like a flash mob).

- ✔ **Choir:** At least six singers with instrumental accompaniment.

- ✔ **Classical ensembles:** An almost infinite range of possibilities exist using various instruments (see Table 16-1 for some examples).

- ✔ **Jazz ensemble:** A trio or quartet consisting of guitar(s), bass and drums.

- ✔ **Organ:** This instrument is an integral part of the ceremony at many churches. Some very grand ones sound like a full orchestra.

- ✔ **Piano:** Either solo or as part of an ensemble; this instrument can be an electric keyboard, a baby grand or an upright.

- ✔ **Small orchestras:** Six or more pieces, such as a double string quartet or a string quartet, organ and flute.

- ✔ **Soloist:** One singer with either instrumental accompaniment or a cappella.

Table 16-1	Classical Ensemble Configurations
Type	*Instruments*
Duets	Flute and violin; violin and cello; two violins; harp and flute; flute and guitar
Trios	Harp, flute and cello; violin, flute and keyboard; two violins and a flute
String quartets	Four violins; two violins and two violas; two violins, one viola and one cello
Woodwind quartet	Flute, clarinet, oboe and bassoon
Brass quartet	Two trumpets, trombone and French horn or tuba
Quintets	String quartet and piano; string quartet and harp

Selecting ceremony musicians

If your house of worship provides the musicians for your ceremony, you won't need a contract, just a confirmation of timing and fees. If you're hiring an independent soloist, quartet or other musical entity for your ceremony, you want to get all the particulars in writing.

When interviewing musicians for your ceremony, be sure to cover the following questions, and take notes:

- ✔ Do they have a sample MP3 you can listen to?

- ✔ Will the musicians on the audio link be the ones playing at the ceremony?

- ✔ Have the musicians worked at this venue or church before? If not, will the leader have a short meeting with the person in charge?

- ✔ Can the musicians give you some direction on musical choices for various parts of the ceremony?

- ✔ If you want a particular piece of music, can the musicians configure it for your ensemble? How long will that take, and for what fee?

- ✔ If you hire a soloist or other group for the ceremony, will the musicians have a rehearsal with them?

- ✔ How many hours are included in the quoted price? If the ceremony goes over the expected time, is overtime available?

- ✔ What will the musicians wear?

- ✔ Do the musicians have any special requests – armless chairs, music lights, gazebos for outdoor ceremonies? (Classical musicians – particularly harpists – insist on some covering. Because these instruments are so expensive, even the threat of a drizzle may keep the harpist from performing unless she's in a building or under a gazebo.)

- ✔ Can they be available for your rehearsal? Do they charge an additional fee? If you're having an elaborate ceremony and feel that the cues are complicated, you may want to negotiate a price to have the group (or at least the leader) be present at the rehearsal. See the later section 'Places Everyone – Time to Rehearse'.

- ✔ Let the officiant know if you're bringing in outside musicians, so their contributions can be woven neatly into the order of service at an early stage. Also, ensure sufficient and suitable seating exists for a choir, if the venue doesn't have specific choir stalls, and for other musicians.

Using downloads or CDs

Choosing to use pre-recorded music for the ceremony enables you to use a song you love in its original format without a live band attempting recreate it. This is normally a little easier in a civil ceremony than in a religious building that may not have the technology needed to play the music. And talking of technology, make sure you ask your ceremony venue what they are set up for – do they have a facility for playing CDs or an inbuilt sound system complete with iPod docking station? – and make sure that you test their system before the actual wedding day.

Using an iPod on the day is easier than taking a CD as the venue staff or wedding planner can operate it. Just create a playlist called 'ceremony' and download the songs into the folder in the order they are to be played – prelude, processional, signing of the register and recessional. If you don't have an iPod or the venue doesn't have a docking station, you may need to bring in CDs. Check whether the venue's system can accommodate just one CD at a time or whether you can load several in at once because you may have five songs you want to play at your ceremony but spread over three CDs. A better idea is to burn your own CD containing the songs in the correct order so that all the music is in one place. If your venue doesn't have a sound system for you to use, hiring a small public address (PA) system that allows you to play your music through a couple of speakers is normally fairly easy.

You don't need to worry about obtaining a licence for playing pre-recorded music in wedding ceremonies, no matter what premises the ceremony itself takes place in. (You can find out more about this online, at www. prsformusic.com/users/businessesandliveevents/Pages/ PRSforMusicchargingpolicies.aspx#7.)

Now for the fun bit: Choosing the tunes

Put on the kettle or pour a glass of wine and flick through your music collection or scour an online music website for options. Hours of fun! Modern, pop, rock or classical – add to your list whatever moves you. You both need to be happy with your choices. (That said, the bride may like to keep the processional music a surprise.)

It's your wedding, but you don't have an entirely free choice with the music. For a church service, you may be referred to the organist and restricted to hymns and perhaps classical music, although some churches are more open. And even for a civil service, you need to submit your specific choices to the registrar so she can confirm suitability for a non-religious ceremony (remember – you can't use any religious music in a civil ceremony).

The following sections offer up some suggestions for kinds of music. To get other ideas, pop on to a music agency website for suggestions and sound bites.

Keeping it classical

Dozens of classical music pieces, although beautiful, have found their places in wedding ceremonies so often that they've lost the ability to inspire. That doesn't necessarily mean that you should be afraid to use such standards. The key is to find musicians who know how to make the music sound as if the pieces are perfect for *your* wedding, or recorded versions that really speak to you.

If you're opting for live music then before you get your heart set on a particular piece of music check to see whether a solo organist can play it or if it works for the number of musicians in the group you've contracted. Some of the musical pieces that you consider may only work for entire orchestras or may call for specific instruments that aren't in your ensemble. Sometimes the best way to truly understand if that piece of music will work with the musicians hired is to go to YouTube (www.youtube.com) and type in the song name plus the musician type (guitarist, pianist, string quartet and so on).

Here are some classical music ideas for the various parts of the ceremony:

✔ **Prelude:**

- 'Andante from Piano Concerto No. 21' by Mozart
- 'Arioso', 'Wachet Auf' or 'Badinerie' by Bach
- 'Barcarolle' by Offenbach
- 'Berceuse' by Fauré
- 'Chanson de Matin' or 'Chanson de Nuit' by Elgar
- 'Intermezzo' by Mascagni
- 'Minuet' by Boccherini
- 'Panis Angelicus' by Franck
- 'Dance of the Blessed Spirits' by Gluck

✔ **Procession:**

- 'Arrival of the Queen of Sheba' by Handel
- 'Bridal Chorus (Here Comes the Bride)' by Wagner
- 'Canon in D' by Pachelbel
- 'Trumpet Tune' by Purcell
- 'Trumpet Voluntary (Prince of Denmark's March)' by Clarke

✔ **Signing of the register:**

- 'Air on the G string', 'Jesu, Joy of Man's Desiring' or 'Sheep May Safely Graze' by Bach
- 'Melody in F' by Rubinstein
- 'The Pearl Fishers' Duet' by Bizet
- 'Salut d'Amour' by Elgar
- 'To a Wild Rose' by MacDowell

✔ **Recession:**

- 'Alla Hornpipe (from Water Music Suite)' by Handel
- 'Trumpet Tune' by Purcell

- 'Wedding March' by Wagner

- 'Wedding March (A Midsummer Night's Dream)' by Mendelssohn

Going for jazz, rock, pop – whatever you fancy

Couples are now putting their own personal stamp on weddings by selecting music that has meaning for them, or music they *like* as opposed to following the classical tradition. Even if you hire a classical string quartet, most players are delighted at the chance to play more rock or pop music. Likewise, a lot of couples are opting for jazz bands for the ceremony and subsequent drinks reception for a more upbeat sound.

Here are some ideas to get you thinking:

✔ **Prelude:**

- 'Beautiful Day', 'Sweetest Thing', 'Electrical Storm' or 'With or Without You' by U2

- 'Better Together' by Jack Johnson

- 'It's a Beautiful Day', 'Haven't Met You Yet', 'Lost' or 'Everything' by Michael Bublé

- 'Love Me Do', 'Can't Buy Me Love', 'A Hard Day's Night' or 'Help' by the Beatles

- 'Love Me Tender' by Elvis Presley

✔ **Procession:**

- 'At Last' by Etta James (or the Beyoncé version)

- 'Chasing Cars' by Snow Patrol

- 'Halo' by Beyoncé

- 'Have I Told You Lately?' by Van Morrison

- 'I Won't Give Up' or 'I'm Yours' by Jason Mraz

- 'Make You Feel my Love' by Adele

- 'Songbird' by Eva Cassidy

- 'Your Song' by Elton John

✔ **Singing of the register:**

- 'Kissing You' by Des'ree

- 'One Love' by U2

- 'Feeling Good' by Nina Simone

- 'What a Wonderful World' by Eva Cassidy and Katie Melua

- 'You're My Best Friend' by Queen

✔ **Recession:**

- 'Dog Days Are Over' by Florence and the Machine
- 'How Sweet It Is (to Be Loved by You)' by Marvin Gaye
- 'It Had to Be You' by Frank Sinatra
- 'One Day Like This' by Elbow
- 'Signed, Sealed, Delivered I'm Yours' by Stevie Wonder
- 'Walking on Sunshine' by Katrina and the Waves

Religious hymns

If you're marrying in a religious building then speak with your minister, who can give guidance on popular hymns for the ceremony. You can also listen to clips via www.yourchurchwedding.org.

Some popular choices include

✔ 'All Things Bright and Beautiful'

✔ 'Amazing Grace'

✔ 'As Man and Woman We Were Made'

✔ 'Be Still for the Presence of the Lord'

✔ 'Come to a Wedding'

✔ 'Give Me Joy in My Heart'

✔ 'Jerusalem'

✔ 'Lord of All Hopefulness'

✔ 'Lord of the Dance'

✔ 'Love Divine All Loves Excelling'

✔ 'Make Me a Channel of Your Peace'

✔ 'Morning Has Broken'

✔ 'One More Step Along the World I Go'

✔ 'Praise My Soul, the King of Heaven'

✔ 'Praise to the Lord, the Almighty'

✔ 'Praise Ye the Lord!'

✔ 'The Grace of Life is Theirs'

✔ 'The King of Love My Shepherd Is'

✔ 'The Lord's My Shepherd'

✔ 'We Pledge to One Another'

Getting with the Programme: Producing the Order of Service

An *order of service* (or wedding programme) serves many purposes – as a lovely memento of the day, a way to honour the participants and a playbook that guides everyone through the steps of the ceremony – and it determines the sequence and spirit of the ceremony. At different points you may have music for drama or scriptural readings for contemplation. You want to keep things moving apace without rushing, and you want each moment to reflect both the seriousness and joy of the occasion.

You may opt to follow the ceremony verbatim as prescribed by your church or register office. However, if you're crafting your own script or having an interfaith wedding, you may ad lib or edit the steps. Chapter 15 looks at a typical ceremony order for a Christian or civil ceremony.

Some churches create orders of service for couples getting married; alternatively, you can design your own. In either case, make sure your minister or the person in charge goes over it before the final printing. Orders of service can be simple or elaborate, photocopied on plain paper or engraved on card stock, written in calligraphy or typeset, unadorned or embellished with artwork, ribbons and colour (for design ideas, head to Chapter 8 on invitations).

A typical layout for an order of service includes:

- **Front cover:** The name of the couple – 'The Marriage Ceremony of Sophie and Henry', for example – along with the date and place.

- **Pages two and three:** The ceremony step by step, complete with music and readings.

- **Back cover:** Printing on the back cover is optional and could feature everyone involved in the ceremony – the officiant(s), the bride and groom, their parents, the wedding party and any musicians you've hired for the ceremony. For a more elaborate order of service with multiple pages, you may have a more detailed programme, especially if you have many guests unfamiliar with the ceremony traditions – for example, when to respond at particular points during a religious service. You may also want to include foreign-language translations; words to the readings, songs, prayers or blessings; or explanations of religious or ethnic rituals, customs or military traditions. Apart from repeating reception site details, don't tell guests more than they need to know about your wedding-day schedule (see Chapter 14).

When listing the music, include the processional, music or songs during the ceremony (including hymn numbers) and the recessional. Also list names of soloists and musicians, indicating who's performing what.

Figure 16-1 shows a typical order of service for a Christian ceremony. Figure 16-2 gives you a structure for planning a programme for a civil wedding ceremony.

ORDER OF CEREMONY

The Marriage of

Sophie Smith-Jones
and
Henry Featherstone

11th August 2014

St Mary's Church, Mayfair

Figure 16-1:
An example
of a simple
order of
service for
a Christian
wedding.
(page 1 of 4)

PRELUDE

*THE PROCESSIONAL – **Bridal Chorus – by Wagner***

THE WELCOME

HYMN
Give Me Joy In My Heart

INTRODUCTION TO BRIDE & GROOM

READING

'The One' by Author Unknown

THE MARRIAGE

THE ADDRESS

READING
Song of Solomon 2:10-13 & 8:6-7

Figure 16-1:
An example
of a simple
order of
service for
a Christian
wedding.
(page 2 of 4)

HYMN
The Lord Of The Dance
THE PRAYERS

The Lords Prayer
Our Father, who art in heaven
Hallowed be thy name; Thy kingdom come;
Thy will be done;
On earth as it is in heaven.
Give us this day our daily bread.
And forgive us our trespasses,
As we forgive those who trespass against us.
And lead us not into temptation;
But deliver us from evil.
For thine is the kingdom;
The power and the glory,
For ever and ever.
AMEN

SIGNING OF THE REGISTER

THE EXCHANGING OF RINGS

RECESSIONAL

The Wedding March – by Mendelssohn

Figure 16-1:
An example
of a simple
order of
service for
a Christian
wedding.
(page 3 of 4)

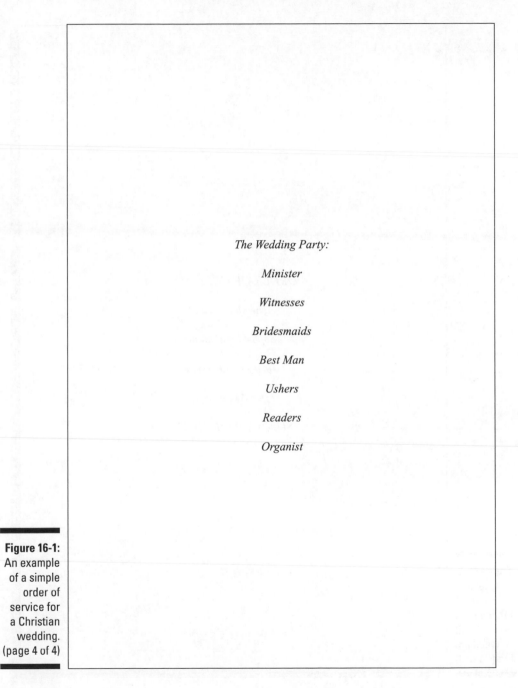

The Wedding Party:

Minister

Witnesses

Bridesmaids

Best Man

Ushers

Readers

Organist

Figure 16-1:
An example
of a simple
order of
service for
a Christian
wedding.
(page 4 of 4)

ORDER OF CEREMONY

The Marriage of

Sophie Smith-Jones
and
Henry Featherstone

11th August 2014

SURREY PARK HOUSE

Figure 16-2:
A sample
order of
service for a
civil
wedding.
(page 1 of 3)

PRELUDE

*THE PROCESSIONAL – **Canon D – J. Pachelbel***

REGISTRARS WELCOME

DEFINITION OF MARRIAGE

INTRODUCTION TO BRIDE & GROOM

READING

*'**All I Ever Really Needed to Know I Learned in Kindergarten'** – Robert Fulgham*

STATUTORY DECLARATION

STATUTORY MARRIAGE CONTRACT

Figure 16-2:
A sample
order of
service for a
civil
wedding.
(page 2 of 3)

THE EXCHANGING OF RINGS

PRONOUNCEMENT

SIGNING OF THE REGISTER

READING

'Yes, I'll Marry You' – Pam Ayres

CONCLUSION

RECESSIONAL

One Day Like This – Elbow

Music Performed by xxx Strings

Figure 16-2:
A sample
order of
service for a
civil
wedding.
(page 3 of 3)

Places, Everyone – Time to Rehearse

Rehearsals not only make the wedding run smoothly, but also tremendously reduce the angst level. If you have children in the ceremony, the rehearsal helps them get a sensory hold on what they'll be doing. (Come to think of it, that's why adults need rehearsals too.)

Attendants may be quite blasé when handed a wedding-day schedule (see Chapter 14) at the rehearsal, and may even make hilarious jokes about the 'mindless minutiae' and the 'control freak' who penned it. These are usually the same folks who ask for a new copy an hour before the ceremony and clutch it as if it were a life-support system.

Having a quick run-through

You usually hold the rehearsal the night before the wedding, ideally where the ceremony is to be. The time should be late enough in the afternoon to accommodate those coming from work, but early enough so you can greet other guests arriving for the rehearsal dinner (if applicable). Now isn't the time to start choreographing your rehearsal. With a delineated schedule, a rehearsal shouldn't take more than 45 minutes, even for an elaborate ceremony. If you have people coming to the rehearsal who haven't seen each other in a long time, allot extra time to get hugs, kisses and gossip out of the way.

Seating your guests

The marriage ceremony can be held in a variety of configurations if you aren't in a religious setting and therefore not bound by house rules. For example, you may face the guests as you take your vows. Another option is seating 'in the round' or in a semi-circle. In such cases, break up the rows with extra aisles that are smaller than the main one. Allow a centre aisle wide enough for double the number of people walking down it. (Make sure that the aisle is of equal width from front to back.)

For a ceremony with chairs arranged in rows chapel style, allow just under one metre from the edge of one chair to the back of the next. Make each row short enough to provide easy access and egress. If you must have long rows,

create a couple of extra aisles so people can get in and out. Long rows across inevitably mean that half the guests have to get up so one person can take a seat in the middle. ('Excuse me. Excuse me. Excuse me. Uh, were those your toes?') Also, have an even number of seats in each row because most people come in couples.

When at the ceremony, guests often feel it looks presumptuous to let ushers know they deserve front-row seats. If you don't apprise ushers ahead of time, you may find yourselves looking at rows of empty chairs during your ceremony. You may also mark reserved seats with small, informal cards.

Rehearsals in a church usually involve the minister as well as the person responsible for the chapel, who puts everyone through their paces. If your minister participates in your rehearsal, invite her (and spouse) to the rehearsal dinner. A minister who's your family clergyperson or a friend should also be invited (with spouse) to the reception. You may ask the clergyperson to say grace.

Sadly, having a civil ceremony rehearsal isn't usually possible as the registrars don't offer this service. That said, if you can get access to your wedding venue, you can conduct a rehearsal without the registrar. Try to nominate someone to lead the proceedings on your behalf – a wedding co-ordinator is the ideal choice (see Chapter 1).

Your wedding co-ordinator may also be in charge of the line-up. If you can't rehearse where your ceremony is going to be, improvise in another space, perhaps where the dinner is being held, timing it so you finish before the other guests get there. Set up the first row of chairs with an aisle in the middle – the point is to give participants an idea of where to stand as well as whom they're walking with and in what order.

When setting up chairs for a ceremony in an off-premise location, be sure that you overestimate the width of the aisle. Test it and retest it and insist that the wedding planner go over it with you. Your ceremony will be completely thrown off if you appear in a wide dress with a parent on either side and you can't negotiate the space between the chairs without resorting to single file.

Getting musicians you've hired to play at the rehearsal as well is usually cost-prohibitive (although the organist is sometimes available). Fortunately, music isn't really necessary for a walk-through. If, however, you'll sleep better having the total experience, bring your music on a portable sound system and have someone cue it at the right moments for the processional and recessional.

You need to give the participants a visual cue so they know when to go next down the aisle. You may tell them to wait until the person(s) ahead of them has reached a certain row. If you don't have a wedding co-ordinator, you need to appoint someone who can cue the musicians and the wedding party.

Going over the rules and expectations

One round of both the processional and the recessional should be sufficient as a run-through. Just make sure you go over these details:

✓ **Prelude:**

- Schedule the prelude music to begin when guests start arriving, 15 minutes to a half hour before the ceremony. After the ceremony, the music should continue until the last person leaves the ceremony area, or as soon as the reception music starts, if the reception is adjacent.

- If you're getting married in a private home or other space where there's a phone, silence the ringer or disconnect the line for the duration of the ceremony.

- Tell ushers to be welcoming and friendly to the guests, not stand in a clump. They should know where the nearest toilets are, and they should have extra directions to the reception.

- Ushers and bridesmaids should attempt to look happy and relaxed when walking down the aisle.

- Make sure all key people sit in allocated seats in the front two rows. Remember to save a seat for the father of the bride and the bridesmaids. Remind readers to sit at the end of pews.

Reserved seating, aside from the first two or three rows for close friends or relatives, is rare these days. Because most couples are joining their family and friends together, having the ushers ask, 'Bride's side or groom's side?' isn't necessary.

- For a Christian ceremony, the bride's mother is the last to be seated. Designate at the rehearsal who will escort her.

- If you have an aisle runner, two ushers have the job of unfurling it after the bride's mother is seated and before the ceremony begins.

✔ **Procession:**

- Practise the processional order so bridesmaids know what order to walk in and, more importantly, where to sit down.

✔ **Ceremony:**

- Walk to the signing-of-the-register table with your witnesses so you all know what route to take.

- When the bride arrives at the altar or registrar's table, she should hand her bouquet to her maid of honour so that her hands are free. If she's wearing gloves, she should remove these before the ring portion of the ceremony and hand them to an attendant. The attendant should remember to give these items back to the bride before the recessional.

- All who are standing should keep their knees relaxed. If your knees lock at the altar for a prolonged period of time, the flow of blood is constricted and you may faint.

✔ **Recessional:**

- Practise the recessional. Think about whether it will be just the bride and groom exiting formally, or whether the wedding party will also proceed in a set order.

- Many churches have heavy doors at the entrance. Make sure that someone is assigned to open the doors and prop them open when the recessional music begins. We hate to see a just-married couple have to stop and wrench the doors open, and then wait for someone to hold them.

✔ **Postlude:**

- If you don't have a wedding co-ordinator and you have several cars going to the reception, appoint an usher-and-bridesmaid-traffic-team to serve as ground control.

Things to throw

Releasing a tide of helium-filled balloons and watching them drift up and out of sight seems romantic but is in fact environmentally unfriendly. The balloons eventually deflate and become random litter, get hung up in trees, or wind up in lakes and oceans, where animals such as whales, birds and dolphins ingest them and die. Rice has also fallen out of favour because it expands in the stomachs of birds and other creatures and can be fatal. And very few venues allow you to throw paper confetti anymore; normally, they insist on biodegradable confetti. Seeing last week's paper confetti at your wedding is not nice. If you feel you must have something thrown, try birdseed, flower petals or having bubbles blown at you instead – ask your ushers to hand your guests 'confetti cones' with your chosen 'confetti' as they leave the ceremony venue.

Part IV
A Rousing Reception

Bar Setup Checklist

❑ Does the caterer charge a service or corkage fee on top of the bar 'setup' fee that includes ice and fruit?

❑ Is it possible for the hosts to personally supply any wines or Champagne at an in-house venue? If so, what is the corkage fee?

❑ Will the liquor supplier take back unopened bottles of liquor and unchilled bottles of wine?

❑ Do you wish to have blended drinks, speciality drinks, or drinks that require special preparation? (For example: drinks such as cosmopolitans, martinis and margaritas that require shaking and particular glasses.) What ingredients and equipment do you need to arrange in advance? Are any of those included in the regular bar setup?

❑ What non-alcoholic beverages will be available? (These might include fruited iced teas, fresh squeezed juices, sangria without alcohol filled with slices of fresh lemons, limes, and oranges and served in glass pitchers, or nonalcoholic beers.)

❑ If you're using a full-service facility, what brands will the banquet manager provide? What is the price difference between inexpensive 'well' brands and 'premium' or 'top shelf,' the most expensive?

❑ Will your site accept liquor deliveries in advance of your reception? Do they have a secure place to keep it?

❑ If you're supplying the liquor, where should leftover open bottles of liquor be left? Who will pick them up for you after the wedding?

❑ Do you feel comfortable serving liquor to suppliers such as musicians and photographers? How do you want to instruct the caterer regarding this matter?

web extras

Toasts are an important part of most weddings. Head to www.dummies.com/extras/weddingplanninguk for some top tips on making them memorable.

Part IV

A Rousing Reception

In this part...

✔ Unleash your taste buds and devise mouthwatering menus for your wedding day.

✔ Ensure that you have the right drinks on hand.

✔ Bring in the 'wow' factor with a stunning wedding cake.

✔ Think about the music you want to hear at different points of your day.

Chapter 17

What's on the Menu?

In This Chapter
▶ Choosing and communicating with your caterer
▶ Letting your taste buds take the lead
▶ Weighing up the main-meal options: sit-down versus buffet
▶ Finding alternatives to the formal dinner reception

The ceremony was splendid – neither of you fumbled your vows and there wasn't a dry eye in the house. Now your guests 'ooh' and 'aah' as they promenade into the reception space, which is aglow with candles and as fragrant as the gardens of Giverny. A brigade of tuxedoed staff appears, choreographed as if in an Andrew Lloyd Webber musical. In unison, 150 hands reach down and each guest plucks an exotic-looking canapé from a gleaming tray, pops the morsel into their mouth – and begins frantically searching for a cocktail napkin in which to spit.

How can you keep all this spitting from happening at your reception? Don't expect to wave your magic wedding wand and turn processed cheese slices into brie en croûte. But creating an imaginative and tasty meal doesn't require magic. All you need is time, determination and trust in your own taste buds.

In this chapter, we examine the many ways you can serve the food at your wedding, no matter what your budget.

Finding and Working with the Perfect Caterer

If you're renting an off-premise space (see Chapter 4), you need to find a caterer. Although asking friends for recommendations may seem natural, taste in food is really, really subjective. Consider these other sources for recommendations:

✔ **Culinary schools:** Ask whether they have an alumni list, association or job bank. Check out the bulletin boards and post a 'caterer wanted' ad.

- ✔ **Preferred list:** Many venues that require you to hire outside caterers have a preferred list that you must select from – ask for references from the venue and an idea of their price range. Contact approximately three from the list and hold interviews.

- ✔ **Professional associations:** If you're planning a long-distance wedding and have absolutely no clue where to begin, consult a professional association in that country.

- ✔ **Restaurant chefs:** Ask the chef at your favourite restaurant whether they cater outside of their premises – or whether they're particularly impressed with any caterer in the area.

- ✔ **Vendors:** The best recommendations often come from other suppliers – wedding planners, bands, florists, party co-ordinators – who've worked with these caterers and know what really goes on behind the kitchen doors.

Call and ask caterers for an information package that includes sample menus. If the packet is stuffed with recommendation letters, as is often the case, the majority should be current. Don't be shy about calling references. Write down your questions before you pick up the phone. Be as specific as possible in relation to the style you have in mind for your reception, as well as how much help you can expect with the ceremony and other aspects not directly related to food and service.

Here are some questions to ask people about their experience with specific caterers:

- ✔ Did the caterer deliver what they promised?

- ✔ Were expensive items, such as prawns, plentiful?

- ✔ Were the staff neat and prompt?

- ✔ Were there enough bartenders and service people? Did guests ever have to wait for anything?

- ✔ Was the food tasty and attractive?

- ✔ What were the downsides, if any? (To get an honest answer, qualify this question by saying, 'Not that your answer would necessarily keep me from hiring this caterer. . . .')

Before making any decisions, meet with caterers in person, preferably at their kitchen/offices. This meeting should give you a fair idea of their manner and workmanship. Are they brusque? Disorganised? Clean? Does their workspace smell yummy? Are they legally licensed? Do they have a certificate of inspection in the kitchen? Do you relate well to the person you'd be working with? Figure 17-1 lists some key questions to ask.

Caterer Interview Checklist

- What ideas, if any, does the caterer have regarding appropriate spaces for your wedding?

- If you have found your space already, has the caterer worked there before? If not, will the caterer make a site visit before writing a proposal?

- What specific menus can the caterer recommend that will work in that facility's kitchen?

- Does the caterer have sample menus? Are there photographs of the work?

- What references can the caterer provide?

- What are the caterer's specialities?

- How flexible is the caterer in planning a menu?

- Can you have a tasting? At what cost?

- How does the caterer price the menus?

- Is a wedding cake included? If not, what are the charges? Can you supply one? Is there a cake-cutting fee?

- What are the specific hourly charges for all staff such as waiters, captains, and kitchen staff? What additional gratuities are suggested? What are the overtime charges?

- How many staff people would they suggest for your event, and how many hours would each staff member work?

- How do they handle the rentals? Must you use a specific company? What choices do you have for rentals, such as glass, silver, china, and linens?

- What does the caterer own that will be included, such as props, platters, or kitchen equipment?

- Will you receive separate food, service, and rental bills?

- How do they handle the liquor?

- Assuming that you are allowed to supply your own liquor, what suppliers does the caterer suggest? Ordering suggestions?

- What do they charge for setups (soda, ice, fruit)?

- How involved will the caterer be in your wedding — just supplying food or helping with the ceremony and other facets?

- What is the caterer's educated estimate on *total* costs for food, liquor, rentals, and staff for your party?

Figure 17-1:
Ask the right questions when interviewing prospective caterers.

Comparing pricing between off-premise sites (where you bring in a caterer) and on-premise sites (where you must use the venue's catering team), such as hotels or banquet halls, is slightly tricky. For an on-premise site, tally the cost of the food, beverages, VAT and service charge. For an off-premise site, combine the site fee with the caterer's estimates on food, alcohol and other drinks, rentals and service. If you interview several caterers for one site, use an average of their estimated costs as the catering charge for that site. (For a full explanation of on- and off-premise sites, see Chapter 4.)

Savouring Your Options: From Concept to Taste

As with other things in life, the greater the interest you take in your wedding meal and the more personalised your choices, the better the results and the more you'll enjoy it. The best way to start designing your meal is to have some idea of what you want to serve.

Whether you're dealing with an in-house catering operation (such as at a banquet facility, restaurant, club or hotel) or hiring a caterer for a site you're renting, before you concoct elaborate haute cuisine wish lists, start with their sample menus, which constitute their greatest hits. Request to meet with the banquet manager and/or catering director and ask them to tell you – for real – the kitchen's strengths and weaknesses.

To focus your search for the perfect meal, take a few preliminary steps:

- **Take a palate poll.** What are your and your intended's favourite restaurants? Favourite meals? What do family and friends like to eat? What may be considered too exotic? Do most of the guests eat meat? (see the later section, 'Considering special dietary requirements').

- **Adapt a recipe.** Go through cookbooks and food magazines for ideas and concepts. Keep in mind, however, that unless you're holding a wedding for ten people, something like hand-rolled pasta carbonara won't translate. Chefs are usually open to using your favourite recipes – as long as they come from reliable sources such as professional cookbooks.

- **Tap your know-it-all pals.** If you have friends who always know the hot new restaurants or actually work in the food business, ask them for their opinions.

Next comes the fun bit: tasting time.

Setting up the tasting

If your wedding is in a restaurant's banquet space, the meal for your reception may be prepared in a banquet kitchen completely separate from the main restaurant kitchen. Therefore, a meal in the restaurant may bear no resemblance to the food you'll have at your wedding. So a tasting session is important.

After you book a space or caterer, we feel that you're entitled to a free tasting, so make sure that point is either spelled out in the contract or in an oral agreement. Schedule the tasting far enough before your wedding date so that you have time for a second one if needed, although not so far ahead that key ingredients are out of season. If your caterer doesn't do a free tasting as standard, ask whether they attend wedding fairs and shows to which you could pop along to sample their wares or, alternatively, make a special request to arrange a tasting.

Your caterer will tell you how many people you can bring to the tasting. Besides you and your spouse-to-be, the banquet manager should be there to offer professional comments and suggestions. You may also want to include your parents or in-laws, or perhaps a trusted 'foodie' friend. Ask how many people can attend the tasting, free of charge. Most caterers and venues include the bride and groom free of charge, but you may have to pay a fee for anyone else to attend. We recommend no more than four people from your side attend the tasting; any more and discussions can get very heated and decisions difficult to make.

Because of the cost of labour and ingredients, places often won't let you taste the canapés unless they're booking huge numbers consistently. In such cases, ask whether they have an event coming up and can make up a 'take-away' tray for you to sample at home. (You will, of course, offer to pay for this.) If they can't accommodate you, can they at least show you photographs and describe ingredients in detail?

Getting the best out of the tasting session

At this stage of the game, you want to keep a few things in mind:

✔ **Ask to taste two or three options for each course.** You may think you're set on filet mignon, but after tasting the chef's specialty lamb, you change your mind completely. In principle, a kitchen should shine at preparing a meal for two or four people. If it doesn't, the meal served to your guests could be even worse.

✔ **Request that the food's presentation be exactly as it would be at your wedding.** If you decide on poached salmon that's beautifully plated, rimmed by a painstakingly drizzled nouvelle sauce and garnished with flowers for your wedding, then it should look the same on your tasting day, not dumped from a tray by a waiter.

✔ **Taste food and wine together.** Either bring the wine you're considering serving or ask the caterer to supply some selections in your price range.

✔ **Go about the tasting professionally.** Don't stuff yourself with every last canapé and lick your plate clean; save room for dessert. Enjoy yourself and consider the experience your guests will have at your wedding.

✔ **Ask questions and take notes.** Is it possible to have this sauce on that dish? Can we have a little less/more seasoning with the vegetables? What if we served this with coffee ice cream instead of vanilla? Take notes, draw pictures and be ridiculously detailed. Yours is probably not the only event that the chef is working on at the moment, and details that are important to you may fall through the cracks unless you furnish notes or a follow-up letter summarising your desires.

Taste with your eyes as well as your mouth – be very specific about how you'd like the food to look.

Ask your caterer to pack a few portions of each course (including the wedding cake) for you to take when you leave your reception to assuage the inevitable 3 a.m. munchies. Now's also the time to ask whether leftovers can go to a local soup kitchen or charity, if this is what you want.

Building rapport with the chef

Find out who's really in charge of cooking your meal – the banquet chef, sous-chef or someone farther down the totem pole. Having a lovely meeting or tasting with a well-known executive chef or the chef for the restaurant kitchen does no good unless one of them is actually involved in the preparation of the meal at your event.

If at all possible, meet with the chef to determine what the kitchen staff can produce well for a group of your size. Although chefs have a reputation for being intimidating, in our experience they're flattered when someone cares what they think, and that can have a decided impact on what comes out of the kitchen. If the catering manager and chef, as well as the references you've called, all recommend a very basic menu, listen to them and keep it simple.

Creating a Memorable Reception Meal

Deciding on how your meal will be served is a matter of your individual tastes, the style or theme of your wedding, what your venue can accommodate and, of course, your budget. Here we discuss the main ways you could serve the food at your wedding reception.

Whether you're serving lunch or dinner, your reception meal can be as formal or as casual as you want. If you're hiring a marquee or a rustic barn in the height of summer you may decide that a buffet with a hog roast would suit the occasion far more than a sit-down four-course meal. Similarly, if you've booked the best hotel in town and asked your guests to wear black-tie, they may be expecting more than a light buffet.

One of your main decisions, therefore, is whether to have a seated meal, served in a formal or casual way, or a buffet, which can be seated or standing. With either option, the quality of your food should still be paramount; you just need to choose the right style for you.

Tucking into the postnuptial nibbles

Between the wedding ceremony and the reception meal is usually a drinks reception at which nibbles are traditionally served with the drinks. What you serve is up to you, but choose something that suits your theme and the type of wedding you've arranged. Crisps and nuts may be all you need for a casual outdoor wedding but for a more formal wedding the usual choice is *canapés*, which are small, bite-sized, savoury morsels of deliciousness often served on bread or pastry. Canapés should be easy for your guests to eat in *one* bite. They are normally served on trays with no knives, forks or spoons, although a toothpick or skewer may be fine and, if necessary, a small plate with a small fork is okay.

We suggest you choose the canapés *after* you choose what you're serving for your main meal so you don't duplicate foods, perhaps by following up salmon rolls served at the drinks reception with grilled salmon at dinner, for example. Also take into consideration the rehearsal-dinner menu (if you have a rehearsal dinner the night before). When in doubt, the wedding meal should take precedence.

Canapés are usually priced per piece or are included in the meal package with a choice of hot and cold options. Ideally, you should have both, and don't forget to include a few vegetarian options, too. Ask how many pieces of each canapé are served within your price level. Between six to eight canapés per person is ample for a one- to one-and-a-half-hour drinks reception. You can find some neat ideas for creating your canapé menu in the 'Creating a winning selection of canapés' section, further on in the chapter.

Serving up a sumptuous sit-down meal

Sit-down dinners or lunches can be served in a formal way or a more casual style, with family fare.

Putting together a formal sit-down menu

If you're serving a formal seated lunch or dinner, typically you'll serve three courses, although some couples opt for a four-course dinner which has the addition of a fish course between the first and main courses. For an even grander dinner you may offer five courses, with one course being a 'palette cleanser'. The number of courses you serve depends both on your budget and how you want to time your wedding. Obviously, the more courses, the longer the dinner.

When putting together a menu, try to keep the first course light and simple so that your guests aren't stuffed to the gills by the time the main course arrives. Cold soup in the spring or summer or a light salad or vegetable terrine are good choices. In the colder months, warm soups, seasonal winter vegetables and warm salads work well.

If you choose to serve a fish course between the first and main courses, choose something that your guests will recognise and can eat easily (we suggest that you keep away from anything on the bone). Salmon, cod or scallops, for example, are always popular. Fish courses have been less popular for the past 20 or so years, as the cost can be prohibitive, but historically this course was a special part of the menu.

Main courses at weddings are often beef, chicken, lamb or fish, with a vegetarian option available, as this is what people generally like to eat. The rule of thumb for *mass catering* (that is, where numbers are higher than at a dinner party) is normally 'keep it simple'. Your caterer can talk you through many ways to serve these staple foods in interesting ways and appropriate accompaniments to have with them for the season.

If you choose to serve a palette cleanser, this course is usually served between the main course and dessert, although, depending on what you choose, it can be served between the first and the main course. *Palette cleansers* (sometimes called *amuse bouche*) are usually small, dainty morsels served in cups, such as a tomato consommé, or in Martini glasses, such as sorbet or a granita – with or without alcohol!

Desserts have become the pièce de résistance for 21st-century weddings. They can be as elaborate or simple as you want (again, depending on your budget), but try to leave your guests with something great by which to remember your wedding meal. In recent times the *trio of desserts* has been very popular, where chefs serve three mini desserts on one plate – perfect for a couple who cannot decide which dessert to choose at their tasting! Great desserts, however, need not be expensive and some firm favourites have been making a comeback lately: apple crumble with custard, lemon, treacle, chocolate or custard tart with double cream, and summer fruit jelly and ice-cream, to name just three. Or, why not skip dessert and serve your cake? You could also consider the option of having a dessert table rather than having dessert served at the table.

Figures 17-2 and 17-3 show samples of three-course summer and winter menus.

Figure 17-2:
A typical summer menu.

Menu

English Asparagus,, Hollandaise Sauce and Poached Egg

Baked Glazed Fillet of Salmon on crushed dill, New Potatoes

Strawberries and Clotted Cream Tart

Figure 17-3:
A typical winter menu.

Menu

Roast Pumpkin Soup, served with Homemade Sourdough

Rack of Lamb,, Mashed Potatoes, Fine Green Beans and a Red Wine Sauce

Chocolate Cheese Cake

Less-formal seated dinners

If done well, menus served in a more casual way can be fantastic for weddings. This style is somewhere between a formal silver service and asking guests to serve themselves at a buffet. Less formal seated dinners are also a way of creating a memorable wedding feast without breaking the bank.

At a casual seated dinner, your guests remain seated and the food is served to the table on platters or in bowls for guests to share between themselves. Again, keep the first course simple and then rev things up for the main course. This type of dinner is a great way to serve international cuisine in particular, such as Italian pasta or lasagne, Indian curry, Lebanese mezze or Spanish tapas. More traditional British fare can also be served in this way with hearty stews, fish pies or steak and kidney puddings.

For authentic ethnic pastries or other specialty side dishes that are time-consuming to make or which require hard-to-get ingredients, consider ordering them separately from an ethnic bakery, deli or restaurant and having them delivered to your reception site. They can be served to the table or be part of your buffet. Most venues will be happy to accommodate you if you'd like something they don't specialise in, though you'll have to ask in advance and may have to sign a disclaimer.

In order to make your wedding dinner even grander, you may want to offer a special wine menu to complement each course. (For the lowdown on drinks head to Chapter 18.)

Serving with style

Be clear with the banquet manager or caterer how and when food is to be served, and how you want the tables to be set. You've spent a great deal of time (and money) on how these tables are going to look when you come into the dining room. One of our personal dislikes: tables that are pre-set with the first course and/or the accoutrements for coffee service. Although sometimes necessary, pre-set food makes people question how long it's been there.

Food is usually served in one of three ways:

- ✔ **French service:** Waiters heat plates and garnish food at a side table or cart called a *guéridon*. If done properly, this technique is very impressive. Although considered for eons the height of elegance, it's rather slow and requires a great deal of space.

- ✔ **Plated or à la carte:** Waiters carry the food out on plates. By far the most elegant way to serve plated food is to have waiters carry two plates at a time and complete one table at a time. The main advantage is that the food arrives at each place the way it was meant to look rather than improvised by the waiters.

- ✔ **Silver (English) service:** The waiters serve the food at the table, transferring from a service dish to the guest's plate from the left.

A ratio of one waiter to ten guests per table is ideal. Skimping on the number of servers can be a penny-wise but pound-foolish decision. If you're trying to save money, this isn't the place to cut corners – getting a waiter's attention shouldn't feel like hailing a cab in a typhoon.

If you're holding your reception in a marquee, the person working with you from the catering company should advise you on the best way to serve the dinner and ensure the service is not slow. (See Chapter 5 for information on marquee receptions.)

Bigging up buffets

Your reception will be much shorter and, in most – though not all – cases, less expensive with a buffet than with a served meal, because you don't need to have so many staff serving the meal and the downtime between courses disappears. If you prefer not to, you don't have to serve the entire dinner as a buffet; you could have a seated first course before inviting a few tables at a time to go to the buffet.

Buffets can be seated or standing (see the later 'When Dinner is not Served' section), hot or cold, and they can be served traditionally on one or two long tables or from buffet stations. Having several stations requires extra plates (assume three plates per person) so that guests can take a fresh one at each station – something to keep in mind if you're renting china. You also need plenty of staff to bus this many plates and man the stations. The success of a buffet really depends on the quality of food you're serving, how it is served and the number of catering staff you have available to assist your guests.

Opting for a traditional buffet

The *traditional buffet* comprises a long table with the food served in sections – salads, main courses, vegetables and perhaps a separate table for desserts (see Figure 17-4). Catering staff often stand behind the table and serve guests from hot plates. Many couples find this a little too casual for their liking and it can, if not managed properly, cause long delays in some tables getting their food.

If you decide on the traditional buffet, your caterer should advise you on the best way to avoid long queues and keep traffic flowing. It may be that you have two identical buffet tables at either end of the room so that you effectively halve the time that it will take for your guests to visit the buffet. Your caterers should also be vigilant in ensuring that the platters or hot plates are never empty. Some dishes may be more popular than others and nothing slows down a buffet service more than running out of the roast potatoes, for instance, with guests waiting for a fresh batch to arrive from the kitchen.

Menu

Carpaccio of Spiced Tuna

Apple & Red Chicory Salad, Lemon & Honey Dressing

Selection of Seasonal Salad

oOo

Selection of Roasts: Beef, Salmon and Turkey

Roasted Potatoes and Selection of Seasonal Vegetables

Ice carving — Chef's choice seafood platter, including prawns, sushi and sashimi

oOo

Selection of desserts including : Chocolate and caramel tart;

champagne raspberry jelly; lemon posset with fresh blueberries

Cheese & biscuits

Figure 17-4:
A traditional
buffet menu,
perfect for
an indoor
wedding
venue.

Going with buffet stations

The in-vogue idea of buffet stations has come from abroad (Italy, Asia and the US prefer this method of serving buffets) and it can be a lot of fun. *Buffet* or *food stations* enable you to serve eclectic and creative meals without creating traffic jams at one single table that is trying to service everyone at the same time. Particularly if you're having a marquee wedding with a lot of outside space, buffet stations are a great way to make use of that large area.

The idea of buffet stations is that you have many stations or tables set up around the room that guests can pick and choose from, each of which offers a different type of food: one could offer carved meats, another seafood, the next fruits, cheeses and stuffed vegetables; still another, seasonal salad combinations. If you and your spouse have a mixture of ethnic backgrounds you could have stations with different international cuisines – an Indian station, a Chinese station and a Thai station, for example. Each station should be manned by a member of staff or even a chef. This can work particularly well on dessert stations – one couple we know had a chef making fresh crêpes suzette on order for guests.

Putting together a buffet menu

Whether you have a traditional buffet or stations, choose your menu with the same care and attention as you would a seated dinner – pick a variety of colors, textures and temperatures of food. Figures 17-4 and 17-5 show some example buffet menus.

Figure 17-5:
A summer buffet menu, perfect for an outdoor, marquee wedding.

> *Menu*
>
> Spit-Roasted Free-Range Pig with Apply Sauce and
> Sage and Onion Stuffing
>
> New Potatoes tossed in Minted Butter
>
> Greek Salad, Pasta Salad, Coleslaw and Mixed-Leaf Salad
>
> Roasted Peppers Stuffed with Herbed Rice
>
> Vegetarian Lasagna
>
> Our Wedding Cake

As well as the food itself, discuss with your caterer how you want your buffet to *look*, too. A line-up of even the spiffiest silver serving dishes can look fairly institutional, so ask to have items served at different temperatures and in a variety of bowls and platters in addition to silver dishes. Ask your caterer who decorates the stations, whether they own interesting vessels from which to serve the food, and whether they have specific props for certain dishes, such as netting for a seafood station. One idea that works well for buffets with an Italian theme, for example, is to casually throw chillies and herbs on the table between serving dishes to add a rustic, authentic feel.

Here are some other presentational ideas for you to consider:

✔ Buying a bolt of inexpensive fabric and puddling the material around the serving dishes.

✔ Using painted backdrops, creative signage and simple props.

✔ Displaying foods at various heights by using tiered candy trays or specially constructed props.

✔ Creating peaks and valleys by using linen-covered milk crates or small hay stacks; tilting platters by propping them up with upside-down plates underneath.

✔ Garnishing tables with bunches of beautiful fruits and vegetables such as grapes, artichokes, chillies and apples.

✔ Making *topiaries* (mini trees) out of foods such as lemons, figs or nuts.

✔ Piling round tables high with dried fruits, nuts, olives or marinated vegetables – anything that guests can help themselves to without creating a mess. (Ask a waiter to keep them looking fresh and appetising.)

✔ Adding a touch of showmanship with food cooked or finished in front of the guests. (Pasta, carved meats, grilled chicken skewers, fajitas and other foods are all the more tantalising when prepared on the spot by a chef.)

✔ Creating mini-vignettes such as a sushi station designed as a Zen rock garden with a tiny fountain and bonsai trees.

When Dinner is Not Served: Nibbles and Nosh for Other Times

Although seated dinners and lunches are the most popular types of receptions, they're not for everyone. The other options include a cocktail party, afternoon teas, wedding breakfasts or brunches and a full-on party. Although these affairs are usually less costly and less fussy, they still require thought and ingenuity.

Cocktail party pointers

Here are some specific guidelines for cocktail parties:

✔ Two-and-a-half to three hours is the optimum length for a cocktail party. Anything shorter is too rushed; anything longer feels dragged out. If you go to four or five hours or decide to have a 'party' rather than 'cocktail party' (see the 'Partying full-on' sidebar), make sure that you have ample food, drink and cake – you may, in fact, prefer to serve a casual buffet rather than just canapés. Consider having a dessert table, which can also function as a mouth-watering decor element. Or perhaps even a chocolate fountain, always a firm favourite.

✔ Stagger the selection of served canapés so guests don't get bored.

✔ Provide enough food so that guests aren't racing to leave for a real meal.

✔ Ensure the entire room set-up is clearly that of a cocktail party rather than a dinner gone awry. Tables should be no larger than 32 inches in diameter (poseur), and you should only have enough seating for about a third of the guests maximum.

✔ Specify on the invitation that the reception isn't for dinner, as in, 'Please join us for cocktails and canapés to celebrate our marriage.' This particular wording also makes it clear that guests aren't invited to the ceremony. Refer to Chapter 8 for more on invitation wording.

✔ Don't give an end time for the party. Serving a wedding cake, dessert and coffee at the beginning of the last hour and toning down the music is usually enough of a hint for guests to wind down the festivities.

Creating a winning selection of canapés

Canapés – lovely little nibbles – are all the rage for the postnuptial and pre-dinner drinks reception (see the earlier 'Tucking into the postnuptial nibbles' section). Many people like them so much that they ditch the main meal altogether and stick with bite-size treats. Serving solely cocktails and canapés, rather than a meal, for the reception is a fine choice in a variety of circumstances; for example, where:

✔ The space you've fallen in love with can seat only a third or fewer of your guests.

✔ Your reception is a celebratory party that's been postponed for several days or weeks after the ceremony.

✔ You're an older or previously married couple and don't feel comfortable having a traditional wedding reception.

✔ You have vast numbers of guests you *must* invite but you can't afford a seated meal for all of them.

✔ You simply want a non-traditional affair.

The trick is not to show that you can afford umpteen canapés, but to design a menu that has broad appeal, is appetising and leaves guests with energy to party.

There are some real favourites where canapés are concerned and most catering companies will happily provide you with an extensive list. Some of our favourite hot canapés include:

✔ Crab cakes with sweet chilli sauce

✔ Crispy pork or prawn or vegetable spring rolls

✔ Crispy tiger prawns with a Thai dipping sauce

✔ Grilled foie gras on brioche with fig butter

✔ Miniature beef Wellingtons

✔ Miniature cones of beer-battered fish and chips

✔ Mini burgers on tiny seeded buns

✔ Roasted or deep-fried calamari with cocktail sauce

✔ Sesame chicken fingers with honey mustard

✔ Spinach-and-cheese-filled filo triangles

✔ Steamed vegetable dumplings with hoisin sauce

✔ Tiny wild mushroom tarts

✔ Vegetable or meat samosas

In addition, you'll want to serve some canapés that are cold or room temperature:

✔ Cheddar cheese straws

✔ Grilled prawns on little gem leaves

✔ Oysters topped with wasabi, served on porcelain spoons

✔ Salmon tartar on black bread rounds

✔ Scottish smoked salmon blinis with sour cream

✔ Shot glasses of chilled pea soup or gazpacho

✔ Vegetable sushi rolls

Tea for two (hundred)

Having a tea in lieu of a full meal is popular for many of the same reasons that having a cocktail party reception is, particularly if you want to have a daytime wedding or include children. The menu may feature many of the classic tea foods – cucumber sandwiches, petits fours, sweet biscuits – but if you have a sizable crowd, you may consider having canapés (see the preceding section) and even include a Champagne toast.

A tea may seem like one of the simplest receptions imaginable, but you can spiff it up by offering several unusual flavoured teas, available at gourmet shops and specialty stores, and using a variety of interesting teapots and mix-and-match vintage crockery.

Other ways to munch: Breakfast, brunch or lunch

You may often hear the term 'wedding breakfast' used for the reception meal that follows the ceremony – in the UK, this term can mean lunch or dinner ('breakfast' simply refers to the idea that it's the bride and groom's first meal together). If you want to have an actual 'breakfast' or brunch then your ceremony will normally take place in the morning. For both brunch and lunch, the drinks reception (if you have one) is often shorter and less elaborate.

Brunch is a modern and fun idea for smaller weddings or for couples who don't want the fuss and formality of a sit-down lunch or dinner. It can be one of the least costly meals to produce. Following a late-morning or midday ceremony, a typical brunch buffet may consist of bagels, cream cheese spreads, smoked salmon, Danish pastries, mini quiches, fruit salad, juices and coffee. Stations may offer omelettes, waffles, blinis and pancakes.

Partying full-on

Many couples who opt for a destination wedding or a smaller, intimate wedding day often decide to have a large party for all their friends weeks or even months after their wedding. At an event like this, you need have nothing remotely wedding related in your decor or your food. Just let your hair down and celebrate! Feel free to serve whatever you love and what you and your friends enjoy eating.

Finesse and impress

Some flourishes to further jazz up your meal:

- A choice of sparkling or still water

- A lush presentation (at each table) of rich chocolates, fresh fruit and biscuits with dessert and coffee

- A small dish of herb-infused olive oil in lieu of butter with bread

- A variety of good breads to complement each course (for example, cheesy puff-pastry sticks with soup, a crusty sourdough roll with a beef course, and a wholegrain walnut toast with cheese and salad)

- Butter moulded into florets or other shapes

- Canapés in baskets, colourful glass bowls or chintz hatboxes, or on unusual serving trays

- Cappuccino/espresso bar

- Finishing touches on canapé trays, such as tiny bouquets or offbeat elements such as miniature brides and grooms, balls and chains, or tennis racquets

- Lemon slices served in iced water

- Multicoloured sugar crystals

- Sprigs of fresh herbs, such as rosemary and tarragon, as garnishes

- Waiters offering freshly grated cheese and ground pepper at the table

Midnight munchies

If your wedding is going on beyond midnight then we recommend having some sort of evening buffet, even if you've served the heartiest and most elaborate dinner. Guests often become hungry after hours of dancing, and nothing's more welcoming than a tasty snack served in a casual way. You may offer sandwiches and cake, or how about bacon rolls, chunky chips, hotdogs, kebabs, macaroni cheese or mini burgers?

Considering Special Dietary Requirements

In our experience, ever more people have *special dietary requirements,* which could mean anything from vegetarian, vegan, kosher or halal, to something even more specific, such as nut allergies or an allergy to onions. If you've asked your guests to let you know if they have any special dietary requirements when they return their RSVP cards (as we suggest in Chapter 8), it is up to you to pass on this information to your caterers (particularly if you're having a seated dinner rather than a buffet) well before your wedding day. Ensure they know the names of the guests, their requirements and what table they will be sitting on (to do this, you need a seating plan; see Chapter 5). Also make sure that your guests with special requirements are served their main courses at the same time as everyone else. Some couples may even want to mention the vegetarian option on their printed menu, particularly if your group of friends includes a high number of vegetarians.

Chapter 18

Let's Drink to That

● ●

In This Chapter

▶ Understanding pricing structures

▶ Stocking your own bar

▶ Serving wine, beer and champagne

● ●

According to the Bible, Jesus performed his first miracle at a wedding in Cana, an ancient town in Galilee, by turning water into wine. Although miracles are wonderful, we believe in using them sparingly. Fortunately, you can also provide drinks with a combination of common-sense planning and good taste.

This chapter is about alcohol and how to serve it at your wedding. Our place isn't to moralise about *whether* to serve wine, beer and spirits, but simply to show you *how* to do so intelligently and graciously. And, of course, we firmly believe that when serving any alcohol, you must do so legally and responsibly. If alcohol is an issue because of religion, recovery or expense, consider having a morning wedding with a breakfast reception, where alcohol is neither necessary nor expected.

Tending Bar

When thinking about drinks, remember the purpose of your wedding day: you, your parents and your future spouse have sent out invitations to have friends and family join you in celebration. We think that this invitation includes food *and* drink for at least part of the day. However, budgets vary and providing free drink all day is not always viable but, by the same token, not providing *any* drink could be deemed bad form. So, in the following sections we provide the info you need to decide what sort of beverage service you want to provide.

Speaking in bar code

Before we get too far along, make sure you're conversant in bar-speak – and we don't mean pick-up lines. Here are a few terms worth knowing:

✔ **Champagne:** With a capital *C*, Champagne is the sparkling wine produced in France's Champagne region. Using the second fermentation in the individual bottle, winemakers have produced Champagne the same way for approximately 300 years. Although you may enjoy sparkling wines, only Champagne deserves to be called Champagne.

✔ **Corkage fee:** The amount the site charges to remove the corks from bottles you supply and to serve the wine. Be warned that at some venues the corkage fee can be ridiculously high. As an alternative, if you want to serve a particular wine ask the venue to how much they charge for it. The cost will be higher than if you bought it, but perhaps lower than the amount you'd pay as a corkage charge.

✔ **Highball glasses:** Caterers usually use 'all-purpose' highball glasses for all drinks except wine and Champagne. These one-size-fits-all glasses make for shorter lines at the bar and are less expensive to hire. (Champagne and sparkling wine, however, are always served in flutes.) If glassware is particularly important to you and your budget can handle it, you may request an assortment of the proper glasses. These include highball (perfect for Pimm's or mixer drinks), short tumbler (perfect for whisky), liqueur glasses (various types but used for brandy or after-dinner liqueurs), shot glasses, and red and white wine glasses, not to mention Champagne flutes.

✔ **House wine(s):** What the establishment serves without an additional charge. Depending on the house, the wine can range from perfectly palatable table wine to rotgut.

✔ **Mobile bar company:** A company that comes to your wedding and operates the bar. The price normally includes staff, drinks, equipment, ice and glasses. Most offer a variety of price options. Confirm in writing exactly what the mobile bar company will be providing, whether it removes rubbish and whether it includes all bar sundries.

✔ **Prosecco:** An Italian sparkling wine that's a fraction of the cost of Champagne. Frequently used in the popular Bellini cocktails for the drinks reception and used in lieu of Champagne for the toasts.

✔ **Sparkling wine:** Produced by using either the Champagne method or a less-expensive method.

When you have your wine and food tasting (see Chapter 17 for details), try the house wine. Far from being a minor detail, a glass of house wine is the first thing many people put to their lips at your wedding breakfast. If you find it undrinkable, ask to try a few others.

In-house pricing

Restaurants, wedding venues, private clubs and other spaces where the catering is on-site usually hold an alcohol licence that allows them to sell alcoholic beverages with food. (See Chapter 4 for more about in-house and venue-only sites.) Their offering full bar service isn't a humanitarian gesture to make your life easier but rather a large profit centre for the facility. Consider the tastes and habits of your guests when planning the bar.

In-house venues typically price wine and spirits in one of five ways:

- **Per consumption:** They charge you specifically either per bottle or by drink and only for what your guests consume. Sodas, juices and bottled water may be served at no additional charge or priced per consumption as well.

  This arrangement is a smart choice if you think your guests won't be drinking much. Advise the front-of-house employee that waiters aren't to clear half-empty glasses (and thus send guests back to the bar for a new drink). Also have your wedding co-ordinator or front-of-house employee apprise you of the consumption level halfway through the party. Doing so accomplishes two things: you have an opportunity to moderate the amount of wine being poured, and the venue knows that someone else is keeping track.

- **Drinks reception included, then per consumption:** This pricing scheme means that whatever guests consume during the drinks reception is included in the agreed-upon per-person price (even if your guests drink like fish) and that whatever they drink *after* that period of time will be charged per drink to your bill. This option is a good one if you're not sure how much people will drink, because booze consumption is heaviest at the beginning of the reception and slows down considerably after dinner. What's more, if you pour wine with the meal, chances are guests won't request additional drinks, which keeps the tab for additional beverages down.

- **All-inclusive:** Many venues offer you a price whereby the food and daytime drink is included within the one price. Most venues ask you to select the drink to be served for the drinks reception from a tiered menu. For example, sparkling wine or buck's fizz is included, but if you want Bellinis or Pimm's, you pay an additional fee. House wine is included during dinner, but if you want a specific brand you need to ask the venue whether this is available and what the difference in price would be. A sparkling wine toast is included but if you want Champagne you pay extra.

  If selecting this option, check how many drinks are allocated per person in the drinks reception and during dinner. You may think you're getting a great deal only to discover that your package allows for just one drink during the drinks reception.

- **Corkage fee only:** You pay a fee for wine and Champagne that you bring in yourself. Calculate this fee carefully because you can wind up paying a huge premium per bottle when the fee is tacked on. If you have your heart set on a wine that the establishment doesn't carry, find out what they would charge you to order it specially. Believe it or not, even when they tack on their markup, this route may cost you less.

- **Cash bar:** One way to help keep the cost of your wedding down is by having a cash bar in the evening. (As hosts, you would normally be expected to provide some drink during the day, though. Generally speaking, this would be one to three glasses of something during the drinks reception, wine during the meal and a glass of something bubbly for the toast.) If you want to provide drink for some guests at night via the cash bar, you could use tokens, poker chips or even a code word that the guest gives to the bar staff when ordering a drink. The bar would know this person is a VIP who doesn't have to pay for their drink and that the cost should go on your bill.

Go through your guest list and note how many invitees are under 18. Have your contract specify a lower price for them.

Venue-only options

One of the main advantages of holding your wedding at a venue-only site where you bring in a caterer – such as a marquee or barn – is that you can also buy and bring in your own drink. In some instances, the site may have an in-house caterer you must use, but you're still allowed to bring in your own drink. In either case, this way you're not locked into an establishment's rigid pricing structure, and you can serve what you want.

Some places where you can shop for alcohol and perhaps find deals include:

✔ **Discount warehouses or superstores** that sell wine at or near wholesale prices, usually only by the case.

✔ **Local vineyards or breweries** where you can visit and taste the wine or beer before having it shipped to you.

✔ **Online wine retailers** that offer lower prices and a larger selection of hard-to-find wines than local supermarkets.

✔ **Specialist alcohol shops** that have special purchases or sales. Quantity price savings can be particularly juicy when buying wine and Champagne.

✔ **Supermarkets** invariably have fantastic deals throughout the year so keep an eye out and buy in bulk.

Alcohol legalities

If your venue does not have a bar licence you may need to organise a bar yourself. If you plan to provide alcohol free of charge at your wedding then you don't need to get a licence. If, however, you do plan to buy the drink yourself and subsequently sell it, you need to apply for a temporary event notice (TEN) from your local licensing authority. If the caterers or a mobile bar company are running the bar for you, they tend to be licensed already to sell alcohol, or can get the licence on your behalf.

TIP

Free glasses are an extra added incentive from some sellers, so compare not only prices of the wine but also whether glasses are included. Check that you can return the glasses dirty and, if not, pay extra for this service.

Also, be sure to follow the guidelines for proper storage of the wine or beer so you don't wind up with several cases of salad dressing.

Figure 18-1 covers what you need to take into account whenever you host a party that includes a bar.

Bar Setup Checklist

❑ Does the caterer charge a service or corkage fee on top of the bar 'setup' fee that includes ice and fruit?

❑ Is it possible for the hosts to personally supply any wines or Champagne at an in-house venue? If so, what is the corkage fee?

❑ Will the liquor supplier take back unopened bottles of liquor and unchilled bottles of wine?

❑ Do you wish to have blended drinks, speciality drinks, or drinks that require special preparation? (For example: drinks such as cosmopolitans, martinis and margaritas that require shaking and particular glasses.) What ingredients and equipment do you need to arrange in advance? Are any of those included in the regular bar setup?

❑ What non-alcoholic beverages will be available? (These might include fruited iced teas, fresh squeezed juices, sangria without alcohol filled with slices of fresh lemons, limes, and oranges and served in glass pitchers, or nonalcoholic beers.)

❑ If you're using a full-service facility, what brands will the banquet manager provide? What is the price difference between inexpensive 'well' brands and 'premium' or 'top shelf,' the most expensive?

❑ Will your site accept liquor deliveries in advance of your reception? Do they have a secure place to keep it?

❑ If you're supplying the liquor, where should leftover open bottles of liquor be left? Who will pick them up for you after the wedding?

❑ Do you feel comfortable serving liquor to suppliers such as musicians and photographers? How do you want to instruct the caterer regarding this matter?

Figure 18-1:
When it comes to the bar, work out a beverage strategy with the caterer.

When stocking a bar, bear several points in mind:

✔ Buy from a shop that allows you to return unopened bottles. Just be sure to instruct the caterer not to *crack*, or open, the seal on every bottle. Neither should the caterer ice all the white wine and Champagne, which causes the labels to soak off, unless she's sure they'll be drunk. Bottles without labels look unappealing and are impossible to return. For a catered meal, however, the caterer can go ahead and open almost all the bottles at once; otherwise service slows down considerably.

✔ Check with whoever is running the bar that the drinks price includes the ice, fruit, juices, mixers and soft drinks. Go over the particulars with the caterer or venue co-ordinator. Don't assume that the bar will be stocked with ingredients and garnishes for Bloody Marys, piña coladas, margaritas, Bellinis and other special drinks that you may want to serve.

✔ Double-check that ice has been ordered.

✔ Offer non-alcoholic drinks that are appetising, varied and festive so non-drinkers don't feel like poor relations. Some possibilities: elderflower cordial, fresh apple juice and pink lemonade. People who don't drink aren't usually that interested in pretend cocktails such as virgin daiquiris.

✔ Make sure that white wine and Champagne are delivered chilled, because most venue-only sites don't have enough space – and you won't have enough time – to chill it adequately. If your wedding is at a venue without suitable refrigeration, you may need to hire in a small refrigeration trailer to store all your wine and Champagne.

✔ To prevent any disappearing surplus, assign a responsible friend to confer with the caterer about what remains and to pick up the unopened bottles within a few days after the wedding (when, presumably, you're on your honeymoon).

Liquid logistics

If you're at the point where you aren't sleeping at all and are obsessing about every detail, here's a little 2 a.m. project to keep you busy: make a quick reference for stocking the bar.

Calculating how much alcohol to have on hand isn't an absolute science. Several factors come into play – the social habits of your guests, your budget, the time of year and the time of day. A summer wedding, for example, may require more beer, Pimm's and vodka than a winter wedding, where people are likely to drink more red wine and whisky.

You may notice that bar arithmetic is akin to doubling recipes – the number of litres you need doesn't necessarily increase in direct proportion to the number of guests and/or bar stations added. As you estimate how much alcohol you need, keep in mind the following guidelines on average guest consumption:

✔ For a litre bottle of alcohol (1,000 millilitres) estimate 40 × 25 millilitres shots/measures – 40 drinks.

✔ For a one and a half-hour drinks reception before the wedding breakfast, estimate three drinks per person. Also include a small percentage of non-alcoholic drinks for the drivers and non-drinkers.

✔ Estimate half a bottle of wine per person for the wedding breakfast. Have a mix of white and red.

✔ A bottle of wine equates to approximately five glasses.

✔ A litre of fizzy drink breaks down to five to seven glasses, depending on glass size and ice.

✔ Allow six Champagne flute glasses per standard 750-millilitre bottle of Champagne. For a Champagne toast, figure on 75 glasses per case.

In Figure 18-2, we show you a typical order of what you'd need for 100 guests with a four-hour open bar. Note that these amounts are only estimates. You're always better off having returns than being caught short with no alcohol shop open within 100 miles.

Bar Checklist	
☐ *Vodka*	*6 litres*
☐ *Gin*	*5 litres*
☐ *Whiskey*	*2 litres*
☐ *Scotch*	*2 litres*
☐ *White rum*	*2 litres*
☐ *Real ale*	*1 keg (88 pints)*
☐ *Lager*	*200 bottles*
☐ *Cola*	*20 litres*
☐ *Diet-cola*	*20 litres*
☐ *Lemonade*	*20 litres*
☐ *Tonic*	*1 case*
☐ *Apple/Orange Juice*	*15 cartons of each*

Figure 18-2:
A typical order for 100 guests for a four-hour open bar.

The drinking habits of your guests will reflect your final bar list. For example, if you know that most of the men drink ale, then decrease the lager and order two kegs of real ale. Likewise, if you want to add shots, don't forget to include this along with the shot glasses.

Even if you want to appear flash by having waiters pour from magnum bottles during a drinks reception or for the speeches, spare a thought on how heavy they are. You'll need big, strapping waiters!

Hard to believe, but true: professional waiting staff do and will arrive at your site without corkscrews. Whether your family is tending the bar or you've hired bartenders, it pays to have half a dozen screwpull corkscrews or waiter's corkscrews – not the wing-type corkscrew that means your helpful family members have to yank at the cork with the bottle between their knees.

Avoiding Traffic Jams

We can't stress enough how important traffic flow is to the success of your day. One way to make guests miserable is to have long lines at the bar, making it impossible for them to get that first drink they've been salivating for. An easy solution is to have waiters parked at the entrance of your reception area holding gleaming trays of Champagne, summer cocktails or wine. Most people are perfectly happy to drink what's offered and consequently avoid stampeding the bars.

Some couples opt to have the full bar open as guests arrive after the ceremony. Arbiters of taste split hairs on the subject, suggesting that to open a full bar is tacky, but to serve Champagne and/or wine is fine. Somehow the nuance is lost on us; how much and what kind of drink you serve is a matter of personal taste. However guests may appreciate having a drink brought to them rather then queuing at the bar during the drinks reception.

You can't serve or consume drinks (or food) in the ceremony room for an hour prior to and during the ceremony. If it's a hot day you can provide some refreshments but in a different area, and guests need to hand back all glasses before entering the ceremony room.

For a drinks reception the standard ratio of wine waiters to guests is 1 per 50 or 75.

Even if waiters are passing around drinks to stave off a crush at the bar as guests are first arriving, contract extra bar staff during this crucial period. If hiring additional bartenders costs more, request that some of the waiters fill in behind the bar until all the guests have had at least their first drink.

Considering the Bar Structure

If you're operating a bar in your marquee or similar venue you may need to hire an actual bar structure. Yes, in some instances a clothed trestle table suffices, but this simply won't be professional enough if you have 100-plus guests. Some bar companies include a bar as part of their price, but if not, do a simple Internet search for a mobile bar in your wedding county.

Many couples opt to hire a mobile-bar company, and although the fee may seem hefty, the hire can be cost effective if your guests are heavy drinkers. The fee includes all staff, glasses, unlimited drinks and in some cases the actual bar itself. Look around for a reputable company, and remember that cheapest doesn't necessarily mean the most professional.

An array of bars is on offer with a style to suit your wedding. In most cases they come in straight and curved sections, meaning you can create long, semi-circular, full circle, oval, L-shaped and U-shaped bars. You may choose an understated wooden bar for a rustic wedding, an LED bar for a funky, colourful effect, a mirrored bar for a contemporary feel or one that's personalised to include a special message or monogram of your wedding.

Many couples like to hire a circular bar structure for a visual impact. They do look stunning, but think about the inside diameter. How many staff can fit in there? Can you fit a fridge inside the bar?

When scouting bar companies, be sure to ask:

- ✔ What is the size of the structure? Remember that the more guests you have, the more bar staff and the larger the size of bar you'll need.

- ✔ What does the price include? For example, does the unit come with any internal shelves (much needed for stock and glasses) and does it have any internal fridges or will you need to hire separate ones?

- ✔ What are the power requirements for the bar and any equipment like fridges?

- ✔ Will the bartenders *free pour* alcohol from open bottles (estimating the amount in a shot) or use *pourers* (bottle spouts that measure per shot)?

- ✔ Are pourers silver-tone or plastic? (Silver looks more elegant.)

- ✔ What will the bartenders use as ice bins? If the answer is huge buckets (often the case), request that they wrap them in tablecloths. Champagne should be kept in ice buckets.

- ✔ What do they scoop ice with? We hope with an ice scoop. Harried bartenders may resort to scooping ice with a glass, sometimes resulting in tasty shards of glass garnish. We won't even discuss bartenders scooping with their hands, and we hope you won't have to either.

Chapter 5 goes into detail on decor, but here are some specific bar aesthetics to keep in mind:

✔ Having 2-litre bottles sitting out on a bar looks like you're expecting an invasion of Huns. A more aesthetic approach: 750-millilitre bottles. If you're serving a variety of beers, a few different wines or margaritas, display the bottles prominently on the bar so that guests know to request them and the selection isn't just a secret between you and the bartenders.

✔ Write a few sentences describing the wines you've chosen and give them to the bartenders so they can speak intelligently about what they're pouring. After you and your fiancé(e) have excitedly chosen the perfect cocktail wines, nothing can make you choke on your 1988 Gevrey-Chambertin like overhearing a bartender reply to a guest's query, 'Let's see, we've got red and we've got white.' Writing some of the available selections on a mini chalkboard and standing it on the bar top is another great idea.

✔ Grand floral creations on the bar inevitably become a target for the bartenders or guests to knock over. A small, tasteful arrangement of flowers in keeping with the overall theme is plenty. The same goes for candelabras and votive candles – an unnerving scenario when dolman sleeves are in the vicinity.

Specialty Drink Stations for Blithe Spirits

Although they require additional well-trained staff, specialty drinks stations can be a treat for guests even at large weddings, and a great way to personalise your day as you bring in you and/or your partner's favourite tipple. Special drinks require special arrangements for the full dramatic effect:

✔ Serve these drinks at a separate station rather than at the main bar, or have waiters pass them around.

✔ Stock each station with the accessories needed for the particular drink. For example, a Martini station should have Martini glasses, matching shakers and a variety of garnishes, including pickled pearl onions for Gibsons.

✔ Plan drinks that look pretty as well as taste good. Try having glasses rimmed with coloured sugars or using unusual garnishes like peppermint sticks or long-stemmed strawberries.

Some festive ideas for specialty bars include:

- **Cappuccino and espresso bar:** Doesn't it seem as though coffee bars have taken over the world? Well, weddings aren't immune. Some caterers now specialise in supplying coffee bars that offer everything from cappuccino to half-caff double-skim mocha lattes. Hot rum toddies, Irish coffee and hot chocolate spiced with chocolate liqueur also fit in nicely.

- **Cocktail bar:** Cocktails have been enjoying a huge revival in recent years, and especially at weddings. Consider having a cocktail bar serving just six to eight pre-chosen cocktails of your choice. You may want to rename them as something fun and personal, using nicknames, hobbies or holiday locations. If budget allows, hire a mixologist to really make an impression.

- **Dessert bar:** After-dinner drinks range from a selection of liqueurs to an assortment of aged Cognacs as well as Armagnacs and digestifs. (For ideas of what to serve, see the 'Luxurious liqueurs' sidebar in this chapter.) Sometimes waiters take orders for these at the table, but if you decide to go all out, carts wheeled to the table with a selection of cordials and dessert wines – and their proper glasses – are an excellent finale to a sumptuous meal. One catch: although immensely gracious, the liqueur cart can be a costly proposition because people who'd never think of having an after-dinner drink make an exception when offered one in this situation.

- **Vodka bar:** With the advent of a multitude of unusual vodkas, from flavoured to triple distilled, vodka bars are another possibility. Deeply chilled in iced glasses is the only way to serve this spirit. Vodka drinks work well by themselves or as an accompaniment to a food station serving blini and caviar or smoked fish. Large canisters holding fruit or herb-infused vodkas behind the bar make the station very enticing.

Luxurious liqueurs

Serving a liqueur/Cognac selection at the end of your reception is a spiffy coda to the festivities. If possible, serve these drinks in brandy snifters or delicate cordial glasses rather than cocktail glasses. A primer of possibilities:

- **B&B:** Benedictine and brandy.

- **Cognac:** From the Cognac region in France, brands such as Hennessy and Courvoisier.

- **Cointreau or Grand Marnier:** Orange-flavoured liqueur.

- **Cordials:** May include either inexpensive or named brands with flavours such as Crème de Cacao (chocolate), Crème de Menthe (mint), peach, apricot, pear, peppermint and banana.

- **Kahlua:** Mexican coffee liqueur, Tia Maria (Jamaican coffee liqueur).

- **Sambuca:** Aniseed flavour, often served with coffee beans in the bottom of the glass.

- **Specialty drinks:** Chocolate Martinis, mud slides and Irish coffees.

Another cost-cutting option for bar service is to serve just beer, wine and one specialty drink. Some of these concoctions lend themselves to pre-mixing all the ingredients, including alcohol, rather than being made as ordered, and others require skilled bartenders. A few possibilities:

- **Coladas** accented with a skewer of mango, kiwi and pineapple.

- **Cosmopolitans** made with vodka, triple sec, lime and cranberry juice – or the white-dress-friendly *white cosmo* made with colourless cranberry juice and usually served in a Martini glass.

- **Margaritas** poured into Martini glasses with salted rims and a wedge of fresh lime.

- **Mojitos** combining rum, sugar, lots of fresh mint and lime juice.

- **Sangria** made with red wine and a dash of brandy, and then garnished with fruit slices and poured from a lovely pitcher.

Selecting Wine, Beer and Champagne

Many people mistakenly think that serving only wine and beer is less expensive and a way to keep guests from getting drunk. Both are fallacies. First, not every catering establishment charges substantially less for house wine and beer. A better-quality wine served in lieu of spirits can, in fact, cost you more money. Secondly, the idea that wine and beer aren't as potent as spirits is preposterous. Trust us, enough of either can get you good and drunk. Should anyone overindulge, remember the immortal words of Dean Martin: 'If you drink, don't drive. Don't even putt.'

Earlier in this chapter we discuss beer, wine and Champagne in terms of pricing and amounts. Now we get into the delicate and rather subjective art of choosing appropriate and delicious bottles to complement your party.

Wining when dining

For many people, a good meal by definition is accompanied by wine. The amount of money and time you spend on selecting your wine depends on how important you rate a taste of the grape. Mark-ups on wine and Champagne are typically exorbitant in full-service venues, so this area is one where going for a venue-only site can really make a difference to the cost of your wedding.

One of the most fun aspects of wedding planning is choosing your wine. If you're purchasing the wine yourself, buy several selections in your price range to try at home with dinner. If you're choosing from the in-house wine list, get a copy early in your planning and purchase your top picks at an alcohol shop to try them out. Some establishments include tastings of wine options with menu tastings.

Although a bit of snobbery exists around choosing wines, we want to make it clear that a good wine needn't be expensive. Choose the wine you like the taste of the most. In fact, we advise doing a blind tasting of wines you can afford so you choose objectively and aren't swayed by cost.

Until recently, when planning a bar, you automatically ordered copious quantities of white wine and a bare minimum of red just to satisfy some pretentious eccentric. As good red wines have become more reasonably priced, they've gone mainstream. Order sufficient red wine for everybody to drink it with the main course if:

- You're serving meat or a fish in a red wine sauce.
- The wine is particularly delicious.
- The wedding occurs in the middle of winter.

If you serve white wine (and no red) throughout the meal, half a bottle per person is usually ample. If you serve white wine for only the first course, followed by red or a choice of white or red with dinner, count on a third of a bottle of white per person.

Should you serve the best wine first or save it for last? Some people believe in the power of first impressions, and that, besides, after guests are somewhat sated, they won't notice that at some point during the party the wine ceased to impress their taste buds as much. Others believe that guests only begin to notice what they're drinking after their taste buds have warmed up, so you should serve the good stuff later. One way to circumvent this tangle if you serve more than one wine is to make sure the wines are comparable and complementary.

Don't worry, beer hoppy

Beer and weddings date back to ancient times. In fact, the word *bride* is derived from the Germanic *bruths* and the Old English *bryd*, which in turn come from the root word *bru*, meaning to cook or brew. In the 15th century, wedding feasts were called *bride-ales* (an ale being a party), and the drinking of copious amounts of beer – the stronger, the better for a robust marriage – was, naturally, a prime activity at these rather rowdy functions. The bride's mother parked herself in front of the church and sold her specially made brew, known as *bridal*, to anyone who passed by. The proceeds benefited the bride's dowry.

Today, beer at weddings isn't requisite, but with the rising popularity of microbreweries and a growing interest in the complexities and nuances of 'the liquid bread', beer is no longer considered too roughneck for weddings. If you're offering beer, include one with a lower ABV and stock up if it's a hot summer's day. A vast selection of lagers and real ales are available in kegs. An 11-gallon keg holds 88 pints and a 9-gallon firkin holds 72 pints. Remember that you have to set up real ale some time before the event in order for it to settle, and you need appropriate chilling equipment for keg beer.

For a special beer bar, you may feature recipes from several local breweries, a selection of exotic imports, beers from countries representing your families' ethnic heritage or a world tour of beers from every continent. One way to impress beer aficionados is to get a local microbrewery to make a special batch of its brew for your big day or a pre-wedding party on which it prints labels with your names and wedding date.

Bring on the bubbly

Guests expect Champagne or good sparkling wine at a wedding celebration, whether served throughout the day or just at the drinks reception, by request, at dinner or with the cake for a toast.

Champagnes can be vintage or non-vintage. Any Champagne without a vintage year on the label, which accounts for 85 per cent of all Champagne produced, is *non-vintage*. Three or more different harvests are blended for non-vintage. A vintage Champagne consists of 100 per cent of grapes from a single year rather than blended with reserves from previous years. Plan on coming into a lot of money if you want to serve vintage Champagne.

Whether vintage or non, Champagne is categorised by sweetness, and the terms aren't self-explanatory, to say the least:

- *Extra Brut* or *Brut Nature* means totally dry (under 0.06 per cent sugar).

- *Brut* is still very dry (under 1.5 per cent sugar) and in general is your best bet for a wedding.

- *Extra dry* is sweeter than Brut and considered medium dry.

- *Sec* is slightly sweet. (In French, however, the word *sec* actually means dry. Go figure.)

- *Demi-sec* is considered sweet but not as sweet as . . . (see the next bullet).

- *Doux* is *really* sweet. This style of Champagne is the sweetest and should only be served with dessert.

A fun personal touch is a cocktail created just for your wedding. For their rose garden reception, one couple we know served rosé Champagne with a rose petal garnish and a strawberry in every glass. As guests entered, waiters offered the drinks from trays adorned with forest-green leaves and roses and announced, 'The "Rose Cocktail" in honor of Loretta and George.'

Rosé Champagne has an undeservedly bad reputation among those who think bartenders make it by mixing a carbonated drink and red wine. Actually, makers do their thing by either adding Pinot Noir in the beginning of the process to a blend of white wines or leaving the skins on the grapes during vinification to impart a pink colour. Rosés are particularly sensuous and romantic for weddings. Unlike many blush wines, rosé Champagnes are brut rather than demi-sec.

If you want to serve Champagne but are concerned about the cost, consider serving *Prosecco*, a dry Italian sparkling wine, for the wedding toasts.

One case of Champagne contains approximately 70 to 75 glasses, so for a Champagne toast you need one case per 75 guests. For the drinks reception, bank on two cases per 100 guests. Some flutes can be deceptive in that they hold less than they appear to, in which case you may get closer to 80 glasses per case.

After your Champagne has made its bumpy journey from shop to wedding, let it rest for several hours before opening, as you would any other carbonated drink. Never remove the wire cages before you're ready to open the bottle unless you want spontaneous cork popping. For the same reason, never use a corkscrew, which releases the carbonation suddenly and much too forcefully. Although the correct procedure for opening Champagne is to gently ease out the cork so it emits a teeny sigh, if you don't mind losing a portion of the contents and are hooked on the Hollywood image of Champagne corks going 'Pop!' then give the cork a good, hard pull. In any case, point the bottle away from any other living creature to avoid implanting the cork in someone's eye.

Chapter 19

A Piece of Cake

• •

In This Chapter

▶ Designing your dream cake

▶ Presenting the cake on the day

▶ Saving a little for later

• •

Since ancient times, cakes have been associated with rites of passage and the wedding cake has been a particularly powerful symbol. Embodying the themes of marriage, fertility, communion and hope for a sweet life, the wedding cake remains an important aspect of most couples' first meal as husband and wife, and the cake-cutting ceremony is a ritual guests look forward to witnessing. However, until recently, the cake was generally white, plain and, dare we say it, a bit boring. Almost an afterthought, it was wheeled out after the speeches with little or no fanfare. Guests who actually ate a piece often risked going into sugar shock.

But no longer. The contemporary wedding cake has evolved into a beautiful centrepiece for the reception, as exquisite to look at as it is delicious. Couples spend as much time choosing the look and flavour of their wedding cake as they do on all the other significant elements of their nuptials. A plethora of designs is available today and many artists who originally worked in other materials have turned their talents to creating edible art. Cakes no longer have to be round or stacked or white. In fact, they no longer have to look like cakes at all. Many bakers specialise in creating grand *trompe l'oeil* masterpieces that look like precious jewellery boxes, balls and chains, mosaic-tiled birdbaths, Victorian birdcages, architectural landmarks, patchwork quilts, wedding-dress lace – just about anything meaningful to the couple.

So when it comes to wedding cakes, you've a wide choice, and in this chapter we give you some pointers to help you pick the *crème de la crème* of the cakes for your day.

Setting the Recipe for the Perfect Cake

The good news is that while lavish baked sculptures *can* be prohibitively expensive, you have less-expensive, yet still delectable, alternatives to choose from. In any case, the cake is usually the last thing that your guests eat at the reception, so send them off with something delicious. In this section, we help you consider who makes your cake, and how.

Finding a cake designer

Unless your Aunt Jenny is a world-class pastry chef and has offered to bake her award-winning *gâteau de mariage* for your wedding, you need to rev up your taste buds and go cake shopping. Or, more precisely, 'cake designer' shopping. To find a cake designer (née baker) who can do the job, you may rely on the same methods for finding a reputable caterer (see Chapter 17) or browse the lists on reputable online wedding directories and in wedding magazines. You can find many inspiring galleries of cake photographs online. Visiting a wedding show/exhibition is also a fantastic way to view hundreds of wedding cakes on display. Or you may have a local bakery that can do an amazing job of designing your cake (although today wedding cakes have become more of a specialist item).

Don't assume that you have to purchase your cake from your caterer; most allow you to supply your own, particularly if they don't specialise in the splendiferous structure you have in mind. Do, however, double-check your venue policy regarding wedding cakes. Even if they allow you to bring in your own cake, they may have to approve the source for insurance reasons. Also, if the venue includes the cake as part of your meal price, you're unlikely to get a rebate if you bring in your own.

As when dealing with the caterer, assess the cake designer's potential and limitations. If you choose one because you've seen and/or tasted the designer's cakes and love them, go through the designer's photo portfolio. And when searching for someone to create the *pièce de résistance* for your wedding, don't overlook pastry chefs at restaurants. They've often been trained in the sugared arts and may jump at the chance to strut their stuff.

Before meeting with a cake designer, amass clippings and photos for ideas. Snapshots of your reception venue, your dress or type of flowers are helpful as well. To become knowledgeable about flavours that go well together, make a point of tasting cakes for dessert when you go out to eat. (We realise that doing so may be a hardship, but try to tough it out.)

Focus on the cake early in your planning, because popular cake designers get booked up quickly. Your cake designer doesn't have to be local. Consider having your cake shipped from anywhere in the UK. Many designers send cakes across the country and supply meticulous instructions for keeping and setting them up. When scouring the Internet, search for 'wedding cake', 'wedding cake designer' or 'bespoke wedding cake'. If you can't arrange a personal tasting, try to sort a 'by mail' taste test.

An option that's less costly than having your entire cake shipped is to order a simple tiered cake from a local baker and transform it with custom-made cake toppers, sugar flowers, satin ribbon and other decorative elements that you can order online and have delivered. Even upscale grocery and deep-discount warehouse stores with in-house baking facilities turn out remarkably decent wedding cakes these days. This can be an economical way to go, particularly for an informal wedding or if having a confectionary masterpiece isn't a high priority. You may consider spiffing up the cake table rather than the cake itself, which is a less-expensive proposition. Drape the table with an ornate cloth, pile petals or fresh flower heads on the table, or set the cake on an heirloom platter or cake plate (see the section 'Cake on Display: No Drooling, Please', later in this chapter).

Totting up tiers and toppers

Tiered cakes are either stacked or separated. You place the layers of *stacked* cakes one on top of another; *separated* cakes use decorative elements (traditionally, miniature Grecian columns) to physically elevate tiers so they're not touching. Consequently, separated cakes are taller than stacked ones that have the same number of tiers. The number of tiers you have depends on the number of guests you want to serve, how the cake will look in the room and whether you will be serving the cake as your dessert or as part of your evening buffet and/or a take-home gift to your guests.

The ethereal look of some wedding cakes belies the nuts and bolts needed to make them last through a reception. Constructing a separate-tiered cake is an engineering feat that requires reinforcing the layers, which can be quite heavy, so they don't collapse into each other. Where wooden dowels or plastic classical columns were once the only structures used to separate tiers, you can now achieve the same effect with sugar topiaries, cupids or garlanded Lucite columns – just about anything that can hold the weight of the top tiers. You then separate each layer with corrugated cardboard. Using an expert in tiered cakes ensures you don't get a wobbly tower in which the top layer falls through and becomes the bottom layer.

Topping the cake is another occasion for you to brainstorm. The formerly universal plastic bride and groom have gone out of style, and cake tops are appearing in myriad ingenious forms. Working from photographs, artisans whose sole business is sculpting edible figurines can replicate the couple in a favourite pose, such as teeing off, skiing or driving their convertible. Companies that produce the typical cake ornaments have become somewhat enlightened, producing brides and grooms of all ethnicities and selling them to be easily mixed and matched for either interracial or same-sex couples. Jewellery companies are producing crystal cake toppers as well as metallic monograms to add glitz to simply iced cakes, and several Internet sites offer custom-made hand-blown glass cake toppers.

Classical cake designers insist that everything on a wedding cake should be edible or at least made out of edible ingredients. For that reason, many purists shun fresh flowers on wedding cakes. A crown of fresh flowers that rests solely on the top of the cake, however, can be inexpensive, delicate, pretty and easy to remove – just be sure to use flowers that are pesticide free. Other options include preserved flowers such as candied violets and rose petals, edible flowers such as nasturtiums, or flowers that are made from icing piped from a pastry tube, which are less time-consuming to make for the decorator and hence less expensive than hand-moulded designs.

Selecting the confection

The types of cake and fillings are limited only by your imagination and the cake designer's prowess. The emphasis is on flavour, from cream-cheese-frosted carrot cake to chocolate cheesecake, from a hazelnut torte enrobed in dark chocolate to classic Victoria sponge with a white-chocolate ganache.

If you're serving another dessert in addition to the cake, choose complementary flavours. Fresh berries with pastry cream go well if the wedding cake is a light butter cake filled with lemon curd, for example. On the other hand, a chocolate truffle bombe is a way too rich dessert if you've opted for a chocolate mousse cake. Take the season into account as well; dense cakes with rich chocolate filling are more suited for cold weather consumption, and in spring and summer berry or citrus flavours are appreciated at the end of a meal.

If you're not keen on having a traditional sweet wedding cake and want to be a little different, opt instead for a cake made of cheese (not to be confused with a cheesecake), sometimes also referred to as a *cheese tower*. A cheese tower comes in many flavour combinations and can be just as pretty as a traditional wedding cake, with a wealth of decorating options like fruit, flowers, feathers and ribbons, so you can easily customise your cake to fit the theme of your wedding. You can serve the cheese tower as a cheese course during your evening meal or as part of an evening buffet. (To find suppliers search online for 'cheese wedding cake' or 'wedding cakes made of cheese'.) Another alternative to a traditional cake is a *macaroon tower* (a cone-shaped tower which has macaroons fixed to it) – very French and quite chic. These delicious almond morsels come in many flavours and are great for after dinner, served with coffee.

Icing issues and filling facts

In planning the texture, flavour and look of your cake, a working knowledge of icing and filling options can make communicating with your cake designer a breeze.

✔ **Butter cream:** Both an icing and a filling that consists of real butter (not shortening or margarine), sugar and eggs; ranges from ivory to pale yellow in colour depending on the number of eggs, the colour of the butter and whether meringue is mixed in for whitening. Also used to pipe out beautiful and realistic-looking flowers. Mixes well with liqueurs and other flavourings.

✔ **Dragée:** Bite-sized, colourful confectionery with a hard outer shell; dragée can be gold, silver or multi-coloured and is often used for decorative balls made of candied sugar.

✔ **Gold and silver leaf:** Used in small amounts as a final touch on iced cakes. Painting with edible real gold and silver is both labour-intensive and expensive but quite beautiful for tinted flowers, leaves and art deco touches.

✔ **Fondant:** An icing that the designer either pours in liquid form on to small cakes and petits fours, or rolls out in a sheet, cuts and wraps around the cake. Its smooth, velvety appearance is a perfect surface on which to apply decoration. Refrigerating fondant is unwise because it tends to *weep*, forming unappetising beads of moisture.

✔ **Marzipan:** Ground almond paste that the designer can roll like fondant to cover the cake or use as a base for the fillings between the layers. Can also be hand-moulded into such realistic-looking decorations as individual fruits, bunches of grapes or figures.

✔ **Modelling chocolate:** Has a consistency similar to that of chewing gum, although it doesn't go rock hard. White or dark, the designer can roll it out like fondant and use it to enrobe a cake or to embellish a frosted cake with bouquets of chocolate flowers or other whimsical touches.

✔ **Pastillage, sugar dough or gum paste:** Used to make hand-shaped fantastical and botanically correct flowers replete with stamens and pistils, as well as other cake decorations. Incidentally, although pastillage flowers are exquisite and supposedly edible, we wouldn't suggest biting into one unless your teeth are made of diamonds.

✔ **Pulled sugar:** Molten sugar syrup that's pulled into such shapes as bows and flowers.

✔ **Royal icing:** Egg whites beaten with confectioners' sugar and lemon juice, and then piped with a pastry tube to make intricate decorative elements – lace, trellises or miniature buds. Very sweet and hardens quickly.

✔ **Spun sugar:** Strands of caramelised sugar thrown to create a magical golden veil over a cake or dessert. You can't refrigerate spun sugar, and it doesn't hold up for long, making it inappropriate for a cake that you intend to display for several hours.

✔ **Whipped cream:** Pure whipped cream isn't the same as 'dairy product'; the latter is mixed with stabilisers that increase its longevity but change the taste completely. Whipped cream must be refrigerated.

For variety, each tier of the wedding cake may be a different flavour and/or may comprise different flavoured layers. Renowned baker Sylvia Weinstock created such a cake for the wedding of comedian Eddie Murphy and Nicole Mitchell. The 5-foot-tall, 400-pound cake featured hundreds of pastel sugar flowers cascading over yellow cake filled with fresh strawberries, fresh banana filling and whipped cream; chocolate cake with mocha mousse filling; carrot cake with cream-cheese filling; and yellow cake filled with lemon mousse and fresh raspberries – guests had their pick.

Size matters

Consider how your cake will look in your wedding reception space. A small cake in a room with high ceilings may look lost. To help, most cake designers can create dummy tiers for your cake. *Dummy tiers* look edible and are decorated beautifully, but are made of polystyrene. (Make sure you tell your caterers about them before they serve it up, though!) If your dream is to have a six-tier, lavishly decorated cake but your budget is being pushed, consider having a complete dummy cake on display for your guests and removed after the cake cutting. You can then have an undecorated 'kitchen' cake to serve after the dummy cake is removed by your caterers.

Table 19-1 gives you an idea of how many portions you can expect to get from a tier, to help you determine how big your cake needs to be. Cakes are measured in inches.

Table 19-1	Tier Portion Guide	
Tier Size/Shape (Inches)	*Round Portions*	*Square Portions*
4	10	15
5	15	20
6	20	25
7	30	40
8	40	50
9	50	65
10	60	75
11	70	90
12	80	100

Here are some popular combinations for round cakes:

- ✔ **Two tier:** 8- and 6-inch cakes (60 portions)
- ✔ **Three tier:** 8-, 6- and 4-inch cakes (70 portions)
- ✔ **Four tier:** 10-, 8-, 6- and 4-inch cakes (130 portions)
- ✔ **Four tier:** 12-, 10-, 8- and 6-inch cakes (200 portions)

At the other end of the spectrum are smaller cakes – single-serving-size cakes, to be precise – which can be as cute or elegant as you desire. Increasingly popular are miniature cakes wrapped in chocolate (white, milk or dark) imprinted with a logo, monogram or other design by using computer technology. Possible mini-cake configurations include:

- ✔ **Cupcake cake:** Multiple tiers of individual cupcakes, each decorated separately and sometimes lavishly, are arranged on a stack of plates in graduated sizes to give the image of one many-layered cake.
- ✔ **Party favour cakes:** Each guest gets a miniature cake for dessert or boxed to take home after the reception.
- ✔ **Centerpiece cakes:** Each table has a miniature, decorated wedding cake as the centerpiece, which the guests then slice up and serve to each other for dessert. Sometimes cakes at each table are of different flavours, encouraging guests to share.

If you want to serve the cake as part of your evening buffet but still want your guests to take some home, buy individual cake boxes. You've many styles and sizes to choose from so you're sure to find one to match your theme. Ask your venue manager, caterer or wedding planner to save a tier of the cake for your boxes and place individual portions inside. Place a table with the boxes near the exit, so guests can collect their gift as they leave.

Slicing and pricing

Cakes are generally priced per tier. The price of the cake depends on the intricacy of the design, the flavour of the cake, and the experience and celebrity status of the cake designer. If you select a very-well-known cake designer then you can expect to pay much more, but you'll have bragging rights: 'Oh, it was made by so and so; they did so and so's cake, you know!'

The more decorations you have on the cake the more costly it can be, too – handmade sugar flower posies, for example, can cost as much as £60, and extra-large roses can cost upwards of £15 each. Taking in all the different factors, your cake can cost anything from £200 to thousands of pounds. On average, a three- or four-tiered cake with some intricate design, from a reputable cake designer will cost around £500 to £750.

Two hearts, two cakes

Sometimes couples have two cakes – the bride's, or the wedding cake, and a groom's cake. Here's where you can have a bit of fun – the groom's cake is frequently a surprise that the bride plans for the groom, and the cake usually reflects a specific theme dear to the groom's heart, so it may be sculpted into the shape of anything from a football to a doctor's bag to his favourite car. If you're interested in a particular design, colour or flavour that you think may be too far-out for your wedding cake, consider using the idea for a groom's cake.

Simple sponge cakes cost less than high-quality chocolate or alcoholic fruit cakes and over a four-tiered cake it can make quite a difference to your costs. Another budget-friendly option is to buy a ready-made wedding cake from a supermarket bakery. The big supermarkets all sell some lovely designs. To spruce it up a bit you can ask your florist to decorate the cake with fresh flowers. These cakes are simple in design, but can be quite lovely and, more importantly, can save you a small fortune.

Cake on Display: No Drooling, Please

The wedding cake is usually displayed from the beginning of the reception, so choose a filling and icing that can hold up for the duration. If you're pin-spotting the room (see Chapter 13 for lighting tips), add a spot for the cake table. Otherwise, place it somewhere well-lit and in full sight of the guests, but off the dance floor, or it may wind up on the DJ's head during a fast dance. Keep in mind the time of year and the length of time the cake will be out, so it doesn't look like a Salvador Dalí watch by the time it's cut.

The base of the cake determines the size of the table. A huge table makes even the stateliest cake look minuscule. Ensure the table is sturdy and is either on wheels or light enough with the cake for two waiters to carry it. The general rule with cake tables is that if your cake is plain, decorate the table, and vice versa – an elaborate cake will look far more elegant on a plain white table cloth. To elaborately embellish the table, wrap picture wire (as if tying a package) around the tabletop. After the tables are covered, you can attach swags, garlands and sprays with safety pins to the wire in the appropriate places. Layer sheets and/or tulle to give the tablecloth fullness and make it look more elegant.

Ask the cake designer what kind of serving piece they deliver the cake on. Some provide a flat silver tray or cake stand; others just deliver it on a plain piece of baker's cardboard that you'll need to cover. Your caterer will probably be able to assist you with a cake stand and cake knife, or you can buy your own online or hire for the day.

Ask your cake designer if they will bring the cake to your venue and set it up on the day or if they just deliver it and someone else will need to assemble and set it up on the table. Your florist, caterer or wedding planner should be able to assist you with this.

A sweet touch that also makes use of those expensive bridesmaid bouquets after the ceremony is to have the head of banqueting at your venue or your wedding planner discreetly relieve the bridesmaids of their bouquets and arrange them around the cake with a studied casualness. The bridesmaids, incidentally, are usually grateful, being at a loss for how to balance the bouquets with drinks, canapés and the arms of their significant others.

Arrange to have the cake delivered at least two hours before the reception begins (or your ceremony, if this is taking place at the same venue). Cakes are rarely transported fully assembled. Make sure that you clarify specifically who's delivering and setting it up. Tell your caterer the delivery time so the cake table can be dressed and ready, and so the delivery person doesn't just leave the cake in its box and disappear.

Cutting the Cake

Traditionally, the first shared piece of cake symbolises the couple's first meal as husband and wife. The cake cutting also used to signal the end of the wedding, because the bride and groom would then change and be off. More often now, the cutting is a natural transition after which people who want to leave may do so, but the newlyweds and the majority of their guests stay and take to the dance floor.

When you cut your cake is entirely up to you. Some couples want to cut the cake before dinner is served so that the caterers can take it away and serve it as dessert. Others cut the cake just before the first dance. Whichever you choose you need a graceful signal that cake cutting is imminent because it's the perfect photo opportunity for your photographer and guests.

When you schedule your wedding day (see Chapter 14), put in bold type exactly when you want to cut your cake, so that your DJ or band can play some appropriate music.

Tradition states that, to symbolise the couple's shared life together, the groom places his right hand over the bride's, which holds the knife. Together they cut a small piece from the back of the bottom tier. The groom then feeds the bride first, a small mouthful washed down easily by a sip of Champagne. Then the bride feeds the groom. Then, if they're feeling particularly nice, the bride and groom serve a piece to their new in-laws. It's up to you whether you want to follow this tradition.

Some couples find this ceremony antiquated and would rather skip it. Although we have no objections if you feel strongly, guests do expect to see you cut your cake. They may feel cheated if they don't. Some even believe the old superstition that the bride must cut the first piece or risk being childless. That said, cut the cake, eat your pieces, put the plate down and move away. After the photos, the venue manager or caterers should have the cake taken into the kitchen to be cut quickly and efficiently without showing the guests the mess this work of art becomes during slicing.

A few venues may choose to charge a cake-cutting fee – usually £1 a slice – allegedly to cover the cost of the set-up (plates and forks). We find this charge inappropriate, so attempt to expunge this clause from your contract. Sometimes, though, the charge is fair – for example, when you're using the cake for dessert and the cake is presented with berries, cream and so on.

Saving the Top Tier

Many couples want to save the top tier of the cake for future consumption on their first anniversary or for the Christening of their first child. If this is something you want to do, take precautions to make the cake as palatable as possible one year later – no mould, freezer burn or other taste treats.

Ensure your wedding planner or venue manager knows to save the top tier, otherwise it will be cut up with the rest of the cake. Make arrangements with a trusted member of your bridal party to take it home and freeze it for you and then have it transported to your freezer upon your return from the honeymoon. Your cake designer can give you instructions on how to freeze the cake, depending on the icing and filling you've selected.

Chapter 20

And the Band Played On

*Y*ou're both giddy with emotion as you glide arm in arm to the dance floor for your first dance together as husband and wife. For a moment you could swear the bandleader, sounding rather like a game-show voiceover, just mispronounced your names in his introduction, but you're too busy readying yourselves for the foxtrot you've spent weeks perfecting. With a flourish, the band begins to play. The melody sounds, well, strangely like Aunt Myrtle gargling in the morning at a furious pace. Tears (but definitely not of joy) run down your cheeks and you pray that you'll wake up in a cold sweat, just as you have several times in the past month.

The point we're making is that music is an extremely important aspect of your ceremony and undoubtedly the element that sets the tone and pace of your reception. People may not remember exactly what they ate on your big day, but they'll remember whether they danced all night or stuffed the dinner rolls in their ears.

So in this chapter, we talk through how to plan your music carefully from the drinks reception up until the evening reception. We cover how to source musicians and the questions to ask to ensure they are suitable for your wedding. And, to help you on your way, we even give suggestions of songs to play at your wedding.

Setting the Tone

To help keep your guests lively and your reception flowing nicely, plan for different types of music during each phase of the party, ending on a high.

Welcoming guests to the drinks reception

As guests arrive for the drinks reception, music should greet them. People tend to drift in, and particularly for the first few guests who enter the space, background music serves as an audible welcome mat. Decide with the wedding co-ordinator where to place the musicians or equipment so as not to interfere with the entrance or exits, canapés or photos.

Depending on the number of guests, have a minimum of two musicians: no one will hear a solo flute or guitar over the clanking of ice in drink glasses, let alone the din of excited post-ceremony chatter. If you have more than 125 guests, seriously consider having three musicians.

Typically, you can strike a deal with the band for them to play for the ceremony and drinks reception. Although this may be a good deal financially, it can be awkward musically and logistically unless you really plan it properly. First of all, make sure the music choice during the drinks reception is different to the ceremony. You can do this by adding different musicians or asking for the repertoire to be more upbeat and modern. For example, you may have a duo for the ceremony with a soloist but during the drinks reception change this to an instrumental quartet only. If your ceremony is in a different venue to your drinks reception we advise you use a different set of musicians to avoid guests arriving at the drinks to the view of the band breathlessly trying to set up their instruments. If however the ceremony is in the same venue you may just get away with it by placing the musicians in strategic positions whereby they can be seen and heard by guests during the drinks reception.

Of course if your budget is healthy consider classical music for the ceremony and something different played at the drinks reception. Even if it's jazz from an iPod, it works well to change the mood from serious to festive. Consider one of the following options:

- ✔ **Two or three pieces from the evening band:** Usually composed of one or two guitars, an electric keyboard, and trumpet or sax. (These instruments are the easiest to move to the room where the evening reception is.) Think in terms of a jazz lounge – Miles Davis, Herb Alpert, Sinatra, Tony Bennett, George Gershwin, Fats Waller.

- ✔ **Piano and singer:** If the site has one or you have the budget to hire it, this combination works best with a baby grand piano. It's also a good icebreaker. If you can't hire a piano then a pianist can't bring an electric keyboard instead, not as grand, but musically still perfect. Think cabaret, à la Billie Holiday or Sarah Vaughan. Be conscious of acoustics; this duo still shouldn't be loud enough to take over the cocktail reception.

  If hiring a piano don't forget it needs to be professionally tuned once it is in the position you want it. And once tuned, it can't be moved!

- ✔ **Spanish Guitarist:** A perfect option if your wedding is more intimate. Spanish guitars have an upbeat but romantic sound from Latino to flamenco.

Making a dramatic entrance into the wedding breakfast

After the drinks reception, guests are escorted to the wedding breakfast and they wait there for the bride and groom to enter, last. Some couples like to enter into the room to music, normally something upbeat and fun, maybe something that reminds you of how you met, such as the theme tune to *The Office* if you met at work or the theme song of the first movie you saw together.

Accompanying the wedding breakfast

If you decide to have music during dinner, just ensure you keep the music low key and non-intrusive so guests don't have to shout to be heard across the table. You can simply plug into the venue's sound system your iPod or MP3 player and set it to play your favourite songs. Another option is a string trio or quartet whose playing is soft enough not to overtake guest conversations.

Taking your first dance

The timing of the first dance varies greatly. We recommend that you don't have the first dance too soon after you finish dinner, because guests invariably want to stretch their legs and you need to allow time for evening guests to arrive. Simply have the band or DJ play background music to start with.

Some couples prefer to dance their first dance to recorded music even if they've hired a band. They feel that only the original artist can do their song justice, or they've rehearsed to this specific version and feel edgy about any possible changes. If you decide to use a recording for your first dance, make sure that the timing is down-to-the-minute so the music blends seamlessly with the band starting the second number.

Although you have zillions of possible numbers to choose from for a first dance, your two main considerations are these: the song should carry special meaning for both of you and you should feel comfortable dancing to it.

Some songs seem romantic enough for your first dance as husband and wife, but listen carefully to the lyrics – not just the chorus – beforehand for their true meaning, which may be inappropriate for the moment. For example, The Police's 'Every Breath You Take' is about a jilted ex stalking his ex-lover; Whitney Houston's 'I Will Always Love You' is a break-up song; and Billy Paul's 'Me and Mrs Jones' is about an extramarital affair. Ballads are notorious for having inappropriate words, so check their lyrics before deciding on a song.

Here are ten popular first dance suggestions for you to consider:

- **Aerosmith:** 'I Don't Want to Miss a Thing'
- **Bruno Mars:** 'Just The Way You Are'
- **Elbow:** 'One Day Like This'
- **Etta James:** 'At Last'
- **Jack Johnson:** 'Better Together'
- **Jason Mraz:** 'I'm Yours'
- **Michael Bublé:** 'Everything'
- **Rihanna:** 'Diamonds'
- **Ronan Keating:** 'This I Promise You'
- **Train:** 'Marry Me'

If your idea of a slow dance consists of hanging on to each other for dear life, start taking dance lessons sooner rather than later!

Dancing with parents

On occasion, whether as the second dance or later in the reception, the father of the bride and/or the mother of the groom may like to dance to a particular song with their son or daughter. Although a popular tradition in the US, the parent dance appears to be a bit of a rarity in the UK these days, but we think it's a rather nice tradition to try to keep.

Choose something meaningful (and, we hope, not foolishly sentimental) to you. Don't forget to check the lyrics of any song you choose! Here are some ideas:

- **Beyoncé:** 'Daddy'
- **Billy Joel:** 'Just The Way You Are'
- **Heartland:** 'I Loved Her First' – a bit of a cowboy song but the lyrics are beautiful.
- **Michael Bublé:** 'Daddy's Little Girl'
- **Stevie Wonder:** 'Isn't She Lovely'

One bride and her father spent weeks choreographing a tango and then performed it with great flair, much to the surprise and delight of all the wedding guests. Don't be afraid to be creative in your choices.

| **Ethnic dances** |
| Don't assume that the band or DJ has a full repertoire of traditional or ethnic selections. If you want a full set of ethnic dancing music, such as | Indian or African, you need to arrange this with the musicians or DJ far enough in advance for them to find or learn the music. |

Making special requests

One way to deal with requests is to ask guests to make a song request on their RSVP card, which you send with the invitation. Then you can collate the song list from guests and send it to the DJ or band, knowing that everyone will be happy on the day.

Some couples stipulate in the contract that the bandleader or DJ not play any special requests without clearing them with the bride or groom. If you're truly concerned that guests will make ridiculous requests that disrupt the mood, you may want to take this route. However, you'll lose some spontaneity –letting human nature take its course is often more fun. A talented musician or DJ should be able to gauge the crowd and create an artful segue. Who knows – doing the Macarena could end up being one of your fondest wedding memories.

Which reminds us, your *Don't Play* list is far more important than your playlist. Seemingly benign songs that remind you of a past love, your school chemistry teacher who hated you or a band you despise on principle may mar your wedding if you don't apprise your bandleader or DJ of such. Check the band's or DJ's playlist.

As a surprise for your new spouse, your guests, or your parents, consider having someone perform a song written expressly for your wedding. To find a songwriter who specialises in customised lyrics, do an Internet search with the keywords 'custom songs'.

You could also have a familiar face perform on the night. Perhaps some of your friends are talented singers or musicians who could add to the festivities by performing a number with the band. Not only does the band need to know about this in advance, but they also need to have the music.

Dancing till dawn

Trying to please everyone musically can be hard when selecting your band. We suggest you have a band that plays a range of songs from different eras for the bulk of the party, and then a DJ who can play your more specialised music into the wee hours.

Booking the Band

Talented musicians, like prime locations, go fast. No matter how much time you allot for planning your wedding, make finding and booking the band one of the first things you do.

Before you begin band shopping, put your thoughts in order. As yourself:

- ✔ **Bride and groom:** Do either of you have strong musical preferences? What do you like to listen to? What can't you bear?

- ✔ **Guests:** Who are your guests? Are they all about the same age, or do they cover several generations?

Get opinions about music from people who are important to you – your parents and friends – and find out what kind of music keeps them on the dance floor. Bear in mind, however, that in the end you can't please everybody. As with other aspects of your wedding, you must determine whose enjoyment is most important and plan accordingly.

When hiring a band, you can opt for eclecticism or virtuosity. A band that offers a full repertoire, from swing to funk to ethnic favorites, is probably not expert at all of it. Generally speaking, the bigger the band, the better the sound.

For most dancing crowds of 100 or more, you probably want to hire six pieces minimum. If you want certain tunes or genres that require specific instruments, discuss with the bands you interview what makes sense and what is overkill. Ask the wedding co-ordinator's opinion for what works well in your venue.

Tracking down bands

To find the perfect band for your wedding, consider the following:

- ✔ **Friends:** Have they been to any weddings or other parties lately where the band kept the crowd on its feet all night? What kind of music did the band play? What sort of reception was it? Can you trust your friends' musical taste?

- ✔ **Hotels:** Call the wedding co-ordinator of the nearest large hotel or check its website for recommended bands.

- ✔ **Internet:** Do a search for 'wedding musicians' ('wedding bands' turns up mostly websites selling rings) to find groups, agencies and individual players.

- ✔ **Music agencies/band representatives:** This route is the most common way to find a band of whatever size and style you're interested in. Just make sure whatever agency you contact listens to all the bands before accepting them on to its books.

- ✔ **Music students:** You can get student musicians from colleges and universities for a fraction of the cost of professionals, but remember the cheaper rate is because the musicians are less experienced. You need to ensure any electrical equipment is PAT tested, arrange temporary insurance for the musicians and possibly hire a sound system if they don't have one already.

- ✔ **Nightclubs and pubs:** Call the person who books the bands for them and ask for recommendations and for ways to get in touch with a favourite band's agent.

- ✔ **Suppliers:** Photographers, caterers and other suppliers who work on-site with bands usually know who's in demand.

- ✔ **Wedding blogs:** Pay attention to blog posts on weddings in your area that feature musicians. You can also look at the supplier advertising on the side of the blogs.

- ✔ **Wedding fairs:** Some bands play at local wedding fairs, which gives you a chance to see and hear them live.

- ✔ **Wedding publications:** Search the listings in wedding magazines, both local and national, for bands.

Looking for the perfect band can bring on audio overload. From time to time you may need a few days off to keep you from hiring the next group you listen to because you can no longer distinguish one from another.

Shortlisting bands

Wedding books delight in advising you to get dressed up and go to hear a band in person before choosing them. We really have a problem with this because it stands to reason that a band who invites you to witness their talent at another wedding would have no qualms about using your reception as a marketing tool as well. The only time you should audition a band at someone else's wedding is if the bandleader assures you that the bride and groom have magnanimously agreed (out of sympathy, no doubt) to have you drop by. When you do, remain inconspicuous.

We appreciate that some of you may be uneasy booking a band without seeing them live first, but the fact is very few bands offer public performances. And don't forget while waiting for a band's next public performance to come up, they could be booked by someone else first. So unless you do gatecrash another wedding, you need to relay on online MP3 or video links to check out suitable bands.

When evaluating bands via online links, you need to find out when the recording was made and under what conditions. If recorded at an event, the quality may be uneven but more realistic. Studio recordings may be technically flawless but bear no semblance to what the band really sounds like. Videos can also be technically enhanced, and unscrupulous music agents aren't above showing photogenic band members dubbed with different, more-talented musicians. Unless you work as a sound technician, this fraud is often hard to spot. You must rely on the group's reputation and your own instincts.

Many contemporary bands use *samples* – digital recordings of specific instruments stored on computer discs and played from a keyboard – to augment their sound. You can't tell from a sound clip whether a band uses samples, so be sure to ask. Otherwise, you may feel confounded when you hear a trumpet solo with nary a trumpeter in sight. In general, sampled pianos, basses, organs and strings are common and sound fine. Sampled guitars, trumpets, saxophones and other instruments that involve expressive playing techniques tend to sound canned. Ideally, bands use samples to enhance instruments they're playing rather than in lieu of them. If a phantom orchestra doesn't impinge on your sense of reality, or if you like the idea of an invisible chorus of angels serenading your guests, you can save oodles by hiring a one-man-sampler band.

In evaluating a band, ask these questions:

- ✔ Does the contract stipulate that the musicians who appear on the video or play on the audio are the ones who perform at your wedding? Always insist on seeing a photograph with audio clips.

- ✔ Is the audio or video recorded live or studio produced? Is the sound technically enhanced?

- ✔ If you're listening to a sound clip, how many musicians are playing on it? How many vocalists? How many instruments?

- ✔ Does the band use techno-tricks on stage such as sampling? (These in themselves aren't bad, but you want to know if they use such techniques.)

- ✔ When was the video or audio clip made? (Their style or players may have changed dramatically.)

- ✔ Does the band bring its own sound system? How large a room can it accommodate? Do they bring a sound engineer with them?

- ✔ Who sets up the instruments, and when do they arrive?

- ✔ What are their power requirements? How many sockets and what voltage do they anticipate using?

✔ Is continuous music in your agreement? Will they provide a DJ or CDs to play between their sets?

✔ What do the band members wear? Does formal dress cost extra?

✔ Do you need to hire a piano, or do they use an electric keyboard?

✔ Does the bandleader or another band member act as master of ceremonies? It's quite usual for some bands to announce the first dance or cutting of the cake for you.

✔ Is overtime based on the hour or half-hour? What leeway do you have? How much is the overtime rate? Some bands charge more if their performance runs past midnight.

✔ Does the band have another gig before or after yours? Are they prepared to play overtime?

✔ If you have an original or esoteric piece you want played, will they learn it, and how much lead time do they need? What would they charge to arrange it?

If the band brings a sound engineer, ask whether the engineer needs an area reserved at the back of the room. Some more modern bands have a sound engineer who controls the sound via an iPad, so the engineer doesn't need an area set aside.

If you hear a band that you feel certain you're going to book, but you need a few days to mull it over, make sure to ask for the right of first refusal. In other words, they'll call you if someone else is waving a cheque under their noses for the same date. If they won't, get out your cheque book.

Personally, we could do without *medleys*, short renditions of a slew of songs of a similar type. If you want to hear *full* versions of the Rolling Stones catalogue or your favourite Motown hits, be sure to mention that to the bandleader.

Getting in tune

After you've written your wedding-day schedule (see Chapter 14), go over it with the bandleader either by phone or in person. Specifically, you want to clarify:

✔ **Additional music:** Ask whether a DJ is included in the price or whether an iPod playlist or CDs will be played during the breaks.

✔ **Breaks:** When and where, based on a consultation with the wedding co-ordinator, the band will eat.

✔ **Etiquette:** Stipulate no eating or drinking on stage (unless you don't mind, of course).

✔ **First dance:** The name of the song, when the band should play it, at what tempo and how you'll be introduced.

✔ **Gag orders:** Be extremely specific about how and when the bandleader makes announcements. At the same time, be reasonable: even if you don't want to risk the bandleader running off at the mouth, *somebody* has to tell people that the evening food is ready.

✔ **Introductions:** If the bandleader is acting as master of ceremonies and you want to have family and wedding-party members introduced, write down their names phonetically and their relationship to you. Make a special note of people who are divorced, deceased or not attending to save the bandleader from making a big 'whoops'.

✔ **Staff area:** Provide a secure place for the band to store their personal effects, get changed, eat and hang out in the breaks.

✔ **Who's running the show:** Be certain that the wedding co-ordinator and bandleaders work together in deciding when guests are dancing and when they're eating.

Although this may be your first wedding, it may be the hundredth that the band has played this year. You can, however, get even jaded musicians to rise to the occasion: look after your band and they go over and beyond the call of duty for their performance. Here's how:

✔ **Be flexible.** Ask the band what they like to play and include it if possible. Don't dictate the playlist down to the millisecond. Trust the pros to get the party moving.

✔ **Feed the band.** Musicians work weird hours and have erratic habits. Although you don't have to serve the band what you feed the guests, a dry sandwich doesn't cut it. A full meal served in a decent place plus a soft drink or beer may make them play better.

✔ **Introduce yourselves.** Early in the reception, you and your betrothed should approach the bandstand. Tell the band how happy you are to have them play at your wedding. This gesture alone may shock them into consciousness.

✔ **Provide special equipment.** If the bandleader or manager specifies certain arrangements, such as a baby grand piano, a two-level platform, extra mics or special lighting, make sure these details are attended to. If you can't supply it, tell them well in advance. Arriving at a gig to find specified items missing unnerves musicians.

Most bands provide a rider that stipulates how many band members need feeding, required stage size, power requirements and whether they prefer beer or wine in their staff room. Make sure you read the rider in advance and raise any concerns before signing – and then, on the day, stick to it.

Setting up

At sites with an inlaid dance floor, the band's spot is usually obvious. If your reception is at an off-premise site (where everything's catered) such as a marquee, you must decide where to place the dance floor. We suggest positioning the band and dance floor behind a reveal curtain to add to the dramatics at night when the band does their first set. If this isn't possible, either have the stage at one end or in the middle with tables forming a semi-circle around the dance floor. In principle, having tables between the dance floor and the stage cuts off the dynamic between the band and the dancers, and can burst the eardrums of guests who happen to be seated in the crossfire.

Try not to have the bar and dance floor too far apart because this is the quickest way to split your party, leaving an empty dance floor.

Some considerations for setting up the band:

- Where is the electrical source?
- Does the band need risers?
- What type of chairs does the band need?
- Is special lighting required so musicians can read their music in a darkened room?

You don't want the band members rolling their instruments through the drinks reception on their way to set up. So if you can afford it, pay for early set-up. If you're hiring more than one band, or a DJ and a band who will be performing at different times, you should still have *all* the equipment set up on stage before the guests arrive.

Sound check

Volume is very subjective. Generally, the younger the crowd, the greater the decibels. Pumping up the jam is fine when guests are revved up on the dance floor. But when people are being served or eating, the music (if any at all) should be low enough so people can speak in conversational tones. Any group always has someone who'd find a harp deafening. All you can do is seat that person as far away from the speakers as possible.

You must decide before the reception who's in charge of the sound level. Nothing annoys a band more than getting mixed orders from you and your parents:

You: 'Turn it up!'

Parent: 'Turn it down!'

You: 'I thought I told you to turn it up!'

Parent: 'Did you see whose signature is on the cheque? I said turn it down!'

Choosing your playlist

When creating a playlist for the band or DJ, keep in mind that you'll need about 50 or 60 songs for a four-hour reception. Try to think about the ages of guests and what songs would get them up on to the dance floor. Bear in mind that sometimes the songs you like aren't necessarily the songs that will get guests dancing, so choose a range of songs spanning different eras. Think back to songs that have a special meaning to you both and go through your old CDs to find your favourites. You can also ask guests on the invites to send the name of one song that is guaranteed to get them dancing. Send your list to the band and ask if the songs listed can be incorporated into their playlist/set list on the night.

Here are 30 popular songs, just to give you some ideas and to get you started:

- **Abba:** 'Dancing Queen'
- **Arctic Monkeys:** 'I Bet You Look Good on the Dance Floor'
- **Adele:** 'Make You Feel My Love'
- **Al Green:** 'Let's Stay Together'
- **Amy Winehouse:** 'Valerie'
- **The Beatles:** 'Twist & Shout'
- **Beyoncé:** 'Single Ladies'; 'Crazy in Love'
- **Black Eyed Peas:** 'I Gotta Feeling'
- **Bruno Mars:** 'Marry You'
- **Chic:** 'Le Freak'
- **Dan Hartman:** 'Relight My Fire'
- **Jackson 5:** 'Blame It on the Boogie'
- **Justin Timberlake:** 'Rock Your Body'
- **Kings of Leon:** 'Sex on Fire'
- **Lionel Richie:** 'Dancing on the Ceiling'
- **Maroon 5:** 'Moves Like Jagger'
- **OutKast:** 'Hey Ya!'
- **Rihanna ft. Calvin Harris:** 'We Found Love'
- **Robin S.:** 'Show Me Love'
- **Robin Thicke (ft T.I & Pharrell):** 'Blurred Lines'
- **Robbie Williams:** 'Rock DJ'
- **Snow Patrol:** 'Chasing Cars'
- **Stardust:** 'Music Sounds Better With You'
- **Stevie Wonder:** 'Signed, Sealed, Delivered I'm Yours'; 'Superstition'
- **Take That:** 'Greatest Day', 'Could It Be Magic'
- **The Killers:** 'Mr Brightside'
- **Wild Cherry:** 'Play That Funky Music'

Keeping time

You typically hire a band for two to three hours playing time with breaks in between. When planning your schedule, think about when you want the band to finish (or DJ if you have one) and then work backwards, incorporating the breaks. We recommend you don't start the evening band too early: give guests a chance to work up to an evening of high-energy dancing.

Bands sent out by an agency sometimes refuse to play until paid in full, so we advise you to pay your balance within the time stated on the contract. Any overtime is billed later. Clarify with the bandleader who's in charge of deciding whether the band will play overtime. If you and your spouse are paying for the band, you don't want one of your parents blithely telling the band, 'Oh, please just keep playing. We're having such a *fabulous* time!'

Spinning with a DJ

A disc jockey at a wedding used to be as low-budget a choice as macaroni and cheese for the main course. Today, that's not the case, but rather a matter of the kind of music you want at your wedding. If your preference in music is mostly current top-40, old-school house or a combination of very different styles of music, a DJ is your best bet.

Although for £100 you may be able to hire your multi-pierced neighbour and his decks, don't risk it. Hire a professional DJ – one adept at weddings rather than one who specialises in children parties. You may not be pleased to have dayglo yo-yos and balloon guitars catapulted at your guests as the DJ urges them to do the 'Hokey Cokey' or 'Gangnam Style'.

DJs are only as good as the music they bring. Even though pros have an inventory of zillions, make a list of specific songs you want to ensure that your DJ brings along. Or offer to furnish the recording yourself. If you want your DJ to also act as master of ceremonies, make sure you explain what announcements are needed and when.

If you can squeeze it into your budget, have a DJ with a live band. That way, the band can play what they're good at, the DJ can offer versatility and you still get that special energy between live musicians and an audience that you sometimes don't have with a DJ alone.

Aside from the obvious musical questions, shortlist DJs the same way you would other suppliers. As with a band, you may go through an agency; if so, ask for photos and clarification that the DJs play at weddings. Your goal is to get past these salespeople and check out the talent. If the company has a reputation for sending out pros, ask to see letters of reference for the individual they plan to send to your reception. Also insist that you get to speak to the DJ by phone before the wedding. Among the things to verify:

✔ What the DJ will wear

✔ Whether the DJ has played at your wedding venue before – always an added bonus if the DJ has because they already know the lay of the land

✔ What the equipment looks like and whether the DJ needs a draped table or is self contained and brings everything with them

✔ Whether the DJ plans on using theatrical lighting or any other effects such as bubbles or smoke

Considering other kinds of entertainment

Many couples now don't stop at just music for the drinks reception or evening party. You can book many other types of entertainment. Here are some ideas that are popular for weddings:

✓ **Artist:** A caricature artist draws fun pictures of guests – exaggerating features, but all in good taste. Alternatively, your hired artist can cut a head-and-shoulders silhouette of a guest in seconds, using only a pair of scissors. Guests love artists at weddings because they get to take something home with them, but be prepared for disappointed guests if they don't get a picture – think about having the artist stay for a good while. Book early, as artists like silhouettists are specialised, and only a few people in the UK have the skill needed.

✓ **Casino:** Some weddings incorporate a casino alongside other evening entertainment. Guests use play money on popular tables like black jack, roulette and craps. The guest who accumulates the most money normally receives a prize given by the bride and groom.

✓ **Circus act:** Popular for drinks receptions, or during the break in an evening band's set. You could hire a simple act, like a juggler or stilt walker, or push the boat out with elaborate aerial performers! If you do go down the dramatic aerial performer route, remember that you'll need someone to liaise with performers about safety procedures and rigging requirements.

✓ **Fairground:** Very popular in recent years. You can hire fairground rides like carousels and stalls (hook a duck, coconut shy, splat the rat, hoopla, and so on). If you have a fair set up for the drinks reception, you may want to increase the length from one and a half hours to two hours to give guests time to get stuck in. Be aware, though, that if you want to hire a carousel just a few authentic companies in the UK are available, so do your research early. When viewing company websites, check their location, as the transportation fee may be steep. Also, check the space needed for the carousel and any restrictions, such as whether it must be positioned on a flat surface. If you're hiring fairground stalls, ask whether staff will set up and man the stalls for you or if they simply drop off the stalls and go. If the latter, you need someone to set it all up for you and supervise the games on the day.

If hiring large-scale entertainment, check how it gets transported – what size vehicle is used, whether the vehicle will fit on the access roads and through gates that lead into the property, and so on. We've had a situation before where an order had to be changed from a full-sized carousel to a children's one because the country lane access was too narrow.

✓ **Fireworks:** Guests love to end the night on fireworks! Just be sure to choose a reputable company. Wedding venues may restrict what company you can use due to safety reasons. Unless it is 5 November or New Year's Eve, finish the display by 11 p.m. And tell neighbours (especially those with animals) in advance of the display if the party is at home.

✓ **Lookalike:** Agencies exist that specialise in lookalikes. A James Bond perhaps? Or a performing tribute act, such as an Amy Winehouse, Frank Sinatra or Robbie Williams?

✔ **Magician:** Choose a nationally renowned magician or one from your local area. Try the Magic Circle (www.themagiccircle.co.uk) for a list of local magicians or, if you're using an agency for your live music, ask them if they have any fabulous magicians on their books. Alternatively, ask for recommendations from the venue or your wedding planner. If possible, arrange to meet the magician beforehand so you can test their skills. Let her know if you're expecting children at the wedding because some magicians perform adult-only tricks.

✔ **Photo booth:** Many types of digital photo booths exist, from ones that look like your traditional passport photo booths to those housed inside a London taxi. All, however, come with a box of crazy props for guests to pose with in the pictures. Each picture normally has four poses on it when printed; guests can take them away on the night and all images are sent to the bride and groom after the wedding.

✔ **Surprise act:** You could hire an actor to pretend to be an unwelcome guest and create a scene during the drinks reception before taking a bow and admitting to being a paid actor, for example. Very popular at weddings are singers who pretend to be waiters; they serve drinks and canapés then halfway through dinner suddenly burst into song, to the delight of guests. A spin on this is singing 'firemen' or 'policemen' who enter the wedding announcing that there's a problem and that the proceedings have to be stopped, but before guests can leave they start singing! Sometimes a surprise act may be more personal to the bride and groom; we've had couples before booking acts from shows like 'Britain's Got Talent'.

Part V
Pics and Trips

Five Ways to Safeguard Your Wedding Photographs and DVDs

- ✔ Store your photos and DVDs in a moderate temperature and humidity.

- ✔ Keep any photos that you put on display away from any direct light.

- ✔ Hold a second copy of your DVD and the negatives of your photos in a separate place – preferably in a fireproof box made especially for photographs and negatives.

- ✔ Archive the photos and videos on your hard drive or external drive, burn CDs, make prints and upload images to a commercial photo website that stores them for you.

- ✔ Every few years, update the storage medium before the technology or software needed to read it becomes obsolete.

For a great way to broadcast your destination wedding to friends and family at home, take a look at www.dummies.com/extras/weddingplanninguk.

In this part...

- Find the photographer and videographer whose style matches your own.

- Plan and savour the honeymoon holiday of a lifetime.

Chapter 21

For Posterity: Photos and Videos

After you return from your honeymoon, write the last thank-you note and retrieve your wedding garb from the dry cleaner, you may wonder if it was all a dream. Until, that is, your photographs or video arrives. These images are the key to keeping each memory as sharp as if you were married this morning. The final products – both your wedding album and your video – should recreate the mood of the day. How effectively that's accomplished depends on who does the shooting, what kind of film and equipment they uses and how skilled they are. Figuring out your options – and you may be surprised at the new technologies available – is what this chapter is all about.

Getting Focused

Photography and videography are two distinctly different fields, and both require extensive training to produce high-quality results. Depending on your personal taste and budget, you may want to capture your wedding in more than one format.

Your photographer and videographer are two people with whom you must painstakingly go over your wedding-day schedule. Send it to them early and then make a point of addressing any questions or important details to make sure they've read it. (See Chapter 14 for tips on creating your schedule.) If you want either of them to document every millisecond of your day, arrange for them to travel in the car with you if your ceremony and reception are in different venues.

Ideally, your photographer and videographer should see your venue well before the wedding or, even better, have worked at the venue previously. In some cases this may not be practical, such as when your venue is many miles away and it would not be cost effective for you to all travel there. If your photographer and videographer don't see your venue before the wedding day, request that they arrive about 30 to 60 minutes before they are required to film you, so that they can scout the space and surrounding grounds before they film you getting ready or any guests arrive. ***Note:*** Some photographers and videographers may charge you a little more for this time, but the cost is well worth paying.

Photographers and videographers often have smart ideas about selecting the perfect spots for posed and portrait shots, positioning background floral arrangements, arranging chair groupings and refocusing lighting fixtures. They also need to know and follow the guidelines for photography and videography at the ceremony and venue location – something that you shouldn't overlook. Some churches have very strict rules on photography and filming which you must be sure to convey to your photographer and videographer well before the wedding day.

If your photographer and videographer haven't worked together before, the three of you should have a meeting either in person or by conference call. You don't want them falling over each other in their zeal to capture key moments such as the cake cutting. Most professionals, though, are used to choreographing their movements in tandem so they can get the shots they need. Be sure to tell the videographer very clearly that, when in doubt, the photographer's shot comes first.

Taking Your Pic

One of the really important choices to make regarding your wedding is who you want to photograph it. The talent and photography style of the photographer is obviously important. But take note: a good photographer is intimately involved with your wedding, helping you think ahead of time about photo opportunities that may arise during the celebration, gauging the mood of the crowd, capturing subtle moments as well as intense emotions and yet all the while remaining unobtrusive. The photographer is also one of the few vendors you'll deal with after the wedding as you order prints and put together albums, so pick someone you work well with, and don't pull any bridezilla numbers on them.

If relatives or friends who are photography buffs suggest that they want to photograph everything as well, tell them politely that you'd prefer them to be true guests and enjoy themselves. Flashes from other cameras may set off lights that the photographer has set around the room, ruining the professional shot and producing a continuous disco light show. If you prefer to have no flash photographs during your ceremony, state your wishes in the order of service.

Finding a photographer you click with

Good wedding photographers, especially those who specialise in particular styles, get booked up early, so start your search as soon as you've set the wedding date and booked your venue. To find a good photographer:

✔ Call recently married couples that you know well enough to ask to see their wedding photos.

✔ Call catering professionals, venues and wedding planners (even those you aren't using), as well as editors at local bridal magazines. They're usually willing to recommend someone whose work they respect.

✔ Look at the wedding portraits printed in your local newspaper and other newspapers. If you love the way a couple looks, check for the photographer's name in tiny print under or alongside the photo.

✔ Check out 'real wedding' features in bridal magazines. Often, talented photographers have shot these, which is why they're being featured.

✔ Obtain a list of wedding photographers in your area by looking online and visiting their websites. You can get a real feel for photographers from the photographs they have on their websites.

✔ Don't discount photographers living in other parts of the country. You have to pay for their travel and accommodation, but doing so may be worthwhile if you love their work.

✔ If you're planning a destination wedding, why not take your photographer with you, rather than hiring a local photographer? You will have to pay for her airfare and accommodation, but many photographers enjoy travelling so rates may be negotiable. (For more on destination weddings, head to Chapter 7.)

Before hiring a photographer, interview as many candidates as time and energy permit. If you're looking for a particular style, ask about their ratio of *candid* shots to *portraits*. (See the section 'Choosing a photography style', later in this chapter.) More importantly, do the photos they show you reflect the style you want? It may seem obvious, but if people tell you they're adept at black and white and you see only colour shots, something's amiss. Look at albums that feature an entire wedding, not just their portfolio. Is the narrative of the day conveyed well? Ask to see shots from weddings in a variety of locations. You also want to see film from weddings in various stages – from proofs or contact sheets to completed wedding albums.

Ask questions that bring out the photographers' feelings about weddings. Note how they refer to brides and grooms – warmly or with great eye-rolling? Do they bad-mouth past clients? Do they seem enthusiastic about their work or burnt out? Among the questions you may ask:

✔ What are your favourite moments to photograph? Which weddings have been your favourites, and why?

✔ Do you come with an assistant? More than one? Does the assistant take pictures, or just carry equipment?

✔ What sort of equipment do you use?

✔ How many weddings have you shot? Where did you learn your craft?

✔ How much do you charge, and what does that price include?

✔ Who owns the negatives or digital images?

✔ If you use the Internet to transmit or post images for viewing, what is your privacy policy with regard to website passwords and email addresses? (Many photographers now have websites where you can view your album and order prints, but you may not want the whole world to have access.)

✔ Do you always come with back-up equipment? How many cameras do you bring to a job?

✔ Will you shoot in colour, black and white, or both?

✔ Do you charge for travel, parking or other expenses?

✔ Are you used to working with videographers? Do you have a plan of action for working together?

✔ Will you work with me to put together the albums after the photographs are ready?

If you like a photographer but feel you need to do more homework, say so. Ask the photographer to hold the date for a short while or at least give you the right of first refusal. Then make your decision as quickly as possible.

Choosing a photography style

Professional photographers understand that their main function is to cover the wedding: they can do the classic shots in their sleep – the first dance, the cake cutting, the bouquet toss and so on. Deciding the style and format, however, is up to you. Think about how invisible you want the photographer to be, the number of formal shots you want, whether you want close-up portraits or candid action shots and whether to get a photograph of every guest.

Many photographers specialise in one or more styles. If photographs are at the top of your priority list (in other words, you've appropriated a large chunk of your budget for them), consider hiring more than one photographer. For example, have one photographer do the formals and another photographer who specialises in candid photos shoot the rest of the wedding. The two main styles are:

✔ **Classic (or traditional):** The best photographers in this genre pose their subjects artfully and use creative set-ups. Their 'candid shots' are obviously more posed than spontaneous, but the subject looks natural and comfortable nonetheless. In other words, you're not getting a trite shot of the bride gazing at her train as if looking for moth holes. The photographer takes the couple's portraits with great care, and then retouches and custom-crops the photos.

✔ **Photojournalistic (or reportage):** The photographer chronicles the day as it unfolds, rather than staging situations. Styles vary – some look for natural situations to occur and then stop the action to get a good shot; others just look for great moments and capture them discreetly. Unfortunately, because this style has become more in demand among couples who have an aversion to classic wedding shots, some photographers who really don't get it are marketing themselves as photojournalists. An attempt to capture the mood of the day by taking a shot of your cat, complete with ragged ribbon around her neck, plopped on a bridesmaid's bouquet and obviously dying to scram, somehow lacks that sweet, spontaneous feeling that a good candid shot captures.

Shot talk

When discussing the way you want your wedding photographed, it's helpful to know the kinds of shots that may be taken:

✔ **Candid:** Results appear unposed and natural, because the subject isn't aware of the camera. Positive aspects include the photographer being less intrusive, capturing some unexpected wonderful moments and everyone looking like their true selves. Downsides include everyone looking like their true selves (if you have a less-than-movie-star profile, you can't hide it), unexpected decor elements showing up, such as scrunched napkins and cigarettes floating in half-empty glasses, and unidentified bits of food captured in people's teeth for posterity. The photographer needs to shoot extra exposures to ensure that enough desirable ones turn out.

✔ **Formal:** These include line-ups of family, attendants and friends, posed individually and in groups. A good classic photographer is very exact, arranging the subjects as a painter does a still life. Photojournalists tend to be more seat-of-the-pants, and the lighting or staging may suffer.

✔ **Portrait:** Close-up photographs of the bride, groom or both. Staged, such as the bride posed on a staircase with her train trailing down the steps as she gazes into the camera. Also, this is the term used for head shots submitted to newspapers.

✔ **Set-up or stock shots:** Classic photos taken during a wedding such as the groom and best man toasting each other, the bride and her attendants lifting their legs cancan style or the two mothers with their arms around each other.

Figuring out the film format

To get the look you want, you should be familiar with the basic types of film and formats, such as:

- **Black and white:** Very much in vogue. Photographers with a photojournalistic approach take the majority of their pictures in black and white. Processing and reprints require precision and are consequently more expensive than colour. Black-and-white photographs should be shot with black-and-white film; those shot with colour film and converted to black and white look grey and white and fuzzy. Specify what percentage of colour to black and white shots you want.

- **Colour:** Traditional photographers shoot mostly in colour with a few rolls of black-and-white film upon request (and often for an extra fee). If you plan to buy the proofs and/or negatives and develop your own film, be sure you go to a quality photo lab that specialises in expert processing of these kinds of photographs.

- **Digital:** Images are stored on computer chips, as opposed to paper film, and printed through a computer. (For more information on digital images, see the following section, 'Going digital'.)

- **Medium format or 2¼:** This format is generally better for formals and portraits, although some adept photographers use the film to take candid shots. Superior for details – the twinkle of diamond earrings and the draping of the bride's dress – as well as colour shots, it allows for really big blow-ups if you want fancy murals of yourselves.

- **35 mm:** Telephoto lenses enable you to stay farther away from subjects, which makes this type of film better for candid shots. Thirty-five millimetre works best when you're not going to enlarge photos bigger than 8 x 10. This film generally results in better black-and-white photos than it does in colour.

Going digital

Nothing has changed wedding photography more than the digital revolution. Many photographers (and videographers) have embraced digital cameras because this format saves time. Because you can see the shot on an LCD screen as soon as you take it, you can decide on the spot whether to discard and re-shoot – without wasting precious film. Digital work also allows for greater flexibility in retouching and formatting. The best photographers who shoot only with film have to scan images to display on a website for the brides and grooms to choose from, but those who shoot digital photographs can automatically download them to a computer.

If your photographer uses a digital camera, ask how long they've been working with that format and that particular camera. You don't want to be part of their learning curve – a press of the wrong button and all your wedding pictures could be history. To be safe, request that they also shoot several rolls of conventional film.

Photo booths and other fun options

About ten years ago the craze was to have disposable cameras on tables for guests to use, but now photo booths are en vogue. Something about a group of people in a dark, enclosed space with lots of props and a camera brings out their fun, wild side. People just love them.

Photo booths now come in all sorts of shapes and sizes – from the glitzy versions of traditional photo booths (as found in underground stations and post offices) to the wacky (London cabs and gypsy wagons). You're bound to find a style of photo booth to suit your theme.

The other option for candid self-portraits is to set up your own studio, with a customised canvas backdrop (which can be anything from an ocean scene to faux marble palace). Adding props and shooting in sepia tones can create a vintage look. Guests pose and pop the camera themselves by using a cable release. As the party picks up speed, the various formations can be hilarious.

With both options the photos are printed instantaneously so guests can see them on the spot and keep them. Another idea, in lieu of a traditional guestbook, is to have guests stick the photos into a special album and pen a greeting or caption. You'll also receive a USB stick containing all the photos from the day.

The very latest trend is to have an iPad on each guest table, set up much like a website, where guests can view information about the bride and groom (how they met, cute things guests may not know about them, and so on), details on the bridal party and even a video that the best man may use in his speech. Guests can take photos and video parts of the day, which are all stored in a central database and then sent to you after the wedding. Perfect for the high-tech couple, but not a cheap option!

Don't mistake the use of digital photography as a means to save money. Although digital cameras save time and labour, you're still selecting a craftsman who's studied the art of photography and is paid appropriately. However, you may be able to save some money by asking your photographer to give you all the digital files on a CD. Then you can view the images on your computer, crop and touch up as you like, and have the photos developed via a commercial photo shop or print them yourself. Some online companies even offer framing and album-making services. (See 'Compiling the wedding album', later in this chapter.)

However, not all photographers are willing to relinquish their digital proofs, because your tinkering may 'ruin' their carefully wrought art. Who can blame them? Their reputation is only as good as the printed product. Considering that you presumably hired a photographer for their expertise, you may want to play it safe and have them make an official album or set of prints, and then upload a bunch of images to a password-protected photo website where you and your guests can order copies.

Just because images are displayed online for everyone to see, don't assume you own them. The issue of who owns the originals – be they negatives or jpeg files – is always tricky. Some photographers may give you the files but maintain the copyright, others may charge you extra to own them and still others may download lower-resolution copies of the images on to a CD for you but keep the original, high-resolution files that would be appropriate for enlargement. Make sure the contract spells out ownership.

Another reason to leave the printmaking to your photographer is human nature – post-wedding procrastination is inevitable. It may be months, even years, before you get around to ordering hard copies. In the interim, you risk losing all those digital files due to computer crashes and the march of technology.

If you do get a CD of your wedding pictures, investing in good photo software is worthwhile. Programs have improved tremendously in recent years, enabling you to do such things as organise images, add text, erase unwanted objects, correct colour, straighten crooked shots, arrange layouts, create photo videos, print index sheets for easy reference and even whiten teeth and vaporise tan lines. Just make sure that you save, save, save – archive the images on your hard drive, external drive or cloud-storage facility, burn CDs, make prints and upload images to a commercial photo website that stores them for you. Every few years, update the storage medium before the technology or software to read it becomes obsolete.

Creating special effects

By using special lenses, your photographer can create unusual photos for your album. If any of these techniques interest you, ask your photographer whether they're available. Some of the different specialty lenses include:

- **Fish-eye lens:** This technique distorts a photo, almost as if shot through a magnified keyhole. These shots are bizarre, but including a few can be fun.

- **Macro lens:** This lens provides extreme close-ups and is great for capturing details such as place cards or wedding rings.

- **Panoramic:** These pictures are shot with a wide-angle or *rotation* lens. Photos are long and horizontal, covering a large expanse.

- **Soft-focus or portrait lens:** Traditional photographers use this technique to make people look younger, 'vaporising' wrinkles. Pictures look slightly out of focus.

You may also want to mix it up by having your photographer alter the images after the fact. Some cool techniques include:

- **Colourising:** Hand-painted detailing of black-and-white shots, usually with soft coloured pencils. This technique works well with infrared shots to beautifully fill in such details as bouquets.

✔ **Cross processing:** By using either special software or by manually developing film in non-compatible chemistry, the photographer produces wonderfully intense over-the-top colours and heightens contrast.

✔ **Infrared:** The photographer shoots outside photos with black-and-white film that reads heat instead of light, giving a dramatic, otherworldly feel. Photos are high contrast – grainy black and white – with no middle tones.

✔ **Vintage:** Vintage style photography has seen a surge in popularity among photographers coinciding with the increased popularity of vintage-styled weddings. The photos are less vivid, the contrast is toned down to create a 'flatter' feel, and the colour and saturation are less intense, perhaps highlighting one or two elements only.

Calling the shots

If you've already chosen a photographer, you probably chose that person because their style matches your style. Still, just to be sure, you should specify types of photos you do and don't want. Although some couples love dressing-room shots, others are deeply offended by the suggestion. Table shots, where half of the guests are asked to get up and pose around the other half of the table, are horrendous to some, but they're an integral part of a wedding album to others. Here are a few suggestions:

✔ **Specify groupings.** For formal shots, give your photographer a specific list of the groupings you want, such as the bride and groom and her family, and the order you want them in (and do so under the advisement of the photographer). Include groupings that may not seem obvious, such as the bride and groom with the bride's stepmother and stepbrothers. Make sure you actually specify the name of each person on your list; don't just say 'bride with ushers'.

✔ **Explain dynamics.** Sharing family dirt with the photographer isn't indiscreet. In fact, not doing so may cause you far more embarrassment. If your parents are acrimoniously divorced, one or both of them is with a second spouse or friend that the other detests or your sister hates your new spouse's brother – whatever the case may be, full disclosure is the best course of action. Otherwise, the hapless photographer or assistant may naively attempt to take an endearing photo and wind up causing an altercation.

✔ **Identify VIPs.** If you don't have a wedding planner, appoint an attendant or close friend to show the photographer the guests who are important to you so the photographer can make a point of including them in candid shots. Do so in advance so that your designee can put faces to names of new acquaintances at the pre-wedding events.

✔ **Shoot the rehearsal dinner.** If you're having a rehearsal dinner, you may want to hire your photographer to take some photographs on the night. Doing so helps loosen up the subjects for the next day and familiarises the photographer with the key players to be shot. The rehearsal dinner usually requires the photographer to be there for two hours at most.

Figuring out fees and packages

Photographers use so many different pricing structures that comparing them pound-to-pound or photo-to-photo is impossible. Although asking how many pictures a photographer typically shoots at a wedding can help you gauge the value of their services, knowing what percentage of those photos are keepers is more important. Because candid shots are less controlled than posed ones, the photographer must shoot substantially more film to get the same number of usable pictures.

You may be surprised to discover that in most cases bottom-line price differences for wedding photographers, with the exceptions of celebrity photographers, may be negligible. Photographers generally charge in the following ways:

✔ **Flat fee, no frills:** You pay a single fee for the photographer's time, film and expenses. The fee is usually based on an estimate of the amount of film to be shot during the event. The photographer gives you proofs and negatives, but the rest is up to you. So if your photos need retouching or *custom cropping* (trimming the photo to emphasise the main action by removing extraneous people or background), you must find a photo lab to do it. You also put together your own album, which requires a great deal of time, creativity and energy. If you aren't up for a big project, be prepared for your wedding photos to remain in their lovely paper print-shop envelopes for years to come.

✔ **Flat fee, including albums:** The albums may include one large and two smaller ones or a combination of albums and enlarged, matted photos. Although the shooting is less expensive upfront, additional prints cost dearly. The album may be of good quality but a standard configuration. If you prefer to supply your own album, the photographer may give you a discount. Some photographers retain ownership of the proofs, meaning that you must return them after choosing the images you want. Some photographers may sell you the negatives for a nominal price.

✔ **Hourly fee or flat fee, including contact sheets, proofs and (usually) an album:** Photojournalists often charge this way. The upfront (hourly or flat) price is hefty, because they don't make much money selling you additional prints at a great mark-up. You typically contract for a specific number of hours and/or rolls of film and pay extra for overtime. Negotiate a generous time frame in advance so you don't feel rushed.

Photographers may take four months or longer to prepare your custom album after you've chosen the shots you want. Be patient. The photographer has to go through every photograph carefully to ensure the quality of colour and cropping.

Ask your photographer to shoot a special roll– perhaps with everyone posed in a special way or a large group shot – and give you the film to develop right away. You can easily have these turned into glossy postcards for thank-you notes, amusing announcements or holiday cards.

Choosing which shots to enlarge

Because developing every shot from your wedding in full size and on quality paper would cost a fortune, you look at all the frames in a less-expensive format and choose only the ones you really want developed. These preliminary formats include:

✔ **Compact disc:** Digital images are loaded on to a disc that you can view on your computer.

✔ **Contact sheets:** This format is a compilation of the shots in miniature sizes, which you then examine with a magnifying glass or photographer's loupe. Mark the photos that you want with a *grease pencil* (also known as a wax pencil, china marker or a chinagraph pencil, these are used to mark glossy or photographic paper), perhaps indicating where you want the photo cropped. Some photographers give clients enlarged contact sheets that are easier to see.

✔ **Internet album:** You view images on a password-protected website and make selections.

✔ **Prints:** Photographs that have been cut and blown up but not cropped or retouched.

✔ **Proofs:** A preliminary set of photos, all numbered and catalogued, from which you choose your album shots. They may be arranged in proof books or boxes. The ones you choose are then enlarged, custom printed and cropped to your specifications.

Compiling the wedding album

Wedding albums come in many styles, and new concepts are constantly being created. Classic photographers often include a *flush* album, where the photographs extend to the edges of the page with no borders. These are most often 8 x 10 inches, but some offer 10 x 10 inches. Often, at least one photo spans two full pages. Candid-style photographs are usually compiled in books that have different-sized matte photos on each page. Some studios prefer archival boxes, and others turn your images into a coffee-table book. If you're designing your own album, go through your photos with your photographer and specify the size and shape you want each one to be.

If you have digital images, you can create an album through online companies that allow you to upload images, add text and order a hardcover or softcover book with just a few clicks. These make great souvenir albums for in-laws or wedding-party members and are an excellent option for documenting your shower, rehearsal dinner or other wedding-related event.

Assembling a dozen or so highlights from the wedding in individual albums for family and attendants can earn you major points. Matte the photos or mount them with photo corners in petite handmade albums or accordion-fold albums that tie with a ribbon, often available in stationery and art stores.

If you're buying your own album, note that an archival-quality album features:

- ✔ A cover made of quality material such as leather, fine fabrics, wood or metal
- ✔ Acid-free pages, double-sided archival tape, mats or photo corners as opposed to rubberised pages covered in cellophane
- ✔ A durable spine with raised ribs

Preserving memories

As your wedding planning progresses, you'll probably (we hope) have a great many moments that are touching, humorous or even weird enough that you want to remember them. Chronicle these by taking snapshots, jotting down conversations and saving notes, menus and other similar items. When the hoopla's all over, you can arrange all this stuff in one big, annotated scrapbook – along with your professional pictures. Or you may turn a special box or other container into a wedding time capsule full of mementos from your engagement through the first year of marriage, including letters from friends and loved ones that are left sealed until you open the capsule a decade or two later.

If you're getting your own film processed, insist that each print have the number of the roll and the negative stamped on the back to facilitate ordering. *Never* cut the negatives yourself.

Scheduling the formal photos

Usually, your photographer takes the formal photographs after your ceremony. The majority of your guests go to the drinks reception while the wedding party and family members go to a pre-agreed spot somewhere at the venue or in the grounds.

Try to limit the time for the formal photographs to 30 minutes. That way you have time to join your guests for the drinks reception, share a glass of bubbly and taste at least a few of those canapés you so painstakingly selected.

Ready for your close-up?

Many people underestimate the degree of stage fright they may suffer at their wedding. If being thrust into the starring role unnerves you, your photos will show it. The most important – and sometimes most difficult – thing to do is relax. Continually remember to breathe from your diaphragm, particularly when the camera is on you. Be aware of your shoulders – are they hunched up around your ears? Shake your arms out and loosen your shoulders. Also, watch your posture; you want to neither slump nor stand at formal attention. And whatever you do, don't lock your knees, which keeps your blood from circulating properly.

During your formal shots, appoint someone to keep guests away, or even better, choose an area away from the main reception area. You don't want guests distracting you or the photographer. Don't feel you have to converse with the photographer during the shoot – your mouth will look strange in the photos if you do.

Remember that looking up at the camera for affirmation during candid shots or while being filmed ruins the sense of spontaneity.

If at all possible, have a friend take Polaroids of each of you in complete wedding gear (brides should definitely have photos when their hair and make-up rehearsal is done) weeks before the wedding. You may very well find things that you want to change – the tiara that looks so good in the mirror may look like a Barbie accessory on film, or the *very* white sleeves that seemed just a smidgen long peeking out from the tuxedo jacket look like gauntlets in a portrait shot. If you'll be kneeling at the altar during your ceremony, consider blackening the bottoms of the groom's shoes with a permanent marker, so they don't pop out in the photos. You may even want to practise smiling, as silly as that sounds. Although scars, pimples and wrinkles can be expunged from your photos, a frozen grimace can't.

If you want to be photographed at a public space such as an atrium, garden or park, you may need to apply for a special licence from a government office such as Royal Parks. Also, don't be surprised if a beautiful public site is crowded with other couples taking wedding photos at the same time.

Videotaping Your Day

If you want your celebration videotaped but are worried about ruining your professional lighting scheme or hate the idea of having your reception lit up like a basketball court, don't despair. The art of video has evolved greatly in the past few years. Unlike old tape, which required floodlights, new super-light-sensitive equipment means that you need much less light than you needed in the past.

Although the newer equipment requires less light, that doesn't mean ultra-dim lighting will achieve the best results. Many reception halls have virtually no lighting – they consider mood lighting a room as making it a place where bats would feel at home. This total lack of lighting assures that both photographs and videos will come out poorly. The videographer may illuminate individual guests, but the room itself may film as a large, black hole. Design your room so that the lighting works to create the mood you want without compromising the quality of your video.

In case you're wondering, videographers *will* present you with a DVD – not a videotape! Many people still use the term 'video', as do we, so it is a term we use in this chapter.

Casting for a filmmaker

Many of the new-style videographers specialise in subtlety and sensitively capturing special wedding moments without getting in everyone's way – and with exceptional results.

Use the same criteria in finding a videographer as you would a photographer: state-of-the-art equipment, a good rapport and an aesthetic style you like (and can agree to in writing). In short, you want a professional videographer who works with professional equipment, not some hack who ran into a deal at a pawnshop and films weddings at weekends. Find out what kind of film, format and equipment the videographer shoots and edits with.

Ask photographers who aren't affiliated with a video company to recommend a videographer. Because many photographers have an aversion to working with any video person, any recommendation they make is probably a stellar one. Also ask wedding planners and venue managers – they know whom their clients (and staff) have loved and loathed.

Thinking like a movie director

Ask to see complete videos – not composites – that the videographer has recently shot. In evaluating the work, note whether the image is sharp, in focus and steady. Is the sound clear? Are the shots varied? They should include the following: long shots, which give a sense of setting from afar or panning horizontally; medium shots, which are a little closer, showing, for example, the entrance to the reception; and close-up shots of the guests. The video should tell a chronological story rather than bombard you with random, disconnected images.

No matter how talented someone is at handling a camera, unless the finished product is edited stylishly and cohesively, the video won't be fun to watch. Pacing is crucial. Does the video open with an *overview* – a sense of the action to come, such as a montage of the city where the wedding was held, or an interview with the bride and groom? Do the special effects look like an amateur music video? For that matter, is the music in sync with the action? Does the end of the tape consist of a recap of the best parts of both ceremony and reception? Do the editors use *time-shifting* techniques, the method Hollywood uses to put scenes that are shot out of order in the proper sequence? If you want to splurge, you may have computer-generated graphics, animated titles, interspersing of still photos and quick-cut techniques, making your wedding video look like a major theatrical release.

You can contribute to the unique flavour of your video by choosing meaningful music and having it dubbed in to cover up background noises, adding photos from your honeymoon or scripting wit-provoking questions for on-camera interviews with guests. You may also want to create a continual reel that includes video footage or stills from your shower, rehearsal dinner, hen/stag nights and honeymoon. Most videographers don't allow clients to participate in the editing process, so you need to be very clear about all the elements you want and how you want them used.

Although most videographers (like photographers) retain rights to their own material, you may save money if you can negotiate with your videographer to give you a first-generation tape that you then have duplicated. Although your family and friends may say they care deeply about reliving every moment of your wedding with you, asking them to wade through four hours of real-time video is pushing it. At most, your tape should be an hour and a half. Ask your videographer to create a *highlight tape* or a selected-scenes section on the DVD. If it's affordable, make duplicates for your fans. Also, negotiate to retain your *master tape* (the unedited version). The videographer really has no need for it, and you may find that this uncut version contains parts that you're happy to have in later years.

Get on the mic

For a ceremony, the optimum place for the microphone is within three to five feet of the bride, groom and officiant. Some churches or temples may not permit recording near the altar. The videographer may be able to put a microphone near the PA system to pick up the ceremony, although doing so can produce inferior results. When that isn't feasible, your videographer should pin a lapel mic on the groom or the officiant. For an outdoor ceremony, hiding a wireless microphone in a tree or other stationary element works best.

Safekeeping the Past for the Future

Heat, light and fumes can damage photographs and DVDs. Taking a few precautions can ensure that they're around for your great-grandchildren:

- Store photos and DVDs in a moderate temperature and humidity.

- Keep any photos that you put on display away from any direct light.

- Hold a second copy of your DVD and the negatives of your photos in a separate place – preferably in a fireproof box made especially for photographs and negatives.

- Archive the photos and videos on your hard drive or external drive, burn CDs, make prints and upload images to a commercial photo website that stores them for you.

- Every few years, update the storage medium before the technology or software needed to read it becomes obsolete.

Chapter 22

Handling the Honeymoon

- -

In This Chapter

▶ Narrowing down your options

▶ Searching online

▶ Going with a travel agent

▶ Stretching your travel budget

▶ Taking care of remaining travel details

▶ Honeymooning overseas

- -

*T*he word *honeymoon* comes from the idea that the first month of marriage is the sweetest. More accurately, the honeymoon is a well-deserved break from the stresses of getting married, a delightful interlude in which you decompress after the hubbub of your wedding. For most couples, this entails a holiday or trip that allows them to adjust to being married free from the pressures of everyday living.

Like a wedding, a successful honeymoon owes much to careful planning and budgeting. The good news, though, is that unlike a wedding, you have only to please yourselves. In this chapter, we show you how to approach this greatly anticipated sojourn, from figuring out the honeymoon that's right for you to finding the best deal. Although this chapter is devoted to traditional honeymoons, many of the tips also apply to destination weddings (see Chapter 7).

Determining Your Honeymoon Style

Devising a honeymoon itinerary is much like planning a wedding. You and your spouse-to-be should start by sharing your fantasies of where and how you envision yourself on honeymoon. Try to recall the last photograph in a travel magazine that knocked you out. Then ask yourselves some questions:

✔ What's the holiday of your dreams?

✔ Do you like active holidays, or do you prefer to move as little as possible?

✔ Do you view your honeymoon as a time to relax, take a grand tour, explore an exotic location or simply spend time alone together?

✔ What are your priorities in terms of romantic settings, privacy, activities, accommodations and mode of travel?

✔ Do you have any special needs in terms of cuisine, physical access or lifestyle?

✔ How much time can you take off from work or other commitments?

✔ What's your budget?

✔ Can you use frequent-flier miles, hotel rewards points or another incentive programme to defray the cost?

Most newlyweds flock to spots where the living is easy – places synonymous with sun and beach life. On the other hand, couples who find sitting on a beach as exciting as learning their multiplication tables may choose an adventurous itinerary that gets their adrenaline pumping. If you and your partner have different ideas about what makes a perfect honeymoon, a compromise may be in order – a cruise that makes stops for rock climbing or heli-skiing, or a long weekend in a rustic cabin followed by a few days at a luxury spa.

Whatever your style of getaway, heed this advice:

✔ **Keep it simple.** Trust us – you've never been as bone-tired as you'll be the day after your wedding. Your jaunt doesn't have to be boring; just don't plan on extremes. Unless you have a full wedding-planning service and your only job is to get dressed and show up, by the next day you may feel like you've just completed eight triathlons. Don't try to squeeze in so many excursions or activities that you'll need a holiday after returning from your honeymoon.

✔ **Know your physical limitations.** If you've never climbed a mountain or scuba dived before (and you haven't been training for a recent Iron Man competition), now isn't the best time to start. Getting married may make you feel like a new person, but you're not bionic. If your goal is to do something totally new and exhilarating together, take time before the wedding to prepare, whether that means training in a particular sport, getting in shape or buying the proper gear.

✔ **Give yourself enough time.** In scheduling, too little realism can spoil the romance. If your idea of fun is to travel the length and breadth of the Australian outback or dine with maharajahs in India, you need more than a week away. And don't compromise quality for quantity: whizzing through 22 countries in nine days is hardly conducive to focusing on each other – one of the main points of taking a honeymoon. If you can't afford the time now, scale back your plans and make the grand tour a goal for later.

If you're passionate about a particular part of the world, cuisine or activity, subscribe to specialised newsletters published (online or direct mail) by various organisations, companies and travel experts. Their insider tips can steer you to little-known spots and good deals.

If you've been somewhere extraordinary with a former significant other, don't go there on your honeymoon. Three's a crowd, especially with the Ghost of Relationships Past.

If possible, reserve tours or appointments for special services before your arrival. You don't want to be playing tennis at 3 a.m. because the courts are booked for the rest of the day. A travel agent can be very helpful with these reservations.

High-pressure jobs and family commitments – sometimes you just can't fit a honeymoon in right after the wedding. Still, don't deprive yourself entirely. Try taking off just two days. A long weekend in a nice hotel, ordering room service, may do wonders to ease you back into reality.

Bringing the whole family

Planning a honeymoon as a family holiday is increasingly common for remarried couples where one or both spouses have children. These *familymoons* can be a valuable transition time for merging families Brady-Bunch style, and they're a powerful way of conveying to all that life is about to become a joint venture.

Large resorts cater to newlyweds who want to include their children in the postnuptial holiday by offering packages that feature both romantic and family-oriented activities. Some things to keep in mind:

- **Pick a neutral territory.** Choose a destination where neither of you has spent a previous honeymoon or family holiday. Experiencing things together for the first time fosters bonding.

- **Live large.** Big resorts and cruise ships often work best because they have flexible accommodation (adjoining rooms, living-room suites, activity areas) where family members can congregate and – just as important – get away from each other. Camping may seem like a great bonding experience, but not everyone (especially teenagers) appreciates the lack of privacy.

- **Be democratic.** Sounds obvious, but pick a place with activities everyone enjoys. Another reason large resorts are popular – they have something for everyone.

- **Balance your time.** Don't dump the children in a kids' camp all day, but also set aside time for just the two of you. And spend time with each child one-on-one.

- **Don't push it.** Give kids time to get to know each other on their own terms.

- **Take two honeymoons.** If possible, take a conventional couples-only honeymoon after the familymoon.

Researching Destinations Online

The Internet is the best place to start your honeymoon research. Type possible destinations, activities or simply the word *honeymoon* into a search engine and see what comes up. You may find that booking everything directly yourself is easy enough, or you may discover a company or agent that can handle all the particulars. Some kinds of sites to scope out:

- ✔ **Bridal publications:** All the major bridal magazines' websites include links and copious information on honeymoons.

- ✔ **Discount fares:** You can often find good fares by booking online through a travel website. Always double-check these fares with those on the airline's site to get the best price.

- ✔ **Travel agencies:** Many companies and agents specialise in honeymoons. Some agencies offer promotions for all-inclusive resorts or specific destinations that are perfect for honeymoons.

As with any Internet shopping site, check the company's track record at watchdog sites and be sure that it has the registrations of reputable travel companies, such as ABTA. ABTA ensures that companies follow a strict code of conduct, which means you receive a high standard of service, fair terms of trading and accurate information. ABTA Members also offer financial protection schemes and can advise you on how to financially protect all of your travel arrangements.

Is making reservations a man's job?

Until fairly recently, all honeymoons were pretty much a surprise for the bride – after all, she planned the whole wedding, so it was only fair for the groom to take care of the honeymoon. He agonised, researched and hypothesised in silence and then prayed that his bride wouldn't find his plan abhorrent. Now, just as many couples plan their wedding together, brides and grooms often plan their honeymoons together. Still, a good many grooms feel that this is *their* primary responsibility, which perhaps explains the trend toward surprise honeymoons. The groom tells the bride what to pack or perhaps tells her to pack everything from ski suits to bikinis to keep her guessing. He may wait until the last possible moment – often right before fastening seat belts – to disclose their destination. This route is for the fearless and confident. If you've lived together for eons and had many holidays together, this may be a way to inject the once-in-a-lifetime feeling into your honeymoon.

Working with a Travel Agent

Trying to plan such an important trip without the help of a good travel agent is an example of penny-wise-and-pound-foolishness. Yes, they work on commission and some may charge a fee or even expenses depending on the sort of place you're interested in. Nonetheless, the good ones steer you to exactly where you want to be and at the very least get you the most for your money.

When interviewing a travel agent, bring a list of your wishes, possible venues and desired amenities such as a Jacuzzi, ocean view or four-poster bed. Have a good handle on your budget parameters. The more work you do before you start your chat, the more helpful the agent can be. Some questions to ask:

- Based on what we've told you, what are the options you'd recommend?

- Have you personally stayed at the site, done the tour, flown the route or sailed the line that you're suggesting?

- Do you have guidebooks or videos we can look at?

- What sort of holidays are your speciality? Do you usually work with individuals rather than businesses or groups?

- Where are the deals? What kind of discounts can you get? Will you research special honeymoon packages?

- How do you work in conjunction with tour operators?

- How quickly can we expect you to return our phone calls when we're working together?

- Will you supply us with references of other couples whose honeymoons you've planned, preferably those with similar budgets and interests?

- Will you help us to obtain visas, passports and other documents we'll need?

- Can we expect you to deliver all tickets, vouchers and necessary papers to us a few weeks before our wedding?

- If something goes awry with our trip, what will you do to straighten it out? Do you have a 24-hour helpline that we can call?

The best way to find a travel agent that suits your needs is through word of mouth – get the name of the particular agent, not just the agency.

Making Your Money Travel Farther

Your honeymoon need not be a *moneymoon* to be memorable and romantic. Here are some possible ways to save a few pounds and avoid travel fiascos:

- **Avoid peak season.** Go off-season. Doing so may mean not taking your honeymoon right after your wedding, but the savings can be substantial.

- **Book ahead.** Buy cruise tickets far in advance – you may save up to 50 per cent off brochure rates and be more likely to get the cabin of your choice.

- **BYOB.** Stock your minibar with your own snacks, soft drinks, bottled water and (preferably duty-free) spirits. Ask the hotel to remove the drinks in the bar so that they don't charge you for anything. Limit room-service orders – the prices are usually exorbitant.

- **Check the tax.** As you call around to get price quotes for accommodation, ask whether VAT and/or service charges are included – if you're going overseas you may be charged city or room taxes.

- **Exchange money carefully.** The first exchange bureau you see in the airport or the kiosk in your hotel usually isn't the best place to exchange money – you'll likely pay a surcharge for the convenience. Cash-machine withdrawals are generally the easiest and cheapest way to get money while travelling. However, carry debit and credit cards in case a cash machine isn't available. Check your bank's rules for foreign currency cash-machine withdrawals before you leave and perhaps get at least a cab fare in the appropriate currency in advance.

- **Follow the headlines.** A resort recovering from a hurricane or a region rebuilding after a war may offer bargain rates in an effort to rebuild tourism. However, avoid areas that have a clear and present danger.

- **Guard against scams.** Don't put down any money on a trip until you've pinpointed your hotel's name and location on a map – some tour operators advertise desirable cities and then stick customers outside of town. And be sceptical of win-a-free-honeymoon contests.

- **Investigate honeymoon travel insurance.** Depending on your investment in your trip, getting insurance may be worthwhile.

- **Limit phone calls.** Many hotels charge significantly higher rates than normal, especially overseas. Bring a mobile or, better still, a phone card. When using a phone card, call from a pay phone or the phone at the concierge's desk, as there may be a connection fee from your room. If you're using your mobile, speak to your provider beforehand to find out how much you'll be charged to make and receive calls and texts. Some mobile companies now offer 'passports' for your phone where you pay a small daily rate (about £3) for using your mobile phone overseas. Check with your provider which countries are included and ensure you have this service set up before you leave.

✔ **Pack accordingly.** Bring enough sun cream and toiletries to last the trip. Hotel and cruise gift shops charge outrageous prices to captive guests.

✔ **Register for a honeymoon.** Some travel agencies and websites set up honeymoon registries where guests can contribute to the airfare and hotel, or buy you specific services such as massages or a tour. (However, please observe proper registry etiquette, which we discuss in Chapter 9.)

✔ **Rent a house.** You may be surprised to know that renting a private home (especially during off-season) or part of a villa in the Caribbean or the Mediterranean, a *palazzo* (apartment) in Venice, a motor home in France or a lighthouse or estate cottage in the UK may be quite affordable, particularly if you buy alcohol and groceries at a local market and prepare most of your own meals. Of course, if you've decided to throw financial caution to the wind, some private villas come complete with a cook and chauffeur. Either way, this option is an exciting way to feel like a native in another place.

✔ **Skip the tour guide.** Limit the number of shore excursions on cruises or else plan your own with the help of a good guidebook and travel agent.

✔ **Take a copy of your marriage certificate with you.** Some resorts and hotels offer extra discounts on a number of additional activities to newlyweds if you can prove you've just got married. Ensure you take a copy and not the original document, though.

✔ **Use miles.** Even if you rarely fly, join the frequent-flyer club of the airline you take most often. Ask for an application form when you reserve your flight; being a member doesn't cost anything, and the miles add up to upgrades and free trips. Also check out telephone programmes that offer free miles for a certain amount of long-distance usage and charge cards where you receive miles for pounds charged.

✔ **Use student discounts.** Some youth hostels have private rooms that may be nice enough for a few honeymoon nights.

✔ **Weigh up the benefits of all-inclusive.** Compare package rates with à la carte rates for your particular needs.

It pays to advertise. When you make your hotel reservations, and then again when you arrive, make a point of telling the reception desk and/or concierge that you're on your honeymoon. Better hotels do something special for honeymooners to encourage them to come back for anniversaries and holidays. Letting everyone know that you're just married (without being obnoxious about it) *may* result in little perks, ranging from extra service to discounts at attractions to a bottle of Champagne in your room – and sometimes even a room upgrade. Do the same when you check in for your flight – you never know, business-class travel could come your way!

When in doubt, bring it

Should you bring stationery to write thank-you notes? Absolutely not. Sure, you'll have all the more to write than when you get home, but nobody expects to hear from you now.

However, you may not think to throw a few items in your suitcase as you're swept into the swirling wedding vortex. Do your essential honeymoon packing far in advance so you make sure you bring all you need. Our suggestions:

- Bottle opener
- Camera, film, batteries
- Contraceptives
- Copies of birth certificates, drivers' licences and vaccination records
- Diarrhoea medicine
- Diary and pens
- Earplugs
- Electrical adapter
- Flip-flops
- Hairdryer and/or straighteners
- Hats
- Indigestion tablets
- Insect repellent
- Lingerie and new sexy underwear
- Liquid detergent (small bottle)
- Manicure set, nail polish, remover
- Massage oil, feathers, special toys
- Mini-steamer (for freshening up your packed clothes)
- Music (favourite CDs)
- Painkillers
- Plasters
- Scented candles
- Sun cream
- Tickets for planes, trains or boats
- Torch
- Travel pillow
- Vitamins

One more thing: resealable plastic bags are handy for stashing snacks and wet bathing suits, organising travel items and rescuing leaking bottles of sun cream.

Hitting the Road (or Sky): Tips for Before You Travel

You may decide to drive to a not-so-faraway destination. If you're hiring a car and your licences don't have the same address yet, tell the agent that you're just married so you don't have to pay an extra-driver fee. (This announcement seems to melt even the toughest of hearts.) Know ahead of time whether you need to buy extra insurance from the car-hire company. Chances are, if you already have comprehensive homeowner or tenant's, car and health insurance policies, you're set. Also, some credit card companies extend coverage when you pay with their card.

If possible, have your honeymoon luggage brought to the hotel where you're spending your wedding night so you can leave the next day on your trip without returning home. Leave your wedding clothes with the concierge and have someone pick them up and take them to be cleaned (or returned to the rental establishment) so you don't have to drag them along on your honeymoon.

Going Abroad

Hiring a car rather than taking a tour bus is often cheaper in other countries, so compare the two. For the best prices, prepay through a travel agent to avoid fluctuating rates. Make sure you return hire cars with a full tank, which is usually less expensive than the hire company's per-gallon charge.

If your travel plans include driving in the US, the three big companies – Hertz, Avis and Budget – all require you to be a minimum age of 25. Alamo rents to drivers between 21 and 24 years old for an additional $20 per day. Otherwise, if you're younger, you may have to rely on small, unknown hire companies.

For your convenience and safety, don't put off certain administrative and health matters:

- ✔ **Passports:** Make sure your passports are current – and won't expire during your trip. *Note:* Some countries require that your passport be valid for at least six months or longer beyond the dates of your trip.

- ✔ **Vaccinations:** Many countries require proof of certain immunisations, which may take several weeks to obtain.

- ✔ **Visas:** If a visa is required, obtain it from the appropriate embassy or nearest consulate of the country you're planning to visit before proceeding abroad. Allow sufficient time for processing your visa application, especially if you're applying by mail. You may need to provide passport-sized photos. Most foreign consular representatives are located in principal cities, and in many instances you may be required to obtain visas from the consular office in the area of your residence. As soon as you receive your visa, check to make sure it doesn't have any mistakes. Processing and visa fees vary, and most aren't refundable.

- ✔ **AIDS/HIV testing:** An increasing number of countries have established regulations regarding AIDS testing, although mostly for long-term visitors. Check with the embassy or consulate of the country that you plan to visit to verify whether being tested is a requirement for entry.

For a current list of foreign entry requirements, go to the Foreign Office website: `www.gov.uk/foreign travel-advice`.

Many countries have departure fees that are sometimes collected at the time of ticket purchase or upon exiting the foreign country.

The first taste of honey

According to some historians, Germanic tribesmen in ancient times, after capturing their future wives, would join them in drinking *mead*, an intoxicating beverage made of fermented honey. This resting period (or perhaps hiding-out period until the bride's family gave up their search for her) usually lasted for a month – or 'moon' – and thus became known as the honeymoon.

If the pressure of thoughts of intimacy on your wedding night has got to you – even if you've been living together long enough to be sharing one bathrobe – you may empathise with the plight of the poor medieval bride and groom. Friends and relatives escorted them into their bedchamber to help in 'bedding the bride' – loosening her garments and tucking the two of them in, and then sticking around during lovemaking to bear witness that the bride was a virgin. The marital bedroom was festooned with ribbons on the bedposts to represent the marriage knot and other symbols of a successful deflowering. People crammed in to cheer on the couple and grab at the tossed-off stockings and other undergarments in the same manner they reach for a tossed bouquet today.

Part VI

The Part of Tens

the
part of
tens

web extras

To get ten top tips for making your day unique and individual, head online and check out the free bonus Part of Tens chapter at www.dummies.com/extras/weddingplanninguk.

In this part...

- Stay on top of planning your wedding with faultless organisation.

- Keep the wolf from the door AND plan your dream wedding by being careful with what you spend.

Chapter 23

Ten Top Tips for Perfect Planning

In This Chapter

▶ Controlling finances from the outset

▶ Putting together essential documents

▶ Getting input and help

Simply getting started is often the hardest point of planning your wedding, and it can be a daunting and stressful experience. The number one question we get asked by couples is, without a doubt, 'How do we get started?'. You may know what you want and what you don't want, but many couples lack the time, confidence and know-how to plan such an important and large-scale event, and have no experience in doing so.

Here, we've put together a selection of top tips for planning to get you on your way to your perfect wedding day.

Set Your Budget

Most brides have a clear vision of their day, but setting a budget is often the last thing they want to think about because doing so is very unromantic. Actually, setting your budget is the first thing you need to do, before finding the venue, the dress, the flowers and so on.

Think about what kind of day you want and then set the budget to create the best wedding you can afford. Budget and vision go hand in hand. Knowing in advance how much your wedding is going to cost and where you need to spend money is essential for reducing stress and allowing you to enjoy the experience.

For more on budgeting, head to Chapter 2.

Find Your Venue

When you've set your budget, the next thing to do is find your perfect venue. The venue is the most expensive thing that you hire for your wedding: if you include food and wine in the cost it can easily take up to 60–70 per cent of your overall budget, so it is sensible to make the venue your first port of call. You also may have to make adjustments within your budget once you know the full cost of your venue.

Be sure to visit only venues you can afford because, just like house hunting, falling in love with a venue that's out of your price range will break your heart.

Some couples get bogged down in the detail of their wedding and start thinking about music, photographers, wedding attire, decor and so on before they find their perfect venue. Don't make this mistake – you may well change your mind about these things after you've booked your venue.

For more on venues, visit Chapter 4.

Create a Timetable

Creating a realistic timetable, with monthly goals, stops you worrying that you're not achieving enough and ensures you don't miss something vital. Write down what you need to do and when you hope to do it – month by month.

The timetable is a 'living' document that you're always referring back to and updating. Each month cross off completed tasks – a great way to feel proud about what you've achieved rather than stressing that you've so much more to do!

See Chapter 1 for more details on timetables.

Brainstorm Ideas with a Mood Board

Interior designers often create mood boards for inspiration when designing living spaces. Mood boards for weddings work just as well.

Place a picture of your venue in the middle of the board and then cut out photos from magazines of your favourite flowers and table decor, and stick on swatches of materials you love. Think about the colours and textures for your wedding.

You should start to see a theme appearing for the style of your wedding, based on the things you like. This is a great way to visualise how you want your wedding to look on the day.

Chapter 5 looks at mood boards in more detail.

Select Your Suppliers

Selecting the essential companies and people to help you plan your wedding and create everything for you on the day is often difficult for couples – particularly if you've never planned an event of this scale.

You need to rely on your own instincts to some extent, and choose people you like and get on with. However, you also need to take a more clinical approach and do your research. Look for online reviews or ask your suppliers for a list of referrals. Ensure that you ring a few people on the list to make sure they were happy with the service, though. You'd be surprised what people really tell you about a company's service if you ask them!

Asking a trusted married friend which suppliers they used for their wedding is often the best place to start, especially if you attended the wedding and loved a particular aspect of the occasion. Of course, if you're hiring a wedding planner, they have a list of trusted suppliers they can recommend to you.

Create a Contact Sheet

Create a detailed contact list with the following details for each of your suppliers so you don't have to hunt around for their details every time you need to speak to someone when planning your wedding. A contact sheet is also invaluable information to have to hand on your wedding day.

Include the following information:

- ✔ Service
- ✔ Name
- ✔ Office number
- ✔ Name of person attending on the day
- ✔ Mobile number
- ✔ Time of arrival
- ✔ Fully paid – yes/no (amount due and payment method)

See Chapter 1 for more details about creating a contact sheet.

Make a Master Schedule

This, together with the contact list (see the earlier section) is probably the most important document you need to ensure your wedding goes smoothly.

Think of your wedding as a live TV show where you go out live to the nation at the exact time of your ceremony. Now, work backwards and think about every element that needs to be achieved on the day of your wedding so that 30 minutes before your ceremony (before you go out live) everything is ready.

Your wedding planner, venue manager or a trusted friend should be in charge of carrying out your master schedule, not you! You should be having your hair and make-up done, with a glass of bubbly in hand and enjoying your day with your bridesmaids – calm and reassured that everything is ready for your arrival just before the ceremony.

For more on the master schedule, look at Chapter 14.

Keep an Eye on the Big Picture

Getting bogged down in the details of your wedding and losing track of the bigger picture is easy to do. So many blogs, magazines and inspiration websites are around now that sometimes brides find it difficult to make final decisions for their day.

Blogs in particular are full of some amazing ideas from featured weddings, but they rarely tell you how much it will all cost. You can't have everything (probably!), especially if your budget is tight, so stick to the elements that are really important to you – for example, do you really need to have the crystal-encrusted napkin holders engraved with each guest's name as part of your table setting?

Trust your instincts and stick with your theme and budget. Then your day will be totally unique.

Work Together

Grooms have come a long way in the 21st century and no longer is the wedding design all about what the bride wants. So work with your partner to create your own unique day.

Why not start the planning process by having a fun session with your partner in which you discuss and share your vision for the wedding? It's the personal and unique things about your relationship that will make your day truly special. There may be certain family traditions that he'd like to include in the ceremony, or a particularly part of the wedding that's really important to him, such as the music or photography. Put him in charge of those areas so that he feels involved.

Get Some Help

Don't underestimate how much time and effort will be needed on your wedding day to set everything up. If you don't have a wedding planner involved in your wedding then you need to ask your caterers or banqueting manager for assistance. Enlisting the services of an organised and trusted friend to oversee everything for you is also a great idea. Try not to choose someone from your wedding party or a family member as they will already have enough to do on the day. Pick someone who you know works well under pressure and loves to organise things.

Ask the person to part be of your 'planning team' so that you involve them in some of the planning before the wedding day and enable them to manage your big day for you.

Remember that the person you ask to help is there to manage the day, not to do everything. If you really do have a lot of bespoke elements to your day and your caterers or banqueting manager can't or won't help, consider hiring a wedding planner to assist you with the final few weeks and to manage the big day.

Chapter 1 has details on the different services wedding planners can provide And Chapter 14 looks at getting other help in greater detail.

Chapter 24

Ten Tricks for Saving Money

*T*here are smart ways and not-so-smart ways to save money. Before you start scaling back your grand wedding vision, consider making these surgical cuts to your budget.

Start with a Budget

The very first thing to do after you get engaged is work out your wedding budget (see Chapter 2). If you have a wedding budget of £20,000 and your dream venue has a hire fee of £10,000, that leaves you just £10,000 to fund the remaining wedding. There's no point having a gorgeous venue if you can't afford to feed or water your guests. Choose a venue you love *and* can afford.

Cut the Guest List

With every person you add to your guest list, the cost of your wedding rises exponentially. You have one more meal to pay for, one more invitation to send – after 10 or 20 people, you have another table and chairs to hire, another center-piece to order and so on. Soon you're talking big money. Rather than cut back on the amenities you offer your guests, cut back on the number of guests requiring amenities.

Be ruthless in paring your guest list. Whom do you consider an acquaintance as opposed to a friend? You shouldn't feel compelled to add 'and guest' to invitations sent to unmarried friends even if they think dating a whole week constitutes 'almost living together'. And beware the 'and family' Pandora's box. Talk about your guest list exploding!

Work out what every guest costs. It sounds heartless, but when you realise that inviting a new work colleague to the wedding equates to £100, the decision to invite or not invite becomes a little easier.

Reduce the Hours

In the UK brides and grooms feel pressure to have a ceremony, drinks reception, wedding breakfast *and* an evening party with food. Understandably, the longer the day, the more strain on the wedding budget.

Think about your priorities and adjust your schedule accordingly. If having a leisurely meal with friends and family is important then have the drink reception and wedding breakfast, but end the day at about 7 p.m., thus no evening food or entertainment. This is an especially good approach for Sunday weddings if guests have work the following day.

On the other hand, if having a party is more important then have a late-afternoon ceremony followed by a longer cocktail reception. Instead of a sit-down meal, have a hors d'oeuvres buffet or keep it informal with a barbeque or hog roast.

Limit the After-Dinner Bar

If you have your wedding in an off-premise location (such as a barn or a marquee) and you're allowed to bring in your own alcohol, take advantage of sales throughout the year to stockpile before your wedding. Keep the selection simple: stick to wine, beer and a few key spirits. If the venue is full service, you may want to provide just the first drink for guests or put a pre-paid tab behind the bar – once it's gone, it's gone.

When bringing your own alcohol and opting for do-it-yourself service, do take into consideration that guests serving their own drinks won't pour standard measures, thus you'll get through a lot of alcohol – and fast – so it can be a false economy. You also need to think about practical considerations, such as ensuring that you have enough glasses and someone to clear dirty glasses away for you. Also think about how you would chill the drink and make it easily accessible for your guests. Having drinks in a refrigerated trailer is great, but you need someone to keep bringing out the cold drinks if your caterers aren't doing this for you.

Some caterers will serve your drinks for you, but you need to pay a fee to cover the bar staff, glasses, ice and refrigeration.

Avoid Overtime

Be realistic when planning your wedding-day schedule (see Chapter 14) so you don't incur overtime charges. Leave some leeway in case the ceremony doesn't start on time (which it almost never does) and the rest of the schedule gets pushed back. Otherwise, for example, if you're running late and the band is set up and waiting to play, you'll be charged for their time even though they won't start playing a single note until the reception starts.

Dress for Less

A glam wedding dress doesn't have to cost thousands of pounds. Most high-end wedding-dress stores and designers have several sample sales each year with savings of up to 95 per cent. If you're not the sentimental type, you can recoup some of the cost after the wedding by selling the dress on eBay or at a consignment shop, or by listing it on specialist websites that sell wedding dresses.

Also, take a look at dresses in eveningwear departments or high street stores like BHS and Monsoon. You may find the dress you're looking for at a fraction of the price. Alternatively, if you're not bothered about being the first person to wear the dress, customise a relative's or buy a second-hand dress.

Skip the Fancy Details

Perhaps it goes without saying that you shouldn't have your wedding in a yawning abyss that needs a Broadway set design team to make it wedding-friendly. Whatever site you choose, spend your decor budget where guests are sure to see the results. That means at eye level and above: entrances, tabletops, marquee poles and so on. Don't fill the tables with disposable cameras, favours, trivia cards, ribbons to match the bridesmaids' dresses and personalised menus. In the grand scheme of things they're not important, and they don't have the same effect as a stunning floral urn flagging the top table or entrance.

The best bang for your buck for an evening reception is candles – votives, gothic, Roman, tapers – which, wick for wick, can add drama and romance to a room as much as flowers do.

Go for an Orchestra in a Box

In lieu of hiring a few classical musicians for your ceremony, have an entire symphony – all you need is a decent sound system, a few CDs and somebody to press the right buttons at the right time. In an offbeat setting, well-chosen music can sound powerful and perfectly natural.

Do Easy Things Yourself

Simple but labour-intensive tasks, such as tying ribbons around napkins, assembling invitations and baking favour cookies, can end up costing you a lot of money if you hire people to do them. Instead, roll up your sleeves and dive in. And don't hesitate to enlist bridesmaids, ushers, prospective in-laws, siblings and any other hapless elves to help.

Get Married Off-Peak and Mid-Week

Depending on your area, you may be able to get a better deal on your reception by booking it for a mid-week date or during a month that's not prime time for weddings.

Index

• R •

Notes

Notes

Notes

Notes

About the Authors

Dominique Douglas has been involved in planning events for the past 25 years. She owns Stylish Events, a London-based wedding and events company, which she launched in 2002.

In 1991, Dominique moved to London from Perth, Australia, where she was an event organiser for the Australian Red Cross Society. Over the 10 years that followed, she was Head of Marketing for three commercial law firms. In the last 12 years, she has planned and styled many spectacular events for her private and corporate clients. A specialist in planning weddings in London and the Home Counties, Dominique has also arranged weddings in Italy, the Caribbean and other fabulous overseas destinations.

Since 2012, Dominique has run monthly workshops training aspiring wedding planners on the realities of being a wedding planner. She is a visiting speaker at a number of UK universities, running event management degree courses.

Dominique is proud to be a member of the UK Alliance of Wedding Planners.

Bernadette Chapman owns Dream Occasions in Essex and has been organising weddings and events since 2002. A lover of spreadsheets, she thrives on weddings which have logistical challenges like marquees. Bernadette is recognised as one of the leading planners in the UK and frequently contributes to wedding stories as an expert, often resulting in magazine quotations, TV appearances and radio interviews.

Recognising the need for a professional organisation of wedding planners in an unregulated industry, Bernadette co-founded the UK Alliance of Wedding Planners (UKAWP) in 2004 and is the Education Director. She has written a number of training courses and articles for people wishing to become wedding planners, and she mentors new planners entering the industry.

Marcy Blum has been designing and producing celebratory events for more than 17 years. An expert on trends, style and the 'new etiquette', Marcy is credited with being among the first in her field to do away with the cookie-cutter wedding, showing couples that creative weddings can be fun as well as elegant. A sought-after speaker and consultant for both consumers and businesses, and a contributing editor for *Modern Bride* magazine, she has been a guest on *The Oprah Winfrey Show, Live with Regis and Kelly, The Today Show* and *Good Morning America*. Marcy Blum Associates Events, based in New York City, coordinates events in the United States, the Caribbean, Europe and Japan.

Laura Fisher Kaiser is a regular contributor to *The Washington Post, This Old House* magazine and *Interior Design* magazine. A former editor at *Yahoo! Internet Life, This Old House* and *Avenue magazines,* she writes frequently about antiques and collectibles, architecture, environmental design and consumer trends. In addition to writing *Weddings For Dummies* and *Wedding Kit For Dummies* (Wiley) with Marcy Blum, Laura coauthored *The Official eBay Guide to Buying, Selling, and Collecting Just About Anything* (Fireside) with her husband, Michael Kaiser.

Dedications

To my husband Dan: Thank you for always being there, as a mentor, a friend and, particularly in the early years, funding my passion to be a wedding planner. To my parents: Bill and Marguerita Douglas, who have always encouraged me to be the best I can be and chase my dreams. To two wonderful and wise ladies who have influenced my life greatly; my Great Aunty Mary and mother-in-law, Jo. To Becca, Angelique and all my wonderful interns: who have helped me so much over the years. And finally to all my wonderful clients: it has been an honour and a privilege to assist you to plan your weddings, and I have loved every minute of it.

– Dominique Douglas

To my husband Paul: Thank you for encouraging me and believing in me, but mostly for funding my book obsession. To my children, Liam, Ethan and Lena, who always understand when Mummy is working, I love you to the moon and back. To all my clients current and past: Thank you for entrusting your special day to me, it's been a privilege.

– Bernadette Chapman

For Tony, Anna and Dani, who make me understand why people want children. And for Destin, of course.

– Marcy Blum

For my parents – best wishes on your golden anniversary.

– Laura Fisher Kaiser

Authors' Acknowledgements

We thank the team at Wiley for their support and encouragement – especially Steve Edwards, for his impeccable patience.

This book benefited greatly by the contributions and insights of several experts, notably: Beverley Nichols from Jades Flower Design; Louise McPherson Wedding Design; Debbie Baisden from iBarco; Louise Perry from One Foot in the Groove; James Robinson from Wedding Creative; Elizabeth from Suit that Fits; Vashi Dominguez from Vashi Diamonds; Janice Tee, hair and make-up artist; Charlotte Bradley, Partner at Kingsley Napley LLP; Alexandra Clay of Alexandra Clay, Finest Quality Cakes.

A huge thank you to Lisa and Paul at Dream Occasions and Becca, Angelique and the team from Stylish Events for their assistance. Thanks also, of course, for the wonderful support from the UKAWP members.

– Dominique Douglas and Bernadette Chapman

Thanks a million to our agent, Sophia Seidner, at IMG Literary for picking up the ball and keeping it in play with such grace and tenacity.

We are most grateful for the talents of our illustrator, Liz Kurtzman, and cartoonist, Rich Tennant. We thank the team at Wiley, including Courtney Allen, Melissa Bennett, Tracy Boggier, Kristin DeMint, Jennifer Ehrlich, Holly Gastineau-Grimes, Mary Goodwin, Michelle Hacker and Joyce Pepple. A hearty thanks also to our project editor, Alissa Schwipps, for staying several steps ahead of us and being a dear.

This book benefited greatly by the contributions and insights of several experts, notably: attorney Scott N. Weston of Nachshin & Weston in West Los Angeles, Gary Heck of Korbel, calligrapher Glorie Austern, Elizabeth Petty of The Catering Company of Washington and Terry DeRoy Gruber of Gruber Photographers. We are also grateful for the insights of our technical editor, Lois Pearce.

We couldn't have survived this process without the love and support of our respective home teams: Sandea Green-Stark and everyone at Marcy Blum Associates Events as well as Howard Blum and Destin; not to mention Michael, Adelaide and the rest of the Grant Road gang.

Of course, our deepest gratitude is for the brides and grooms who made our first book, *Weddings For Dummies,* an unqualified success. We feel honoured to have contributed to their weddings.

Publisher's Acknowledgements

We're proud of this book; please send us your comments at http://dummies.custhelp.com. For other comments, please contact our Customer Care Department within the U.S. at 877-762-2974, outside the U.S. at (001) 317-572-3993, or fax 317-572-4002.

Some of the people who helped bring this book to market include the following:

Acquisitions, Editorial, and Vertical Websites

Project Editor: Steve Edwards

Commissioning Editor: Sarah Blankfield

Assistant Editor: Ben Kemble

Development Editor: Charlie Wilson

Copy Editor: Charlie Wilson

Technical Editor: Nicola Jones

Proofreader: Emily Kearns

Publisher: Miles Kendall

Cover Photos: ©michael1959/iStockphoto.com

Project Coordinator: Melissa Cossell

Take Dummies with you everywhere you go!

Whether you're excited about e-books, want more from the web, must have your mobile apps, or swept up in social media, Dummies makes everything easier .

FOR DUMMIES

A Wiley Brand

BUSINESS

978-1-118-73077-5

978-1-118-44349-1

978-1-119-97527-4

MUSIC

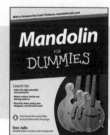

978-1-119-94276-4

978-0-470-97799-6

978-0-470-49644-2

DIGITAL PHOTOGRAPHY

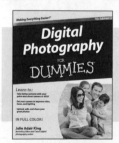

978-1-118-09203-3

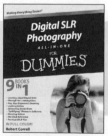

978-0-470-76878-5

978-1-118-00472-2

Algebra I For Dummies
978-0-470-55964-2

Anatomy & Physiology For Dummies, 2nd Edition
978-0-470-92326-9

Asperger's Syndrome For Dummies
978-0-470-66087-4

Basic Maths For Dummies
978-1-119-97452-9

Body Language For Dummies, 2nd Edition
978-1-119-95351-7

Bookkeeping For Dummies, 3rd Edition
978-1-118-34689-1

British Sign Language For Dummies
978-0-470-69477-0

Cricket for Dummies, 2nd Edition
978-1-118-48032-8

Currency Trading For Dummies, 2nd Edition
978-1-118-01851-4

Cycling For Dummies
978-1-118-36435-2

Diabetes For Dummies, 3rd Edition
978-0-470-97711-8

eBay For Dummies, 3rd Edition
978-1-119-94122-4

Electronics For Dummies All-in-One For Dummies
978-1-118-58973-1

English Grammar For Dummies
978-0-470-05752-0

French For Dummies, 2nd Edition
978-1-118-00464-7

Guitar For Dummies, 3rd Edition
978-1-118-11554-1

IBS For Dummies
978-0-470-51737-6

Keeping Chickens For Dummies
978-1-119-99417-6

Knitting For Dummies, 3rd Edition
978-1-118-66151-2

FOR DUMMIES

A Wiley Brand

SELF-HELP

978-0-470-66541-1

978-1-119-99264-6

978-0-470-66086-7

LANGUAGES

978-0-470-68815-1

978-1-119-97959-3

978-0-470-69477-0

HISTORY

978-0-470-68792-5

978-0-470-74783-4

978-0-470-97819-1

Laptops For Dummies 5th Edition
978-1-118-11533-6

Management For Dummies, 2nd Edition
978-0-470-97769-9

Nutrition For Dummies, 2nd Edition
978-0-470-97276-2

Office 2013 For Dummies
978-1-118-49715-9

Organic Gardening For Dummies
978-1-119-97706-3

Origami Kit For Dummies
978-0-470-75857-1

Overcoming Depression For Dummies
978-0-470-69430-5

Physics I For Dummies
978-0-470-90324-7

Project Management For Dummies
978-0-470-71119-4

Psychology Statistics For Dummies
978-1-119-95287-9

Renting Out Your Property For Dummies, 3rd Edition
978-1-119-97640-0

Rugby Union For Dummies, 3rd Edition
978-1-119-99092-5

Stargazing For Dummies
978-1-118-41156-8

Teaching English as a Foreign Language For Dummies
978-0-470-74576-2

Time Management For Dummies
978-0-470-77765-7

Training Your Brain For Dummies
978-0-470-97449-0

Voice and Speaking Skills For Dummies
978-1-119-94512-3

Wedding Planning For Dummies
978-1-118-69951-5

WordPress For Dummies, 5th Edition
978-1-118-38318-6

Think you can't learn it in a day? Think again!

The **In a Day** e-book series from **For Dummies** gives you quick and easy access to learn a new skill, brush up on a hobby, or enhance your personal or professional life — all in a day. Easy!

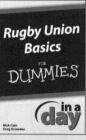